California and Hawaii's First Puerto Ricans, 1850-1925:

The 1st and 2nd Generation Immigrants/Migrants

(2nd Edition, with an INDEX and an expanded Bibliography)

(11/01/16)

This is the 2nd printed Edition of this book (with a full Topical INDEX, an Epilogue, and an expanded Bibliography, which the 1st Edition did not have). The 1st Edition of this book has the same title as this 2nd Edition, but had no INDEX, nor Epilogue. This publication is organized as follows:

- **Table of Contents (Chapters 1-27)**
- Biography: Daniel M. López, M.S.
- 2010 U.S. Census Bureau's Puerto Rican Population Figures
- Preface to this 2nd Edition (June 2016)
- Why I Wrote this Book
- The Cover Page Description of this Book
- Acknowledgements and "Permission Granted"
- Abstract
- Key Words
- Selected Quotes from Important Sources
- **Exhibits 1 through Exhibit 21** (pages 141-168)
- **Table 1** (pages 169-170)
- **Bibliography** (pages 171-191) (from. Bib. #1 - #315) (03/28/13)
- **Bibliography Addendum** (pages 191-194) (from: Bib. #316 - #367) (03/28/13)
- **EPILOGUE** (06/16/2016; pages 195-198)
- **INDEX** (06/16/16; pages 199-206); **TOPICAL INDEX** (06/16/16; pages 207-238)
- **June 17, 2016:** "New" Reference Citations in this book, (pages 239-243, Bibliography #368 - #416); Oral History Interviews (for future Researchers and Scholars, pp. 243-245, Bib. #417 - #422); and Special Genealogical Primary Sources Relating to S.M. Mezes' Birthplace being in Puerto Rico (pp. 245)
- **June 17, 2016:** Exhibits 22 through 26 (pages 246-250)

Copyright © 2016, 2012 by Daniel M. López. All Rights Reserved.

Author: López, Daniel M. [*born as:* Daniel López Velazquez, in Ponce, Puerto Rico in 1950)

Title: *California and Hawaii's First Puerto Ricans, 1850-1925: The 1st and 2nd Generation Immigrants/Migrants* **[2nd Edition** / Expanded & Updated / Fully INDEXED]

2nd Edition (with a comprehensive and general **INDEX, TOPICAL INDEX, an EPILOGUE**, along with an expanded and new **Bibliography**, several Lists, which includes 50 plus new additional bibliographic references added) **(June 2016)**

Inquiries should be addressed to the author at his e-mail address: **DLopez777@aol.com**.

2nd Edition ISBN is: 978-0-9887692-2-9 (Paperback)

Library of Congress Control Number: 2016910417 [2nd Paperback Edition]

(**E-book** ISBN Number: 978-0-9887692-1-2) (The 1st Edition *e-book* version of this book is on *Amazon.com* and on *Barnes & Noble.com*) / 1st Edition digitized version placed on 03/28/2013

This 2nd Edition also Includes the original 367 Bibliographical References of the printed 1st Edition of this Book of March 28, 2013 (see pages: 171-194, Bibliography sources: #1 - #367)
Printed in the United States of America

Printed & Bound by:
ValMar Graphics & Printing
1010 Coolidge Avenue
National City, CA 91950

2nd Edition Paperback Edition (June 17, 2016)

    1. Puerto Ricans/Porto Ricans in California and in Hawaii. 2. Emigration/Immigration.
    3. U.S. Federal Censuses. 4. Race & Ethnic Relations. 5. Puerto Rican Genealogy.
    6. Surplus Labor. 7. Racialization. 8. State of California 1852 Census. 9. U.S. Labor History.
    10. S. M. Mezes' birthplace and his **Genealogical Baptismal** records in/from Puerto Rico and Spain. 11. San Francisco Bay Area. 12.European, Chinese, and Japanese immigration.

Cover Photo Source: *Exporter's Encyclopaedia: Seventh (1911) Edition*, Maritime Exchange Building, N.Y. (pages: 621, 620-626) (Accessed via: *Google Books,* May 2016). The **Arkadia Steamship** was the first ship that departed from Porto Rico on Nov. 22, 1900 with the recruited reported 114 emigrants from San Juan, Puerto Rico to Hawaii to work in the sugar cane fields.

TABLE OF CONTENTS (Chapters)

1. INTRODUCTION 17
2. **PART I: A Review of the Literature** 21
   Why Did Puerto Ricans Immigrate to Hawaii?
3. United States Immigration History and the "Puerto Rican Disapora":
   Are they Related? 51
4. My Research in a Social Context 55
5. The Definition of a "Porto Rican/Puerto Rican" in 1910 for the
   Purposes of this Book 57
6. My Research Proceeded as Follows 59
7. Horowitz, O'Neill, Antonelli, Power: "That's Funny,
   these Names don't 'sound' Spanish?" 61
8. The United States Puerto Rican Population Numbers Between
   1900 through 1910, and Beyond 63
9. The First Puerto Ricans that Decided to Stay in California and in the
   San Francisco Bay Area In Particular 67
10. Scope of my Sources and a Major Limitation: No Contemporaneous
    Letters or Diaries found from the California Puerto Rican Immigrants 71
11. **PART II: The 1910 U.S. Federal Census (for California) and the
    "Extraction" of the Puerto Rican Population Data** 77
    California's Puerto Rican Enclaves and Communities:
    U.S. Federal Census Population Figures for 1900 and 1910
12. California's "Original Puerto Ricans": "Pre-1900s Puerto Rican Immigrants"
    – the *1852 State of California Census* 79
13. The San Francisco Puerto Rican Immigrant Population: 1900-1925 85
14. **December 14, 1900:** The Beginning of Puerto Rican Immigration
    "en masse", to California, and the Immigrants' Respective Names 87
15. Norma Carr's Identification of 44 Puerto Rican Immigrants' Names,
    who were "voluntarily" left behind and subsequently "dispersed" in
    Northern California: December 14, 1900 93
16. The 1900 Federal Census and California's Puerto Rican Immigrants:
    The Census Data 95
17. 1901: The "Year of Immigration" for the California Puerto Ricans
    in the San Francisco Bay Area 99

18. The infants and children of the first California Puerto Rican Immigrants of 1900-1901: The First and Second Generations 101

19. Children and young adults of Puerto Rican Immigrants, who were born in Puerto Rico and also cited in the 1910 Federal Census for California (Alphabetized by Surname): 103

20. The names of infants and children, born in California of Puerto Rican Immigrant Parents, from 1900-1910: The Second Generation 105

21. The names of Hawaiian born children of Puerto Rican Immigrants who lived in California in 1910 109

22. The "Racialization" of the San Francisco and California Puerto Rican Immigrants: 1900-1910.. 111

23. San Francisco County and the Puerto Rican Population: "Pre" and "Post" 1906 San Francisco Earthquake Relief 117

24. San Francisco, California: the 1910 Federal Census population figures for Puerto Ricans...121

25. The beginnings of San Francisco's Puerto Rican Enclaves and *Colonias*: 1910 Census Districts and Beyond till 1925...125

26. The Book - *Exodo Puertorriqueño: (Las Emigraciones Al Caribe Y Hawaii: 1900-1915)* 131

27. NOTES (Footnotes) 133

EXHIBITS 1 through EXHIBIT 21 (plus **TABLE 1**) (pages 141-170)..........................141

BIBLIOGRAPHY + BIBLIOGRAPHY ADDENDUM (pages 171-191; 191-194)...............171

EPILOGUE (*documentation* of **Simon M. Mezes having been born in Puerto Rico**) (pp. 195-198) / (the 2nd Edition part of this Book) **(June 2016)**.............................195

INDEX [General Index], (pp. 199-206) and a **TOPICAL INDEX** (207-238) 199

2016: "New Reference Citations not cited in this book nor in the 2013 Bibliography, nor in the "Bibliography Addendum" Section (pp. 191-194) of this Book 238

ORAL HISTORY INTERVIEWS (for future research for Researchers and Scholars) (pp. 243-244) 243

Special Genealogical Primary Sources Relating to S. M. Mezes' Birthplace in Puerto Rico, (pp. 244-245) 244

Biography: Daniel M. López, M.S.

I was born in Ponce, Puerto Rico, and was raised in the South Bronx area of New York City. I am currently the Editor and Staff Writer of *El Boricua* newsletter for the House of Puerto Rico-San Diego, in San Diego, CA. I worked for the U.S. Equal Employment Opportunity Commission (EEOC) for almost 30 years, as a Federal Senior Enforcement Investigator (EEO).

I earned my B.S. Degree in Sociology from the University of Wisconsin-La Crosse in 1973, and my M.S. degree from the University of Oregon. I published my first articles relating to the Puerto Rican *diaspora* while I was a Graduate Student at the University of Oregon in 1975. Since 1997 I have written numerous articles for the *El Boricua* newsletter for the San Diego County Puerto Rican community, which numbers just over 20,000 as of the 2010 U.S. Federal Census (for California). I am a "Nuyorican" who lived in the "South Bronx" area of New York City during my years at De Witt Clinton H.S., Bronx, N.Y.

I am a current member of the California Genealogical Society (Oakland, CA), the Maui Puerto Rican Association (Paia, Hawaii), and a former member of the San Diego Genealogical Society. I am a current member of the Hispanic Genealogical Society of New York (HGSNY).

2010 U.S. Census Bureau's Puerto Rican Population Figures:

The 2010 Federal Census has identified a total Puerto Rican population (or of Puerto Rican heritage) for the **State of California** as being just over 189,000.

The 2010 Federal Census also has identified a total Puerto Rican population (or of Puerto Rican heritage) for the **State of Hawaii** as being 44,116 (Silver, Patricia and Carlos Vargas-Ramos. 2012. "Demographic Transitions: Research Brief").

This brief article by Silver and Vargas-Ramos focuses on the ever-continuing history of Puerto Rican **migration**, not only to the United States, but the return migration back to Puerto Rico as well. It identifies the population figures of Puerto Ricans in the different geographical regions of the United States, i.e., between the Northeast and the Southeast, etc., areas of the United States. This article points out that, according to the U.S. Census Bureau, the overall 2010 population in **Puerto Rico** was 3,725,789 [with 3,560,838 being **Puerto Rican**, and 164,951 being "Foreigners", i.e., born outside Puerto Rico].

Preface to this 2nd Edition

Importantly for researchers, this 2nd Edition of this printed book, *California and Hawaii's First Puerto Ricans, 1850-1925: The 1st and 2nd Generation Immigrants/Migrants* (November 2016), in contrast to the 1st Edition (March 2013), contains an **INDEX** (the 1st Edition did *not* have), as well as newly researchd material.

Also, the 2nd Edition has a new section titled "EPILOGUE" which documents Simon M. Mezes' having been born in Puerto Rico (pp. 195-198) including primary source documents from Puerto Rico, as well as one primary source document from the *Archivo General de Indias* in Sevilla, Spain. When taken together these documents unequivocally show that one of the first, if not the first, recorded person that was born in Puerto Rico, and who had immigrated to San Francisco, California, as early as December 1849, had in fact been born in Puerto Rico, and not in continental Spain as a number of writers had written without any supporting documentation.

This 2nd Edition includes a comprehensive, general "INDEX" (pp. 199-206), as well as a detailed and comprehensive "TOPICAL INDEX" (pp. 207-238). There are eight (8) separate sections (i.e., Lists) of this general "INDEX". Additionally, both the "INDEX", as well as the "TOPICAL INDEX", includes an alphabetized listing of selected "Primary Sources" (along with the page number in the text of this book for the source location), and consisting of both digitized (such as *Ancestry.com*), as well as printed sources.

Also, this 2nd Edition of the book contains an added and expanded "Bibliography" which contains over 50 new source citations in the section titled "2016: 'New' Reference Citations not cited in the 1st Edition of this book" (cf.: pp. 239-243). It also contains a new section titled, "ORAL HISTORY INTERVIEWS" which should be useful for future research by California and Hawaiian historians, labor history historians, genealogical researchers, scholars and writers (pp. 243-245). There is a new section titled, "Special Genealogical Primary Sources Relating to S. M. Mezes' Birthplace in Puerto Rico" (p. 245). This 2nd Edition also contains 11 new "Exhibits" (i.e., Exhibit 22 through Exhibit 32) (pp. 246-256), which the 1st Edition did not have.

Particularly noteworthy for historians, researchers, scholars, and genealogists is that this 2nd Edition has several additional alphabetized lists of names of the Puerto Rican (i.e., "Porto Rican") immigrants, along with those of their their children's, to both California, as well as to Hawaii, which can be found in the "TOPICAL INDEX" section of the book (pp. 207-238; pp. 216-219, 223-224, 227, 231-238, in particular). This makes it considerably easier for someone to locate a particular person by their name. These lists are in addition to five alphabetized lists of immigrant names already cited in the first edition of the book (see: pp. 28ff.-127). This 2nd Edition of the book contains the incorporation of a number of changes and additions to the printed 1st Edition of this book. Whereas the 1st Edition of this book contained a total of 194 pages, this 2nd Edition contains a total of 256 pages. Finally, this new edition provides a list of 16 towns in Porto Rico which experienced varying degrees of emigration of Porto Ricans to either California, and/or to Hawaii, (pp. 223-224).

Why I Wrote This Book:

I moved to California in 1979. As far as I have been able to determine, I have not found a published **book** which has provided a detailed, comprehensive, or historical account of the **beginnings** of the California Puerto Rican community.

However, it should be noted that an article by authors Jacqueline Lazú and Marisol Negrón, published in 2000, in the ***Centro Journal*** of the Center for Puerto Rican Studies (Hunter College, N.Y., N.Y.), referenced an exhibit which was sponsored by the California Historical Society, the Hayward Area Historical Society of Hayward, California, and the Western Region Puerto Rican Council, entitled: "California *Century: Puerto Ricans and the San Francisco Bay Area, 1900-2000*" (Lazú and Negrón. 2000: 117; see also: Curator Aurora Levins Morales' web site, which she described in what appears to have been her "resume").

This *California Exhibit*, while being a "temporary Exhibit", can still be accessed on-line at the following website: http://www.calirican.org/. (This author accessed this site as recently as: 11/05/12; also at: http://search.yahoo.com.search; Puerto Ricans in San Francisco –Yahoo! Search Results).

In short, the web site stated:

"In 1998, Puerto Rican historian and writer Aurora Levins Morales and historian/archivist Nitza Medina obtained funding from the Western Region Puerto Rican Council and began collecting oral histories, photographs and documents about the history of that community [i.e., the San Francisco, California Puerto Rican community]. Photographer Barry Kleider was commissioned to take portraits of community elders. Additional funding from the Hayward Historical Society allowed Dr. Levins Morales to collect additional oral histories, documents, historical recordings from early radio broadcasts, and to commission additional portraits. The exhibit *California Century: Puerto Ricans in the San Francisco Bay Area, 1900-2000,* opened in the summer of 2002. On this site, you can explore the exhibit, listen to excerpts of oral histories, visit our image galleries and learn about organizations, publications and other resources on California Puerto Ricans" (<http://www.calirican.org/>; accessed on: 11/05/12) (cf.: Exhibits 20 and 21 in this book, following Chapter 27).

I contacted the Hayward Area Historical Society (22701 Main Street, Hayward, CA 94541), and the Curator/Archivist kindly mailed me a packet which provided the following: the exhibit text, a press release, an exhibit card, a brochure, and a couple of newspaper clippings about the exhibition (consisting of a total of 49 pages, apparently taken from the web site itself, i.e., from the *California Puerto Rican History Project* home page) (cf.: Exhibits 20 and 21).

In contrast, a writing of the history of the development of the California Puerto Rican community from its inception, by Norma Carr, in her dissertation entitled, *The Puerto Ricans in Hawaii: 1900-1958* (Carr. 1989), provided a detailed, comprehensive, and historical account of the development of the Puerto Rican community in what was then known as the Hawaiian Territory. However, my book seeks to **add** and **expand** upon Dr. Carr's work relating to the Hawaiian Puerto Rican community.

This author has also made the concerted effort to make the historical **connection** between the beginnings of the California Puerto Rican community and its population with the Hawaiian Puerto Rican community and its ever-growing population. Thus, a substantial amount of U.S. Federal Census data/figures for both the California and the Hawaiian Puerto Rican populations were researched, retrieved and reviewed, and is presented in this book.

Background Information:

This author has found from the U.S. Federal Censuses, covering the time periods from 1850 to 1900, as well as the *1852 State of California Census*, that the genealogy-related *Ancestry.com* software program had identified and "extracted" the names in the form of "lists" for each Census decade. California had 13 individuals who were identified by *Ancestry.com* as having been born in Puerto Rico, and who were also residing in California during the time period of 1850 and 1900, on the respective dates which each Census were taken. The 1910 U.S. Federal Census for California identified 342 persons who had been born in Puerto Rico and were residents of California as of April 1910 (cf.: Exhibit 11); Also refer to "Table 1" of this book, after "Exhibit 21".

The first group of *at least* 64 (and **NOT** 56, as had originally been widely reported, although, in all fairness, the newspapers correctly reported the total of 56 adults, and/or working *children* plantation workers, and did not reference the non-working children and babies --- this point was presented to me recently by Dr. Ellen Fernandez-Sacco, who is Puerto Rican and is also the Vice President of the California Genealogical Society (Oakland, CA)). Puerto Ricans **(i.e., persons)** arrived *en masse*, to San Francisco, CA, on December 14, 1900, while the remaining portion of the **original** group of <u>over</u> 114 Puerto Ricans continued on their voyage to Hawaii to work, predominately, in the sugar cane fields and plantations of Hawaii (see: Exhibit 12 and Exhibit 13), (*San Francisco Examiner.* December 15, 1900: 1, and the Photograph on the front page; see also: *San Francisco Chronicle.* December 16, 1900: 2; *San Francisco Chronicle.* December 2, 1900: 11). **1/**

7

This book provides a more detailed description, by focusing on and reviewing **primary** and secondary sources, of the two types of group migrations which the Puerto Rican immigrants participated in during the period from 1900 through 1925. The emigration of the first **eleven groups** of Puerto Ricans from Puerto Rico on November 22, 1900, to San Francisco, CA, arrived in Hawaii on December 23, 1900. This first wave of Puerto Rican emigration to Hawaii, consisting of these eleven groups, continued until October 1901.

The second migration involved those Puerto Ricans who, after having initially arrived in Hawaii, and due to their perceived, as well as their actual poor working conditions on the Hawaiian sugar plantations, decided to return from Hawaii to California, primarily, to the San Francisco Bay area during the period from 1901 to 1925. This book identifies the ever increasing Puerto Rican population in California during this period. Thus, this author wanted to show the **direct connection** between the Puerto Rican immigrants that had initially emigrated from Puerto Rico to Hawaii directly, and thereafter, and those Puerto Ricans that left Hawaii, and then returned to California to start the beginnings of the Puerto Rican communities (*colonias*) in California in general, and in the San Francisco Bay Area in particular.

It is undisputed that of the original group of over 114 Puerto Rican contract laborers, 56 of these contract laborers **did** arrive on December 23, 1900, to work in the fields and plantations of Hawaii, according to an article entitled "Porto Ricans Arrive" on the first page of the newspaper *The* Hawaiian Star (Honolulu [Oahu]) (December 24, 1900a: 1; see also: *The Honolulu Republican*. December 25, 1900a; *The Hawaiian Star*. January 16, 1901: 1); this December 24, 1900 *The Hawaiian Star* article provided the following facts:

"After weeks of annoyance the agents of the Planters' Association succeeded in bringing **fifty-six [56]** Porto Ricans to the islands to work on the sugar plantations. This was less than half the original number which started from Porto Rico to find new homes in [the] Hawaiian Islands. The Porto Ricans arrived Sunday on the *Rio Janeiro* [sic]" [which was the name of their travelling Steamship] (see: *The Hawaiian Star*. December 24, 1900a: 1; see also: *The Hawaiian* Gazette (Honolulu, Hawaii), December 26, 1900: 8; **Note:** These historical Hawaiian newspapers are a part of the Library of Congress' "digitized" copies of its "U.S. historical newspapers" collection, see: "Chronicling America- The Library of Congress"; see: Schmitt. 1995: 6, 3). **2/** (emphasis added)

The Honolulu Republican newspaper of December 25, 1900, in describing the Porto Rican immigrants' arrival to Hawaii on December 23, 1900, had the revealing headline on the front page of this issue as:

"Held for the Time as Real Prisoners. Porto Ricans not Allowed a Minute on Shore. Arrived Early Sunday Morning…Large Number Deserted in California…" (*The Honolulu Republican*. December 25, 1900c: 1).

The article went on to report that:

"The party of Porto Rican laborers on board the steamer *Rio de Janeiro* arrived in port early Sunday morning and in an hour and a half, without a single one of them being allowed to set foot on shore, they were hurried off to the Spreckelsville plantation on the island of Maui by the steamer *Lehua* which came up alongside for the purpose…. The inhumanity of this phase of their treatment amounts to the same thing as a brief imprisonment at the end of the line for if they were not forcibly detained that was the effect… Her load of human freight had been diminished perceptibly. [The article reported, albeit incorrectly, the following numbers]: Of the 114 who started originally only twenty-five men and eleven women and eight children arrived here [Hawaii]. The others were induced to desert by the Spanish people of San Francisco.... The men claim to have signed no contracts but to have received assurances of free fare with no hold out for the same on future wages" (*The Honolulu Republican.* December 25, 1900c: 1; see also: *San Francisco Chronicle.* January 2, 1901a; *San Francisco Chronicle.* January 2, 1901b: 5).

It should be noted that the journey from San Francisco to Hawaii in late December 1900, via their steamship the *Rio*, for the first group of Puerto Rican immigrants, was a rather harrowing experience fraught with danger. For example, The *Hawaiian Star* issue of December 24, 1900 had the foreboding headline in another one of their articles: "The Rio Was In Danger". It reported that:

"Passengers who came here on the steamship *Rio* give terrible stories of the experiences the vessel passed through [*sic*]...for a time the *Rio* was in real danger. Not many of her passengers knew that at one time the firemen below deserted their posts and that out of five pumps only one was left in condition to be of any use when the storm was at its height.... The experience of the voyage was hardest upon the Porto Rican laborers who came here for plantation work. They were all in the steerage together and the rolling of the vessel filled them with terror." (*Hawaiian Star, The.* December 24, 1900b: 1; see also.: Exhibit 17).

The Hawaiian newspaper, the *Evening Bulletin*, of December 26, 1900, in a dispatch from San Francisco, reported that, "Some of the Porto Ricans who arrived in San Francisco Friday in a destitute condition, after having been prevailed upon to refuse to go to the Hawaiian Islands to work on the sugar plantations, were taken to the Almshouse yesterday, where they will receive temporary care" (*Evening Bulletin* [Oahu, Hawaii], in an untitled column. December 26, 1900: 1; see also their other column in this same issue titled: "Porto Ricans are in the Poor House", *Ibid.* page 1).

It is important to note that the reason why the Hawaiian Sugar Planters originally sent their recruiters to Puerto Rico at least as early as November 1900, to recruit Puerto Rican workers to work in their sugar plantations was because the Planters perceived that they had a "labor shortage." For example, the January 2, 1901 issue of *The San Francisco Call*, in their article titled, "Porto Ricans Reach Hawaii: Secretary of the Planters' Association Speaks of the Experiment", had the following quote:

"The planters have had great difficulty in settling this labor question. We have found [the] Japanese unreliable and have experimented with Italians and Portuguese. The Porto Rican business is an experiment, and if the laborers brought here prove to be good we shall send for more... The Porto Rican laborers...are to work on the Pioneer Mill Company plantation (in Lahaina, Maui)" (*San Francisco Call.* January 2, 1901: 2).

Norma Carr, in 1989, succinctly summarized why in 1900 the Hawaiian Sugar Planters Association (HSPA) began to recruit agricultural laborers from Puerto Rico, as follows:

"The [the Hawaiian Sugar Planters] had a very clear definition of the ideal laborer. He should be destitute so that he would work for low wages; healthy, so that he could work long and hard hours; and docile, so that he would not challenge authority. By all reports the **Puerto Ricans** seemed to meet their expectations. The island had been devastated by military invasion and the forces of nature [the August 1899 hurricane]. The labor force numbered in the hundreds of thousands and jobs were few. Many were experienced cane cutters, almost universally illiterate, humble and law-abiding. Although there were a few caveats on their health, the assumption was that they had suffered neglect and malnutrition under the Spaniards and would greatly improve under American beneficence" (Carr. 1989: 331). (Emphasis added)

The low wages of the Puerto Rican laborers in Puerto Rico, covering the time period from 1899 to

1906, was summarized by the 1907 *Report* by the U.S. Dept. of Commerce and Labor, namely, that:

"**WAGES AND STANDARD OF LIVING**: Wages in Porto Rico are very low. In the sugar plantations the average rate for ordinary unskilled work is from 50 to 55 cents a day. In the coffee plantations it is 30 cents a day, though in the picking season, when wages are paid by measure, the rate is somewhat higher. In the tobacco fields the wages average slightly over 40 cents a day. These wages are practically those of the average workingman... With wages so low, savings are practically out of the question, except in a few favored industries. *The workman needs his entire wage for the support of himself and his family*.... Thus almost the entire earnings of the laborer go to provide food for himself and his family" (U.S. Dept. of Commerce and Labor. 1907: 11). (emphasis added)

Illiteracy in Puerto Rico in 1899, which contributed to mass poverty the year immediately before the first emigration *en masse* began, can also be demonstrated by the number and percentage of the total working population on the Island. For example, according to the 1899 *Census of Porto Rico*, Joseph B. Seabury reported in relevant part that:

"There are only about 2200 **professional** men in the island. Of these 200 are lawyers, 220 physicians, and 800 teachers. Nearly 200,000 of the people---two thirds of them are **women**---have no employment whatever" (Seabury. 1908: 164).

Additionally, the U.S. Dept. of Labor in 1919 reported that:

"In 1899 the percentage of illiteracy for the entire population was 79.6 while in 1910 it was [still] 66.5. Of the entire population in 1910 only 3.9 per cent of the white population could speak English, 4.9 per cent of the blacks, and 2.6 per cent of the mulattoes" (see: U.S. Dept. of Labor. 1919: 12).

The Devastation Caused by the August 8, 1899 Hurricane in Puerto *Rico*

Specifically, the 1899 hurricane's destruction of Puerto Rico was sadly summarized by Puerto Rico's then Military Government's Brig. General Geo. W. Davis, U.S.A., in a 1902 published report, entitled *Annual Reports of the* War *Department for the Fiscal Year Ended June 30, 1900... Report of the Military Governor of Porto Rico on Civil Affairs,* he wrote as follows:

"On August 8, 1899, Porto Rico was visited by a disastrous hurricane and flood, the immediate result of which was the killing and drowning of nearly 3,000 people, the destruction of millions of dollars' worth of property, including the greater part of the food supply of the island, and the threatened starvation of many thousand inhabitants. In order to fully understand the extent of this disaster, a glance at the economic conditions in Porto Rico immediately before and after the storm is necessary. On August 7, 1899, the population of Porto Rico was about 950,000...of this number, perhaps 750,000 belonged to the peon or poor laboring class. The island's main source of revenue for many years had been the coffee industry...."

"On August 8, 1899, 90 per cent of the coffee crop was wiped out of existence, the plantations themselves were severely damaged, nearly all the plantations and banana trees were broken off at the roots, and the fruit strewn around to spoil unless used at once, while the minor crops, such as corn, potatoes, etc., a large proportion, including even some that had been harvested, was blown or washed away. In addition to this, much damage was done to buildings and property in general, the roads were rendered impassable, and business was paralyzed."

"Under these conditions, it seemed that the only course open to the military governor was to appeal, on behalf of the island of Porto Rico, to the Government and people of the United States for assistance, and to apply the funds and supplies received to the distribution of food to prevent actual starvation…. Food in great quantities had to be obtained and promptly distributed or wholesale starvation would follow" (Military Governor of Porto Rico. 1902: 210, 211).

According to the 1899 *Census of Porto Rico*, it should be noted that coffee was the major agricultural crop, certainly by the percentage of land use and acreage of the Island, as evidenced by the fact that in 1899, the relative importance of the various farm products (crops) in percentage of the total area of cultivated land was **at 40%**, while Sugar Cane was at 15 per cent and Bananas was at 14 per cent (Referenced in: Seabury. 1908: 163).

In short, the devastation of Puerto Rico by this 1899 **hurricane** was a major, if not the major, cause of the subsequent emigration of Puerto Ricans leaving Puerto Rico to Hawaii, which began in November 1900 (with the 1st ship departing from Puerto Rico on November 22, 1900), and continued at least throughout the first decade of the 20th Century.

Ironically, Carr pointed out that "before the end of 1901, HSPA [Hawaiian Sugar Planters Association] was complaining that the Puerto Ricans [i.e., the plantation laborers in Hawaii] had not fulfilled their expectations. Nevertheless, the HSPA **continued to [still] find them useful**" (Carr. 1989: 331). (emphasis added)

This is borne out by the fact that, by the end of 1901, the *Report of the Commissioner of Labor on Hawaii. 1901* (issued in: 1902), reported that by the end of the first full year of the Puerto Rican immigrants being in Hawaii as sugar plantation laborers, the number of Puerto Rican "Unskilled Plantation Laborers" for the year ending in 1901 was at 2,095 (U.S. Bureau of Labor. 1902: 19). By comparison, by the end of 1901, some of the other nationalities of "Unskilled Plantation Laborers" were as follows: 1,470 Hawaiians; 2,417 Portuguese; 27,537 Japanese; 4,976 Chinese; 55 Negroes; 46 South Sea Islanders; 342 Americans; 169 British; 163 Germans; and 317 of "All others", for a total of 39,587 "unskilled Plantation Laborers" (Ibid.: 19, 175, 139ff.).

In addition, in this same publication, the *Report of the Commissioner of Labor on Hawaii. 1901*, the Hawaiian Commissioner of Labor stated that "Porto Rican immigration, which was due entirely to the solicitation and aid of the [Hawaiian Sugar] planters, had ceased…in 1902" (U.S. Bureau of Labor. *(1902):* 428).

The 1904 *Report of the Governor of the Territory of Hawaii* stated that a "round-trip ticket between San Francisco and Honolulu costs $135. Distance traveled, 4,200 miles", and that the trip [should take] 12 days to make (Secretary of the Interior. 1904: 135). The 1906 *Report of the Governor* reported that the rates of fare to go from San Francisco to Hawaii were as follows: First class: $75.00; Second class: $50.00; Steerage: $30.00 (Secretary of the Interior. 1906: 43).

Puerto Rico in a Very Brief Historical Context:

University of Puerto Rico Professor Jorge Duany, succinctly summarized one interpretation of Puerto Rico's political, legal, historical, economic and global (or lack thereof) relationship(s) with the United States when he referenced some of the most important historical events that transpired between these two countries. He wrote the following:

"On July 25, 1898, U.S. troops invaded Puerto Rico during the Spanish-Cuban-American War and have retained a strong presence there ever since. In 1901, the U.S. Supreme Court paradoxically defined the Island as 'foreign to the United States in a domestic sense,' neither a state of the

American union nor an independent country.... The court later ruled that Puerto Rico was an 'unincorporated territory' 'belonging to but not a part of' the United States, meaning that the U.S. Congress would determine which parts of the U.S. Constitution applied to the Island. In 1904, the Court declared that Puerto Ricans were not 'aliens' for immigration purposes and could not be denied entry into the U.S. mainland.... In 1917, Congress granted U.S. Citizenship to all persons born on the Island, but did not extend them all constitutional rights and obligations, such as having Congressional representation or paying federal income taxes" (Duany. 2010b: 225). [For one Porto Rican's analysis of the first decade of the United States' effect and its control over Puerto Rico's economy, and which was reported in 1909, see the: *San Francisco Chronicle. 3/26/1909: 15; S.F. Call. 8/12/1902: 7:* (Morín. 2000: 11, 10, in the "Bibliography Addendum" section of this book, pp. 191 - 194). (Bib. #355)].

For a critical, and insightful, description of the comparison and similarities between the historical development of Puerto Rico and Hawaii and their respective relationship(s) to the United States during the first decades of the 20th Century (1898-1930), including what the legal phrase that Puerto Rico "belongs to but are not part of the United States" meant/means, see: (Morín. 2000: 11).

With respect to Puerto Rico's population, Demographer José L. Vázquez's dissertation indicated that the first U.S. Census of the Puerto Rican population was taken in 1899. He wrote that:

"One year after the American invasion of Puerto Rico [1898] a census was taken under the supervision of the United States War Department. Since 1910 the Island has been included in the United States census area, and population counts have been made every ten years" (Vázquez. 1964: 27).

Additionally, Vázquez, in discussing "migration trends" from Puerto Rico in an historical context, i.e., emigration **from** Puerto Rico, pointed out that:

"Migration is not a new phenomenon in Puerto Rico [at least since the late 1800s]. Shortly after the American invasion of the Island (1898), many Puerto Ricans **emigrated** to Hawaii, Cuba, and Santo Domingo as a result of the economic crises created by the *San Ciriaco Hurricane* (1899), and the operation in the Island of emigration agents" (Vázquez. 1964: 116; see also: Vázquez Calzada. 1978: 274-314, 277, 280, 301, 302, 304-305; Vázquez Calzada. 1968: 7-8, 1-41; Vázquez Calzada and Zoraida Morales del Valle. [Undated]: 1-2). (emphasis added)

Additionally, Professor Jorge Duany, of the University of Puerto Rico, summarized the continual emigration from Puerto Rico to the United States after the early 1950s when he wrote that:

"In 1952, Puerto Rico became a U.S. Commonwealth (or *Estado Libre Asociado*, in Spanish) with limited autonomy over local matters, such as taxation, education, health, housing, culture, and language. Still, the federal government retained jurisdiction in most state affairs, including ***citizenship***, immigration, customs, defense, currency, transportation, communications, foreign trade, and diplomacy. By most accounts, Puerto Rico remains a colony because it lacks sovereignty and effective representation in the federal government" (Duany. 2010b: 225).

For an early view and description of Puerto Rico being a colony of the United States at the turn of the 20th Century, within the context of whether to give the people of Puerto Rico citizenship, the *San Francisco Call* newspaper of December 20, 1900 had the headline of, "The Court and the Colonies":

"The expansive results of the **Spanish [American] war** [1898] have put upon the country burdens and responsibilities that have to be borne or gotten rid of.... The great issue raised [of the granting of citizenship] can be settled only by the Supreme Court....The **Porto Ricans** and Filipinos cannot be citizens by the result of one election and returned to alienage by the adverse result of the next...." (*San Francisco Call.* December 20, 1900: 6). (emphasis added)

While there have been numerous researched books written over the years about the **immigration** of many other ethnic groups to California, as far as this author is aware, there have been no comprehensive book which has been written thus far about the historical **beginnings** of the Puerto Rican community in California. **3/** This book is my attempt to bridge this long overdue gap. Also, I provide census data and figures, taken from the *Report of the Governor of Hawaii* (the 1900-1926 editions), which shows the number of Puerto Ricans who decided to migrate from Hawaii to the [West] "Coast", most likely to California in general, and to the San Francisco Bay Area in particular. **4/**

Norma Carr lamented in her 1989 dissertation that:

"There is much more archival material on the Puerto Ricans of Hawaii than one might at first expect. However, very little is readily available [as opposed to today, in 2012], and it is this small body which has become the standard reference on the group. It consists of a few government documents, a few statistical reports, some mention in general studies on the ethnic groups in Hawaii, and two exploratory surveys by professors plus several student papers and Master's theses produced at the University of Hawaii between 1936-1960" (Carr. 1989: 394).

However, this author believes that with further research, and with the utilization of the internet and computer databases, I have expanded the available references/resources which future researchers and scholars will be able to use to further expand on the development of the "history of Puerto Rican immigration to Hawaii", the Puerto Rican sugar plantation workers residing in Hawaii, and the Puerto Rican migration from Hawaii to California during the period from 1900 through 1925. (cf.: this author's extensive Bibliography, wherein I utilized numerous government documents, both from the mainland, as well as from the Hawaiian Government, e.g., the many different *Reports from the Governor of the Territory of Hawaii*, from the: 1900-1926 editions, and the citations from a number of Hawaiian-based newspapers from the first years of the 20th Century).

With this book, I hope to expand on the history of both U.S. and California Puerto Ricans, and hope it is a welcomed addition to the subject of U.S. Puerto Rican history and genealogy as well. In short, this book should add to the existing overall history of both U.S. and California ethnic group history. Any comments can be provided to Mr López's e-mail address at: **DLopez777@aol.com**.

The Cover Page Description of This Book:

The photograph on the cover page of this book is from the front page of the December 15, 1900 issue of the **San Francisco Examiner** newspaper. The descriptive (and unsettling) caption beneath the photograph reads as follows (see also: Exhibit 17):

"In a choppy [?] sea, off Black Point the Porto Ricans were transferred from the *Caroline* to the *Rio De Janeiro* [Steamship]. A gang-plank was let down from the steerage deck of the big ocean steamer and lashed to a plank extending from the deck of the *Caroline.* Up this gangway the unhappy Porto Ricans were driven to the ship that is bearing them to **Hawaii**. The man under whom a cross is marked in the picture is Frank Alves, who piloted the party across the continent. He is shown in the act of forcing up the gangway to the *Rio* a woman who was unwilling to go and who protested energetically until her child was taken from her arms. Then she went aboard. The photograph was taken from the deck of the *Caroline*." (Italicize and bold added)

Acknowledgements and Permission Granted:

I would like to thank and **acknowledge** the following persons for their comments and suggestions on an earlier draft of this researched book, namely:

Dr. Ellen Fernandez-Sacco; Dr. Victor M. Rodríguez; Jose Reyes; Dr. Aileen Alvarado-Swaisgood; Charlie Fourquet Batiz; Rosario Camacho; Johnny Saldivia; Clifford Pagan; Dionisio Flores; Orlando Bodón; Helen Velazquez; Angela Rivera; Emily Vélez-Confer; Kyle Eddinger; the Library Staff at the San Diego County Library in Spring Valley, CA , in particular Philip Shopoff, Christine Plante, and Joshua Mitchell; Fred Rosen (Librarian), San Diego County Library (Poway); as well as the Library Staff at the Family History Center at the Church of Jesus Christ of Latter-Day Saints, in San Diego, CA, for the use of their *Ancestry.Institution.com* and their invaluable library of genealogy books; Linda Meckler; the House of Puerto Rico-San Diego; to my older brother, Roberto López, for reading and editing the entire final manuscript, and providing invaluable ideas and suggestions; and finally to Corazon N. Garcia for being with me for the over three years of the final completion of this book.

Of course, any limitation(s) that may appear in this book are strictly those of the author, and he alone is responsible for such.

Also, I would like to **acknowledge**, and to thank, the following institutions, for providing approval to allow me to include in this book the following "images"/"Exhibits" (See: ***after*** Chapter 27, Exhibits 1 – Exhibits 21):

"Ancestry.com", via the Legal Department, personal e-mail and telephone correspondence (Provo, Utah) (See: Exhibits 1, 2, 3, 6, 8, 9, 10, and 11);

The Bankcroft Library at the University of California, Berkeley, for the "images" from The "*San Francisco Examiner*" newspaper, via personal e-mail and telephone correspondence (Berkeley and San Francisco, CA) (See: Exhibits 12, 13, and 14); and

The San Mateo County Historical Association, 2200 Broadway, Redwood City, California 94063 (See: Exhibits 5, and 7); (<www.historysmc.org>). Phone No.: (650) 299-0104, ex. 222.

Hayward Area Historical Society, 22701 Main Street, Hayward, CA 94541. (510) 581-0223.

ABSTRACT

This book deals with, among other things, the identifying of as many "Porto Ricans" -- Puerto Ricans, by name, age, number of children (if any), occupation/profession, spousal names, year of immigration, etc., as well as the identification of other social characteristics (variables), for the first Puerto Ricans that arrived in **California** from 1850-1900, initially in small numbers. Beginning on December 14, 1900, and thereafter in larger numbers, Puerto Ricans began to immigrate to California and to the San Francisco Bay Area in particular, from 1900 to 1925, and later, well into the 20th Century.

The specific names, as well as their social variables, i.e., the "hard data", of these **immigrants** were obtained from the U.S. Federal Census, *primarily* from the 1910 U.S. Federal Census for the State of California. Utilizing current genealogical technology, specifically, the Library edition of *Ancestry.com*, has allowed this author to identify and verify, via reviewing the digitized version of the 1910 U.S. Federal Census (or the *Thirteenth Census of the United States*), the names of at least 151 Puerto Ricans, who migrated from Hawaii to California, and their family members who had immigrated to the

United States and were living in California and specifically, in the San Francisco Bay Area in 1910 (cf.: Exhibit 11). This book also covers the evolution of the California Puerto Rican community up to 1925, apparently, in large part, based upon the continual return of Puerto Ricans from Hawaii to California.

As a result, these immigrants, along with their children, became the first Puerto Ricans, in any meaningful numbers, who created the beginnings of California's first Puerto Rican ethnic enclaves or *colonias*.

Importantly, many of the names of the children of these early Puerto Rican immigrants to California, namely, "**the Second Generation" Puerto Rican** in California, have been identified in this book.

For a historical comparative analysis of Puerto Rican labor migration to New York City, as opposed to California, refer to the Master's Thesis entitled, "Labor Migration from Puerto Rico 1900-1930 and the origins of the Puerto Rican community in New York City" (Sanabria. 1985). Mr. Sanabria also covers Puerto Rican emigration to Hawaii, Mexico, St. Louis, Cuba, the United States, and Arizona. (*Ibid.* 9-38).

Finally, this book details the historical forces which led to the beginnings of Puerto Rican immigration to **both** California and Hawaii, as well as their migration from Hawaii to California, during the period from December 1900 to 1925. The reason(s) for this, which is important to reemphasize, was that *a significant portion* of the California Puerto Rican population from 1910, through 1925, was a direct result of Puerto Rican migration from the then Territory of Hawaii to California, primarily to the San Francisco Bay Area due, in large part, to the Puerto Ricans' *dissatisfaction* with the working conditions on the Hawaiian Sugar plantations, both economically and socially speaking. The initial intent of the first Puerto Rican immigrants was to go to Hawaii, and **not** to California.

KEY WORDS:

Puerto Ricans; Porto Ricans; California; Hawaii; *Ancestry.com*; Puerto Rican Genealogy; Emigration; Migration; U.S. Immigration; U.S. Federal Census; Race & Ethic Relations; American Ethnic History; Racialization; *State of California 1852 Census*; U.S. Labor History; Surplus Labor; San Francisco

Selected Quotes From Important Sources:

- From: **The United States Constitution**. ARTICLE I, Section 2. (Sept. 17, 1787) (from *The United States Constitution and other American Documents* (The National Archives. 2009: x, 4)):

"The actual [Census] Enumeration shall be made within three Years after the first Meeting of the Congress of the United States, and within every subsequent Term of ten Years, in such Manner as they shall by Law direct. The Number of Representatives shall not exceed one for every thirty Thousand, but each State shall have at Least one Representative...."

- From: **The United States Constitution – 14th Amendment**

"1. All persons **born** or naturalized **in the United States**, and subject to the jurisdiction thereof, **are citizens** of the United States and of the State wherein they reside. No State shall make or enforce any law which shall abridge the privileges or immunities of citizens of the

United States; nor shall any State <u>deprive</u> any person of life, liberty, or property, without <u>due process</u> of law; nor deny to any person within its <u>jurisdiction</u> the equal protection of the laws." (Underline in original) ("U.S. Constitution – Amendment 14 – The U.S. Constitution Online – USC Constitution.net"). (http://www.usconstitution.net/xconst_Am14.html). (Accessed: April 13, 2012) (emphasis added)

- From: Bernardo Vega, Cigar Worker "*Tabaquero*", Quoted by Juan Flores, from *Memoirs of Bernardo Vega*, (Flores. 1984: xii):

"Without a doubt, in order to stand on our own two feet Puerto Ricans of all generations must begin by affirming our own history. It is as if we are saying---we have roots, therefore we are!"

- From: Manuel Maldonado-Denis, *The Emigration Dialectic: Puerto Rico and the USA*, (Maldonado-Denis. 1980: 67):

"The history of our [Puerto Rican] people is also the history of those who have had to leave. To omit this reality in any historic account of our people not only perverts the analysis, but constitutes an act of crass historic irresponsibility."

- From: Charlie Fourquet Batiz, *"Puerto Rico…en los tiempos de 'ante:* A Photo Essay, Part 1 – Home, Sweet Home." (**Nuestra Herencia**. Spring/Summer 2009: 1. Volume 12.2):

"The 1910, 20, 30 and 35 censuses provide listings of our ancestor names, their physical descriptions, what they did, but cannot fully describe daily life in that bygone era."

Finally, the *San Francisco Chronicle* on October 9, 1902, reporting on whether or not the courts ruled if Porto Ricans [Puerto Ricans] were "aliens" or not, quoted the U.S. Constitution:

"The Fourteenth Amendment to the Constitution of the United States provides that all persons born or naturalized in the United States and subject to the jurisdiction thereof are citizens of the United States [and therefore, the courts ruled that Porto Rican **immigrants** in 1902, as opposed to those few Puerto Ricans who has already been born in the United States, were **not** citizens]."

- From: Stephen Caruso, San Diego

"I have known Daniel López for 12 years and he has been a good writer for the local Puerto Rican newsletter each month but little did I realize just how good a compiler and assembler of interesting and vitally important facts and history that he is! Daniel has used in depth and painstaking research to provide a fascinating trip through time as you are compelled to read the great human story of the Puerto Rican migration west and how little known this story is to the American public. I imagine most people feel Puerto Ricans are east coast immigrants but their Western story seems almost more fascinating and riveting. I like the way Daniel ties the thread together in a beautiful knot and I hope the reading public and especially the cultural historian, will delve into this well written book. Thank you Daniel López!"

September 2016: see the new "Exhibits 27 - Exhibits 32", pp. 251-256, for letters from Libraries, Universities, and Cultural Institutions relating to the 1st Edition of this book which was initially printed in 2013.

CHAPTER 1

"The Puerto Rican migration to Hawaii [and to California] in 1900-1901 was the first organized transfer of laborers between two possessions newly acquired by the United States." Norma Carr, *The Puerto Ricans in Hawaii: 1900-1958,* (Carr. 1989: v).

INTRODUCTION:

Prior to 1899, people born in Puerto Rico were referred to as Puerto Ricans, while after 1899, those born in Puerto Rico, were called "Porto Ricans," due to the United States' officially changing the name of the Island to "Porto Rico." As Dr. Clarence Senior pointed out "the spelling of the name of the island [Puerto Rico] was changed to an anglicized form, Porto Rico" (Senior 1965: 13). Surprisingly, there were a number of Puerto Ricans whom had actually immigrated to the United States, as well as to California and in particular, the city of San Francisco, **before** December 1900 (cf.: U.S. Bureau of the Census. 1902: 54; see below; cf.: Exhibit 1, Exhibit 2, Exhibit 3, Exhibit 5, and Exhibit 6).

For example, the United States imposed duality of names for the Island of Puerto Rico/Porto Rico is epitomized by the 1899 publication of the two volume book entitled: *Our Islands and their People: As Seen with Camera and Pencil* (De Olivares. 1899: 257-384) wherein the chapter entitled "A Day in San Juan" (page 257-384), consistently refers to "Porto Rico" (and hence, the reference to Porto Ricans), while the map of the island is titled "Puerto Rico." Notwithstanding, this colonial imposition of the name change of the island by the United States in 1899 was not able to change the name of the map of the Island, which was still called, in the De Olivares book, Puerto Rico. The reason for this is that if one looks closely at the Rand McNally & Co. map, the copyright date for this map was 1898, or one year *before* the Island's name change, (cf.: De Olivares. 1899: 256).

However, the major distinction between "**pre**-December 1900", and "**post**-December 1900," is that beginning in December 1900 and going into October 1901, and into at least the next two decades, Puerto Ricans began to immigrate to Hawaii, and thereafter, to the State of California, relatively speaking, ***en masse***, where they eventually formed the basis of California's emerging Puerto Rican enclaves (i.e., *colonias*) and community whereby the 1910 Federal Census of California listed a total of 342 Puerto Rican immigrants (cf.: U.S. Bureau of the Census. 1913a: 185), with the San Francisco area having a total of 213 Puerto Rican immigrants (U.S. Bureau of the Census. 1913b: 778). A decade later, in 1920, California had 935 Puerto Rican immigrants, while San Francisco had a total of 474 immigrants (U.S. Bureau of the Census. 1922: 630, 678).

Historical Context of Puerto Rican Migration to Hawaii:

Puerto Rican historian Norma Carr placed the beginning of the Puerto Rican migration to Hawaii within the historical migration of labor of a number of different ethnic groups which supplied the Hawaiian sugar plantations with a source of cheap surplus labor. For example, Carr's table entitled "Importation of Labor to Hawaii for the Sugar Plantations" identified the following migrations of (selected) groups to Hawaii, namely:

"Chinese: 1823 – Skilled workers arrived to help set up sugar mills. 1852 – Second group of Chinese arrived. 1886 – Last Chinese contract laborers entered Hawaii. 1900 – Chinese Exclusion Act."

"Japanese: 1868 – First small group arrived. 1884-1907 – About 140,000 came, predominately males.... 1907 – Gentlemen's Agreement restricted further immigration of Japanese laborers. 1907-1924 – More than 14,000 picture brides arrived. 1924 – Japanese were excluded by the National Origins Quota Act."

"Portuguese: 1878-1887 – About 12,780 came from Madeira and Azore Islands.... 1906-1913 – At least 5,000 more arrived...."

"**Puerto Ricans:** 1900-1901 – More than 5,000 arrived in family groups. First from one new American colony to another new American colony." Also, Dr. Carr writes: "1921 – Second and last recruitment by HSPA [Hawaii Sugar Planter's Association] in **Puerto Rico** – 683 arrived."

"Spaniards: 1907-1913 – About 8,000. By 1920 only about 1,500 still in Hawaii" (Carr: 1989: 448, 449; cf.: Secretary of the Interior. 1902: 5-7, 16, 41, 47, 48, page 448). (emphasis added) **Note:** For a comparison between Spanish (Spaniards from Spain) and Puerto Rican immigration to Hawaii, see the **section** of the 2008 dissertation from Ana María Varela-Lago, titled: "Andalusion farmers in Hawaii and California" (Varela-Lago. 2008: 147ff.).

A major reason why Puerto Ricans specifically immigrated to Hawaii beginning in December 1900 was the fact that the Hawaiian economy was overwhelmingly dependent on the sugar plantation economy. Since the plantations were what is today referred to as a "labor intensive" economy, the Hawaiian Sugar Planters were always seeking, and recruiting for, a source of "cheap labor" who were able to conduct the long arduous work required in the hot sun. Thus, at least as early as mid-1900, recruiters were sent to Puerto Rico to recruit a plantation labor force; "sugar [was] King" in Hawaii (Bib. #405) For example, The *Pacific Rural Press* (San Francisco, CA) newspaper of May 1909, reported that:

"To understand Hawaii [e.g., in December 1900] we must understand one thing in mind---that is sugar. Wherever land can be planted to [sugar] cane, cane is grown.... What we see usually is large fields of sugar cane, hardly broken by a tree, and bounded by the ocean on one hand and the mountains on the other.... Besides these, we have Koreans, Porto Ricans, some Spaniards, some Italians and people from almost every other race" (*Pacific Rural Press*. May 22, 1909: 388).

*21st Century **Research Technology**, Tools and Advances:*

It should be noted that as late as 1984, Blasé Camacho Souza, writing in *The Hawaiian Journal of History*, lamented the fact that "acquiring information about [the] Puerto Ricans" who had immigrated to Hawaii [as well as to California], "has been difficult due to the following factors" cited by her, namely:

• "Since they were not aliens, as Puerto Rico became a territory of the United States in 1900, there are no lists of names of Puerto Ricans who came as laborers to Hawaii [as well as to California], as there were lists of aliens kept by consulates of other countries....

• They are not listed on the California to Hawaii Ships' passenger lists.

- News accounts of the time (late 1890s and early 1900s) in various newspapers in Puerto Rico and the continental United States give differing data regarding the number of persons who came and of circumstances surrounding the journeys.

- The misrecording of their names by sugar plantation and Hawaii school personnel resulted in incorrect spellings, with names often being given a Portuguese spelling or Anglicized.

- Birth and death dates were not always accurately recorded" (Camacho Souza. 1984: 156).

Ms. Camacho Souza went on to point out in her article that:

"continued interest in the migration of Puerto Ricans and their life in a [then] new homeland has led to research being done in Hawaii, Puerto Rico, and in the continental United States" [including California] (Camacho Souza. 1984: 157).

By taking advantage of the advances of 21st Century research technology this book was able to be researched and written by this author, with the advent of contemporary computer-related tools and technologies, thereby overcoming to some degree, the limitations which Ms. Camacho Souza outlined above (cf.: Exhibits1 through 3, 6, 8, 9, 10, and 11).

Specifically, I was able to ascertain the names of many of the immigrants that had emigrated from Puerto Rico, to both California and Hawaii---via the utilization of the computer based software and the genealogy-related **Ancestry.com** subscription service, as well as the use of the *Google books.com* web site, which allowed me to access many of the Federal Government's "digitized" early immigration-related **Reports, Bulletins, Pamphlets**, and the **Census Forms** themselves, etc., covering the period from 1850-1925, of the Puerto Rican *diaspora* to both California and Hawaii (see: Exhibits 10 and 11).

Another 21st Century research tool which was not readily available to the public in 1984 was the Library of Congress' "Chronicling America: Historic American Newspapers" web site which allows a researcher to, and I quote:

"Search America's newspapers from 1836-1922 or use the *U.S. Newspaper Directory* to find information about American newspapers published between 1690-present. *Chronicling America* is sponsored jointly by the National Endowment for the Humanities and the Library of Congress…is…an Internet-based, searchable database…." (http://chroniclingamerica.loc.gov/1ccn/ sn83025121/1900-12-28/ed-1/seq-5/;words= RICAN…). (Accessed over several weeks in 2012)

Another research tool which this author was able to utilize was similar to the above referenced Library of Congress' *U.S. Newspaper Directory* web site, namely, the *California Digital Newspaper Collection* web site, Center for Bibliographic Studies and research, University of California, Riverside, http://cdnc.ucr.edu. This web site allowed me to search, and then review, several historically-related, (and significant to this author's subject), California newspapers covering the time period from 1900-1925.

Note: for a bibliography of resources of the historically, and important role that **sugar** has played in Hawaii, refer to: *Sugar in Hawaii: A guide to Historical Resources*, (Compiled and annotated by Susan M. Campbell, Edited by Linda K. Menton). The Humanities Program of the State Foundation on Culture and the Arts in cooperation with The Hawaiian Historical Society, Honolulu, 1986; see also: "An Overview of the History of Sugar in Hawaii", pp. xiii-xv). (cf.: *The Chicago Sunday Times*, Dec. 11, 1910, p. 4, "Census Totals…Stars and Stripes Float over One-Sixteenth of World's Inhabitants").

CHAPTER 2

PART I: A Review of the Literature
Why Did Puerto Ricans Immigrate to Hawaii?

The Historical Connection of Puerto Rican Immigration:

"Everything that affects the Hawaiian Islands, in so far as labor is concerned, has a direct reflection in California. Whenever the people of the Hawaiian Islands have imported laborers, no matter where they came from, we have always had a backwash in California, particularly in San Francisco" (Committee on Immigration and Naturalization. 1921. (Part 1): 361).

The above quote from a Congressional Hearing held in 1921, showed the **direct connection** between Puerto Rican immigration to Hawaii, as well as Puerto Rican migration from Hawaii to California (which is presented and discussed in greater detail in this book.)

The pioneering historical scholarship of Virginia Sánchez Korrol describes the "evolution of Puerto Rican communities in the United States" which primarily covered the New York City community, and justly so, (cf.; Sánchez Korrol 1994a: 281-301; Sánchez Korrol 2005), while Teresa Whalen covered the history of the Puerto Rican community in Philadelphia (although California and San Francisco were briefly mentioned in her article) (Teresa Whalen 2005: 8-11, 24-25, 32; 1-33; The Historical Society of Pennsylvania (n.d.), their article titled: "Early Enclaves", author unknown).

In contrast, this book will describe the "evolution of Puerto Rican communities in California", and the City of San Francisco in particular, from 1850-1925, as well as the Puerto Rican community in Hawaii from 1900-1925. From December 14, 1900 onward, these Puerto Ricans emigrated from Puerto Rico to the United States as *"contract laborers"*, on their way to the Hawaiian sugar plantations, although about half, or 56 arrived in Hawaii on Dec. 23, 1900, while 56 (it was, in reality, at least 64, according to *this* author's counting) of the originally more than 114 immigrants, opted to **stay in** San Francisco, CA. (*The Hawaiian Star*, December 24, 1900a: 1).

A Brief Description of Why the Puerto Ricans Immigrated to Hawaii:

Blasé Camacho Souza succinctly summarized the reasons why Puerto Ricans immigrated from Puerto Rico to Hawaii during the period from December 1900 through 1902 when she wrote in her article entitled, "Trabajo y Tristeza—'Work and Sorrow': The Puerto Ricans of Hawaii 1900-1902", as follows:

"In…1898, Hawaii became a territory of the United States through annexation. Hawaii's sugar industry had been recruiting labor world-wide 'to get enough workers, to get them cheaply, and to keep them on the plantations.… The Hawaiian sugar planters were looking for a new source of labor. A **strike** at Pioneer Mill in Lahaina, on April 4, 1900, and another at Olowalu Plantation near Lahaina, shortly thereafter, by Japanese laborers, successfully elicited some concessions from their managers. The Organic Act of 1900 which established the labor contract system; thus, Japanese laborers felt free to make demands for higher wages, reduced hours, Japanese instead of white *lunas*, abolition of the docking system, and other concessions. This was the situation that the first group of Puerto Ricans to arrive in Hawaii, in December 1900, encountered when they were assigned to work at Pioneer Mill. The Hawaiian Sugar Planters' Association looked to Puerto Rico to supply new cheap labor" (Camacho Souza. 1984: 158). (emphasis added)

For example, the official Hawaiian government analysis and description of the direct **connection(s)** between Chinese, Japanese, and Puerto Rican labor, and why the Puerto Ricans were recruited to work in the plantations of Hawaii in 1900 [and in 1901], was capsulated in this 1902 *Report*, namely:

"From the planter's point of view an important result of the **Porto Rican immigration** was the moral effect that their arrival had upon the Japanese. The latter had begun to fancy that with the enforcement of the Federal Chinese exclusion and contract laws after [Hawaiian] annexation they were complete masters of the labor situation in Hawaii. They formed temporary combinations for the purpose of striking at critical periods of the planting and grinding season, and in this way had succeeded in forcing up wages. This is sufficiently shown by the rise in the average wage of field hands from 60 to 76 cents a day, an increase of over 25 percent, during the time ending June 30, 1901--the first twelve months following annexation. The regular arrival of monthly expeditions of **Porto Rican laboring people** throughout an entire year largely disabused them of this sense of monopoly and made them much more reasonable in their relations with their employers" (cited in, Carr. 1989: 333). (emphasis added)

Puerto Rican Immigration and Hawaii's Continuing Need
for International Labor for their Sugar Plantations:

The 1900 *Report of the Territory of Hawaii to the Secretary of the Interior* summarized the importance of sugar production to the total economy of Hawaii, and its need for plantation laborers in 1900 when it stated that:

"There is a strong feeling among sugar men [i.e., the Hawaiian Sugar Planters' Association] that some **source of labor supply outside of the Territory [e.g., like Puerto Rico]** is essential to the continued prosperity of local sugar enterprises (Secretary of the Interior. 1900: 16). (emphasis added)

Note that the 1900 *Report of the Governor* did not cite, or reference, any Puerto Ricans among its 10 cited "nationalities" who lived in Hawaii in 1900.

Historical Context of Hawaii's International Labor Request Needs (1852-1899):

Prior to the first Puerto Rican agricultural immigrants' arrival to Hawaii in December 1900, Hawaii had made concerted efforts in recruiting international labor from many different countries throughout the world. For example, the 1921 dated publication entitled "Labor Problems in Hawaii", has a Table ("unnamed") wherein it listed the nationalities and numbers of the various immigrants which had immigrated to Hawaii during the period from 1852 through 1899. From 1852 to 1864, a total of 704 Chinese agricultural immigrants arrived in Hawaii (this number was calculated by this author). Thousands of Chinese immigrants continued to arrive in Hawaii till 1886. From 1887 to 1890 the Table had no number(s). Basically, from 1891 to 1899 over 9,000 Chinese immigrants immigrated to Hawaii (Committee on Immigration and Naturalization, The. 1921 (Part 1): 542).

In addition, from 1855 to 1899, Hawaii immigration increased yearly from a number of different world-wide countries. For example, immigrants arrived in Hawaii from (at least) the following countries (identified by "nationality"): Japanese (who first arrived in 1858) (a total of over 60,000 thousand immigrants as of 1899); Portuguese (over 8,000 thousand); Germans (1,403); South Sea Islanders (2,444); Galicians (372); Americans (14 in 1898); and Norwegians (615 in 1881). Japanese immigration did not begin in large numbers till 1885 (1,946). Note that "Legislative appropriations for the encouragement of immigration" to Hawaii was begun in 1854, according to this Table (Ibid.: 542). **Note:** These number calculations were added by this author, (CF.: Bibliography #171)

The Puerto Rican Historical Context For Immigrating To Hawaii:

The 1901 *Report of the Governor* recognized that:

"Upon the successful and economical production of sugar depends the prosperity of the islands.... Since the annexation of the Hawaiian Islands as a Territory of the United States, while many of the Japanese and Chinese have returned to their native countries. Between June 14, 1900...and the 31st day of August, 1901, 4,079 Japanese have left the Territory, while only 589 have arrived. This condition of affairs presents a most serious question as affecting our principal industry. All sugar plantation stocks have fallen far below their former value, owing to the uncertainty of the labor supply" (Secretary of the Interior. 1901: 63).

Additionally, the government of Hawaii, at least as reported in the 1901 *Report of the Governor*, expressed a racially-oriented explanation for why the "white", as opposed to the "non-white" plantation laborers could not continue to work on the Hawaiian sugar plantations when it reported that:

"It is simply a physical impossibility for the Anglo-Saxon [i.e., "white"] satisfactorily to perform the severe labor required in the sugar fields" (Ibid.: 63).

At least as early as 1900, the Government of Hawaii acknowledged their need for an ever continuing supply of international labor to be able to work on their Sugar Plantations. Thus, the Governor of Hawaii, in his *Report of the Governor of the Territory of Hawaii to the Secretary of the Interior*, provided a Table wherein it listed "the ratio of nationality and of contract and day laborers for 1899". It indicated that:

"The number of sugar plantation laborers...in 1899...increased to 35,987" (Secretary of the Interior. 1900: 16). The nationalities were as follows: Hawaiian (1,326); Portuguese (2,153); Japanese (25,654); Chinese (5,969); South sea islands [*sic*] (79); "Other nationalities" (806); Total: 35,987 (Secretary of the Interior. 1900: 16).

Further, this same 1900 *Governors Report* provided a Table wherein it identified a total of 10 categories of nationalities of "skilled labor" [i.e., laborers] which were then working "on Hawaiian sugar plantations [on] October 31, 1899", namely: Americans (405); Hawaiians (219); British (252); Germans (218); Portuguese (305); Australians (16); Scandinavians (71); Japanese (416); Chinese (94); "Other nationalities" (23). Total: 2,019 (Ibid.: 16).

As a direct result of the above, Puerto Rican immigration and sugar plantation labor was needed, and recruitment began in Puerto Rico around the later part of calendar year 1900.

For example, the 1901 *Report of the Governor* stated that up to the fiscal year ending June 30, 1901, there were a total of 1,772 men, and 323 women, for a total of 2,095 Puerto Rican immigrant laborers on the Hawaiian sugar plantations. For comparison, as of June 1901, there were a total of 1,470 Hawaiians, 2,417 Portuguese, 342 Americans, and 169 British laborers. The 1901 *Report* indicated that these Puerto Rican immigrants were considered, and listed to be, "unskilled plantations laborers", among the Hawaiian Islands' 58 plantations (Secretary of the Interior. 1901: 66, 64).

This same 1901 *Report of the Governor* acknowledged that "the **cost of living** [in Hawaii] *is much higher* then in most localities on the mainland, owing to the fact that nearly all our supplies are shipped to us from long distances", thereby adversely affecting all of the Puerto Rican laborers and immigrants, as well as all the other inhabitants of Hawaii as well (Ibid.: 69). (emphasis added)

At least as early as July 1901, the California *Amador Ledger* newsletter reported that Puerto Rican immigration to Hawaii beginning in December 1900 and thereafter, was viewed by at least some sectors, as being the "solution" to the labor problem in Hawaii. Thus, the *Amador Ledger* wrote the following:

"With the advent of the **Porto Ricans** there seems a solution of the labor problem which has been vexing the sugar planters of the Hawaiian Islands. There are now 5000 **Porto Ricans** established on the various islands, and they are not only giving satisfaction to the planters, but are happy and contended in their new homes" (*Amador Ledger*. July 5, 1901: 1).

It should be noted that the 1902 *Report of the Commissioner of Labor On Hawaii. 1902* (issued in: 1903), had a section of this *Report* entitled: "Labor Conditions in the Sugar Industry in Hawaii, California, Texas, Louisiana, Cuba, and Puerto Rico", wherein it discussed, and compared, the working conditions in these aforementioned countries (*Report of the Commissioner of Labor On Hawaii. 1902* (1903): 90ff.).

This referenced 1902 *Report*, listed a total of 1,679 Puerto Rican male Field Hands, and 175 Puerto Rican female Field Hands, with each gender working six days per week (Ibid.: 162), although it also reported that "the Porto Ricans, when they arrived, gave the least promise, either as citizens or as laborers, of any immigrants that ever [albeit only **recently** having] disembarked at Honolulu" (Ibid.: 25). This 1902 (1903) Commissioner's *Report* listed detailed Tables of the different Occupations which were utilized on the Sugar Plantation, idenified by: Occupation, Nationality, Years, Number of Employees for each Occupation, Days per week worked, Hours per week worked, Wages per day earned, etc. (Ibid.: 162ff).

At least as early as 1905, the *Report of the Governor of the Territory of Hawaii to the Secretary of the Interior*, reported the Hawaiian Islands' concerns regarding strikes which had occurred on the sugar plantations. For example, the Governor of Hawaii acknowledged the problem of labor strife when he indicated:

"One of the most important events during the year was the strike at Lahaina plantation, on the island of Maui, which occurred on May 20, 1905. Seventeen hundred Japanese refused to work and became riotous by breaking the windows and doors of the 'sugar mill' and gathering together at night, striking terror to the private residents of the town of Lahaina, and making an attack on the house of one of their own countrymen" (Secretary of the Interior. 1905: 61).

Also, the *Third Report of the Commissioner of Labor on Hawaii. 1905* (issued in 1906), reported that as of 1905, there were a total of 1,907 Puerto Rican laborers working on the Hawaiian Sugar Plantations, or 3.95% of all of the plantation workers, down from a high of 5.29% in 1901. This report also provided the "distribution of [Puerto Rican] labor on [the] Hawaiian Sugar Plantations" in 1905 as being involved in the following job occupations, namely:

4 involved in Administration; 1,722 in Cultivation; 70 in Manufacture; 4 in Mechanical trades; 7 in

"Superintendence"; 79 in Transportation; 21 in an "Unclassified" occupation, for a total of 1,907 (U.S. Dept. of Commerce and Labor. 1906: 11) [see: Bibliography #301].

Even as late as May 1909, the Hawaiian Sugar Planters were using the Puerto Ricans, along with other "ethnic groups", to **break up strikes** which were going on in the sugar plantations. Thus, the *Los Angeles Herald* had the informative headline in their May 1909 issue: "Japanese Strike Appears Broken. Many Laborers are Hired to Take Places. Hawaiians Are Determined to Replace Orientals...." The *Los Angeles Herald* newspaper reported that:

"A determined effort is being made to break the **strike** of the Japanese plantation laborers, of whom more than 5000 have walked out to enforce demands for increased **pay**. Six hundred strike breakers, composed of Hawaiians, Portuguese, **Porto Ricans**, and Chinese, have been put to work in the large mill on the Honolulu plantation, grinding cane which already had been cut when the Japanese went on strike" (*Los Angeles Herald.* May 16, 1909: 3). (emphasis added)

Additionally, in April 1901, Santiago Iglesias, a representative of the Federation of Labor of Porto Rico, went to Washington, D.C.:

"with a petition signed by 6000 Porto Ricans praying for relief from the distressing [economic and physical] conditions alleged to exist on the island, presented the petition to the President today.... Iglesias told the President that the destitution existing in the island could be relieved if the Government would expend liberal sums in the building of roads" (*San Francisco Call.* 4/16/1901: 2).

An often overlooked contributor for why the Puerto Rican agricultural immigrants emigrated from Puerto Rico to Hawaii (and also to California), at least as early as 1900, was due to **the ever increasing cost of the standard of living** on the Island after the United States assumed "possession", i.e., the "acquisition", of Puerto Rico via the ***Treaty of Paris*** of December 10, 1898. Thus, the *Sacramento Daily Union* [Sacramento, CA] reported in April 1899 the following (cf.: Exhibit 14, Exhibit 15, and Exhibit 16) (see also: *San Francisco Call.* December 20, 1900: 6):

"...there is much dissatisfaction among the lower class of natives throughout the island and there has been a good deal of violent talk by the ignorant against the new regime. The chief cause of this anti-American feeling is the **increase in the cost of living** since the American occupation began.... But, as things have turned out, the prices of all kinds of commodities have advanced considerably: and the **cost of living is very much higher now** than it was in the days of Spanish dominion. The merchant, moreover, is uncertain as to what customs he will have to pay and he does not care to order more than is actually necessary. Nor is the agriculturist in a mood to extend his cultivation until he can be assured of a safe market for his products...." (emphasis added)

The April 1899 article went on to report that:

"Many, who are without employment, are lying hungry about the towns and they constitute the material which mischief-makers use in working up irritation against the Americans.... Give our commerce and agriculture a chance" (*Sacramento Daily Union.* April 6, 1899: 6).

The magnitude and the devastation of much of Puerto Rico, especially in the interior coffee farming areas due to the August 1899 hurricane, was capsulized in an August 26,1899 article with the headline: "Suffering Porto Ricans. **Californians** Appealed To For Help", in the California newspaper, the *Sacramento Daily Union*. It reported the following:

"The appeal made to **Californians** through Governor Gage by Secretary Root, for aid for the suffering Porto Ricans, is as follows.... I enclose herewith copies of two telegraphic dispatches ... from the Governor General of Porto Rico, by which it appears that the devastation wrought by the recent hurricane in that island is even greater than was at first supposed. It is evident that a great multitude of people rendered utterly destitute by this awful calamity must be fed and cared for during a considerable period until they can have the opportunity to produce food for themselves. Enormous quantities of supplies of the kinds indicated by the Governor General must be produced.... I beg you to ask the people of your State [California] to contribute generously to the relief of the people of Porto Rico" (*Sacramento Daily Union.* August 26, 1899: 3). (emphasis added)

To summarize the historical transformation of the Puerto Rican agricultural worker, as well as Puerto Rico's agriculturally-based economy during the period from 1899 through 1910, the book titled *Sources for the Study of Puerto Rican Migration – 1897-1930*, provided the following factual summary description:

"Census data show that between 1899 and 1910 the number of landless farmers increased considerably as the number of farms smaller than nineteen acres fell from 87.8 per cent to 72 per cent of all farms and as the number of farms over one hundred acres increased from 2.2 per cent to 6.5 per cent of all farms. By 1910, one quarter million people on the Island lived on family owned farms but over half a million were without land. Under these circumstances there developed in Puerto Rico a large relative surplus population that manifested itself as a growing problem of unemployment [i.e., these were those persons who were probably more likely to want to, and/or had to, emigrate]...."

"It was these workers who, lacking any means of subsistence except for their labor power, were forced into a process of migration....The movement of workers from Puerto Rico that began with migrations to Hawaii [and to California] in 1900 and which culminated with the presence of thirty four thousand Puerto Ricans in New York City by 1930 was a consequence of the dramatic changes that occurred on the Island as a result of the United States intervention [in Puerto Rico beginning in 1898]. Add to this the effects of the hurricane of 1899, *San Ciriaco*, and it is easy to see why many Puerto Ricans were eager to accept the promises of agents who were actively recruiting workers for labor scarce Hawaiian sugar plantations.... The migrations of workers from Puerto Rico to Hawaii between 1900 and 1901 thus became the first in a long series of migrations under contract that took place up to 1930 and continues to this day" (History Task Force. 1982: 3, 4).

Thus, it was the combination of Puerto Rico's devastated economic and physical condition of the Island, especially the interior farming regions, which prompted many Puerto Ricans to make the gut-wrenching decision to emigrate from Puerto Rico and take a journey of literally thousands of miles to Hawaii (or to cut their journey short---so to speak), to decide to stay in California, and not to continue the additional 2,100 miles to Hawaii.

Thus, at least as early as May 1901, in an article entitled "Labor Conditions in Porto Rico", by Azel Ames, M.D., in the *Bulletin of the* U.S. Department of Labor, Dr. Azel reported that "...the transfer of a few thousands of the islanders to the Hawaiian Islands **under contract to labor** on the sugar plantations, may under wise management prove of value to all concerned" (cited in: Ames, Azel, M.D. May 1901: 410). (emphasis added) (cf.: Maldonado 1979: 115; also on the role of contract labor in the evolution of these communities in the U.S., and San Francisco; *N.Y. Times*, 3/21/1917: 10, Bib. #325).

In short, these aforementioned Puerto Rican contract laborers emigrated from Puerto Rico due to economic and natural disaster-related reasons. For example, *The New York Times'* May 5, 1900 article, "Porto Rican Relief", reported that:

"The committee appointed last August by Secretary of War Root to receive and disburse funds for the relief of the Porto Ricans who suffered from the great hurricane last spring has made its report.... The committee states that in its opinion the Government should continue the issue of rations until the 1st of June. It is set forth in the report that the committee...has decided to use the balance of the fund for the benefit of the large number of children who were made orphans by the hurricane" (*New York Times*. 5 May 1900: 2; see also: *San Francisco Chronicle*. December 23, 1900: 9).

Disputed Figures of the Number of Puerto Rican Immigrants to Hawaii *(1900-1901):*

In a similar vein, Professor Anthony Castanha of the University of Hawaii wrote in his 2004 Dissertation, that:

"From November 1900 to September 1901, eleven expeditions carrying 5,203 Boricuas ["Porto Ricans"] departed from [Puerto Rico] to the sugar plantations [of Hawaii].... Most of the Puerto Ricans who emigrated there were Jíbaros from the mountain regions of Yauco, Lares, Utuado, Adjuntas and Maricao. Most of them were coffee **farmers** whose homes and crops had been destroyed in 1899 by the hurricane *San Ciriaco*. Others came from the coastal regions of Ponce and Mayaguez.... The [Puerto Ricans] were recruited by the Hawaiian Sugar Planters' Association (HSPA) to work on the lucrative sugar plantations scattered throughout the major islands of the Hawaiian chain" (Castanha 2004: 253-254; cf.: Bulletin of the Department of Labor. 1903a: 703, 767-772). (emphasis added)

However, the Spanish language newspaper, *El Problema* (Sept. 6, 1901) (Puerto Rico), cited the immigration numbers for the combined first 10 (out of the <u>eventual</u> total of 11 Group expeditions), to be a total 5,203 immigrants. However, **after** the Sept. 6th issue, the 11th and final expedition left Puerto Rico on Sept. 29, 1901, and arrived in Hawaii on Oct. 19, 1901. It should be noted that the 1902 (published in: 1903) *Report of the Commissioner of Labor On Hawaii,* reported the total cost for transporting the first "about 5,000" Puerto Ricans from Puerto Rico to Hawaii for the eventual combined 11 expeditions was as follows:

"The Porto Ricans arrived in Hawaii in **11 expeditions** beginning in December, 1900, and continuing until October 19, 1901. There were about 450 in each party, the total number of immigrants being about 5,000, of whom 2,930 were men and the remainder women and children. The exact cost of recruiting and bringing them to Honolulu was $564,191.68, or more than $100 per capita---a sum amply sufficient to assure their comfortable transportation and entertainment while en route" (U.S. Bureau of Labor. 1903: 26; see also: Bulletin of the Department of Labor. 1903a: 703; Bib. #23).

Note: The literature unequivocally shows that there have been some discrepancies with the immigration figures, i.e., with different figures obtained, depending on the source(s) one is reviewing.

It should be noted that the *El Problema* newspaper actually mis-counted, and incorrectly reported, the number of immigrants in their September 6, 1901 column/article. For example, the newspaper identified the following 10 expeditions (out of the **eventual** total of 11 Group expeditions to Hawaii), the number of Puerto Rican immigrants on each of these 10 expeditions, and the day and the month for each of the 10 expeditions which the article cited. (reprinted in: Centro de Estudios Puertorriqueños. 1982: 45; see also: Camacho Souza. 1984 165, 166; Rosario-Rivera. 2000). Therefore, the following figures represent the day, the month, and the number of immigrants which were in <u>each</u> of the aforementioned 10 cited expeditions just listed:

Nov. 22, 1900: 114; Dec. 26, 1900: 384; Jan. 24, 1901: 776; March 03, 1901: 551; March 26, 1901: 894; April 24, 1901: 534; May 21, 1901: 775; June 14, 1901:708; Aug. 12, 1901: 169; Aug. 29, 1901:

398; for a **Total: 5203**. (**Note:** Whereas the *El Problema* newspaper cited the 3rd expedition as departing from Puerto Rico on January 24, 1901, Norma Carr, in contrast, cited the 3rd expedition as departing from Puerto Rico on February 6, 1901 (Carr. 1989: 90)).

However, when you count the above cited immigrants from the 10 expeditions, the correct figure is 5,303, or exactly 100 more immigrants than what *El Problema* reported on September 6, 1901. Thus, the ***average*** for the 11 expeditions was 482 Puerto Rican immigrants who emigrated from Puerto Rico per each expedition (*Pacific Commercial Advertiser*. May 14, 1901: 12; *Pacific Commercial Advertiser*. January 17, 1901: 1 3; *Pacific Commercial Advertiser*. April 19, 1901: 5; see: *San Francisco Call*. April 14, 1901: 17)).

Also, Norma Carr identified the following 11 expedition **Groups**, from their *departure date* from Puerto Rico to Hawaii, as follows: I) Nov. 22, 1900; II) Dec. 26, 1900; III) Feb. 6, 1901; IV) March 3, 1901; V) March 26, 1901; VI) April 24, 1901; VII) May 21, 1901; VIII) June 14, 1901; IX) Aug. 12, 1901; X) Aug. 28, 1901; and XI) Sept. 29, 1901, (Carr. 1989: 90-91, 92-145ff.).

Professor Carr's dissertation identified the 11th Group as having departed from Puerto Rico on September 29, 1901 and arriving in Honolulu, Hawaii on October 18, 1901, with 300 Puerto Rican passengers (cf.: Carr. 1989: 145, 90-91, her "Migration Chronology Journey/Source" Table/Chart; Camacho Souza. 1984: 165, 166). Therefore, if you add the 300 to the *El Problema* figure of 5, 203, than the total corrected figure is 5,603, i.e., the 5,203 + 100 + 300 figures = 5,603 immigrants. For comparative figures see: (Rosario-Rivera. 2000: 1-26).

Norma Carr's Citations of the Names of Puerto Rican Immigrants to Hawaii from 1900-1925:

Norma Carr's dissertation also identified the names of a number of these Puerto Rican immigrants from among the 11 Groups which were mentioned above, and therefore departed from Puerto Rico beginning in November 1900 and thereafter, and either arrived in Hawaii, or died during transit sometime between December 23, 1900 and October 1901. For example, Car (1989) identified the following names:

The mother [her name was not identified] of the child, Juan Perez (p. 104); Ezequial Rodriguex (*sic*, written in the original) (15), died on December 25th and Pedro Andujas (22), died on December 29th, with "both deaths attributed to anemia. They were buried at sea." María Jose Torres, "the 80-year old mother of the Garcia sisters, died on January 2nd [1901] and was buried in New Orleans…" (page 108).

She also identified additional names of those that either arrived in Hawaii, or had died on their way to Hawaii, namely:

Frederick Beltran (20), and Vicente Cruz, both died and were buried at sea. Juan Bautista Dominis and his wife (not named), became parents of a girl on March 17 [1901] and named her Zealandia [she was named after the ship they were traveling on to Hawaii] Patricia Dominis." Ana Muniz and Ramon Patinao, Maria Pagan and Francisco Beauchamps, and Dolores Beauchamps and Lorenzo Jimenez. All three couples were married on the *Zealandia*, on their voyage to Hawaii (page 122). F.J. Madura "had made the trip as the only passenger in Cabin Class and had been waited on like a king. Madura was an employee of the labor brokers…" (Carr. 1989: 122-123).

Norma Carr also identified the following additional names of those that <u>arrived</u> in Hawaii among the first 11 expeditions (December 23, 1900 - October 1901), as follows:

"...Seven Puerto Ricans in steerage were P. Sanchez, C. Velazquez, F. Caedeno, M. Caedeno, M. Ruiz; M. Cartes, and J. Jesus. An earlier account about the reluctant passengers gave their names as Eselle Rivera and Maria Cheovana, Nancisco Santiago, Pablo Sago, Martin Cortes and Baldo Velsope. So much for consistency. First class passengers included Q. Bargas [?] and I. Blanco... Judge Wilcox committed Jose Ricardo Centerio to the insane asylum... In 1903 Carlos Santiago appealed to the Governor of Puerto Rico to intervene to secure the bonus or the Puerto Ricans [plantation workers]..." (Carr. 1989: 154; 194).

Norma Carr further identified other Puerto Rican immigrants who arrived in Hawaii after 1906, as:

"In 1906 Captain A.O. Winters of the Salvation Army preached to the Puerto Ricans on the island of Kauai and invited them to join the march for Christ. Within three years a group of energetic Puerto Ricans preached the gospel in Spanish throughout the Territory [of Hawaii]. The first to join the Salvation Army were Francisco C. Salsules, Juan C. Feliciano, Jose Pagan, Nicolas Aguilar, Candido Cencel, Miguel Velez and Emergirdo Quinones. The California-based Pentecostal Church established a mission in Hawaii and recruited Hawaiians and Portuguese as well as Puerto Ricans" (Carr. 1989: 209).

Carr went on to identify "the first Puerto Rican ministers [in Hawaii] in the Pentecostal Mission" as the following persons:

"Rev. Juan (Juanito) Feliciano, the Rev. Ramon Quinones, the Rev. Jose Pagan and the Rev. Juan Castro. They preached the gospel everywhere, on plantations, in the open next to the volcanoes, under trees, in private homes, hospitals and prisons..." (Carr.1989: 209).

She further wrote that a Puerto Rican Pastor's name was Pancho Ortiz, and that:

"In 1913 Juan [Lugo] and the pastor's son, Panchito, were selected to go to San Francisco for special training as pastoral missionaries. The two young men preached in Spanish in San Francisco, San Jose, and Los Angeles" (Carr. 1989: 229-230).

Carr identifies the important role played by the Puerto Rican immigrants to Hawaii after 1900, and their subsequent critical role in the future development of the Pentecostal movement in Hawaii, when she wrote:

"Panchito Ortiz, Salomon and Dionisia Feliciano, who were also from Hawaii, joined [Juan] Lugo by late October. Lorenzo Lucena arrived in 1917. These five native-born Puerto Ricans who had been immigrants to Hawaii initiated the Pentecostal movement on their home island, but Lugo in particular is credited as its founder..." (Carr. 1989: 230).

Other Puerto Ricans identified by Carr that were in Hawaii at this time were: Manuel Guzman (p. 231); Alfred "Freddy" Santiago; Manuel Olivieri Sanchez (p. 235); Juan Cancio Martinez (p. 256); Jesus Taro; and Johann Maltines [sic, in the original]. She also identified the following names of those Hawaiian Puerto Ricans who were required to register for the draft [for WW I], namely: Lorenzo Camacho, Ramon Mendez, Ramon Mitta, Pedro Fino, Manual O. Sanchis (sic, in original), his brother Milliano S. Olivieri, John F. Rosa, and Hermohenes Montijo. "Manuel Olivieri's Sanchez advised his fellow countrymen to refuse the draft call as long as they were not allowed to vote... Hilda Ortiz was at Ookala School in 1924-25, and in 1927 Margaret Maldonado was teaching at Honomu. Both women had long careers as teachers in Hawaii" (Carr. 1989: 236; 246).

Carr reported that the "three Kauai poets-Carlos Fraticelli, Justo Perez Peña and Nicolas Caravallo

Vegas—were respected and acclaimed within their small communities…. The tree Kauai poets and [Andalecio] Trochez of Kahuku were all born in Yauco [Puerto Rico]… The Troche family was in Kauai [Hawaii] until 1915 or 1916" (Carr. 1989: 252). [For a description of the role played by Puerto Rican poet **Carlos Fraticelli** in Hawaii, see: (Austin Dias, *"Carlos Mario Fraticelli: A Puerto Rican Poet on the sugar plantations of Hawai'i"*, the **Centro Journal**. Vol. XIII, Num. 1, 2001, pp. 96-109; Center for Puerto Rican Studies, CUNY), Bib. #356].

Note: Carr pointed out in a footnote in her dissertation that, "Adalecio Trochez added 'z' to his name believing that it was its proper spelling. It was not. The rest of the family continued to use Troche" (Carr. 1989: 257).

It should be noted that Austin Dias describes Carlos Fraticelli, arriving in Hawaii in 1901, as the voice and the poet of a generation of people, who gave expression for those that emigrated from Puerto Rico to Hawaii, during the first decades of the 20th Century, and therefore, "he [Fraticelli] reveals himself to be a keen observer and chronicler of the immigrant experience". Therefore, Fraticelli "… is the spokesperson for his Puerto Rican people" (Dias. 2001: 98, 102). In other words, "Fraticelli's works are a celebration and an affirmation, in poetry and music, of his Puerto Rican Culture" (Dias. 2001: 105).

Austin Dias goes on to summarize the historical importance of Carlos Fraticelli to the Hawaiian Puerto Rican experience, as follows:

"Fraticelli's testimony of the Boricua experience in Hawai'i at the beginning of the twentieth century is both particular and universal. His concerns are common to all immigrants, regardless of time and place: assimilation, loss of ethnic identity, alienation between immigrant parents and children born in the new county. The social problems he addresses are still with us today: quality of public education, crises of the family, crisis of values. At the same time these are issues the Puerto Ricans in Hawai'i continue to face today." (Dias. 2001: 107).

Hawaiian Puerto Ricans and U.S. Citizenship:
The Historical Role Played by Manuel Olivieri Sanchez:

It should be noted that a *Wikipedia* article titled "Manuel Olivieri Sanchez", reported the historically significant role played by Mr. Olivieri Sanchez, particularly for the Hawaiian Puerto Ricans. For example, this article pointed out that:

"Olivieri Sanchez was born in Yauco, Puerto Rico, when the island was still a Spanish possession…. [Mr.] Olivieri Sanchez's family…moved to Hawaii [in **1901**] with his mother. He became fluent in both English and Spanish and worked as a court interpreter. At the time both Puerto Rico and Hawaii were territories of the United States. However, with the passage of the Jones-Shafroth Act of 1917, [the same year that the U.S. entered World War I], the United States granted U.S. Citizenship to the Puerto Rican residents in Puerto Rico and excluded those who resided in Hawaii. Even though Puerto Ricans in Hawaii were excluded from U.S. citizenship, they were assigned draft numbers along with those who were citizens."

The above referenced *Wikipedia* article went on to report that the:

"*Struggle for U.S. Citizenship:* In 1917, Puerto Ricans in the island, believing that they were entitled to the same rights that every other U.S. citizens had, tried to sign up to vote in a local Hawaiian election and were denied their rights by David Kalauokalani, the county clerk, who claimed that early immigrants [the Puerto Ricans] were not covered by the Jones Act. Olivieri Sanchez became enraged in what he viewed as a violation of the civil rights of his fellow countrymen. He encouraged his fellow Puerto Ricans to protest by telling them that 'If you are not allowed to vote, don't answer the draft.' Olivieri Sanchez took a mandamus suit to court with the claim that all Puerto Ricans were United States citizens and entitled to the civil rights guaranteed by the Constitution of the United States, however the lower court ruled in favor of the county clerk."

Finally, this *Wikipedia* article reported that:

"Olivieri Sanchez hired two liberal lawyers. Together they presented the case to the Territorial Supreme Court. The case known as **'IN THE MATTER OF THE PETITION OF MANUEL OLIVIERI SANCHEZ FOR A WRIT OF MANDAMUS AGAINST DAVID KALAUOKALANI'** No. 1024, which was decided on October 22, 1917, reversed the lower court's decision. The Territorial Supreme Court recognized that all Puerto Ricans in Hawaii were citizens of the United States and were entitled to all rights of citizenship" (*Wikipedia* article; author: unknown; Title: "Manuel Olivieri Sanchez, accessed: November 21, 2012; http://en.wikipedia.org/wiki/Manuel_Olivieri_Sanchez).

The Hayward Area Historical Society and Archives:

The Hayward Area Historical Society (Hayward, CA) (HAHS), provided a number of documents from their 2002 "travelling exhibit" entitled: "*California Century: Puerto Ricans in the San Francisco Bay Area, 1900-2000.*" The Society's Curator/Archivist provided this author, in their 50 page packet of October 18, 2012, a copy of the Exhibit's "Press Release", dated July 13, 2002, wherein it reported that: "The exhibit was guest curated by scholar Aurora Levins Morales and included photographs of [by] Barry Kleider." This Exhibit was also co-sponsored by the California Puerto Rican Historical Society (cf.: Exhibit 20 and 21 in this book).

What is noteworthy, for the purposes of this book, is that the exhibit provided a brief narrative description of several members of the **1st Hawaii Expedition** (or what Norma Carr cited as being the "1st Group" to California/Hawaii). These documents (although some are not dated, and citing no specific author, or reference(s)), states that:

"Mingo Perry, Born May 15, 1911, Honolulu, Hawaii: Mingo Perry was born Domingo Perez. His mother, Juana Ramos Borrero, was from Peñueslas and his father, Domingo Perez Troche, from Yauco. In 1900, in their early twenties, *the couple joined the first expedition to Hawaii and settled on Ewa plantation*, near Honolulu. In 1906 the family lived briefly in San Francisco where Mingo's sister Christine was born, but returned to Hawaii following the great earthquake [of April 1906].... In 1925, when Mingo was fourteen, the family moved to San Francisco's Bayview area, and then to DeCoto, now Union City" (Hayward Area Historical Society. 2012). (emphasis added)

"Josephine Rodriguez de Santiago, Born January 8, 1921, Adjuntas, Puerto Rico: Josephine's mother, María Serrano was probably born in Adjuntas in the late 1880s. Orphaned young, she was raised with her brother in a convent orphanage.... She became the postmaster of Adjuntas, possibly the first woman to hold such a post in Puerto Rico. José Rodriguez was also from Adjuntas. In 1900, when he was ten, *his family joined the first expedition to Hawaii*, where the men went to work in the cane fields of Maui.... At eighteen, Josie married a Hawaiian Puerto Rican named Tony Santiago, whose family came from Yauco." Tony was a former cane worker. (Ibid.) (emphasis added)

"Matilda 'Tillie' Pacheco, Born September 10, 1922, San Francisco, California: Both of *Tillie's parents left Puerto Rico in November, 1900 on the first contract labor expedition to Hawaii.* Her father,

Emilio Avilés was nineteen, from Arecibo. He was one of the group of immigrant (*sic*) who refused to board the ship from San Francisco to Hawaii. Instead, he stayed in San Francisco, working as a carpenter and later as the first Puerto Rican civil servant in California, when he began working for the Post Office in 1906." (Ibid.) (emphasis added)

Some of the documents provided by the Hayward Area Historical Society, identified a number of the Puerto Rican immigrants that went to Hawaii beginning in 1901 and thereafter. For example, the document titled, "Exodus", identified the following names of those Puerto Ricans who went to Hawaii, and who either stayed in San Francisco, or migrated from Hawaii to San Francisco during the first and second decade of the 20th Century:

Paula Garcia (from Lares); Jesse Pagan's grandfather died on the journey [to Hawaii]; Tillie Pacheco's father, Emilio Avilés, "he refused to board the ship [in San Francisco] to Hawaii"; Don Emilio (from Arecibo), who lived in San Francisco; Rafael and Catana Morales met and married on board the ship to Hawaii. By 1904, they had resettled in San Francisco, along with many others who did the same. Julia Rodriguez de Olivera was brought to Hayward [CA] in 1923 by a sister; "Mingo Perry's family came to DeCoto in 1925."

The HAHS's document titled "War Time," identified the following names:

"When ten year old Jose Tomás Rodriguez' *family left for Hawaii in 1900*" [i.e., in the 1st expedition to Hawaii].... "José Rodriguez was one of many Puerto Ricans who went to war [World War I]"; "José's oldest sister, Catana, turned back to San Francisco... [and was] a skilled seamstress, she became a dressmaker...and when the family joined her in 1904, they flourished."

The HAHS's document titled "Religious life," identified the following names:

"**Juan** Lugo...had *come on the 1900 migration from Yauco*. Other Hawaiian Puerto Rican missionaries included Francisco Ortiz, just four years old at the time of the Hawaiian exodus, and Lorenzo Lucena, who had gone to Hawaii with an uncle at fourteen. These men were among the first to bring Pentecostalism to Puerto Rico. In 1916 Juan Lugo, who had spent three years preaching in Northern California, went to Ponce, Puerto Rico, and was the first to introduce the Pentecostal faith in his homeland. Hawaiian Puerto Rican preachers traveled back and forth between California and Puerto Rico throughout the 1910s and 20s. Domingo Cruz (from Peñuelas), a "Hawaiian Puerto Rican carpenter" who married "Judith Orsatelli, a Puerto Rican Corsican immigrant to the islands." "At age 101 [in 2002?], Julia Olivera is Templo de la Cruz' oldest living member. She came to Hayward [CA] from Adjuntas in 1923, sent for by her older sister. She joined Templo that same year, and her daughter and son in law are missionaries.... Josie Lopez' **parents** came in the **first Hawaiian migration** and resettled in San Francisco just before the 1906 earthquake." (emphasis added)

Note: Norma Carr wrote that: "Ten-year old **Juan Lugo** arrived in Hawaii with his mother and sister in 1901 from Yauco, the principal coffee center of Puerto Rico. He was from the area called Pina, near the neighborhoods known as Vegas, Naranjo and Rubias, which sent many laborers [to the Hawaiian plantations] as well. Six-year-old Julia [Juan's sister] died before they reached New Orleans and was buried at sea. The mother [of Juan Lugo] and [her] two children were placed on a plantation on Oahu" (Carr. 1989: 229).

The HAHS's document titled "Social Clubs," identified the following names:

"***Emilio Avilés, a member of the first contract labor expedition***, was a 'natural leader' that helped organized networks and social clubs". "A talented musician and ardent participant in political debates, his home in San Francisco's North Beach quickly became the unofficial center of the small Puerto Rican *colonia* [in original]...." "**Jesse Pagan** was born in Hawaii in 1924 of Puerto Rican parents ***from the 1900-1901 contract labor expedition***. His parents worked on a sugar plantation, but moved to Honolulu shortly after his birth, and he grew up in Kalihi Valley.... An active member of Puerto Rican clubs in Hawaii, when he moved to the Bay Area in 1957, Jesse Pagan joined PRUMA [The Puerto Rican Union of Mutual Aid] and has been president thirteen times." (emphasis added)

The HAHS's document titled "Sports," identified the following names:

"Julio Santiago was born in 1927 in Peñuelas, Puerto Rico. His uncle, Liborio had gone to Hawaii around 1904. Eventually Liborio settled in Danville where he owned a ranch.... Eventually most of the [Santiago] family settled in Hayward [CA]," where "Julio has been an active member of Templo de la Cruz for fifty years, and directed their radio program for many years."

The HAHS's document titled "Music", identified the following names:

"Mingo Perry was born Domingo Perez in Hawaii in 1911. He grew up in Honolulu and in 1925, when he was fourteen, his family moved to Decoto in the East Bay. Like most musicians, he learned by listening to others. At sixteen he began performing professionally...."

Regrettably, notwithstanding the actual correct number of immigrants that survived their arduous journey either to California, and/or to Hawaii, a number of these Puerto Rican immigrants died before they reached either California, and/or Hawaii. For example, on one such journey, the *San Francisco Call* had the somber headline in their April 9, 1901 issue which read as follows: "Porto Ricans Die on the Way to Hawaii":

"Dysentery is said to have caused seven deaths east of here [El Paso, Texas] among 865 Porto Ricans emigrants bound for Hawaii...and at this point the bodies of two children who had died were taken charge by an undertaker" (*San Francisco Call*. April 9, 1901: 1).

Additionally, the *San Francisco Call* of April 14, 1901 reported that, "Two deaths occurred between here [Los Angeles] and Indio [California], attributed to anaemia. One of the victims was a boy aged about 9 years and the other a young man probably 23 or 24. The bodies were left here [Los Angeles] for burial" (*San Francisco Call*. April 14, 1901: 17).

It should be noted that the publication entitled *Sources for the Study of Puerto Rican Migration – 1879-1920*, commented on the Puerto Rico newspaper, *El Problema*, that:

"An effort to counter both liberal and labor press opposition to these migrations can be found in ***El Problema***, a newspaper published by agents of the company that recruited workers for Hawaii, see especially Vol. 1 number 1. September 6, 1901." (Centro de Estudios Puertorriqueños. 1982: 223, Footnote 2., 4, 10-101).

It is important to note that some researches have posited that, "the actual [immigration] figure [figures] is not known and varies with each accounting" (Arroyo. 1977: 64).

At the time some argued that "the only reasonable objection advanced so far to their emigration from Porto Rico is that the island's best laborers are leaving" (*Pacific Commercial Advertiser*. April 19, 1901: 5).

The 1902 publication entitled *Report of the Governor of the Territory of Hawaii to the Secretary of the Interior. 1902,* reported in a statement of the department of public works from July 1, 1901, to June 30,

1902, that there were **two** Puerto Ricans that were in this department, out of a department with 1,230 employees. It also reported that there were a total of 539 Puerto Ricans attending Public schools and 57 attending Private schools in the Territory of Hawaii, even "though [the Puerto Ricans are] only about two years in the country" (Secretary of the Interior. 1902: 16, 41).

Interestingly, this same 1902 *Report* listed four Cubans, i.e., "foreign-born" persons, as well as 18 persons who were born in the "West Indies", and whom were also living in Hawaii in the year 1900, with three of the four Cubans living in Honolulu alone (*Ibid.*, 5, 7, 6). Also, this 1902 *Report* pointed out that there were a total of 10 Puerto Rican children who were in "Reformatory School", out of a total of 63 boys, within the Hawaiian system of the department of education. Three of these Puerto Rican boys were in the Reformatory School for truancy, with three for larceny, and four for vagrancy (Secretary of the Interior. 1902: 47, 48).

Additionally, the 1903 U.S. Department of Labor lamented that:

"The Porto Ricans, when they arrived [to Hawaii], gave the least promise, either as citizens or as laborers, of any immigrants that ever disembarked at Honolulu. The men had been carelessly recruited at a time when the laboring population of Porto Rico was in a condition of acute distress. It is probable that few of them were in a physical condition to make a long voyage when they went on shipboard. They were mostly people from the coffee country of their own island, and who had been starved out of the mountains when that region was devastated by the hurricane of 1899" (Bulletin of the Department of Labor. 1903a: 702, Bibliography #23).

This Governor's *Report* went on to reveal that:

"the first three expeditions ["Groups"] passed through San Francisco in the winter, and although they [the Puerto Ricans] were brought across the country by the southern route, the lightly clad members were subjected to the inclemencies of what was to them almost an artic climate" (Bulletin of the Department of Labor. 1903a: 702, Bibliography #23).

Put another way, Azel Ames, M.D., writing in 1901, reporting from data obtained from the *1899 Porto Rico Census*, wrote that:

"In Porto Rico, where agriculture is basis; where 78.6 per cent of the entire population is practically rural and essentially agricultural…it is plain that 'labor problems' relate almost wholly to the agricultural toiler, his interests, condition, and needs" (Ames, M.D. 1901: 380).

Dr. Ames went on to report that: "'Agriculture' is so absorbent and inclusive as practically to comprise directly or indirectly the body of the working population of the island….Laborers—The peons or day laborers, who stand in relation to agriculture overwhelmingly preponderant numerically. They constitute, of course, the great bulk, over 68 per cent, of the agricultural breadwinner" (Ames, M.D. 1901: 389, 394).

Finally, Dr. Ames pointed out the working class nature of the Puerto Rican laboring class when he wrote that: "with over three-fourths of the *breadwinners* of the island engaged in agriculture, and of the total number of the *breadwinners* four-fifths [were] laborers…." (*Ibid.*: 395). (emphasis added) (cf.: Exhibits 14-16).

Put another way, Jóse L. Vázquez stated that, that in 1899, that out of the Puerto Rican population of 953,243, the rural population was at 814,540, while the urban population was at only 138,703 (14.6%), and in 1910, that out of the Puerto Rican population of 1,118,012, the rural population was at 893,392, while the urban population was only 224,620 (20.1%), (Vázquez. 1964: 34). For historical comparison, the population in Hawaii in 1900 was 154,001, and in 1910, it was 191,874 (U.S. Bureau of the Census. 1975: 9, "Series A 9-22").

In a related vein, Vázquez wrote in his sub-section titled "The Working Population", that:

"Toward the end of the Nineteenth Century Puerto Rico was still a typical agrarian society. Subsistence farming was common, although commercial agriculture showed some development.... In 1899, for example, 63 per cent of all 'gainfully occupied' workers were engaged in agricultural pursuits. 'Domestic and personal services' were second in importance. These two 'industries' were the source of employment for 83.3 per cent of all breadwinners" (Vázquez. 1964: 93, 103, 104).

Although most of the Puerto Rican immigrants, both in California and in Hawaii, worked in agriculturally-related jobs, the *Pacific Commercial Advertiser* reported that some Hawaiian families were utilizing females as domestic servants. For example, its headline on May 2, 1901 read as follows: "New Idea in 'Help'. Porto Rican Girls for Domestic Servants. Waialua is Experimenting" (*Pacific Commercial Advertiser.* May 2, 1901: 6). The *Advertiser* reported that:

"Many of the young girls who have arrived here at different times with the various lots of Porto Ricans are now in comfortable homes in the neighborhood of the plantations, getting wages that they would not likely to get working in the cane fields for a long time to come. At Waialula, where a considerable number of immigrants went to toil in the fields, there are several private families who have secured young girls, some of them whose parents are not living and who are in need of a good home, as nurses and cooks and housemaids. They are reported to be good workers, clean and tidy in their habits, and anxious to please. Their greatest difficulty, at first, is the matter of language" (*Pacific Commercial Advertiser.* May 2, 1901: 6).

Put another way, the Porto Rican emigrants to both California and to Hawaii represented the "surplus labor", i.e., "working class" laborers, that had been increasingly accumulating in Puerto Rico when the United States took possession of the Island in December 1898. For example, the Governor of Porto Rico, in his *First Annual Report* in May 1901, confirmed the surplus labor issue which existed in Puerto Rico when he acknowledged the serious unemployment problem as follows:

"The great army of the unemployed has a corps amounting to 183,635 in this tropical island. Of these about one-third are men and two-thirds are women" (Allen. 1901: 35).

On December 17, 1901, the Hawaiian newspaper, the *Pacific Commercial Advertiser*, had the related headline article entitled: "Labor of Porto Rico: Its Surplus Needs a Chance in Hawaii. We Can Take About 12,000" (*Pacific Commercial Advertiser.* May 17, 1901: 5)

The *Advertiser* went on to point out that:

"When General W. Davis was military governor of the island he made a careful investigation of **wages** and of the labor question generally the conclusion he reached was that there were too many people for **wages** to reach a high level, though he thought that under the United States there would be some advance.... The million inhabitants of the island are not well off as the mass of the population in the United States... The truth about Porto Rico is that the trouble is due to economic causes... [and] that permanent relief would only come from two sources. One was **emigration**..." (*Ibid.*: 5). (emphasis added)

A "racially-related" reason for the Puerto Rican Migration to Hawaii

A historically overlooked secondary reason why the Hawaiian Sugar Planters began to request, and to have recruited, the Puerto Rican immigrants to Hawaii, had a "racial element" to it. For example, the Hawaiian *Pacific Commercial Advertiser* newspaper of September 1901 had an article with the racially tinged headline of: "A Test of White Men. An Old-Time Labor Experiment on Maui…It Started in for Ten Years and Did Not Last Two—The reasons." The article went on to report, at least as early as 1870, that the Hawaiian Planters experimented with having "white labor" (as opposed to what was considered at that time to be "non-white labor", like the Puerto Ricans) work as field laborers on the Hawaiian Sugar plantations. The article stated that:

"In 1870…white laborers were imported to Hawaii [possibly from California]… [and that] a contract for ten years was made…[but] before the two years had gone by, only one man of the [original] eighteen remained to reap the benefit of his labors…. [Thus ended] the first experiment with white labor" (*Pacific Commercial Advertiser.* September 2, 1901: 9).

This racially-tinged attempted justification for the supposed necessity of non-white labor, such as Puerto Ricans, Chinese, Japanese, etc., as opposed to so-called "white labor", is summarized in an article in the August 1901 issue of the *Pacific Commercial Advertiser*, when it reported a quote which was addressed to the paper's Editor, namely, the following:

"I think it's very generally admitted that white men cannot work in the cane fields of Hawaii as field laborers. At least that has been the experience of nine-tenths of the planters in the past, and is liable to be so in the future. It is therefore evident that we must look elsewhere for men who can do this class of labor, unless we want to see this industry ruined…. When men talk of white men working in the cane fields of a tropical country like this [Hawaii] they don't know what they are talking of, and we think, if [white men were put in this] class of work for a single day, they would very quickly find out that it is not a job for white men" (Pacific Commercial Advertiser. 1901: 2).

A more current interpretation of the role that Puerto Rican "**surplus labor**" played in spurring emigration from Puerto Rico to the United States after 1898 (and by extension, to California and to Hawaii) was outlined in the article entitled, "The Emergence of Imperialist Capitalism and Puerto Rican Emigration: 1879-1901" (*Journal of American Ethnic History.* 1984: 54-66; see in particular: the section titled, "Early Emigration Under United States Control (1898-1901): 60-65).

A related reason to the role played by surplus labor in the Puerto Rican immigration to Hawaii is the fact that they were specifically recruited to offset what the Hawaiian Sugar Planters' perceived problems that were created, over time, with the Chinese and the Japanese field laborers (such as **labor strikes**), as well as from the implemented restrictive contract labor law. Thus, the *Pacific Commercial Advertiser* of August 1901 reported that:

"The sugar-planters of Hawaii, cut off from their supply of coolies by the contract labor law, find in the Porto Ricans an acceptable substitute. Porto Rico is overpopulated, and while the planters of that island profess some alarm at the exodus of laborers, the loss to the labor supply is not so extensive as to portend serious inconvenience" (*Pacific Commercial Advertiser.* August 23, 1901: 11; see also: *San Francisco Call.* May 16, 1901: 3).

Similarly, the August 12, 1901 issue of the *Pacific Commercial Advertiser* added a racially-related justification for the Puerto Rican immigrants going to Hawaii when it reported that:

"Now that we are a part of the United States the alien contract labor law is enforced in the Hawaiian Islands as well as in the other portions of our country, so that *we can no longer draw upon*

Chinese and Japanese for our labor. Consequently the planters have had to look elsewhere. They seemed to have settled upon **Porto Rico** as a country from which they might draw a timid and ignorant element easily imposed upon and subdued" (*Pacific Commercial Advertiser.* August 12, 1901: 4; see also: *Pacific Commercial Advertiser.* February 25, 1902: 4; *Pacific Commercial Advertiser.* December 11, 1902: 1, 3). (emphasis added)

This emigration from Puerto Rico, therefore, was the beginnings of the Porto Rican *diaspora*, both to California and Hawaii. Castanha cites anthropologist James Clifford who wrote, "Diasporas usually presuppose longer distances and a separation more like exile: a constitutive taboo on return, or its postponement to a remote future" (Castanha. 2004: 255).

The January 10, 1901 issue of *The Honolulu Republican* newspaper summarized the two primary reasons overall that created the conditions for the beginnings of the Puerto Rican migration to California, and then Hawaii:

"The change from Spanish to American rule affected **business** in Porto Rico very adversely. It disturbed and completely upset normal trade and industrial conditions. On top of this came the big **hurricane** in 1899. In one day seven-twelfths of all growing crops was wiped out of existence" (*The Honolulu Republican.* January 10, 1901: 8). (emphasis added)

It is important to know that the newspapers of the day basically had two competing explanations for their readership as to why this particular group of Puerto Ricans decided to emigrate from their homeland in Puerto Rico and travel to their original destination of Hawaii. In short, one school of thought argued that the emigration from Puerto Rico was voluntary, while the other was that it was involuntary and based upon deception, deceit, and lies disguised as false promises. For example:

The *San Francisco Chronicle* newspaper reported, as early as December 7, 1900 that the Porto Rican immigrants while in transit to San Francisco contended:

"…that they are being taken against their will, and are giving the [train] guards no little trouble…. The Porto Ricans, however, contend that they were loaded on a boat in Porto Rico with the understanding that they were going to the opposite side of the Island [i.e., Puerto Rico] to work, but after six days they were landed in New Orleans and rushed on to a train. They learned in San Antonio where they were being taken to, and **have since been trying to escape**." (*San Francisco Chronicle.* December 7, 1900: 1). (emphasis added)

Also, the *San Francisco Chronicle* reported and emphasized the rather sensational position that these Puerto Ricans were "kidnapped from the Islands to be taken to Hawaii to work on sugar plantations…." (*San Francisco Chronicle* December 14, 1900: 4).

Rosario-Rivera wrote that among the letters which she reviewed in the Puerto Rican archives (in Puerto Rico), there were indications that the Puerto Rican immigrants left for Hawaii due to wonderful offers having been presented to them by the North American companies that were established in the Hawaiian Islands. However, she also reported that the reality of the immigrants' working conditions in Hawaii could be exemplified in a letter written by Eusebio Torres while working in Hawaii when "Mr. Torres complained in his letter that they had the Puerto Rican immigrants working like 'slaves, and that the boss (the *maiordome* or *mallordomo*) gets them up [in the mornings] with a whip; that they got sent to solitary for three months chopping rocks for the government if you did not work in the plantation. (Rosario-Rivera. 2000: 2; 16) **[Note:** translated by Rosario Camacho on 7/30/12; cf.: *"Carta* *de Eusebio Torres a su madre"* (*Esta carta la escribió un emigrados de Hawaii a su madre aquí en Puerto Rico* in: Rosario-Rivera.2000:16.]

In contrast to the *San Francisco Chronicle*, the *Honolulu Republican* in their article on December 25, 1900, combined both the "voluntary" argument, as well as the "deception" argument(s), to explain this new Puerto Rican immigration to Hawaii. They reported:

"That the Porto Ricans who came here in the *Rio* came of their own volition seems apparent but that in no wise [*sic*] lessens the objectionable manner in which they were induced to come here through deception and false promises... If the entire party were free and willing emigrants why was it necessary to keep an armed guard about their train during the two days at Sanderson, Texas, and at other points en route. And too why was it necessary to put them aboard a tug at Port Costa, forty miles from San Francisco, and take them to the *Rio* after that vessel had left her wharf and pulled into the stream" (*The Honolulu Republican.* December 25, 1900b: 4).

The *San Francisco Call* had the informative headline in their November 13, 1901 issue which reported the false promises which were made to the Puerto Rican immigrants as follows: "Porto Ricans Deceived By False Promises: Stone Masons Lured to Honolulu on Promise of Being Paid $5 a Day" (*San Francisco Call.* November 13, 1901:4).

Thus, Dr. Castanha's 2004 dissertation had a section in Chapter 6 entitled, "Reluctant Exodus, Kidnapping and Slavery", describing the plight of the Puerto Ricans from their first arrival in the city of New Orleans by steamship until they were transported onto a train which took them to Los Angeles, and subsequently to San Francisco, CA (cf.: Castanha. 2004: 262-268, 269-271).

Finally, in 1902 the American Federation of Labor adopted a resolution wherein it was declared that the Puerto Rican immigrants went to Hawaii based upon the false promises which had earlier been made to them (Bib. #5, p. 88). For example, the *Pacific Commercial Advertiser* reported, "that the United States government be asked to return to Porto Rico those people who were induced to leave that island for Hawaii under the promise of better industrial conditions" (*Pacific Commercial Advertiser.* November 24, 1902: 1; Bib. #5, p. 88; cf.: p.15).

In dramatic contrast to the *San Francisco Chronicle*, the *San Francisco Call* reported a more positive outlook when it reported that the Puerto Ricans who were passing through Los Angeles, on their way to San Francisco, and then onto Hawaii:

"all are in the best of spirits," and that the "Journey so far has been a pleasant one and they offer no complaints regarding their treatment" and that they are "Happy, well fed, ragged, joyously jingling small change...and not a word of evidence that they were being mistreated could be obtained."

The *San Francisco Call* also reported that these Puerto Ricans were going to Hawaii because they "sought to improve their [economic] conditions." (*San Francisco Call.* December 14, 1900). (see: <http://cdnc.ucr.edu/ newsucr/cgi-bin/newsucr? a=d&d=SFC19001214. 236&c1=search&srpos...>)

A subsequent article in The *San Francisco Call* reported that the Puerto Ricans were "duped" into not going to Hawaii, while those that did travel onto Hawaii were "anxious to be sent to Hawaii to Fulfill their **Contracts** with the Plantation Owners" (*San Francisco Call.* December 16, 1900: 37). (emphasis added)

In the *San Francisco Call* issue of March 7, 1901 it was reported that:

"A number of the Porto Ricans who were **induced** by the Examiner to violate their contract and **remain in California** while on their way to the Hawaiian Islands are about to become county charges. These people were led to believe they would practically become slaves, and they refused to ship from San Francisco to the islands.... Several persons took the Porto Ricans upon the representation that they would make good orchard laborers [in San Jose, CA]" (*San Francisco Call*. March 7, 1901: 9). (emphasis added)

Some newspapers outright labeled the *San Francisco Examiner* as **"liars"** in their reporting of the plight of the newly arrived Puerto Rican immigrants. For example, the newspaper *The Pacific Commercial Advertiser* [aka: the PCA] on December 27, 1900, had in one of their articles a headline entitled: "Porto Ricans are Public Charges: Conditions Wrought By the Lying Examiner of San Francisco." The PCA [in Honolulu, Hawaii] also went on to report that:

"The Porto Ricans whom the [*San Francisco*] *Examiner* deluded into staying at San Francisco, instead of going to Hawaii where good wages and good treatment were in store for them, are now flocking to the poorhouse [in San Francisco]. Thanks to the absurd yellow journal, the people of San Francisco will have to care for them at large expense, or buy them at large expense, or buy them tickets to some other place to which they may be persuaded to go." (*Pacific Commercial Advertiser* [Honolulu, Hawaii]. December 27, 1900: 3, 4).

The Hawaii *Pacific Commercial Advertiser* newspaper probably had a vested interest in wanting as many of these Porto Rican immigrants to go to Hawaii to work on its plantations.

Similarly, The *Hawaiian* Gazette (Oahu, Hawaii) in their December 28, 1900 issue, labeled the *San Francisco Examiner* as being outright liars in a headline entitled: "Porto Ricans Are Public Charges: Conditions Wrought By the **Lying** Examiner of San Francisco", (*The Hawaiian Gazette*. December 28, 1900: 1, 5). It wrote: "Some of the Porto Ricans who arrived in a destitute condition, after having been prevailed upon to refuse to go to the Hawaiian Islands to work on the sugar plantations [by the *San Francisco Examiner*...]." (emphasis added)

Also, the *Hawaiian Star* (Honolulu [Oahu]) issue of December 26, 1900, reported in their article entitled "The Porto Ricans", that:

"The *San Francisco Examiner*, having by systematic and persistent misrepresentation thrown a large number of Porto Ricans destitute and homeless upon the charity of the people of California, is now seeking to create the impression that the Planter's Association is responsible for the present plight of these unfortunates, and to bully and coerce the planters into providing for them" (*Hawaiian Star*. December 26, 1900: 4).

On the other hand, contrary to the reporting of the *Hawaiian Gazette*, *The New York Times*' April 4, 1901 issue, in an article entitled, "The Porto Rican Exodus: Men and Women Anxious to Leave the Island for Hawaii, Best Laborers Flee from the Distress Said to Exist in their Native Land", summarized the poor economic condition of Puerto Rico as a major reason for the ongoing emigration of the population to Hawaii. It reported that:

"The number of Porto Ricans who have lately so willingly emigrated to Hawaii, there to seek a livelihood under unknown conditions, is regarded as conclusive proof that want and even starvation exist here [In Puerto Rico, due to the immediate effect of the August 1899 devastating hurricane, San Ciriaco], and as a direct and emphatic contradiction of statements to the effect that the island is enjoying prosperity and comfort. The argument is made that no man will leave his native land unless forced to do so by stress of circumstance, and that under Spain Porto Ricans never emigrated" (*New York Times*. April 4, 1901: 5, "A" and "B"; History Task Force. 1982: 34-35).

Puerto Rican Plantation Labor in Hawaii, June 1901:

Norma Carr, citing the *Report of the Governor of Hawaii 1901* (pages 65-66), in her Table entitled, "Plantation and Puerto Rican Labor June 1901", reported that there were a total of 1,772 Puerto Rican men, and 323 Puerto Rican women, for a total of 2,095 Puerto Ricans working on the plantations, out of the "total of all nationalities" of 39,587 [5.2%], among the 58 Hawaiian Plantations the *Report* identified (Carr. 1989: 450-451); CF.: Bibliography #254).

Importantly, within one year of their arrival to Hawaii, many, if not most, of these Puerto Rican immigrants desired to leave Hawaii (see: below for a detailed description of this historical event; cf.: Rosario-Rivera's (2000: 1-16) article wherein she **quotes** several letters that were written by the parents of the Puerto Rican immigrants who went to Hawaii, and who were dissatisfied with the **wages**, and the working conditions in Hawaii). For example, Rosario-Rivera refers to one letter wherein she wrote that one person complained that the Hawaiian Puerto Rican immigrants were paid only 50 cents a day when they had been earlier promised good wages. She also reported that 40 Hawaiian Porto Rican immigrants lost their job(s) because they did not want to work for such low **wages** (Rosario-Rivera. 2000: 14).

A brief "sample" of names which were identified by Rosario-Rivera in her article, beginning with the letter "A", and alphabetized are as follows (spelled exactly as they appear in her article): Acevedo, Francisco* [Kaanisco Azexedo]; Agostini, Julio; Alas, Providencia; Alvarado, Manuel (Alvarodo)*, etc. **Note:** The asterisk indicates that these names appeared in the official lists, which shows it being not well written---it is not clear to the translator what the sentence means in her article] However, the **original** Spanish sentence reads as follows: *"El asterisco indica que asi apareci en las oficiales, lo que justifica que estuviera bien escrito"* (Rosario-Rivera. 2000: 26).

However, it should be noted that there was a contrary position, namely, that the Puerto Rican immigrants in Hawaii were "happy" with their working conditions, and with their overall situation(s), on the sugar plantations. For example, the *Pacific Commercial Advertiser* of August 1901 had the following headline: "Many Glad They Came. Porto Ricans Feel Satisfied With Work..." (*Pacific Commercial Advertiser*. August 6, 1901).

Ronald Arroyo wrote in his dissertation that:

"The first Porto Rican to go to the Hawaiian Islands and earn enough money to return to the mainland was Celestino Garcia. He and an unidentified companion returned to San Francisco in November 1901. Garcia gave further testimony to the plight of his comrades. He had been disenchanted with the wages on the plantation and had gone to Honolulu where he worked breaking stones for roads.... He was interviewed by the United States District Attorney Woodworth and his story was told in the newspapers" (Arroyo, Ronald. 1977: 142). [**Note:** Unfortunately, Dr. Arroyo did *not* provide a specific reference for the facts that he presented in the paragraph which I cited above].

However, my research located the most likely source from which Dr. Arroyo made the argument, so to speak, that Celestino García, was the first Puerto Rican that had migrated from Hawaii to California. The Puerto Rican newspaper, *La Correspondencia*, reported in its December 5, 1901 issue, that:

"Two Puerto Ricans, one named **Celestino García**, and the other, not identified by the U.S. Attorney's Office, arrived here [i.e., San Francisco, CA] yesterday from Hawaii. They said that they had been taken to that country as slaves and that they were put on a plantation from where escape was impossible because of the heavy guard. According to García and his companion, an agent took them to Hawaii under false pretenses.... They arrived in this city [San Francisco] 15 days ago...." (Cited in: Centro de Estudios Puertorriqueños. 1977: 41; see also: *San Francisco Examiner.* November 13, 1901; *San Francisco Call.* November 13, 1901: 4). (emphasis added)

However, it should be noted that there existed an opposing viewpoint which argued that the Puerto Rican immigrants working on the sugar plantations were pleased with their working conditions and that any statements to the contrary were misrepresentations.

For example, the May 15, 1901 issue of *The Hawaiian Star*, in a dispatch from San Francisco, and in their article simply entitled "Porto Ricans", reported that:

"Contrary to various distressing reports of the discomfort of the Porto Ricans imported into the sugar fields of the Hawaiian Islands, Mariano Abril, a prominent **Porto Rican**, now at the Californian Hotel, says that his countrymen and their families are well established, pleased with conditions and in a way to make more money than they ever could have earned at home. Abril is editor and proprietor of *La Democrata*, published at Carguas [*sic*], Porto Rico. He has just returned from an inspection of the Hawaiian plantations and the new homes of the 6000 Porto Ricans who are there. He wished to learn the conditions. He is well pleased.... They are peculiarly suited for sugar culture" (*The Hawaiian Star.* May 15, 1901: 1; *The Hawaiian* Gazette. May 17, 1901: 5). (emphasis added)

It is noteworthy that Mr. Abril, notwithstanding being Puerto Rican, simply did not live in Hawaii, and therefore, his impressions of the working conditions of the Puerto Rican agricultural class immigrants, may not have been fully accurate, and possibly even be tainted, since he actually was not working in the sugarcane fields himself. Therefore, he was more inclined to receive "second-hand" information, and possibly may have had "limited first-hand" information himself.

Mr. Abril's motives, or ability to observe accurately, may be called into question when you consider the fact that more than a year after his above cited observations, the [*Hawaiian*] *Evening Bulletin* of November 1902, referencing the ***first-hand*** experiences of the Puerto Ricans themselves, reported that:

"The *San Juan News* (Puerto Rico) of October 12 publishes, with editorial comment, a long letter from Porto Ricans in Hawaii, detailing their woes. This letter is signed by a number of Porto Ricans.... The News has been honored by a communication which it received *addressed by* **500 Puerto Ricans** who are employed on the plantations in Hilo, Hawaii. Their letter is one long wail against the abuses which are being inflicted upon them by the men in charge of the plantations. They claim that they are treated worse than beats and are driven away from these places when they utter a word of complaint. They have no one to help them; not a soul to console them nor any one [*sic*] to appeal to except their fellow countrymen who live in Porto Rico. The conditions assumed such proportions that the people of the United States finally learned of them" ([Hawaiian] *Evening Bulletin.* November 14, 1902: 1; see also: *Ibid.*: page 4, "Porto Rican Complaints"). (see also: *Pacific Commercial Advertiser.* January 17, 1902) (emphasis added)

In short, The [Hawaiian] *Evening Bulletin* quoted an unnamed source questioning the Hawaiian Governor's understanding of the working conditions of the Puerto Rican immigrants, as follows:

"It is what it is and not what Mr. Cooper and Mr. Dole would like it to be" (*San Francisco Call.* November 14, 1902: 4). [Hawaiian Governor, Sanford B. Dole, 6/14/1900-11/23/1903].

Additionally, and again in dramatic contrast to the above referenced Mr. Abril's rather positive (and rosy?) description of the working conditions of the Puerto Rican immigrants, the 1902 publication entitled, the *Proceedings of the American Federation of Labor 1901-1903*, described the much more serious, onerous, graphic, and appalling conditions for the Puerto Rican workers in Hawaii, when it reported:

"Resolution No. 82.-By Delegates Santiago Iglesias… [and] Porto Rico Unions:

WHEREAS, … Porto Rican workingman have been conducted to the Hawaiian Islands as emigrants, being deceived with false promises of honest and remunerative work; and

WHEREAS, The Porto Rican workingmen emigrated in Hawaiian Islands are being maltreated, whipped and treated like criminals by the bosses of the sugar plantations; and

WHEREAS, The Porto Rican workingmen in Hawaii are being robbed, shot and taken to jail when they protest or make any reclamation…" (The American Federation of Labor. 1902: 88).

Similarly, even as late as at least March 1903, the *Pacific Commercial Advertiser* continued to report how a seemingly significant number of the Puerto Rican immigrant plantation laborers in Hawaii continued to complain, via testimony, to Washington, D.C., i.e., to the Commissioner of Immigration, of several major concerns, namely that the:

"taking of the testimony of those Porto Rican plantation laborers who have made complaint of their treatment since coming to the islands, and of the alleged misrepresentation of conditions leading them to come here…. They charge that they were induced by the planters' agents, in Cuba and in Ponce, to come to the Hawaiian Islands under several misrepresentations as to conditions here. In the first place, they were told that the work was not that hard. Secondly, they were given to understand that they would be paid more than they have been paid. Other alleged misrepresentations were to the effect that they would be better housed, better fed, and generally better treated than they say that they have been…. Besides all this, they say that they have been cruelly treated by the lunas on the plantations, driven to work at unseemly hours and compelled to work without sufficient food" (*Pacific Commercial Advertiser.* March 8, 1903: 1).

Another objective indicator of how stressful and difficult it was to immigrate from Puerto Rico to Hawaii was illustrated by the Hawaiian publication titled, "*Report of the President of the Board of Health of the Territory of Hawaii*, published in 1905, wherein it unfortunately listed a total of 7 Puerto Rican patients who were "admitted during the six months ending June 30th, 1905" to the Oahu Insane Asylum, out of the total of 175 patients in the Asylum, while 2 Puerto Ricans died in the Asylum. By contrast, 2 Spaniards, 6 Germans, and 6 Americans were admitted to this same Oahu Asylum. On the positive side, during this same aforementioned time period, two Puerto Ricans were discharged from the Asylum (presumably being medically satisfactory) (Hawaii Board of Health. 1905: 67, 68).

It should be noted that the Puerto Rican population in Hawaii in 1910, according to the U.S. Federal Census numbered 4,828, which made it second only to New York City as having the largest Puerto Rican population outside of Puerto Rico itself (see: The *San Francisco Call*. November 16, 1910, for the ethnic breakdown of the population in Hawaii as of 1910).

Also, the February 1910 issue of the *Sausalito News* [Marin County, CA] reported that by 1910, what could be considered the first great "wave" of Puerto Rican immigration to Hawaii was coming to an end. Thus, it wrote, from a dispatch from Honolulu, Hawaii, that:

"Hawaiian Sugar Planters' Association, yielding to threats made by members of the Legislature, decided to abandon the scheme of importing several thousand [additional] **Porto Ricans** as laborers on the plantations. The plan was very unpopular and had aroused vigorous opposition both here and at Washington, but the planters declined to give it up until an efficacious threat was whispered in their ears by members of the Legislature" (*Sausalito News* [Sausalito, Marin County, CA]. February 5, 1910: 1). (emphasis added)

It should be noted that 10 years after the arrival of the first Puerto Rican immigrant laborers, at least some of the Hawaiian newspapers continued to publish extremely derogatory articles about this so-called "experiment in labor migration," which the Puerto Ricans were involved in. Thus, *The Democrat* [Honolulu. T.H.), in November 1910, reported the following:

"If the importation of the Russian immigrations is a serious mistake, the bringing into the country of about 5,000 Porto Ricans was a *blunder* that was hardly less than a crime…. A considerable number were petty criminals, wharf-rats and prostitutes from Ponce and other coast towns…so a considerable number of them became strollers and vagabonds, and whenever possible flocked into the towns" (*The Democrat* [Honolulu]. November 1, 1910: 3).

Finally, and it is noteworthy, that Norma Carr, a social historian, writing 82 years *after* the first Puerto Rican immigrants arrived in Hawaii on December 23, 1900, argued that the negative, and racially oriented newspaper articles that were written about the Puerto Ricans between 1900 and 1910, and thereafter, continued to have an adverse effect on the Puerto Ricans in Hawaii, even 82 years later. Thus, Carr wrote in her article (published in 1987) that:

"Puerto Ricans have been in Hawaii for 82 years and have two public images: negative and nonexistent….Of all the labor groups recruited to serve the plantation system, the Puerto Rican is now the most invisible…" (Carr. 1987: 97, 97-106).

How Far was the Puerto Rican Immigrant's Journey and How Did it Compare to that of European Immigrants?:

Similar to the European immigrants that came to America during the late 19th and early 20th Century, the Puerto Rican immigrants who traveled to America beginning in December 1900, and thereafter, via steamship traveled the following distance(s): From San Juan, Puerto Rico to New Orleans (in nautical miles) was 1,539 miles (U.S. Dept. of Commerce and Labor. 1911: 756). They then traveled by train from New Orleans to San Francisco, for an additional 2,482 miles. A combined distance of 4,021 miles. Those that continued to Hawaii, according to the distinguished Puerto Rican historian Dr. Norma Carr, (López and David Forbes 2001: 110), traveled a total of over 6,500 miles from Puerto Rico to Hawaii.

For historical comparison, the immigrants that sailed in 1900 from London, England to New York [e.g., Ellis Island] traveled a total of 3,233 miles (nautical miles). From St. Petersburg, Russia to New York it was 4,632 nautical miles; from Hamburg, Germany to New York it was 3,652 nautical miles; from Gibraltar, Spain to N.Y. it was 3,207 miles (U. S. Department of Commerce and Labor 1911: 756, 755).

The U.S. Immigration Commission, also known as the Dillingham Commission of 1911, wrote that "the cost of recruiting and bringing the 5,000 Porto Ricans to Hawaii was $564,191, or $112 per capita", while "the least expensive European immigration cost $83.60 per capita, and about $160 per man" (*Reports of the Immigration Commission* 1911a: 703, Vol. I). It is *noteworthy* that many of the Puerto

Ricans that initially immigrated to Hawaii, from at least 1901 to 1920, decided to return to California to live and work (cf.: Senior 1947: 44-46).

By 1910, each of the 342 Puerto Rican immigrants to California had their own respective life story, and were much more than a statistical number in the U.S. Immigration Commission Report of 1911 which was headed by Senator Dillingham (of Vermont) (cf.: *Reports of the Immigration Commission.* 1911a, Vol. I, and Vol. II; Reports of the Immigration Commission. 1911b, Vol. I: pages 320, 703, 663, 713, 715, 105, 109; Vol. II: 84, 85, 154, 233, 779, 780).

*The **Employment Contract** Presented to the First Puerto Rican Immigrants Dated – April 16, 1901:*

A copy of the *first* "contract", or Agreement, which was [apparently] presented to the first Puerto Rican immigrants from Puerto Rico to Hawaii was reprinted in the Hawaiian government's publication of 1903 and titled, "*Report of the Commissioner of Labor On Hawaii. 1902* (1903) with the descriptive title of the Agreement being "Agreement For The Employment of Laborers For The Islands of Hawaii". (U.S. Bureau of Labor. 1903: 26-27). (see: a complete two-page copy of this **original April 16, 1901** "Agreement", or contract, from the *Report of the Commissioner of Labor on Hawaii. 1902,* in "Exhibit 19" in this book).

This Agreement/Contract was "signed" as follows:

R.A. Macfie, W.D. Noble, T*he Agents, San Juan, Ponce, Adjuntas.* (U.S. Bureau of Labor. 1903: 27).

Importantly, the 1902 (published in: 1903) *Report of the Commissioner of Labor on Hawaii* reported that:

"An English translation of the notice in Spanish, posted by agents recruiting laborers in Porto Rico for the Hawaiian Planters' Association, and known as the "Contract under which the **Porto Rican** laborers went to Hawaii", follows [see: below]", (U.S. Bureau of Labor. 1903: 26). (emphasis added)

It should be noted that a copy of the Agreement [or Contract] which was presented to the Porto Rican immigrants for work in Hawaii was also reproduced in the *Bulletin of the Department of Labor in* 1903, and again in 1908. (Bulletin of the Department of Labor. 1903a: 703-704; 1903b Bulletin).

This Agreement/Contract had a total of **6 provisions**, with the "introductory paragraph" reading as follows (written verbatim):

"The Planters' Association of the Hawaiian Islands needs laborers for the cultivation of cane and the manufacture of sugar, and therefore makes the following offer to working people and their families who will go to that country:

1. To furnish such laborers, their wives, children, and relatives free passage from **Porto Rico** to Honolulu, including subsistence and medical attendance during the journey.

2. To furnish such laborer upon his arrival with agricultural employment for the period of three years from the date of actually commencing work; also furnishing employment to his wife and elder children if they so desire.

3. To guarantee the laborer the following wages for each month of 26 working days of actual labor…

4. The laborer and his family will receive, free of cost, living apartments, fuel and water for domestic use, medical attendance, and medicines.

5. The laborer shall be exempt from personal taxes, he and his family will enjoy the full protection of the laws of the Territory of Hawaii, and his children under age 14 years of age will be provided with primary instruction in the public schools.

6. At the conclusion of three years from the time of actually beginning work the planter will pay the laborer a $72 bonus, providing always that the laborer shall have worked continually during the period upon the plantation to which he was assigned an average of not less than 20 days in each month.... Ten hours constitute a working day in the fields and 12 hours in the mill...."

The Agreement/Contract went on to outline that:

"The journey will be made as follows: The laborers will embark upon comfortable steamers for New Orleans, a trip of 4 days; from there they will travel by rail to San Francisco, which will require 4 days more, and from California they will embark in a Pacific liner, which will take them to Hawaii in 6 more days. The whole journey will occupy about 14 days....

The workmen and their families will be provided by the Planters' Association upon embarking with *clothing, underclothing, footwear, and blankets*....

From cablegrams and letters received we know that the **Porto Ricans**, who have gone to Hawaii in the **first five expeditions**, have been given satisfactory employment upon the plantations of the islands, as well as their wives and children. This is corroborated by letters which the emigrants have sent to their families in **Porto Rico**.... These letters are on file at the Hawaiian agency, at the disposition of any who care to examine them...." (emphasis added)

It should be noted that **contrary** to the Hawaiian Planters' Association positive description of the Puerto Rican immigrants' experiences in Hawaii, at least until April 16, 1901, the article written by Rosario-Rivera uncovered other letters wherein some of these same Puerto Rican immigrants strongly complained of their treatment, the alleged false promises which were presented to them, and their experiences in Hawaii during this same time period. She read a number of these letters in her research at the Archives in Puerto Rico (Rosario-Rivera. 2000).

Note, however, that this above cited Agreement/ Contract was dated April 16, 1901, or several months ***after*** the first group of Porto Rican immigrants arrived in Hawaii on December 23, 1900. Additionally, the Puerto Rican immigrants departed from Puerto Rico on November 22, 1900, and arrived on December 23, 1900, for a total of 31 days, or more than **twice** the amount of time that the Agreement/ Contract specified.

Note: For a relatively contemporary description of some of the **positive contributions which Puerto Ricans** made to Hawaiian society and culture, the Ethnic Resource Center for the Pacific College of Education, Educational Foundations, University of Hawaii, produced a book appropriately entitled:

A Legacy of the Hawaiians, Chinese, Japanese, Portuguese, Puerto Ricans, Koreans, Filipinos and Samoans in Hawaii (1975) (cf.: the chapter titled: "The Puerto Ricans in Hawaii", by Blasé Camacho Souza, (Camacho Souza. 1975: 55-66)).

In summary, Porto Rican emigration to Hawaii was due to a confluence of very specific historical, economic, geographical and sociological factors summarized above. Importantly, however, the newspapers did agree on one central fact, namely, that the Puerto Rican immigrants left Puerto Rico to better their respective economic lives. For historical comparisons, the Master's Thesis titled, "Subjective Factors in the Migration of Spanish From Hawaii To California", by George F. Schnack in 1940, described the different reasons why the Spaniards left Spain for Hawaii in 1907 through 1925, and thereafter, and then from Hawaii to primarily the San Francisco Bay area in California, (see: Schnack. 1940). One similarity between the Puerto Rican and the Spanish immigrants to Hawaii is summarized by Schnack in his Chapter titled, "The Spanish in Hawaii", when he wrote, "The recruiters sent to Europe by the Hawaiian Sugar Planters Association [HSPA] naturally looked for their recruits among the poorer classes of people" (Ibid.: 34).

Puerto Rican Hawaii Plantation Laborer Figures:

It should be noted that in 1911 the publication titled the *Fourth Report of the Commissioner of Labor on Hawaii. 1910*, was published. It cited the number and percentage, of Puerto Rican sugar plantation workers in Hawaii covering the period from 1901 through 1910, as follows:

1901: 2,005 (5.3%); 1902: 2,036 (4.8%); [1903 was not reported on] 1904: 2,066 (4.5%); 1905: 2,029 (4.5%); 1906: 2,017 (4.8%); 1907: 1,878 (4.2%); 1908: 1,989 (4.2%); 1909: 2,024 (4.9%); and 1910: 1,869 (4.3%) (Report of the Commissioner of Labor. 1911: 23).

This same 1911 *Report of the Commissioner of Hawaii* also identified the following number of Puerto Rican **children** that were enrolled in Public and Private Schools of Hawaii during the period from 1900 to 1910, as of the months of December for each of the following years:

1900: [N/A]; 1901: 596; 1902: 593; 1903: 538 [June]; 1904: 437; 1905: 405; 1906: 392; 1907: 368; 1908: 355; 1909: 438; and 1910: 372 (Report of the Commissioner of Labor. 1911: 16).

Five years later, in 1916, another government report, titled *Labor Conditions in Hawaii*, reported the number and percentages, of the Puerto Rican sugar plantation employees in Hawaii, which included the time periods from 1910 through 1915, as follows:

1911: 1,918 (4.3%); 1912: 1,822 (4.0%); 1913: 1,608 (3.5%); 1914: 1,480 (3.2%); and 1915: 1,423 (3.2%) (U.S. Bureau of Labor Statistics. 1916: 18).

Interestingly, this same 1916 report, *Labor Conditions in Hawaii*, identified the number of Puerto Rican "Skilled Sugar Plantation Employees" during the period from 1904 through 1915. The U.S. Bureau of Labor Statistics' 1916 definition of a "skilled sugar plantation employee" was as follows:

> "In plantation statistics employees receiving $50 a month or more, excluding the earnings of contractors and of persons receiving in excess of this sum on account of overtime, are classed as skilled without regard to occupation" (U.S. Bureau of Labor Statistics. 1916: 19).

This above cited 1916 Report identified the following number of Puerto Rican "skilled employees" as follows:

1904: 8; 1905: 5; 1906: 4; 1907: 7; 1908: 9; 1909: --- [no number here]; 1910: 10; 1911: 9; 1912: 9; 1913: 6; 1914: 11; and 1915: 12 (U.S. Bureau of Labor Statistics. 1916: 19).

Additionally, this aforementioned 1916 Report also cited the following occupational positions which the Puerto Rican sugar plantation workers held for the year of 1915 in their Table titled: "Occupations, Rates of Wages, Hours of Labor, and Nationality or Race of Employees on 50 Sugar Plantations", namely:

Blacksmiths helpers: 1, out of a total of 116 Blacksmiths helpers; Brakemen, railroad: 13, out of 124; Camp cleaners: 10, out of 206; Cane cutters: 99, out of 3,172; Cane cutters and carriers: 41,out of 915; Cane cutters, carriers, flume layers, and flumers: 7, out of 266; Cane cutters, loaders, and haulers: 6, out of 583; Cane cutters, seed cane: 1, out of 230; Cane loaders: 23, out of 2,045; Carpenters: 1, out of 216; Carpenters helpers: 1, out of 462; store Clerks: 2, out of 223; Contract cultivators: 185, out of 7,717; Dairymen: 1, out of 18; Drivers, auto truck: 1, out of 36; Engineers' helpers, steam plow: 1, out of 14; Engineers, locomotive: 8, out of 110; Engineers, steam plow: 4, out of 126; Engineers, traction engine, assistant: 1, out of 8; Field hands: 619, out of 14,279; locomotive Firemen: 3, out of 96; Foreman, stablemen: 1, out of 46; Freight handlers: 4, out of 45; Laborers, general: 45, out of 169; Laborers, railroad: 4, out of 494; Laborers, road: 1, out of 23; Machinists' helpers: 1 (a boy), out of 145; Masons' helpers: 1, out of 49; Oilers, mill: 1, out of 86; Overseers: 5, out of 377; Overseers, assistant: 7, out of 345; Painters: 2, out of 53; Stablemen: 2, out of 285; Steerers, steam plow: 7, out of 105; Surveyors' helpers: 1, out of 17; Teachers, kindergarten, apprentice: 1, out of 8; Teamsters and cultivators: 180, out of 2,279; Water tenders, steam plow: 3, out of 36; Wharf hands: 8, out of 78; Wood choppers: 1, out of 12; and Yard boys: 1, out of 111; etc., (U.S. Bureau of Labor Statistics. "Labor Conditions in Hawaii...." 1916: 78-118).

Therefore, the above listing of the 41 varied occupations which were held by Puerto Ricans in Hawaii in 1915, shows that they performed a wide variety of employment services, although only a few of the occupations dominated most of the Puerto Rican employees' jobs, such as: Cane cutters: 99; Cane cutters and carriers: 41; Contract cultivators: 185; Field Hands: 619; Laborers, General: 45, and Teamsters and cultivators: 180, (*Ibid*). In short, this 1916 publication, entitled *Labor Conditions in Hawaii....*, at least according to this author's calculations, identified a total of 191 separate occupations, which were distributed among 50 Sugar Plantations in Hawaii, with the Puerto Rican immigrants working in 41 of these varied occupations (*Ibid*.: 78-118)

The Concentration of Wealth and Land in Puerto Rico:

It should be noted that even as late as at least 1919, wealth in Puerto in Puerto Rico was overwhelmingly concentrated in the hands of a relatively few, while poverty and landless workers and laborers, was widespread. This was another contributing cause of Puerto Rican emigration. Thus, the U.S. Department of Labor's 1919 *Report* entitled *Labor Conditions in Porto Rico* unapologetically pointed out the **per capita** as:

"It is estimated that the total **wealth** of the island is in the hands of 15 per cent of the population. A member of the Porto Rican Legislature recently stated on the floor of the house that only 14 per cent of the wealth of the island is in the hands of native Porto Ricans. Of the remaining 86 per cent, **Continental Americans** own 67 per cent and the rest is in the hands of Spanish, French, and other foreigners. According to statistics of 1909, Porto Rico had the lowest **per capita wealth** of the 14 countries given below: Great Britain ($1,442); France (1,257); Australia (1,228); **United States (1,123)**; Denmark ($1,104); Canada ($949); Belgium ($734); Germany ($707); Spain ($548); Austria-Hungary ($499); Greece ($485); Italy ($485); Portugal ($417); Russia ($296), and **Porto Rico ($182)**. (U.S. Dept. of Labor. 1919: 13, 14). (emphasis added)

Additionally, this same 1919 U.S. Dept. of Labor *Report* also represented that **land** was extremely concentrated among an exceedingly few persons or entities, so that:

"Hence we find that of the best land of Porto Rico 537,193 acres are owned and 229,203 acres leased by [only] 477 individuals, partnerships, or corporations. Of this land **Continental Americans** control the largest area, 357,799" (*Ibid*.: 13). (emphasis added)

The 1921 *Report of the Governor of Hawaii* reported that the Puerto Rican population in Hawaii in 1920 was 5,602, of which 1,215 were "Laborers" on the sugar plantations. They were classified as follows: 8 were "Skilled men"; 772 were "unskilled" men; 48 "unskilled" women; 116 unskilled male minors, and 16 unskilled female minors, for a total of 952 "unskilled" Puerto Rican plantation laborers; 234 Contractors, and 21 Planters, (Secretary of the Interior. 1921: 38).

In contrast, in 1921 there were a total of 173 Spanish (i.e., Spaniards), 888 Americans, 924 Hawaiians, 2,433 Portuguese, and 18 Russian laborers (*Ibid.*: 38).

The 1921 publication titled "Labor Problems in Hawaii" listed that there were a total of 1,917 Puerto Rican "children below age of 12" in Hawaii as of January 1, 1920 (Committee on Immigration and Naturalization, 1921 (Part 1): 547).

Further, Norma Carr (Carr: 1989: 454-455) provided the following figures summarizing "Plantation Labor and School Attendance" for the Puerto Rican immigrants for the period of 1901-1939. However, for the purposes of this book, I will provide the figures for the Puerto Rican population for only the following selective years: (See also: Committee on Immigration and Naturalization. 1921: 545).

Puerto Rican Population and Plantation Laborers:

1901: 5,000 Puerto Ricans; 2,095 Laborers;

1902: [This line is left blank]; 2,036 (1,955) Laborers;

1910: 4,828 Puerto Ricans; 1,820 (1,224) Laborers;

1920: 5,602 Puerto Ricans; 1,422 Laborers; and

1925: 6,382 Puerto Ricans; 1,066 Laborers.

Puerto Rican School Attendance (Public/Private):

1901: - [This line is left blank; although there were Puerto Rican students in school in 1901];

1902: 539 Public/57 Private [Students];

1910: 309 Public/63 Private [Students];

1920: 1,068 [Students]; and

1925: 1,043 [Students].

Puerto Rican "Departures" from Hawaii to the [West] "Coast":

The 1914 government publication entitled *Report of the Governor of Hawaii to the Secretary of the Interior For the Fiscal Year Ended June 30, 1914*, provided a Table which identified the number of steerage passengers--- Puerto Ricans in this case---that had migrated, i.e., "departed", from Hawaii to the [West] "Coast" (most likely to California), for four fiscal years since the census of April, 1910, or for the period from 1911 to 1914, namely: 1911: 232; 1912: 13; 1913: 33; 1914: 105; Total "departures" being 383 (Secretary of the Interior. 1914: 34). [*Note:* The 1905 *Report of the Governor* (page 26) pointed out that the "arrivals", and the "departures" statistics [for Puerto Ricans and for the other "nationalities"], are *from* the port of Hawaii [i.e., Honolulu]].

The 1914 *Report of the Governor of Hawaii to the Secretary of the Interior For the Fiscal Year Ended June 30, 1914*, reported that 46 men, 25 women, and 34 children, or a total of 105 Puerto Ricans "departed" (i.e., left) Hawaii for the [West] "Coast" of the United States, most likely to California. This *Report* did not provide any figures for whether or not any Puerto Ricans had "arrived" (as immigrants) to Hawaii (Secretary of the Interior. 1914: 35).

It should be noted that Hawaii: "was unprepared for the **influenza epidemic** which occurred in 1918. Puerto Ricans did fall victim to it but not as extensively as other groups. The death toll of 93 was the group's fourth highest in the decade. That year the birthrate was their second highest for the period [1911-1919]" (Carr. 1989: 234). (emphasis added)

Similarly, the 1919 *Report of the Governor of Hawaii* identified the number of Puerto Ricans that migrated from Hawaii to the [West] "Coast" of California during the period from 1915 to 1919 (again, most likely to California), for the period up to the census of April 1919, namely: 1915: 50; 1916: 210; 1917: 41; 1918: 57 [55?]; 1919: 43; Total "departures" from 1915 through April 1919 was: 401. Therefore, the total number of "departures" to the "Coast" during the period from 1911 to April 1919 was 784 Puerto Ricans (383 + 401) (Secretary of the Interior. 1919: 36).

Note: Norma Carr identified a total of 784 Puerto Ricans that had "departed" from Hawaii [presumably to the West Coast, most likely, to California] during the period from 1911 through 1919, while there were a total of 1,976 births, and 764 deaths, which equated to "a net gain of 435 over deaths and departures [of Puerto Ricans]" (Carr. 1989: 234).

The 1920 *Report of the Governor of Hawaii* reported a total of 14 Puerto Ricans that "departed" to the [West] "Coast for the year ending June 1920 (Secretary of the Interior. 1920: 36). The 1921 *Report of the Governor* shows that 9 Puerto Ricans "departed" to the "Coast" [i.e., California] "for the year ending June 30, 1921" (Secretary of the Interior. 1921: 39). The 1922 *Report of the Governor of Hawaii* shows that 22 Puerto Ricans "departed" to the "Coast" "for the year ending June 30, 1922" (Secretary of the Interior. 1922: 34).

The 1923 *Report of the Governor of Hawaii* reported a total of 149 Puerto Ricans "departed" to the "Coast" "for the year ending June 30, 1923" (Secretary of the Interior. 1923: 40).

The 1924 *Report of the Governor of Hawaii* reported that the Puerto Rican population in the Territory of Hawaii (i.e., "Citizens") was at 6,347, with a total of 2,178 Puerto Rican Laborers in three distinct work categories, working on the Hawaiian Sugar Plantations (Secretary of the Interior. 1924: 37).

Most importantly, for the purposes of this book, is that this 1924 *Report* listed a total of 112 Puerto men, 88 women, and 98 children, a total of 298 Puerto Ricans who "departed" from Hawaii for the [West] "Coast", most likely, to California, while a total of "only" 51 Puerto Ricans "arrived" in Hawaii (as immigrants) (*Ibid.*: 38).

Finally, the 1925 *Report of the Governor of Hawaii to the Secretary of the Interior.1925,* reported that the Puerto Rican population in the Territory of Hawaii (i.e., "Citizens") as of 1925 was 6,382. This same *Report*, in its Table entitled "Labor report of 42 plantations of the Hawaiian Sugar Planters' Association for the month of May, 1925, by racial classification", listed that there were a total of 1,088 Puerto Ricans who were "employees on pay roll", with 22 being the "Number on a monthly basis", and the remaining 1,066 being the "Number [of] employees not on monthly basis" (Secretary of the Interior. 1925: 40).

This aforementioned 1925 *Report* listed that there were a total of 11 men, 9 women, and 15 children, for a total of 35 Puerto Rican "Arrivals" from the [West] "Coast" to Hawaii for the year ending June 30, 1925, and a total of 81 Puerto Rican "departures" from Hawaii to the [West] "Coast" also for the year ending June 30, 1925 (Ibid.: 41).

This 1925 *Report* also reported a total of 1,043 Puerto Rican pupils attending public schools in the Territory as of June 30, 1925. During this period 107 Puerto Ricans had died and 315 were born (or a "Birth rate" of 40.40 ?---this figure is difficult to read), with the "Infant mortality" rate for Puerto Ricans being at 35, or 111.11 "deaths per 1,000 births" (Secretary of the Interior. 1925: 71, 88, 90).

This 1925 *Report* also described the **Hawaii National Guard**, which was "organized under the provisions of the national defense act (and amendments thereto) of the United States Congress and the Revised Laws of the Territory of Hawaii", and it indicated that "the racial composition of the guard on June 30, 1925" had 74 Puerto Ricans in it, out of its total of 1,486 members (Secretary of the Interior. 1925: 104, 105).

Finally, the 1926 *Report of the Governor of Hawaii* reported that the "Estimated" Puerto Rican population in Hawaii as of December 31, 1925 (mid-year) was at 6,443, while as of June 30, 1926, it was at 6,504 (Secretary of the Interior. 1926: 81). Meanwhile, according to the 53rd *Statistical Abstract of the United States,* Puerto Rico itself had a population of 1,430,792 in 1925 (midyear), and a population of 1,549,868 in 1930 (U.S. Department of Commerce. 1931: 3).

It should be noted that the State of Hawaii's Superintendent of Education, Charles G. Clark, reported in 1980 that Hawaii had celebrated:

"the **80th anniversary** of Puerto Rican immigration to Hawaii," by having the Hawaii Department of Education present "an artmobile **exhibit**, called, 'Puerto Rican: One Identity from a Multi-Ethnic Heritage'" (cited in: Carr. 1980: Forward: ii).

NOTE:

June 2016 - For a list of names of immigrants to (into) Puerto Rico from 1815-1820, including the name of (most likely), Simon M. Mezes' father, who arrived in Puerto Rico in 1811 from Louisiana (cited as: Juan Simon Mesas, p. 269), see: Raquel Rosario Rivera, *La Real Cédula de Gracias de 1815 y sus primeros efectos en Puerto Rico: Incluye Registro de Emigrados.* (1995), (San Juan, Puerto Rico), (page 237, 283, 285).

For a listing of the 58 Hawaiian Sugar Plantations, on June 30, 1901, in which Porto Rican Laborers (i.e., immigrants) were working on 41 of them, See the: "Report of the Governor of the Territory of Hawaii to the Secretary of the Interior. 1901", (Bib. # 254; see the Table titled, "Number and Nationality of all Laborers on Hawaiian SugarPlantations June 30, 1901", pp. 65-66).

This Table listed a total of 1,772 men, and 323 women Porto Rican laborers as of June 30, 1901.

The table also listed the following "nationalities" as working on said plantations, 1,470 Hawaiians, 2,417 Portuguese, 27,537 Japanese, 4,976 Chinese, 317 Negroes, 46 South Sea Islanders, 342 Americans, 169 British, and 163 Germans.

Finally, this same Table listed the "Grand Total" of Laborers working on these sugar plantations as being at: 39,587.

CHAPTER 3

United States Immigration History and the "Puerto Rican Diaspora": Are they Related?

The answer to the question above is: Yes! In short, their connectedness was succinctly summarized by Professor Edna Acosta Belén, in her appropriately titled article: "Puerto Rican Diaspora in the United States," when she wrote:

"The United States is often described as a 'nation of immigrants.' Throughout its history, different nationalities and races have made their own vital contributions to U.S. society [e.g., U.S. Supreme Court Justice Sonia Sotomayor who is of Puerto Rican heritage] with their productive labor and creativity. For more than a century and a half, the Puerto Rican Diaspora has participated in this process by establishing its own historic and cultural legacy within the United States. Similarly, this population has maintained its ties to the island; has made important economic, cultural, and political contributions to Puerto Rican society; and continues to reassert its Puerto Ricanness within the context of U.S. society" (Acosta Belén 2010: 7).

While a number of books have outlined the histories of different ethnic groups in California, and San Francisco in particular, no comprehensive book has been written regarding Puerto Rican immigration to California or San Francisco. For example, the following ethnic histories have been written: *The Italians of San Francisco 1850-1930* (1978), by Deanna Paoli Gumina; *Russian San Francisco* (Images of America Series) (2009), by Lydia B. Zaverukha; *Jewish San Francisco (CA)* (Images of America Series) (2006), by Edward Zerlin, Ph.D.; *Irish San Francisco* (Images of America Series) (2008), by John Garvey; and *Filipinos in San Francisco* (Images of America Series) (2011), by the Filipino American National Historical Society.

For a contemporaneous detailed description of the social conditions and economic causes of emigration which the "European Ethnic Groups" and the Puerto Ricans had during the approximate period from 1898-1910, see the following government Report by the **Committee on Immigration,** entitled: (Reports of the Immigration Commission. *Emigration Conditions in Europe.* 1911e: 53-67, Chapter IV).

In short, the Committee on Immigration concluded in 1911 in their Chapter titled, "Causes of Emigration From Europe. Primary Causes," that:

"The present movement of population from Europe to the United States is, with few exceptions, almost entirely attributable to economic causes. Emigration due to political reasons and, to a less extent, religious oppression, undoubtedly exists, but even in countries where these incentives prevail the more important cause is very largely an economic one…. But the present movements results, in the main, simply from a widespread desire for better economic conditions rather than from the necessity of escaping intolerable ones [therefore, this author believes that this fact is a **demon-**

strable difference than what had occurred in Puerto Rico in August 1899---the hurricane---with its attendant economic and social devastation (like famine) and widespread unemployment]. In other words the emigrant of to-day comes to the United States not merely to make a living, but to make a better living than is possible at home" (Reports of the Immigration Commission. 1911e.: 53).

The 1911 **Reports of the Immigration Commission** specifically listed a total of 29 "race or people" [or what today are likely to be referred to as "ethnic groups", or "nationalities"], of persons from different countries, such as: English, French, German, Hebrew, Irish, Italians, or Spaniards, in their publication/report (see: Reports of the immigration Commission. 1911e: 59).

Another similarity between Puerto Rican and European imigration is the role that *agriculture*, or lack thereof, had in creating the conditions for emigration. Thus the **Immigration Commission** reported that: "A large proportion of the emigration from…Europe…may be traced directly to the inability of the peasantry to gain an adequate livelihood in agricultural pursuits, either as laborers or proprietors" (*Ibid.*: 54).

The similarities, and connectedness, between U.S. immigration history and Puerto Rican immigration history is exemplified by the following historical example(s):

The white-European ethnic groups, like the Italians and the Irish, etc. [Note: they were not considered "white" until later; (cf.: *How The Irish Became White*, by Noel Ignatiev, 1995)], as well as the Chinese and the Japanese immigrants [what in some circles today are called "people of color", or "ethnic minorities"] who came to the United States throughout the 19th Century and the first decades of the 20th Century, came to America for one fundamental reason, namely, to improve their respective lives, not only for their families, but for themselves. Similarly, the Puerto Rican *Diaspora* to California, and to Hawaii, first <u>began</u> during the first ten years of the 20th Century, (namely 1900 to 1910), and was predicated on these immigrants' wanting to improve their lives, even if it meant traveling thousands of miles from Puerto Rico to either California, and/or to Hawaii, and oftentimes, back to California (*San Francisco Call.* Dec. 14, 1900: 1; *San Francisco Call.* May 28, 1905; *San Francisco Examiner.* December 16, 1900: 39, (Bib. #345); *San Francisco Examiner.* Dec. 19, 1900: 4; (Bib. #164)). **5/**

Professor Virginia Sánchez Korrol succinctly summarized the relationship between the historical reality and relationship between Puerto Rican immigration to the United States and the historical reality of 19th and 20th century European immigration to the United States when she wrote the following:

"In recent years, the media has tended to portray U.S. Latinos of Hispanic Caribbean ancestry as new immigrants. But this characterization ignores the long connections between these immigrants and the United States. And because Puerto Ricans, who have also had a prolonged presence in the U.S… their experiences have often been entirely excluded from accounts of U.S. immigrant communities."

Professor Sánchez-Korrol went on to write that:

"In fact, the Hispanic Caribbean role in American history originated long before the nineteenth century, and it is well documented in recovered chronicles, letters, and other firsthand accounts and primary sources. These can be found in projects such as the *Recovering the U.S. Hispanic Literary Heritage Project* of Arte Público Press and in published works such as the *Memoirs of Bernardo Vega* (1984)…. Vega believed that 'in order to stand on our own two feet, Puerto Ricans of all generations must begin by affirming our own history'…" (Sánchez Korrol 2005: 1).

It should be noted that the 1920 U.S. Federal Census explained the then newly created "Porto Rican citizenship"; Puerto Ricans became U.S. citizens in 1917, as follows:

"Country of Allegiance – Under the act of March 2, 1917, all persons born in Porto Rico are treated as **citizens of the United States** unless they (or their parents in case of minors) have declared their intention to retain Porto Rican citizenship, Spanish citizenship [from Spain], or citizenship of other countries" (U.S. Bureau of the Census. 1922: 1197). (emphasis added)

Regarding the pre-1917 time period, Dr. Clara E. Rodríguez, writing in her dissertation in 1974, posited that there were some major differences between European immigrants and Puerto Rican immigrants, which I believe still exists into the 21st Century, when she wrote that:

"…certain Puerto Rican characteristics, e.g., race and citizenship [as of 1917], will make the Puerto Rican experience in the U.S. different from the previous immigrant groups…. Immigrants came to this country with different resources, but all seeking to optimize their situations…. One cost of entry common to all immigrants was: shedding ethnicity or learning to publicly be non-ethnic… The time which individuals spend before they pass through a gate is called 'waiting time.' Here again, this has relevance to the immigrant situation; for there is the implicit expectation in the American culture that the greater the time in the U.S. of a particular group, the better [over-time] will be their socio-economic position. There is, however, an important exception to this 'waiting time' expectation. That is race. It may be that there are two distinct sets of entry gates: one for Whites and one for Nonwhites" (Rodríguez, Clara E. 1974: xvi, xvii, xviii).

She went on to write that:

"For Americans want, have always wanted, to maintain an ideal self-image that does not admit those racially or visibly culturally different ethnic groups [such as Puerto Ricans]. This ideal has changed but slightly with the passing of centuries" (Rodríguez, Clara E. 1974: 1).

Dr. Sánchez Korrol summarizes the important historical, and the current continual role, which Hispanic Caribbeans, including Puerto Ricans, have had on the United States when she wrote the following:

"But historians and students of history should remember that the story of Hispanic Caribbean's and their contributions to United States culture and society begins long before the mid-twentieth century" (Sánchez Korrol 2005: 4).

In addition, it is important to always keep in mind that, "Latino History", in its broadest context, and *Latino immigration history* in particular, does matter and are an important part of U.S. History, and the current "Latino immigration debate" issue. In a related vein, the "teaching of U.S. Puerto Rican History" is also important, especially in light of the historical reality of the ever increasing U.S. Puerto Rican population increase(s) for more than a century (cf.: Sánchez Korral 1999; Silvestrini-Pacheco and Castro Arroyo 1981; Sánchez Korral 2005; Reimers 1999: 12; Ruiz 2006; History Task Force. 1982). In short:

"Latinos represent the largest minority population in the United States, a diverse mosaic of cultural backgrounds, generations (e.g. immigrant, U.S. born children of immigrants, grandchildren of immigrants), and historical experience…. The term Latino refers to all people of Latin American birth or heritage who live in the United States…" (cf.: Ruiz 2006: 655-672; Ruiz 2009: 7, 7-26).

Dr. Lawrence R. Chenault, a former Economics Professor at the University of Puerto Rico, writing in 1938, summarized how the 1910 Federal Census identified the Puerto Rican population within the continental United States when he wrote:

"Since there is no separate classification in the census covering the Puerto Rican people in the United States, we can only judge the total number of people of Puerto Rican origin by the number **born in Puerto Rico** and living in the continental United States" (Chenault 1938: 53; Preface). (Emphasis added)

However, by the 21st century, Professors Jorge Duany and Patricia Silver, citing U.S. Census Bureau 2008 Figures, ranked California eight (8th) in the number of individuals of "Puerto Rican Origins" who live within its state boundaries with a Puerto Rican , i.e., **"Puerto Rican origins"** population, of 172,978 out of a total United States Puerto Rican population of over four million, thereby documenting, "the growing dispersal of the Puerto Rican diaspora throughout the United States" (Duany and Patricia Silver. 2010: 6, 7; Duany. 2009a: 59, 58; López. 2009a)

Note: the 2010 Federal Census cited a total of 189,000 Puerto Ricans residing in the State of California as of April 2010 (See: Footnote #5 in the "Notes" section of this book).

NOTE: September 2016 - For an historical comparison(s) between "European White Immigrants" (aka: "White Ethnics") and that of "Immigrants of Color" (aka: "Ethnic Minorities", or "People of Color"), such as immigrants from the Caribbean (oftentimes Porto Ricans, even well after 1925, including into the 21st Century), and its racially discriminatory impacts BECAUSE of this difference, see the book titled:

Working Toward Whiteness: How America's Immigrants Became White, The Strange Journey From Ellis Island to the Suburbs, (by David R. Roediger, 2005, Basic Books; via Amazon.com e-books. Kindle Books Edition).

See: Chapter 22 in this book (pages 111-116), titled, "The 'Racialization' of the San Francisco and California Puerto Rican Immigrants: 1900-1910".

NOTE: The government Report titled, *Abstract of of the Twelfth Census of the United States 1900* (1902; Bib. #277), in its Glossary, "defines" the "Colored Population" in Porto Rico in 1899/1900 as being, "used in the Census of Porto Rico, taken by the War Department, to include Negroes, Mongolians, and persons of Mixed Race," (pp. 387, 388).

Mongolians are defined as being: Chinese and Japanese, (p. 388).

Note: For a comprehensive listing of the "Destination of immigrants admitted to the United States, fiscal years 1899-1910, inclusive, by race or people" [and/or by "Nationality" or Country], this Table has 39 such separate listings, see: Bib. #167, pp. 106-109, 319ff., which includes such areas as these immigrants going to California, Hawaii, Porto Rico, as well as to New York State; (see also: Bib. #42, p. 542 (Table); Bib. # 254, p. 4)

Note: For a listing of "Aliens admitted to and departing from the Territory of Hawaii between the years 1910 and 1921, inclusive", see: Bib. #42, p.. 546 (Table) (Serial 7 - Part 1); this lists at least 31 separate "Race or people" ("Nationalities" or Countries) of these "Aliens" [i.e., Immigrants]. Also, see: Bib #42, p. 542 (Table) (Serial 7 - Part 2) which lists the number of Immigrants to Hawaii, by Nationality or Country, from 1852 (293 Chinese) to 1899, including American, Chinese, Japanese, Portuguese, German, Norwegian, South Sea Islanders, and Galician Immigrants.

(cf.: The article by Dr. Samuel Betances, "The Prejudice of Having No Prejudice in Puerto Rico", (*The Rican*, Winter 1972: 41ff, see both: Part I and Part II).

CHAPTER 4

My Research in a Social Context

Thus far there has been relatively limited detailed research on the historical beginnings and eventual development and growth, of the Puerto Rican community in California, beginning from 1850 to 1925 and thereafter, and to Hawaii from 1900 to 1925. Dr. Clara E. Rodríguez astutely observed, that there exist:

"...the incorrect assumption that the history of the Puerto Rican community in the United States [especially in California] has been undistinguished and of fairly short duration...." (Rodríguez, Clara E. 2001: 230).

In short, the principal guiding light and inspiration of this research is summarized by Professor Virginia E. Sánchez Korral, referencing educator Jesse M. Vázquez's insightful and inspirational words, when she wrote:

"If American scholars study American culture and society through American studies that is considered scholarship. However, when a Puerto Rican researcher studies Puerto Rican culture---any aspect of it---it is not seen as quite scholarly enough" (Sánchez Korral 1994b: Preface, xviii).

Thus, one of the aims of my research is to locate the historical "facts", basis, and social and economic conditions, which accounted for the beginnings of the Puerto Rican diaspora and immigration, to both California (from 1850 to 1925) and Hawaii (from 1900 to 1925), although the research of this book primarily covers the period from 1900 to 1925.

September 2016:

This 2nd Edition of this book was a truly social process in that it was stongly advised to me by professional (Puerto Rican) Genealogist, Tony Rivera Maldonado (Association of Professional Genealogists (APG) Member and a Member of the Sociedad Puertorriqueña de Genealogia) (see: pp. 195-198), that I should definately add/include an INDEX to this 2nd Edition book for Reserchers and Genealogists.

This was truly a social and collaborative effort in that without Mr. Rivera Maldonado's research, assistance, editing input, translation help and encouraging me to complete said INDEX, this INDEX by me would not have been undertaken, nor completed. For this I am extremely grateful, and most appreciative, for Mr. Rivera Maldonado's assistance, time and high-level scholarship skills and standards. Thank you Tony!

I would like to thank the continued advice, research assistance, and translation skills of two Members of the Hispanic Genealogical Society of New York (HGSNY), namely, Orlando Bodón-Echevarria (p. 245), and of Charlie Fourquet Batiz.

October 2016-

My research, of course was conducted within, and was influenced by, my particular life experiences and currrent social context and social interactions. The following quote(s) hopefully will show the reader of this book the conscious decisions I made in the preparation of this book in my selection of particular historical "facts". For example, social historian and social activist, Professor Howard Zinn, in his book titled, *A People's History of the United States: 1492-Present*, (2003, HarperCollins Publishers, N.Y., N.Y.), insightfully wrote the following:

"Thus, in that inevitable taking of sides which comes from selections and emphasis in history [i.e., of "certain "facts", as oppposed to others], I prefer to try to tell the story..." of the Porto Rican immigration to California and Hawaii from, from as much as I was possibly able to, from the immigrants perspective, as oppposed to from the perspective of the Hawaiian Sugar Planters and their "historians", (page 10).

"It is not that the historian can avoid emphasis of some facts and not of others. This is as natural to him as the mapmaker, who, in order to produce a usable drawing for practical purposes, must first flatten and distort the shape of the earth, then choose out of the bewildering mass of geographic information those things needed for the purpose of this or that particular map", (page 8).

Professor Zinn further writes that:

"My argument cannot be against selection, simplification, emphasis, which are inevitable for both cartographers and historians. But the map-maker's distortion is a technical necessity for a common purpose shared by all people who need maps. The historian's distortion is more than technical, it is ideological; it is released into a world of contending interests, where any chosen emphasis supports (whether the historian means to or not) some kind of interests, whether economic or political or racial or national or sexual," (page 8).

Finally, Dr. Zinn astutely points out that:

Furthermore, this ideological interest is not openly expressed in the way a mapmaker's technical interest is obvious.... No, it is presented as if all readers of history had a common interest which historians serve to the best of their ability. This is not intentional deception; the historian has been trained in a society in which education and knowledge are put forward as technical problems of excellence and not as tools for contending social classes, races, nations," (page 8).

CHAPTER 5

The Definition of a "Porto Rican/Puerto Rican" in 1910 for the Purposes of this Book

Although it may seem self-evident, the historical record shows that the definition of ethnicity, and/or of race, has changed over the years, and oftentimes, from one Census to another (Rodríguez, Clara E. 2000; Rodríguez, Clara E. 2005: 291, 288-293). For the purposes of this book, a "Porto Rican," or "Puerto Rican," was defined by the U.S. Census Bureau as follows:

"... Figures for 1910-1950 are for **persons born in Puerto Rico**. Those for 1960-2000 are for persons of Puerto Rican birth or **parentage**" (Teresa Whalen 2005: 3, Table 1-2; Duany 2003: 426, Table 1, "Note"; U.S. Bureau of the Census. 1999: 2, "Footnote 2"; cf.: U.S. Bureau of the Census. 1913a: 185). (Emphasis added)

On November 17, 1907, the *San Francisco Call* had the headline, "A People Without Nationality", referencing the "Porto Rican Immigration" as the social and political issue of the day, as well as attempting to provide its own "definition" of a Puerto Rican immigrant to the San Francisco Bay area. The reporter wrote as follows:

"**What is a Porto Rican?** He is not a citizen. He is not a subject. Possibly he may be a new form of **property.** There is neither means nor any way by which a native of Porto Rico may become a citizen of the United States. He is not exactly a man without a country, but he has no nationality and therefore cannot renounce that which he has not. In a word, even if he remove (*sic*) to the United States he cannot be naturalized. In our own country he has no political status...." (*San Francisco Call*. November 17, 1907: 1). [Emphasis added]

This reporter went on to write that:

"While Spaniards and foreigners [i.e., "White European ethnic" immigrants] may become American citizens in the United States or in Porto Rico by simply following the regulations of the law, the native of Porto Rico, who has been under the American flag for over nine years now, has no legal way of becoming a citizen of the United States or the right of receiving the blessings of that same constitution he has sworn to support. Even if the Porto Ricans tried to become American citizens in this country they could not, for the simple reason that they have no nationality to renounce. I know of no other people in the civilized world who are in the same position" (*San Francisco Call*, November 17, 1907: 1).

CHAPTER 6

My Research Proceeded as Follows

After keying in two separate search terms into the computer, "Porto Rico," and "Puerto Rico," the web site **AncestryInstitution.com** 6/ generated two separate lists of names -- those who were born in "Porto Rico," and those born in "Puerto Rico" as of 1910. Thus, the sons and daughters of these first generation Puerto Ricans were not defined by the 1910 Census as being "Porto Rican/Puerto Rican," if they were not actually born in Puerto Rico (Teresa Whalen 2005: 3, Note). However, I **DID** count these second *generation* children as also being Puerto Ricans for purposes of this book and by *today's* 2010 Census definitions (cf.: Exhibit 10 and Exhibit 11, in this book).

Therefore, the 1910 Census had a narrower and a more restrictive definition of who was "Puerto Rican," at least by today's standards, which are currently more inclusive and less restrictive, than it was in 1910. Regardless of this limitation, this author was able to identify the names of numerous sons and daughters of these first generation Puerto Ricans to California from the digitized 1910 census forms.

Another important part of my *methodology* was to focus on **primary sources** as much as possible, while also reviewing relevant secondary sources, as well.

For example, I reviewed the 1850, 1860, 1870, 1880, 1900 and 1910 U.S. Federal Census pages (using Ancestry.com). The 1890 Census was destroyed by fire.

I reviewed several <u>contemporaneous</u> **primary source newspapers** from the turn of the century, i.e., from 1900 through 1910, which covered <u>both</u> the Puerto Rican ("Porto Rican") immigrants in Hawaii and California, such as:

A total of 21 issues, from several different Hawaiian newspapers, such as the: *Hawaiian Evening Bulletin*; the *Hawaiian* Gazette; *Honolulu Republican*; and the *Hawaiian Star*.

Additionally, I also reviewed 20 issues of another Hawaiian based newspaper, the *Pacific Commercial Advertiser* [Honolulu, Hawaii Territory].

Report of the Governor of *Hawaii to the Secretary of the Interior* (This author reviewed issues from 1900 through 1926). (see the issues in the "Bibliography" section under the name of: "Secretary of the Interior", the "1900 through the 1926" individual Reports of the Governor of Hawaii), after "Exhibit 21" of this book.

I reviewed several <u>contemporaneous</u> **primary source newspapers** from California, from the early 20th Century which focused on the Puerto Rican immigrants of California (primarily in the San Francisco Bay area), as well as additional source citations which appear in the "Addendum Bibliography" section of this Book.

The *San* Francisco *Examiner* (24 issues); *San Francisco Chronicle* (18 issues); *San Francisco* Call (27 issues); the *Los Angeles Herald* (3 issues), the *Los Angeles Times* (5 issues), the *Sacramento*

Daily Record-Union (3 issues); the *Amador Ledger*, the *San Mateo Gazette*; the *Sausalito News* [Marine County, CA] and the *New York Times* (16 issues).

It is important to note that while my methodology did not consist of any "oral histories", (at least as it relates to California) and/or interviews, the Hawaiian Puerto Rican, Blasé Camacho Souza, along with Alfred P. Souza, did publish a book in 1985 entitled *De Borinquen A Hawaii Nuestra Historia: From Puerto Rico to Hawaii,* wherein they were able to identify many of the **descendants** (via conducting oral histories) of many of the Puerto Ricans that first arrived in Hawaii, beginning from 1901 through 1921. This book contains:

"...a list of donors who symbolically commended their forefathers for their vision and bravery and recognized their contributions to the multi-ethnic Hawaiian community. This document provides scholars, researchers, and persons searching for their 'roots' with needed information about the early 1900s exodus of Puerto Ricans to Hawaii. Listed are names of the emigrants, where they came from, and year of arrival. This list is not all-inclusive as only those names voluntarily submitted were included" (Blasé Camacho Souza and Alfred P. Souza, 1985. *De Borinquen A Hawaii Nuestra Historia: From Puerto Rico to Hawaii.* Puerto Rican Heritage Society of Hawaii. Honolulu: Hawaii [the Library of Congress, Copyright Office edition], Bib. #365).

For example, they identified a total of, according to my counting, 494 Puerto Ricans that had emigrated during the years from 1901 through 1921 from Puerto Rico to Hawaii, of which a **total** of 181 came from the village of Yauco; 74 came from the city of Ponce; 47 came from Lares; 36 from Adjuntas; 33 from Peñuelas; 23 from Aguadilla; and 12 from Juana Diaz (these are a selective citation of the number of villages and municipalities which were cited in this book).

In 1901, 181 immigrated to Hawaii from Yauco, while 32 emigrated from Adjuntas. The book also identified, by name(s), a total of 13 Puerto Ricans who emigrated in 1903; 10 Puerto Ricans who emigrated in 1910; and 76 Puerto Ricans who immigrated to Hawaii in 1921.

All told, the book identified well over 600 names of the Puerto Ricans that had immigrated to Hawaii from 1901 through 1921.

A sample of some of the names which the Souza's provided in their Chart/Table portion of their book, from among the 1901 emigrants from Puerto Rico to Hawaii, were as follows (their Birthplace is in parenthesis):

Jose Rodriues Acevedo (Birthplace: Lares); Juanita Torres (Adjuntas); Luis Rodrigues Almodovar (aka: Luis Rodrigues Almadova) (Yauco); Margara Andujar Lopes (aka: Margaret Lopes Almadova) (Ponce); Juan Angel (aka: John Angel) (Mayagüez); Juana Feliciano Santiago (Aguas Blanca); Dominga Ramos (Peñuelas); Juan Caraballo (San Juan); Francisco Garcia (Quebradillas); Eudalia Rivera (Guayanilla); Maria Josino (aka: Maria Hosino) (Arecibo or Adjuntas); and Fernando Schmidt and Olga Torres Schmidt (Juana Diaz).

Note: Concencion Lopez [López] (Guayanilla) immigrated to Hawaii in **1900**). [Name in original] this is the verbatim way which the name for Concencion Lopez was spelled in the Souza's book. (see their book: *De Borinquen A Hawaii Nuestra Historia:* From Puerto Rico to Hawaii. 1985: 46).

CHAPTER 7

Horowitz, O'Neill, Antonelli, Power: "That's Funny, these Names don't 'sound' Spanish?"

It is noteworthy that the 1910 Census identified that Puerto Rico had a total of 11,766 immigrants who had earlier immigrated *to* Puerto Rico before 1910 (e.g., from the mid to late 1800s), and they were listed by the census as being "foreign born" (U.S. Bureau of the Census. 1913b: 125), thereby helping to account for a relatively sizable number of Puerto Ricans with non-traditional "Puerto Rican" or Spanish surnames.

Consequently, many of the last names that I have identified in this book are in fact not your typical Spanish or Puerto Rican last names. Clara E. Rodríguez wrote about the following informative and not commonly known fact that:

"As the population grew, it became more and more diverse. Although most of the nineteenth-century [foreign] immigrants probably came from Spain and its possessions, a great many came from other European countries. Common present-day Puerto Rican surnames, for example, Colberg, Wiscovitch, Petrovich, Franqui, Adams and Solivan, reflect that diversity" (Rodríguez, Clara E. c. 1989: 1). (cf.: *13th Census of the U.S. Taken in...1910: Statistics for Porto Rico.* (1913), p. 23).

Dr. Clarence Senior had pointed out earlier what the 1910 federal census showed: that a sizable number of the Puerto Ricans listed in the federal census for California, have these non-traditional sounding/spelling Puerto Rican names. As Dr. Senior wrote:

"In Puerto Rico, as in the United States, it is not at all uncommon to find names which reflect a history of immigration: Antonelli, Brown, Buscaglia, Cox, Descartes, Franklin, Howowitz, Kilgore, LaFitte, Lee, Luchetti, O'Neill, Palmer, Peterson, Power, Stahl, and many others" (Senior 1965: 7).

Specifically, the 1900 Federal Census (*The Twelfth Census of the United States*) in its Table 73, titled "Population of Porto Rico Classified by Sex, Race, and Place of Birth: 1899", provided the following figures for the immigrants who had moved to Puerto Rico during the 19th century: Of the total Puerto Rican population in 1899 of 953,243, of whom a total of 939,376 were born in Porto Rico; 7,690 were born in Spain; 1,693 were born in "Other West Indies"; 1,069 were born in the United States; 2,433 were born in "Other Europe"; 348 were born in "Spanish America"; and 634 were born in "Other countries," (These figures "includes 5 persons of unknown birthplace") (U.S. Bureau of the Census. 1902: 95; U.S. Bureau of the Census. 1904: 95, cf.: Google books for many of these early 20th Century Government issued publications).

Therefore, many of the surnames of the first California Puerto Rican immigrants, as well as for their children, which were identified in the 1910 Federal Census, and also identified in this book, did not have **"Spanish"** surnames (see below for the specific names of these Puerto Rican immigrants).

Finally, the official 1910 U.S. Bureau of the Census definition (or category) for Puerto Ricans born in the United States was as a part of the "native population" of the United States, **7/** and this was indicated as follows:

"The term 'native population' as ordinarily used by the Bureau of the Census comprises all persons born in the United States, including those persons born in Alaska, Hawaii, **Porto Rico**, and other outlying possessions of the United States flag, and persons born at sea under the United States flag, and persons of native parentage born abroad and designated as 'American citizens born abroad'" (U.S. Bureau of the Census. 1910a: 169; See also: U.S. Bureau of the Census. 2010). (emphasis added)

October 2016 - see the following source: "U.S. Bureau of the Census. 1913. *Thirteenth Census of the United States Taken in the Year 1910: Statistics For Porto Rico Containing Statistics of Population...,* "Place of Birth and Year of Immigration" (Table 19, p. 23).

Country of Origin - The country of birth [i.e., those who live in Porto Rico **in 1910**] of the "foreign-born" population is given in Table 20, (p. 23).

For example, a *selective sample* of the foreign-born population who resided in Porto Rico in 1910, according to the 1910 U.S. Federal Census, are as follows:

Spain - 6,630;	Germany - 192;	Russia - 31;	Belgium -12;
France - 681;	Canada - 72;	China - 21;	Ireland - 37;
Italy - 362;	Denmark - 100;	Netherlands (Holland) - 76;	Portugal - 23.
England - 221;	Africa - 65;	Japan - 20;	

Total: "All Foreign Countries" - Foreign-Born Population 1910 [Porto Rico] - 11, 766 (100%).

For historical comparison(s) purposes, the **1930 Federal Census** (for the population in Puerto Rico], listed the population for the "Foreign White Stock by Country of Origin and by Sex, for Puerto Rico, Urban and Rural, 1930, with 1920 Figures for the Foreign-Born White Only" population (page 145) [note: this was the only Table (i.e., Table 12) that was listed in this 1930 Federal Census relating to the number of the "Foreign-Born" population who were residing in Puerto Rico in 1930]. Below is a *selective sample* of the Countries listed in this 1930 Census Table for "Foreign-Born", i.e., the "Total Population" (including from "Spanish-speaking Countries"), in Puerto Rico, for 1930, (see: page 145) (note: for "research purposes", the 1920 figures are similarly listed in this same Table 12) (source: *Fifteenth Census of the United States: 1930 - Outlying Territories and Possessions, Number and Distribution of Inhabitants...,* (1932)):

England – 302;	Irish Free State – 88;	Italy – 796;	Poland – 12;
Czechoslovakia – 28;	Palestine and Syria 468;	Sweden – 41;	Portugal – 22;
Scotland – 52;	Norway – 14;	Denmark – 69;	Austria – 25;
Austria – 25;	Canada (French) – 16;	Spain – 18,596;	Russia – 25;
Northern Ireland - 15;	France - 2,406;	Netherlands – 95;	Other Asia – 46.
Greece – 18;	Canada (Other) – 87;	Germany – 391;	

NOTE: The above referenced "Table 12" did *not* list the similar "Foreign-Born" population figures for the "Non-White" population who were also residing in Puerto Rico in 1930.

CHAPTER 8

The United States Puerto Rican Population Numbers Between 1900 through 1910, and Beyond

According to the publication titled *Abstract of the Twelfth Census of the United States: 1900*, published in 1902, the census listed a total of 680 Puerto Ricans (i.e., only persons *born in* Puerto *Rico*, according to the 1900 U.S. Census definition) that resided within the United States, with the *State of California having had a total of 6 Puerto Ricans* residing there (see and compare, Chapter 8, below). Importantly, the State of New York had a Puerto Rican population, in 1900, of 336. By comparison, the Island of Puerto Rico in 1900 had a population of 953,243, according to the U.S. War Department (U.S. Bureau of the Census. 1902: 54, xii, 7, 54; U.S. War Department, Office Director Census of Porto Rico. 1900: 40; United States Census Office. 1901: 689).

Similarly, according to the publication titled *Thirteenth Census of the United States Taken in the Year 1910: Abstract of the Census*, published in 1913, a total of 1,513 Puerto Ricans resided within the United States in 1910, with the *State of California having had a total of 342 Puerto Ricans*, while the Pacific Division (including California), having a total of 352 Puerto Ricans. Again, for historical comparison, Puerto Rico in 1910 had a population of 1,118,012 (cf.: U.S. Bureau of the Census. 1913a: 185, 24; see also: U.S. Bureau of the Census. 1913b; U.S. Bureau of the Census. 1914: 39; see also: Duany 2004: 1057; Duany 2003: 426; Duany and Pantojas-García 2006: 27; Chenault 1938: 53; Senior 1947: 48; U.S. Bureau of the Census. 1999: 2, "Footnote 2").

Further, for the sake of historical comparison, the 1910 Puerto Rican population for New York City was 554 (or 36.6%), and for New York State it was 641 (42.4%), of the total U.S. Puerto Rican population of 1,513 (U.S. Bureau of the Census. 1913b: 779; U.S. Bureau of the Census. 1913a: 185). Thus, "in 1910, 37% percent of all Puerto Ricans in [the] continental United States were living in New York City" (U.S. Bureau of the Census. 1953: 3D-4). It is noteworthy, that in 1947, Dr. Clarence Senior, then Director of the Social Science Research Center of the University of Puerto Rico, wrote that "children born in the United States [of Puerto Rican parents] were not counted [as being "Porto Rican" in either the 1900, nor in the 1910 Census]" (Senior 1947: 44, 48).

In December 1904, the *Los Angeles Daily Times* [later the *Los Angeles Times*] newspaper published an article about the Puerto Rican immigrant population in San Francisco as being 500 when it indicated that (cf.: *Los Angeles Herald*. December 15, 1904: 3, Bib. #320):

"...in the squalor of Hinckley Alley and the narrow streets of Telegraph Hill [in the city of San Francisco], 500 Porto Ricans are destitute and near starvation. In a short time they will number 5,000 helpless people in a strange land. They have come from the sugar plantations of Hawaii, where, three years ago, 5,000 Porto Ricans were taken under contract to sugar planters" (*Los Angeles Times*, December 15, 1904: 3), [AKA: *Los Angeles Daily Times*].

In April 1905, Physician Herbert Gunn, M.D., gave a speech, which was then published in the *California*

State Journal of Medicine, in which he presented what he knew of the Puerto Rican population in the State of California:

"It is estimated that there are in this state [California] over 1000 Porto Ricans, 600 located in San Francisco and the rest scattered throughout the state. Many are working in the vegetable gardens around San Francisco bay, as in San Leandro, San Lorenzo, Niles, etc. Quite a number have gone to Los Angeles and from there probably out into the surrounding farming country. Nearly every steamer from Honolulu [Hawaii] brings from 15 to 30 Porto Ricans, and, as before stated, there are several thousand there to draw from" (Gunn, M.D., 1905: 212). [Note: Dr. Gunn's medical practice was in the City of San Francisco].

The May 1905 issue of *The San Francisco Call* supported Dr. Gunn's figures when the paper reported on the "Porto Rican Colony" that, "there are in San Francisco to-day 600 native Porto Ricans still waiting" (*San Francisco Call*. May 28, 1905: 1).

Further, just a scant seven months after the devastating April 18, 1906 San Francisco Earthquake and Fire, on November 17, 1906, Dr. Gunn, of the Hospital Department in San Francisco, was cited as providing a "communication" to *The San Francisco Chronicle*. This newspaper article indicated that: "about 500 Porto Ricans are living in the city, 200 of whom are at Lobos square...." (*San Francisco Chronicle*. November 17, 1906: 7).

Where Did All These California Puerto Ricans Come From?:

The obvious answer to the above question---Puerto Rico---is NOT the correct answer. Instead, apparently the California Puerto Rican population from 1900 to at least 1908, came directly from Hawaii, when they decided to migrate from Hawaii to the "Coast", mostly to California. For example, the publication entitled *"First Report of the Board of Immigration to the Governor of the Territory of Hawaii... For the Period Beginning April 29, 1905, and Ending January 31, 1907"*, in their Table called "Arrivals and Departures of Immigrants at Honolulu", listed Porto Ricans for both the 1905 and 1906 calendar years, but left "blank" their actual numbers, unlike the numbers it provided for the other cited "Nationality" [Nationalities], namely, the Japanese, Koreans, Chinese, and Portuguese (Board of Immigration. 1907: 34).

However, the Board of Immigration in their *Second Report*, issued in 1909, reported that in 1907, a total of 490 men, 305 women, and 532 children, or a total of 1,327 Puerto Ricans "departed" from Honolulu, to the [West] "Coast", presumably, mostly to California. Similarly, in 1908, a total of 214 men, 132 women, and 204 children, or a total of 550 Puerto Ricans "departed" from Honolulu, to the [West] "Coast", again, presumably, mostly to California (Board of Immigration. 1909: 18).

This data alone leads this author to suspect that the 1910 U.S. Federal Census, which listed the 1910 California Puerto Rican population as being at 342, possibly may have substantially undercounted the Puerto Rican populations, both in California, and the San Francisco Bay area. This continual historical undercounting by government officials, and/or by the Federal Census, of the U.S. Puerto Rican population apparently continues till this day!

Similarly, the *Report of the Governor of Hawaii to the Secretary of the Interior. 1925,* listed the number of Porto Ricans that had "departed" from Hawaii to the "Coast", for the year ending June 30, 1925, as being: 81 men, 48 women, and 79 children, or a total of 208 Puerto Ricans (Secretary of the Interior. 1925: 41).

Further, in 1947, Professor Clarence Senior, wrote that the City of San Francisco, CA, in 1910, was second behind New York City in Puerto Rican population.

"[It] had the second largest concentration of Puerto Ricans on the continent… The 1910, '20 and '40 figures were 213, 474, and 603 respectively. No other city comes close to having the same number. Oakland's 194 in 1940 should be added to the metropolitan city's total since it is virtually the same area" (Senior 1947: 44). [**Note:** Oakland, CA is located in Alameda County]

Dr. Senior went on to point out that: "the Puerto Rican-born population of New York City was 554 in 1910 and 7,364 in 1920… [and that] the 1930 data were not published" (Senior 1947: 44). He published his findings in 1947 while he was at the Social Science Research Center, University of Puerto Rico.

However, Lawrence R. Chenault, Professor of Economics at the University of Puerto Rico, presented the Puerto Rican population figures compiled by the Federal Census for the years of 1920, 1930, and 1935. In the "Tables" of his book can be found the following Puerto Rican population figures, (i.e., persons born in Puerto Rico and living in the Continental United States): 1920 - 11,811; 1930 - 52,774; and 1935 - 58,200. Professor Chenault also indicated that in 1920 **California** had 935 Puerto Ricans and in 1930 had 1,795 (Chenault 1938: 53, n. 5, p. 58).

October 2016 - In contrast to the above cited Porto Rican population figures, the figures below shows the Porto Rican population figures for selective U.S. States, according to the: U.S. Bureau of the Census. 1913. *Thirteenth Census of the United States Taken in the Year 1910: Statistics For Porto Rico.* (1913), (page 23, Table 19), namely, as follows:

The "State of Birth" section of the 1910 U.S. Federal Census shows the following "Native Population: 1910" Porto Rican population figures broken down by ones "Place of Birth", and where the Porto Rican population figures were distributed within the U.S., namely in:

Total Native (Population of Porto Rico) in 1910 was - 1,106,248;

PORTO RICO (their "Place of Birth") - 1,103,746;

United States, Exclusive of Outlying Territory - 2,303;

New York - 552;

Pennsylvania - 207;

Massachusetts - 175;

Ohio - 120;

Louisiana - 107;

Other States - 1,142;

Hawaii - 17;

Philippine Islands - 19;

American Citizens Born Abroad - 157; and

Born at Sea - 4.

For a contemporaneous write-up of the 1910 U.S. Federal Census figures for the U.S. Population, by individual States, and also of the then Territories of the U.S., including for California, Hawaii and for Porto Rico, see:

The Chicago Sunday Times, (December 11, 1910, page 4), "Census Totals Are Made Public. Bureau's Announcement Gives 102,000,000 Residents of All U.S. Possessions. 91,972,266 on Continent: Stars and Stripes Float Over One-Sixteenth of World's Inhabitants".

For example, a selective 1910 population Census figures shows as follows:

Hawaii Population -	191,909;
Porto Rico *Population* -	1,118,012;
California Population-	2,377,549;
Military and Naval pop. -	55,608;
Alaska population -	64,356;
New York population -	9,113,614.

"The total population of the world is estimated at 1,637,168,247, so that the American nation has within its boundaries at home and abroad more than one-sixteenth of the total."

For historical comparisons, the following 1910 Census figures shows how the U.S. total population compares with the other "Great Nations" respective populations, in 1910, which are as follows:

China -	407,253,030;
The British Empire -	392,846,835;
Russia -	146,796,600;
United States -	162,000,000;
France and colonies -	92,531,323;
German Empire -	72,851,000;
Japan, including Corea -	59,636,131
(*spelling of Corea in original*)	

CHAPTER 9

**The First Puerto Ricans that Decided to Stay in
California and in the San Francisco Bay Area in Particular**

*Who Were these Puerto Rican Immigrants who
arrived in California on December 14, 1900?*

In what appears to be a representative example, Jose Morales, a youth of 18 years, was interviewed by the *San Francisco Chronicle* and seems to have summarized the feeling of these first Puerto Ricans that opted to remain in San Francisco, CA on Dec. 14, 1900, since he was the "principal spokesman" for this group. (cf.: Exhibits 12-14):

"When asked why they had left the main party he said: 'A man came to us and told us that they were going to be taken to Honolulu and sold as slaves... He said that there were neither Americans nor Spanish on the islands at Honolulu ...and would get only get 25 cents a day and would have to live on that. He said the islands were full of fever and that the work was very hard. He said that California was a fine place for us to live and told us that the people of San Francisco would take care of us and we could get plenty of work and make $2 or $3 a day... He said that when we got on the ship [for their voyage from San Francisco to Hawaii] where we could not get away we would be treated like slaves and would get very little to eat...' " (*San Francisco Chronicle.* December 15, 1900: 14).

According to the Governor of Puerto Rico, Charles H. Allen, prior to December 1900, "...emigration [had] been almost unknown [from Puerto Rico]" (Allen. 1901: 74). However, as a group, and statistically speaking, the first Puerto Ricans that had emigrated *en masse* **from** Puerto Rico and who arrived in San Francisco in December 1900, and thereafter, were most likely agricultural workers, as well as also being "contract workers" (U.S. Department of Labor. 1901: 410).

These Puerto Rican immigrants, even before their arrival to California, were being reported as being **"contract laborers"** by some newspapers. Thus, *The Pacific Commercial Advertiser* (Honolulu, Hawaii Territory), (December 10, 1900, p. 1), reported:

"Under direction from Washington the Porto Rican immigrants who arrived here [i.e., to New Orleans] on the Arradia (*sic*) [Arcadia] under contract to work on sugar plantations in Hawaii, were allowed to land and today took a special train for **San Francisco**.... The authorities took the position that Porto Ricans are people of the United States, and therefore not subject to the restrictions placed on foreign immigrants by the immigration law, which shuts out all **contract labor**. It was admitted the Porto Ricans came to this country [the U.S.] under **contract**, and the only issue was as to their rights as American citizens." (emphasis added)

Statistically speaking, these immigrants to California were very likely poor agricultural laborers from the Island. For example, at least as early as 1902, the Military Governor of Puerto Rico described, in his *Annual Report*, the population in the Island as follows: "...the population of Porto Rico [in 1899] was about 950,000 ...of this number, perhaps 750,000 [or 78.9%] belonged to the peon or poor laboring class." (U.S. War Department. 1902: 210). Governor Allen summarized this immigrant population when he wrote: "most of the emigrants are of the very poorest class of laborers" and the reason(s) for their departure was "with the hope of bettering his financial condition...." (Allen, Charles H. 1901: 75).

Citing *1899 Porto Rican Census* data, the U.S. Department of Commerce reported that the "Porto Rican population is [was] preponderatingly *[sic]* agricultural [with 62.8%]...breadwinners...engaged in agriculture...while in the United States only 38 per cent of the entire number of breadwinners are [were] engaged in agriculture..." (U.S. Dept. of Commerce and Labor. 1907: 11). Similarly, the 1899 Porto Rico Census data in the *Abstract of the Twelfth Census of the United States 1900* showed that 67.9% of those that were actually *born* in Porto Rico (as opposed to "those born elsewhere") were engaged in agriculture, with fishing and mining being a real small portion of this latter figure, regarding the "population [that were] at least 10 years of age" (U.S. Bureau of the Census. 1902: 99).

Similarly, the Puerto Rican population, according to the 1899 Puerto Rican Census, was 85.4% rural, while 14.8% was urban. (U.S. Bureau of the Census. 1913a: 570).

It is noteworthy that Puerto Rico from 1899 to 1900 had a very high rate of unemployment among the working class population. Thus, the Secretary of Puerto Rico in December 1905 (while citing 1899 Puerto Rico Census data) reported that the population in 1899 was at 953,243, and "of the **entire** population, 636,878 were without gainful occupation [or 66.8%; presumably a substantial number were non-employable children]. There were 146,000 who could neither read nor write..." (Porto Rico, Executive Secretary. 1905: 8). Thus, the first Puerto Rican immigrants, **en masse**, to Hawaii, beginning in December 1900, and thereafter to California, particularly from December 1900 to October 1901, were statistically more likely to have had an agricultural and a rural background, and be unemployed at the time of their respective emigration from Puerto Rico to California and/or to Hawaii.

Finally, as late as May 1901, Governor Charles H. Allen, in his *First Annual Report* of *Porto Rico* pointed out the high rate of unemployment in Puerto Rico at this time when he wrote: "the great army of the unemployed has a corps amounting to 183,635... Of these about one-third are men and two-thirds women. These facts, of course, complicate the labor problem already sufficiently difficult" (Allen. 1901: 35).

In August 1901,The *New York Times,* reporting on the continuing Puerto Rican exodus from Puerto Rico to Hawaii, identified an ever growing problem for the Island of Puerto Rico when it stated that: "The only reasonable objection advanced so far to this emigration from Porto Rico is that the **island's best laborers are leaving**.... In all events, it is not likely that they will ever return. It is considered that Porto Rico is over-populated, and the sooner this population is thinned out, the better off Porto Rico will be" (*New York Times.* April 4, 1901: 5). (emphasis added)

The 1900 – 1910 Time Period in California:

During the very first decade of the 20th century, or from December 1900 through December 1910, the State of California had the second highest number of Puerto Ricans of any *State* (342), with the exception of New York (which had 641), residing in the United States in 1910. In 1910, the entire United States had a total Puerto Rican population of 1,513 (Teresa Whalen 2005: 11).

Carmen Teresa Whalen summarized the 1910 population figures, as follows:

"By 1910, the largest concentration of Puerto Ricans---3,510---lived in Hawaii....with 213 Puerto Ricans living in San Francisco.... Although the then United States 'Territory' of Hawaii had a 1910 Puerto Rican population of 3,510, it was not a State of the United States at that time; it became a state in 1959" (Teresa Whalen 2005:11). [**Note:** see, however, the *Fourth Report of the Commissioner on Labor On Hawaii: 1910.* (1911: 12), which listed a total of **4,890 Puerto Ricans living in Hawaii** in 1910); (see also: U.S. Bureau of the Census. *Thirteenth Census of the United States Taken in the Year 1910: Statistics For Hawaii.* 1913d: 9, 10, 18)]. Thus, the census data for Hawaii shows the distribution of the "native population according to state of birth" in 1910... [that] 3,510... were born in Porto Rico" (see: Table 16), but that the **total Puerto Rican** population in Hawaii was **4,890** (and not 3,510) in 1910, which was *larger* than either the Korean, Filipino, and "Negro" populations in Hawaii as of 1910, (Table 4,page 9; see also: Schmitt. 1977: 25, 26)].

Several contemporaneous California newspapers covering the California "Puerto Rican immigration issue," reported that the first Puerto Ricans that migrated to the state as a group, arrived by railroad via the Southern Pacific Railway, first to Los Angeles, then on to San Francisco, CA, and for almost half of them, a continuation to their final destination, Hawaii, as "contract laborers." This relatively unknown event, although a historically significant journey, took place during December 1900.

The contemporaneous newspapers (***incorrectly***) reported that among the original group of 114 (it was really *at least* 120) immigrants that departed from Puerto Rico on November 22, 1900, an initial group of 56 Puerto Ricans decided to stay in California, and not to continue on to Hawaii, (*New York Times*, December 7, 1900: 1; *San Francisco Call*, December 14, 1900: 1; *San Francisco Chronicle*, December 7, 1900: 1; *San Francisco Chronicle*, December 15, 1900: 14; *Los Angeles Times*, December 15, 1900: 3; *Los Angeles Times*, December 14, 1900: 3 (Bib. #106)). (**Note:** my research identified *at least* 64 immigrants, **not** 56, that stayed in California on Dec. 14, 1900).

A plausible explanation for the newspapers' incorrectly counting the number of Puerto Ricans as being 56, and not the correct figure of *at least* 64, is because the newspapers most likely **did not** include in their figures the three newborns, and the several infants who were with their respective parents.

Dr. Norma Carr labeled this "first Group" of Puerto Ricans "Group 1", i.e., those [about] 114 or so immigrants that initially arrived in San Francisco on Dec. 14, 1900 (Carr 1989: 92ff.). Thereafter, 10 additional Puerto Rican immigrant Groups proceeded to their scheduled final destination to the sugar cane fields of Hawaii up until October 1901. Note that although different figures were cited in the newspapers at the time, between 50 to 66 immigrants stayed in California (cf.: Medina 2001: 88; see also: Below). My book posits that a total of *at least* 64 immigrants stayed in California after December 14, 1900 from Dr. Carr's "Group 1." However, from these 10 subsequent additional "Groups", it is not known how many of these Puerto Rican immigrants may have stayed in California, and not continue on to Hawaii---so further research is needed to address this.

Importantly, Sánchez Korrol specifically identified Dr. Norma Carr's 1989 dissertation as representative of a "new historiography" [relative to Puerto Rican immigration to Hawaii and the United States] (Sánchez Korrol 1994b: xxii, xxvi, "Footnote 12").

CHAPTER 10

Scope of my Sources and a Major Limitation: No Contemporaneous Letters or Diaries found from the California Puerto Rican Immigrants

It is unfortunate to note that my research was not able to locate contemporaneous letters, diaries, and/or journals by the first Puerto Rican immigrants that stayed in California beginning from December 14, 1900 through December 1925. However, Rosario-Rivera located letters in the *Archivo General de Puerto Rico*, San Juan, P.R., which were written by Puerto Rican immigrants whom had arrived **in Hawaii** after April 23, 1900. A few of these letters were cited by Rosario-Rivera in her seminal research in this area, which she referenced in her article entitled: "*Pasaporte A La Angustia. Sufrimientos de los emigrados y familiares con destino a Hawaii (Incluye registro de emigrados hasta ahora localizados)*" (Rosario-Rivera. 2000: 1-26).

The on-line digitized census on *AncestryInstitution.com* allowed me to access the 1910 U.S. Federal Census for both the State of California (in general), and for all of California's 58 separate Counties, including the City of San Francisco in particular, to locate specific individuals (See: *AncestryInstitution.com*. 1910).

The City of San Francisco is most relevant to my research because: (a) The very first group of these California Puerto Rican immigrants arrived in the City of San Francisco on December 14, 1900; and, (b) The City of San Francisco maintained the largest concentration by far, of the first Group of "Puerto Rican immigrants" that arrived in California *en masse*, from December 1900 to April 1910.

Thus far, only a small number of research studies and articles (but not any books), have only briefly addressed the early Puerto Rican **immigration history** to California covering the first decade of the 20th century, although Medina's article did deal with what she called the first 56 California Puerto Rican Immigrants of December 14, 1900, as did Dr. Carr's dissertation (cf.: Medina 2001: 85-95; Carr 1989: 103-105, 452-453; Leyland 1980: 3-4, 15-19, 63-64, 69-70, 72-75, 81, 92; Feldman 1978: 3-4; U.S. Civil Rights Commission 1980). However, most of these aforementioned authors had not identified, at least to any significant degree, the names of the immigrants themselves, aside from the initial listing of 44 of the original "56 escapees" (i.e., the *at least* 64 immigrants that decided to stay in California on December 14, 1900, according to this author). The notable exception is that Norma Carr identified 44 (at least according to my count), and Medina 20 names of those Puerto Ricans which stayed in California, and whom did **not** continue on to Hawaii---Medina cited 20 of the names which Carr had earlier cited in her 1989 dissertation.

While Carr and Medina both posited that 56 stayed in California, in contrast, my research and evidence posits that a total of at least 64 immigrants stayed in California on December 15, 1900 (when you **add** the children, infants and the newborns that were with their immigrant parents).

Thus, I have addressed this formerly overlooked area, by extracting the names, ages, addresses, "Year of Immigration", Spouses Names and Place of Birth, Occupation, etc., from the 1910 U.S. Federal Census for well over 100 of these pioneer Puerto Rican immigrants to the San Francisco, California area, focusing on the time period from 1900 to 1910, and based on data from the 1910 Federal California Census.

As a result, this book is now a part of a broader U.S. Ethnic History research, and the more specific subject area of U.S. Latino Immigration History.

One major limitation of this book thus far (although creating an area for future research) is the need to obtain primary sources of the **California, as well as the Hawaiian, immigrant experience** through copies of whatever letters and/or diaries may have been written by the immigrants themselves, and/or by someone writing on the immigrants' behalf. However, one important potential hurdle to overcome is the fact that, according to the 1900 U.S. Federal Census for Puerto Rico, out of a total Puerto Rican population of 659,294 persons that were "at least 10 years of age" in Puerto Rico in 1900, the 1900 Census identified 524,877 (79.6%) who were "illiterate," while for the (so-called) "colored population" the figure was 217,818 persons (87.7%) (see: U.S. Bureau of the Census. 1904: 97; U.S. War Department, Office Director Census of Porto Rico, 1900. *Report on the Census of Porto Rico, 1899*: 72-75; War Department, U.S.A. 1900: 5; see also: Vázquez Calzada. 1990: 1-9).

The 1900 U.S. Census Bureau's official definition of illiterate was: "Persons at least 10 years of age unable to write any language" (U.S. Bureau of the Census. 1904: 446).

Therefore, since nearly 80% of the population in Puerto Rico was illiterate, one can reasonably expect that most, if not practically all, of the December 1900 California Puerto Rican working class immigrants were also illiterate. Thus, the opportunity to obtain any copy, or copies, of any such letters and/or diaries is somewhat limited. Unfortunately, attempts to locate them have been unsuccessful thus far (cf.: the encyclopedic, *American Diaries: An Annotated Bibliography of Published American Diaries and Journals*, First Edition, Vol. 2 – *Diaries Written from 1845 to 1980*, (1987), by Laura Arksey, Nancy Pries, and Marcia Reef, Gale Research Group, Detroit, MI). Although this book listed 3,263 Diaries and Journals as sources, and covered topics dealing with Emigrants and Emigrant Journeys to different States, including California, and Hawaii, **not one** of these sources related to a Puerto Rican immigrant's Diary or Journal! (cf.: Bib. #181, #417, #418, #421)

However, it is important to note that based upon newspaper reporting accounts of the *San Francisco Examiner,* it **DID identify three** Puerto Rican immigrants of the at least 64 who were able to write in Spanish (see latter on in this book for their names). Future research can possibly locate whatever letters, diaries, and journals, they may have written.

Interestingly, Dr. Norma Carr provided a footnote for Chapter IV of her 1989 Dissertation which pointed out that the Puerto Ricans within the first year of their *arrival to Hawaii*, DID have access to someone who was hired to write letters on their behalf. She wrote:

"José Ramón Vandrel, hired in March 1901 for a period of three months **to write letters** for the Puerto Ricans and articles for publication in newspapers back on the island…apparently stayed much longer. Instead of writing letters praising the plantation system, he helped the laborers write complaints to officials" (Carr 1989: 215, 134). (emphasis added)

At least as early as April 1901, the Puerto Rican newspaper, *La Correspondencia*, had an article entitled, "Cartas del Hawaii" [Letters from Hawaii], when it [apparently] reproduced a copy of a letter attributed to a Hawaiian Puerto Rican immigrant, Julio Montes, who wrote, in relevant part:

"Dear friend… I am far away from my country…I was in a sad situation, so, I said, let me emigrate and see if I can better my situation, and that's just what I did. We arrived in Honolulu on March 25th [1901] and because of the recommendation that I brought with me I landed a job in a store that sells food and merchandise and I am not treated badly…. I tell you that here a clerk or a peon can work in a store; we are all equal…. I will write every month and I hope that you answer my letters since my only wish is to receive correspondence" (Cited in: Centro de Estudios Puertorriqueños. 1977: 34).

It is noteworthy, however, that my research was able to locate a letter that was written by the Puerto Rican immigrants who were working on the Hawaiian Sugar Plantations during July 1902. This letter was translated by the Centro de Estudios Puertorriqueños, and it was apparently obtained from the *Fondo Fortaleza, Archivo General de Puerto*. These Puerto Rican immigrant workers were complaining about their working conditions while having been employed in the plantations in Hawaii in 1902; the letter was signed by a total of **58** Puerto Ricans. For example, this letter reads, in relevant part (cited in: Centro de Estudios Puertorriqueños. 1982: 52-53, 51-52; typed verbatim):

"Manifestation made by the Puerto Ricans at present at the Plantation Paauilo to the Hon. Civil Governor of the Island of Puerto Rico…. With the greatest respect we address you begging for protection, we, the Puerto Ricans at the Plantation of Paauilo, to bring to your knowledge what is happening to us in the said plantation. We, Puerto Ricans, that happen to be here, find ourselves more than trampled on even to the point of wishing ourselves dead (?), we are like slaves, and we beg you to see if we can obtain from your goodness that you should take measures so that we can return to our country so as not to be maltreated because we do not deserve it; they treat us like one who is in prison to the extent that it is good policy (?) to take us away from those that we meet in the said plantation, so it is that being terrified we send supplication to our Hon. Sir that he may illumine the way we favor to see if we cannot return to our beloved Borinquen which for the first time we have left to seek our prosperity and have met our perdition to the territories of Oceania, which although under the dominion of the stars and stripes, we do not consider as under your orders."

This July 1902 "complaint" letter went on to point out, that:

"And for those reasons we turn to you in order not to see ourselves obliged to cause that the associates of the sugar companies be compelled to put us into our dear country and that later on no trouble should arise between the Puerto Ricans and the associates of the companies, because the said gentlemen wish that we should work like animals and whether right or wrong, sick or well they wish that no one shall stay in the house. We are more than slaves here and we cannot longer resist the savagery that is coming to every one of us Puerto Ricans; they are every day inflicting more barbarities on us. The first thing is that the pay is small; it is not according to what was offered us before we left Puerto Rico; the second is that the store book stands us for half of our day's wage, and the result for us is not what it should be. For these reasons, we, the undersigned, have recourse to your Honor and place ourselves at your orders."

Therefore, the above cited July 1902 letter signed by the 58 disgruntled Puerto Ricans begins to explain why Puerto Rican immigrants began to migrate from Hawaii to California soon after their initial respective arrival(s) to Hawaii on December 23, 1900.

As a result, the 1903 weekly publication entitled *The Louisiana Planter*, which was "devoted to the

Sugar, Rice and Other Agricultural Industries of Louisiana", wrote the following about the Puerto Ricans in Hawaii:

"The Porto Ricans *in Hawaii* **frequently write to Porto Rico** a tale of woe but this comes closer [to] home and will doubtless have immediate attention" (*The Louisiana Planter and Sugar Manufacturer, A Weekly Newspaper.* June 6, 1903: 366, Vol. XXX, No. 23). (emphasis added)

Dr. Raquel Rosario-Rivera's Archival Research in Puerto Rico and
the Identification of over 285 Hawaiian Puerto Rican Immigrant Names:

Whereas my research was unsuccessful in locating any letters that were either written by, or on behalf of, the Puerto Rican immigrants that were residing in **California**, however, Dr. Raquel Rosario-Rivera published an article in the *Revista de la Pontificia Universidad Cathólica de Puerto Rico (Ponce, Puerto Rico)* wherein she described having gone through many boxes in the archives in Puerto Rico which contained a number, if not many, letters that were written by the relatives and family members of those Puerto Ricans that had departed for Hawaii (**Note:** This article is in Spanish and was translated for me by Rosario Camacho). I believe that Dr. Rosario-Rivera's [not related to Rosario Camacho] research used the archives of the "A.G.P.R.", i.e., the Archivo General de los Puertorriqueño, San Juan, Puerto Rico, in the Puerta de Tierra Jail (in Old San Juan) (cf.: Rosario-Rivera. 2000; Platt. 1998: 11, 189; cf.: *La Real Cedula de Gracias de 1815 y sus primeros efectos en Puerto Rico: Incluye Registro de Emigrados*, by Raquel Rosario Rivera, 1995).

The title of this article, translated into English, read: "Passport to Anguish...." ["Passaporte A La Angustia"] The article did reference at least one letter that was written by one of the Hawaiian Puerto Rican immigrants who complained, quit strongly, of the abhorrent way in which the Puerto Ricans were being treated on the Hawaiian plantations. Her article cited that there were over 300 boxes that have not been cataloged or archived (at least as of 2000). Thus, in 2000 Rosario-Rivera wrote that, "There are about 300 boxes of the Fund in the General Correspondence AGPR which have not been yet, cataloged" (see: Rosario-Rivera. 2000: 11, "Footnote 25"; see also: Carr. 1989: 156).

Importantly, Dr. Rosario-Rivera listed the names of over 285 Puerto Rican immigrants, presumably extracted from these letters, and/or [unnamed] lists which she refers to, which had emigrated from Puerto Rico to Hawaii. She indicated that these (many) letters were written by immigrants' family members who wanted to know, among other things, the whereabouts of their loved ones. The article indicated that the Governor of Puerto Rico had his secretary respond to only **one** of these family member's anguishingly written letters. Importantly, this article also listed the ages and towns where these Puerto Rican immigrants came from, as well as the plantation(s) that they were sent to work. Finally, she listed the source (i.e., the Box 17; "Caja 17") for each of the 287 names which I counted.

Rosario-Rivera also provided a brief portion of Governor Allen's response letter (English in original) wherein she indicated that this letter read as follows:

"He sympathizes with your misfortune, but no appropriation is available with which to pay the passage of your daughter from Hawaii to Porto Rico. The emigration was, as in all other cases, voluntary, and as the Government has nothing to do with sending people away from the island, it cannot undertake to return them" (Rosario-Rivera. 2000: 9).

Note: Apparently, the boxes of these letters are/were located at the following [archival] site: "A.G.P.R. Fondo Oficina del Gobernador.Serie: Correspondencia General, Caja 17. Carta de Victoriana Sanchez al Gobernador Allen con fecha 1 de Octubre de 1901. [This was one example]. (Rosario-Rivera.

2000: 1, Footnote 1).

Similarly, Norma Carr identified in her dissertation her archival primary sources as being from the following site (Carr. 1989: 156):

"General Archives of Puerto Rico. Letter. Allen, Charles H., Governor of Porto Rico. The Great Round World. 21 January 1901. Documents of the Executive Mansion Box 70. File 1309. Documents of the Executive Mansion Box 70, File 1421: Items 1, 3, 4, 14, 15, 20, 26, 28, 31, 33, 36, 40, 41, 43, 44, 45, 47, 48, 52, 53, 54, 58, 71. Hawaiian Sugar Planters Association.... Minutes of Meetings of the Trustees from May 11, 1900 to Oct. 14, 1901."

The 1920 Census provides future researchers with more promising information since the percentage of the Puerto Rican population that was defined by the U.S. Census Bureau as being illiterate, had dropped down from 80% in 1910 to 55.0% in 1920 (for persons 10 years of age and over) (U.S. Bureau of the Census. 1922: 1205).

Hopefully, future research may uncover California's equivalent to the New York City Puerto Rican immigrants' "chronicler of events", that began in 1916, epitomized by the Puerto Rican pioneer and cigar worker (*Tabaquero*), Bernardo Vega's *Memoirs of Bernardo Vega: A contribution to the history of the Puerto Rican community in New York*. In short, "Bernardo Vega's text contains the most detailed and politically coherent account of Puerto Rican life in New York for the three formative decades, from 1916 to the aftermath of World War II" (Flores 1984: ix, "Translator's Preface").

CHAPTER 11

PART II: The 1910 U.S. Federal Census (for California) and the "Extraction" of the Puerto Rican Population Data

California's Puerto Rican Enclaves and Communities:
U.S. Federal Census Population Figures for 1900 and 1910

Background and Historical Context:

In contrast to the California Puerto Rican population (see: below), Puerto Rico's population in 1900, according to the U.S. War Department, shows that, Puerto Rico had a population of 953,243, and in 1910, the population figure was at 1,118,012 (U.S. Bureau of the Census. 1902: 7; U.S. Bureau of the Census. 1913b: 22). For historical comparison, the Puerto Rican population for the "continental" United States in 1900 consisted of 678, and in 1910, 1,513 Puerto Ricans (U.S. Bureau of the Census. 1902: 54; U.S. Bureau of the Census. 1913a: 185; Duany 2004: 1057).

The California Puerto Rican Population:

Utilizing the *Ancestry.com's* 1900 California State census, I identified **7** persons that the 1900 U.S. Federal Census list as Puerto Rican. However, the publication *Abstract of the Twelfth Census of the United States 1900* listed **6** Puerto Ricans in California in 1900 (U.S. Bureau of the Census. 1902: 54).

The 1910 California Puerto Rican population figures were as follows: California had 342 (U.S. Bureau of the Census. 1913a: 185) and San Francisco had 213, while both Oakland and Los Angeles had 10 persons who were "born in Porto Rico" (U.S. Bureau of the Census. 1913b: 778). (See also: "Exhibit 4", which was compiled by this author, entitled, "The Puerto Rican Population of the United States, the State of California, and San Francisco: 1900, 1910, and 2000 Census Figures").

The New York Puerto Rican Population:

In contrast to California's Puerto Rican population, the New York State Puerto Rican population in 1900 was at 336, while in 1910 it was 641, with 554 living in New York City, whereas the State of California had a Puerto Rican population of 342 as of 1910 (U.S. Bureau of the Census. 1902: 54; U.S. Bureau of the Census. 1913a: 779; U.S. Bureau of the Census. 1913b: 779; Teresa Whalen 2005: 11, 3).

October 2016   *Hawaiian Puerto Rican Population:*

See: Page 214 in this book which provides the Hawaiian Porto Rican population figures from December 23, 1900 to 1930 (fom the 1930 U.S. Federal Census).

CHAPTER 12

California's "Original Puerto Ricans": "Pre-1900s Puerto Rican Immigrants" – *The 1852 State of California Census*

An individualized visual review and confirmation of the digitized Census Forms for each identified "Puerto Rican", covered the Census years for 1860,1870, 1880, and 1900 (*note*: "Over 99 percent of the 1890 population schedules were destroyed in a fire... in January 1921" (Dollarhide 1999: 58)), was reviewed by me. During the time period from the 1850 Census through the 1900 Census, there were 13 Puerto Ricans identified as residing in California from 1850 through the 1900 Federal Census (cf.: Exhibits 1, 2, 3, 5, and 6); I did not identify any Puerto Ricans in California in the 1850 census.

Upon reviewing the California portion of the U.S. Federal Census, specifically, for the years of 1860, 1870, 1880, and 1900 I was able to identify, by name, the following "**pre**-December 1900" Puerto Ricans that had earlier immigrated to the United States, and were in fact living within the State of California during these cited decades. Upon typing the two separate keywords, i.e., "Porto Rico", and "Puerto Rico," a list of "Porto Ricans," and a separate list of names for "Puerto Ricans," for the State of California was generated; no two names on either of these two separate lists were the same.

A review of the digitized U.S. Federal Census revealed that there were a handful of Puerto Ricans that had immigrated to the State of California "**pre**-1910 Census", since it may never be known as to how many may have actually emigrated to California at some point in their lives, and may not have appeared in any Federal Census either due to death, or to migration to another state, or were ever identified in any California City Directory, nor in any California State Census. Nevertheless, the following California residents, along with their names, and their Country of Birth, are identified as "original California Puerto Ricans", i.e., only those individuals identified as having been born in Puerto Rico/Porto Rico in the Federal Census (See: below)).

For example, the review of the Censuses showed that there were four immigrants born in Puerto Rico who had presumably migrated to the continental United States during the 1850s (see: below). California was admitted to the Union (the "Date of Act of organization or admission") on Sept. 9, 1850 (U.S. Department of Commerce and Labor 1911: 21); (cf.: *Ancestry.com 1850 United States Federal Census*).

The 1852 State of California Census:

Mr. Simon Mezes' name appeared in the ***1852 State of California Census***, although it was cited as being: S M Mazie, but his "Place of Birth" was still cited as being **Porto Rico**. Most importantly, at least for the purposes of this book, is that this same *1852 State of California Census* also had a column wherein it recorded/listed the person's "Last Residence." Mr. Mazie's "last residence" was listed as being, **"Porto Rico."** It also listed Mr. S M Mazie as residing in the county of San Francisco in 1852. The 1852 California Census lists him as being 24 years of age, making his estimated year of

Birth "abt 1828", and his residence "San Francisco" (see: Exhibit 6, Exhibit 5).

Importantly, Mr. S.M. Mezes appears in the **1852 *San Francisco City Directory*** as*:* Mezes, S.M. (Hinrichsen, Beincke & Co.) 1221 California [which was the address of this company] [Page 153] [P. 43]. (San Francisco City Directory, Sept. 1852: 153). (emphasis added) (see: Exhibits 3, 5, 6, 7, and 18, after Chapter 27 of this book, all relating to Mr. Mezes).

The **1852** State of California Census also lists a Ms. R V Spence as born in "Porto Rico", and she also resided in San Francisco County. Ms. Spence was born "abt 1847." She was 5 years old in 1852, and her "Race" was cited as being "White" (*Ancestry.com.* California State Census 1852); cf.: Lainhart. 1992: 22-3, "State Census Records).

Ann S. Lainhart pointed out that:

"The 1852 Special Census is similar in format to the 1850 federal census with one major and important difference: instead of an estimate of the property value, *the previous **residence** of each individual* is recorded. This allows a researcher to follow [people's] migrations..." (Lainhart. 1992: 22, 23). (emphasis added)

Additionally, the **1900 Census** shows that Clara Blair was born in "Porte Rico" [*sic*] [Porto Rico] and immigrated to the United States in 1850, at age five; she lived in Sacramento, CA, and was listed as a "wife". Mr. Edward Dufish (Black) was born in Puerto Rico, and immigrated to the United States in 1852; his name appeared in the 1910 California Census (although not in the 1900 CA Census). His occupation was a Barber and he lived in Los Angeles in 1910. Importantly, Edward Dufish's name appears in the *Los Angeles City Directory (1892)* which cited his residence as being: "barber shop, 427 5th, r same" (this residence address is cited verbatim) (*Los Angeles City Directory 1892*: 856). Mr. Dufish's name appeared in the *1894 Los Angeles City Directory*, with the same address and occupation (see*: Los Angeles City Directory. 1894*: 1347).

However, it is not known which State Mrs. Blair and Mr. Dufish had initially immigrated to (cf.: Ancestry. com. 1860. United States Federal Census). Mr. Simon N. Mezes [A.K.A: Simon M. Mezes] immigrated to California on February 22, 1850, after moving to the U.S. from Puerto Rico; his name and census information appeared in the 1860, 1870, and in the 1880 Federal Census (for California), (see: Millard. 1924a).

Interestingly, both Mr. Mezes or Mr. Dufish were likely prominent, and economically very successful. For example, Mr. Mezes was a Banker in Puerto Rico, possibly the bank's President, before he [apparently] immigrated in February 1850 to the San Francisco Bay area (Millard. 1924a, 1924b). Also, the 1860 Federal Census, in a book published in 1864, listed a total of only 124 persons with the occupation of Banker throughout the entire State of California, (Washington, Government Printing Office. 1864: 34). The 1860 Federal Census also listed the "Value of Real Estate" owned by Mr. Mezes as being worth $50,000.00 and the Value of his Personal Estate" as being worth $20,000.00 (in 1860s dollars!).

Also, the publication entitled San Francisco Municipal *Reports* (1873) listed the following:

"The names of persons, firms, and corporations assessed for sums over $20,000, on the Assessment Roll of the City and County of San Francisco for the fiscal year 1873-74, as returned by the Assessor to the State Board of Equalization" (Board of Supervisors. 1873: 461).

Further, this publication listed Mr. S.M. Mezes as having $42,850.00 on their "Assessment Roll." (*Ibid.*: 470).

Also, Mr. Mezes was cited in the *San Francisco Chronicle* newspaper in the May 21, 1871 issue (page 1), when it wrote, "Now for Belmont, and farewell to Mezes, the great... landowner...." (See: <www.footnote.com/image 60108773>). The July 2, 1900 issue of the *San Francisco Chronicle* mentioned that Mr. Edward Dufish and his wife, Jennie Dufish, had both arrived on the "Pacific Mail steamer", the *Acapulco*, from Panama after a 22 day trip. (*San Francisco Chronicle*, July 2, 1900: 9). Earlier, Mr. Mezes' marriage was cited in the December 24, **1859** edition of the *San Mateo County Gazette* (Redwood City, San Mateo County); his name appears as: S.M. Mezes, Esq. (San Mateo County Gazette. 1859).

The 1860 Federal Census of California: Accessed via *ancestryInstitution.com 1860 United States Federal Census*, two individuals as having been born in Puerto Rico. These were: John M. Van Ryn and S.N. Mezes (S.M. Mezes) see: (*Ancestry.com*. 1860. United States Federal Census [database on-line]) (see: Exhibits 1, 2 in this book).

John M. Vanryn (Male) [also cited as: John M. Van Ryn], (21), who lived in "Los Angeles, California." His "Profession, [or] Occupation..." was listed in the 1860 census as: "Professor of Languages." Most impressive is the fact that the 1860 Federal Census listed a total of only 58 persons in the occupation of Professor in the entire State of California (Washington: Government Printing Office, 1864: 35, Google books; cf.: Dilts, B.L. 1984: 887, "1860 California Census Index). Similarly, Dilts (1984) also listed Mr. Van Ryn as residing in Los Angeles, CA (page 887).

While Mr. Mezes is identified in both the 1860 and 1870 Federal Census as having been born in Puerto Rico, for some unexplained reason, he is listed as having been born in Spain in the 1880 Census. It is noteworthy, however, that the San Mateo County Genealogy (*SF genealogy.com*) web site published a Table titled, "1870 Federal Census San Mateo County..." which specifically identified Mezes' birthplace as: "Porto Rico [sic.]" (This is taken verbatim from the site) (Filion and Pamela Storm 2003: 2; see also: *San Mateo County Gazette* 1859: 1-2; *digitized* copy). (**Note**: Mezes lived in San Mateo County California --- just outside San Francisco --- for over 20 years, in the city of Belmont, California) (See: Exhibits 3, 5, 6, and 7).

Most importantly, at least as it directly relates to Mr. Mezes, is that in an article published in *La Peninsula*, Journal of the San Mateo County Historical Association (May 1967), the following information regarding him is provided (see also: Millard 1924a: 382-383):

"Mezes arrived in California on February 22, **1850**, having moved to the U.S. **from Puerto Rico** where it is believed he had been president of a bank. He soon developed a large legal practice as counsel for claimants of Mexican land grants who were required to establish titles to their property under American law [following the Treaty of Guadalupe Hidalgo of 1848]" (See: Millard 1924a, 1924b: 1; *La Peninsula*, 1967: 1). [**Note:** unfortunately, Mr. Millard did **not** provide a *source* for the information of Mr. Mezes' immigration arrival date of February 22, 1850 to CA]. (emphasis added)

However, it should be noted that Mr. Mezes' (Mazie's) name did **not** appear in the *1850 U.S. Federal Census* (Jackson and Gary Ronald Teeples. 1978. **Note:** "Part or parts of the census are missing for this year [1850]"; see the section titled: "Census Schedule Taken").

For some background and *historical* context of the struggle for land in the San Francisco area during the period from 1846-1866, see the article entitled, "Politics and the Courts: The Struggle Over Land in San Francisco 1846-1866", which appears in the *Santa Clara Law Review* in 1986 (cf.: Fritz. 1986: 127-164).

Additionally, Mr. Millard, in his book entitled *History of the San Francisco Bay*, wrote that Mr. S.M. Mezes was, "born of pure Spanish lineage...having come to Porto Rico while a boy, he became, at the age of twenty-one, the president of the largest and most influential bank in the island" (Millard 1924b). (**Note:** Once again, Mr. Millard did **not** provide a single resource, or reference, for his suggestion that Mr. Mezes may not have been born in Porto Rico, although the 1852, 1860, and 1870 Censuses ***unequivacably*** lists Mr. Mezes as having been born in Porto Rico/Puerto Rico "about 1828". (cf.: *San Mateo Times-County Fair Supplement.* July 23, 1976). (see: Exhibit 5, for several documents that confirms that Simon Mezes was in fact born in Puerto Rico, and also that Mr. Mezes had emigrated to the United States "circa 1848"). (cf.: Looseley. 1927, *Foreign Born Population of California, 1848-1920*, especially, pages 1-14, Bib. #364).

Finally, Mr. Millard's previously cited article identified the important role played by this Puerto Rican immigrant, Mr. Mezes, in the history of the San Francisco Bay area (e.g., Redwood City, CA). He wrote:

> "Simon Montserrate Mezes helped to establish Redwood City and was one of San Mateo County's most prominent citizens, yet we know very little about his personal history... Mr. Simon Montserrate Mezes died at his home in Belmont [California], December 6, 1884.... He was buried in Union Cemetery, in a lot he had purchased in 1859 at the time of the cemetery's founding," (pages 1-3).

Thus the above reference shows that Mr. Mezes is one of the first, if not the very first prominent and documented Puerto Rican to have arrived in California, according to the U.S. Federal Census, and the 1852 State of California Census records.

Finally, the *Sacramento Daily Record-Union* newspaper of December 9, 1884, reported the death of Mr. Mezes as follows: "S.M. Mezes, an old resident of this country and for whom this place [i.e., Redwood City, CA] was originally named Mezesville, died at his residence near Belmont...." The article reported that the death was due to an accident. (see also: *Redwood City (Cal.) Tribune*, June 3, 1978: 6, two different pages---one of these page numbers is "unknown" to this author; see also: *Redwood City (Cal.) Tribune.* November 29, 1951:2).

The 1870 Federal Census of California: Accessed via *AncestryInstitution.com*. The 1870 census cited two persons as being born in Puerto Rico, and living in California, namely, Simon M. Mezes, and William Tate (44). Mr. Tate's occupation was cited as having been a Wood Chopper, and he lived in San Rafael, Marin, CA (cf.: Ancestry.com. *1870 United States Federal Census* [database on-line]), (cf.: Exhibit 3, for an example of the 1870 Census page). Interestingly, the 1870 Federal Census also identified a total 235 persons who were born in the "West Indies" and who were also residing in San Francisco, California as of June 1870 (Secretary of the Interior. 1872: 449, *A Compendium of The Ninth Census (June 1, 1870)*: 449).

Mr. Mezes is cited in the 1870 Census as being born in Puerto Rico and his Profession as being a: "Capitalist."

It should be remembered that Mr. Mezes' occupation in Puerto Rico was that of a banker, and that the Ninth Census of the Population of the United States for 1870 listed a total of "only" 455 Bankers (and brokers of money and stocks) in the entire state of California, among a total of only 10,631 Bankers in the entire United States. (Secretary of the Interior. 1872: 676).

The 1880 Federal Census of California: It was accessed via AncestryInstitution.com. It cited one individual in California, born in "Puerto Rico Island" (in addition to Simon M. Mezes): he was Rafael Hernandez who lived in San Francisco, California. Although both of his parents were born in Spain, Mr. Hernandez himself was born in "Puerto Rico Island." His "Occupation" was: "Cigar Maker" (cf.: Ancestry.com. 1880. United States Federal Census [database on-line]).

The 1890 Federal Census for the State of California: Since the 1890 Federal Census was destroyed by fire, it could not be determined how many Puerto Ricans lived in California. Further research is needed here (cf.: Ancestry.com. 1890 United States Federal Census).

The 1900 Federal Census of California: It was accessed via *AncestryInstitution.com*; it identified a total of *seven (7)* individuals who were living in California which the Census cited as having been born in either "Porto Rico", or in Puerto Rico. (see: Exhibits 8 and 9, for "sample blank pages" from the 1900 U.S. Federal Census, which identifies the Questions which were asked by the U.S. Federal Census Enumerators). These were as follows:

Charles F. Benzon (19), (CF.: Exhibits 10 and 11) lived in San Francisco, CA; Ben Camacho (24), and his family lived at: "Soquel Township, Santa Cruz, California. Clara Blair (55) and her family lived in: "Sacramento City, Sacramento, California." Mrs. Blair immigrated to the United States in 1850, when she was five years old (cf.: Ancestry.com. 1900. United States Federal Census [database on-line]). Mrs. O Munroe (65); and B L A Munroe (48) [the Census' spelling] lived in San Diego County. Mcenty Portorico (48) [the census' spelling of the name] lived in San Francisco, CA; and Charles Rodigez (57) [The census' spelling] lived in San Francisco, CA (cf.: Exhibit 10).

According to the publication: *Great Register [The Great Register of San Diego County for 1894]*, "An alphabetical list of registered voters in San Diego County, California 1894", Mr. B. L. A. Munroe is listed as: No. 4951; Munroe, B. L. A.; Age is 43; height is 6 foot; complexion is Dark; **Nativity as Porto Rico**; Occupation as Clerk; Local Residence as: 7 Ward 1 pret; Naturalized: "By naturalization of father"; Post Office Address: Hotel De Europe; Date of registration in 1894: July 30, 1894" (San Diego County. 1894: 78, *The Great Register of San Diego County for 1894*).

Upon a review of the *San Diego City and County Directory: 1895* ("An Alphabetical List of Business Firms and Private Citizens"), Mr. B. L. A. Munroe was listed as a "salesman, res Hotel d'Europe" (San Diego City. 1895) (Note: that the 1893-94 edition, titled *Directory of San Diego City and County for 1893-94*, did not list Mr. Munroe, nor was Mr. Munroe (nor Mrs. Munroe) cited within its pages) (cf.: San Diego City. 1893-1894). Thus, this suggests that they may have first arrived in San Diego sometime in late 1894. (NOTE: Mr. Munroe's race was listed as being "Black", see: Bibliography #13).

In a review of the microfiche *"California Deaths: 1905-1929"* (California. u.n. [Unknown Date]. Vital Search-CA: Deaths - 7748), and the book titled *"Index to Obituaries and Death Notices in the San Diego Union (1868-1915)"* (San Diego Genealogical Society. 2010: 239, 244)...Mr. Munroe is listed as being 60 years old at the time of his death on April 22, 1910; he appears in the *Index* as: Alphonso B.L. Munroe (NOTE: the 1910 Federal Census listed Mr. Munroe's Race as being "Black", Bib. #13).

Mrs. M O Munroe (his Mother), unfortunately, was only listed in the *1906 San Diego City and County Directory*, which simply indicates for her: "Munroe Mrs M O, h Newton av and 22d" (cf.: California. Unknown Date, VitalSearch-ca; San Diego City. 1868-1915; San Diego City 1906). Mrs. M O Munroe was also cited in the microfiche, *"California Deaths: 1905-1929"*, and in the Table/Chart cited as the:

Index to Obituaries and Death Notices in the San Diego Union (1868-1915) (San Diego Genealogical Society. 2010). Her Date of Death was Sept. 16, 1908; she appears as: Mary O. Munroe in this publication.

It should be noted that Mr. B.L.A. Munroe was earlier cited in the California Voter Registration (1866-1898) publication (aka: *Great Registers, 1866-1898*) and he is listed as follows:

Name: Mr. B.L.A. Munroe; Residence Year: 1888; Age: 37; Birth Year: abt 1851; Residence Place: Los Angeles, California. Importantly, Mr. Munroe's "Country of Nativity" is (again) cited as: **Porto Rico**. His "Voting No.: 7450; Occupation: Teacher; Local Residence: Hayes St.; Naturalized: 'by Naturalization of Father'" (No date cited); Date of Registration: Sept. 11, 1888, (California State Library, California History Section. 1866-1898: 81) (*Ancestry.com - California*) (emphasis added) (http://search.ancestry.com/content/viewerpf/aspx?h=6067895&db=CAGreatRegisters&iid=32421).

Finally, the publication entitled, *San Diego County California Census Index 1900* listed the name of B.L.A. Monroe (North San Diego County Genealogical Society and Carlsbad City Library. 1981: 84. Evelyn Jean White, Editor, Bib. #135). However, Ms.White acknowledged that while "this index is an alphabetical listing of heads of households... there will be discrepancies in the index... [due to] the census takers' phonetic... spelling [of ones' name]". (Note: there is no page number in this book which is listed on <u>this</u> page).

6/16/2016: A contemporaneous example which showed that S. M. Mezes was a "Rich Man", and therefore, a highly prominent and economically sussessful man while he lived in California in the 1860s, is in the brief article titled, "Rich Men of San Mateo" in the *Marysville Daily Appeal (CA)* newspaper (September 25, 1862), wherein this article indicated that:

"The following is a list of the persons, companies and firms which stand highest in the amount of their taxable property on the assessment roll to San Mateo County...Mezes & Arguellos, $81,000..."(pages 80-81).

06/17/2016

EPILOGUE (documentation of Simon M. Mezes having been born in Puerto Rico)

This **Epilogue** can be read at the end of the **Bibliography** section (page195ff.). This **Epilogue** presents the new research, and write-up, which was conducted <u>after</u> the 1st printing of this book in March 2013, wherein the genealogical <u>documentation</u> of the birthplace of Simon M. Mezes (aka: S.M. Mezes), as well as his parents birthplace as well. Much of this <u>documentation</u> was obtained from the church in Mayagüez, Puerto Rico where Simon M. Mezes was born, as well as one document from Spain (from the Spanish Archives, i.e., the *Archivo de Indias*).

Thus, the genealogical research relating to Simon M. Mezes was primarily conducted after March 2013 till June 2016, and therefore, is presented in this **EPILOGUE**. Particularly, see the bibliographic sources cited in the section titled, "Special Genealogical Primary Sources Relating to **S. M. Mezes**' Birthplace in Puerto Rico", (see: Bib. #419 - #422; cf.: Exhibit 24, Exhibit 25, and Exhibit 26, pp. 248, 249, 250). (See also: Exhibit 22, and Exhibit 23, pp. 246, 247). Finally, see: S. E. Mezes' book titled, "Ethics: Descriptive And Explanatory", (1901), (by S. E. Mezes, Ph.D., Professor of Philosophy, University of Texas, New York: THE MACMILLAN COMPANY.

CHAPTER 13

The San Francisco Puerto Rican Immigrant Population: 1900-1925

*Summary of Puerto Rican Migration from
Hawaii to San Francisco, California: 1901-1925:*

While a number of researchers and scholars have previously written and posited that the California Puerto Rican population directly grew out of the direct migration of Puerto Ricans to California in general, and to San Francisco in particular, there was a paucity of figures and census numbers to substantiate this assertion, i.e., there were few, if any, source citations (or references) cited. Recently this author was able to identify specific numbers regarding this migration process from Hawaii to the "[West] Coast", mostly likely to California. For example, the *Report of the Governor of Hawaii to the Secretary of Hawaii* (Secretary of the Interior. 1919: 36), in their Table entitled "Steerage arrivals and departures and births and deaths 9 fiscal years since census of April, 1910," listed the following figures of Puerto Ricans that <u>departed</u> from Hawaii, presumably to the [West] Coast, i.e., California:

1911: 232 "departures"; 1912: 13; 1913:33; 1914: 105; 1915: 50; 1916: 210; 1917: 41; 1918: 57; 1919: 43; for a "Total departures" of 784. However, the total number of Puerto Rican "Arrivals" from Puerto Rico to Hawaii during this period from 1911-1919 was only 8. Thus, this report indicated that the increase in the Hawaiian Puerto Rican population during this aforementioned period was due to an "excess of births over deaths" (Secretary of the Interior. 1919: 35).

Similarly, this above cited 1919 *Governor's Report*, in its Table entitled "Arrivals and departures of steerage passengers for the year ending June 30, 1919" [presumably covering only a one year time period], listed the following figures for the number of Puerto Ricans who had "departed" from Hawaii for the "Coast" [presumably most, if not all, of whom went to California], namely: 14 Men, 9 Women, and 19 children, for a total of 42 Puerto Ricans in total. One Puerto Rican Women was listed as departing for the "Orient"! (Secretary of the Interior. 1919: 37).

The "estimated" Puerto Rican population in Hawaii as of June 30, 1919, was 5,400, while the 1910 Puerto Rican population in Hawaii was 4,890. It also listed a total of 1,976 births, and 764 total deaths (*Ibid.*, 35, 36)

By the end of 1901 the City of San Francisco had the largest concentration, by far, of "Puerto Rican immigrants" within the State of California, and therefore, I began an analysis of the 1910 California Census Population names, in general, and for the City of San Francisco (San Francisco County), in particular. Thus, a review of the on-line database for the 1910 Federal Census for the City of San Francisco presented a good starting point to begin this research project.

Several writers have speculated that the ever expanding San Francisco Puerto Rican population was the direct result of Puerto Ricans being unsatisfied with their working conditions and their life situations in Hawaii. Their disatisfaction developed soon after the first arrivals in December 1900. For example, at least as early as 1902, the *Report of the Governor on Hawaii-1902 (1903)* identified this ever-growing discontent, when it reported that:

"The Porto Ricans, on their part, have not been uniformly contended with the **conditions** they have encountered in Hawaii. **Complaints** of ill usage and injustice were made. It was claimed that they were charged exorbitant prices at the plantation stores, and were obligated to be at work at unreasonably early hours…. The cost of living is relatively higher in Hawaii than in Porto Rico…. But the conditions of the Porto Ricans in Hawaii have another and a pleasanter side. The hopelessly ill have died, some of the **discontented have left for California**…." (*Report of the Commissioner of Labor on Hawaii-1902* (1903): 29). (emphasis added)

R.C. Leyland's Master's Thesis in Geography, entitled *Puerto Ricans in the San Francisco Bay Area, California: An Historical and Cultural Geography,* posited that the first Puerto Ricans that arrived in California after 1900, particularly in San Francisco, made the decision to settle "near [other] Latinos [within their communities], [as they were] attracted by a common language [Spanish]," (Leyland 1980: 6). Leyland further posited that:

"[…] Puerto Ricans from Hawaii pioneered the San Francisco Bay Area settlements…. During 1901 to 1925 the Puerto Rican emigration to California flowed through Hawaii. This flow represented a return migration as a result of the failure of these early expeditions to fulfill promises… Most Puerto Ricans that came to San Francisco via Hawaii arrived first in Los Angeles and then traveled by land north to San Francisco…. The plan to return [to Puerto Rico] was later postponed or abandoned for settlement on the Pacific Coast [and in particular, the San Francisco Bay Area]… San Francisco Bay Area's *Colonias* [ethnic enclaves] were founded from 1901-1925, the period during which the return expeditions from Hawaii to Puerto Rico took place" (Leyland 1980: 66, 70, 69, 72, 81, 92; see also: Feldman 1978: 4, 3-5).

Using 1910 Federal Census data, the 1911 U.S. Federal Committee on Immigration in their publication titled *Reports of the Immigration Commission. Immigrants In Industries…* (Vol. III) identified a total of 35 Puerto Ricans in their Table/Chart entitled "Immigrant Labor in the Manufacture of Cigars and Cigarettes in San Francisco, Cal. Races Employed", 21 of whom were females, and five (5) of whom were "Foremen and Bosses", among the eight (8) establishments which the Commission had investigated for their Reports in San Francisco. (See: *Reports of the Immigration Commission.* 1911d: 409, 410, 411, 414, 416, 417 Part 25).

Note: For a contemporaneous article describing what the **"cost of living"** was in San Francisco in 1904, see: *The San Francisco Chronicle.* October 20, 1904: 7, "Cost of Living: Some Facts About the cost of Living in San Francisco"; http://www:sfgenealogy.com/sf/history/hgcol.htm, (accessed: 5/20/2010).

September 2016:

The first known documented case of a Porto Rican immigrant leaving Hawaii to return (back) to California (and possibly back to Porto Rico) happened in November 1901, namely, Celestino Garcia, (Arroyo, Ronald. 1977: 142) (see: page 40 of my book)

CHAPTER 14

December 14, 1900:
The Beginning of Puerto Rican Immigration *"en masse"*,
to California, and the Immigrants' Respective Names

The sensational front page headline of the December 15, 1900 edition of the *San Francisco Examiner* reads: "Threats and Force Put 66 Porto Ricans on Rio, But Fifty Others Escape." However, a review of a series of articles and columns that appeared over a two week period from December 14 through December 26, 1900, shows that the *San Francisco Examiner* (see: Bibliography under the *San Francisco Examiner*), identified the names of **at least** 64 of the Puerto Rican immigrants that made the difficult decision to stay in the City of San Francisco, as opposed to continuing their journey on to Hawaii, beginning with their December 15, 1900 edition. (**NOTE:** the 64 *included* children and infants which the *San Francisco Examiner* made a reference to over this two week period). In dramatic contrast, the *San Francisco Chronicle* (December 15, 1900) published only one name of these Puerto Rican immigrants, namely, Jose Morales (18). (cf.: Exhibits 17, 12 and 13).

The following issues of the *San Francisco Examiner* newspaper provided names of the immigrants, a brief description, and the names of which city in Northern California the Puerto Rican immigrants were dispersed to, if known. Their names are listed below spelled **exactly** how they appear in the *San Francisco Examiner* series of articles in December 1900. They cited a total of *at least* 64 persons in their articles (although several names were misspelled). The following excerpts were taken from these newspaper articles/columns, with their names cited (spelled) **exactly** as they were published in the December 1900 newspaper(s):

The Names and the Newspaper's Descriptions of the "First Group" of
Puerto Ricans that Stayed in California on December 14, 1900: "Group 1"

Background: A newspaper article reported that on December 14, 1900 a total of 56 Puerto Ricans stayed in San Francisco, and did not travel onto Hawaii, since "they were the last of the fifty-six Puerto Ricans who escaped involuntary deportation to Hawaii on the 14th instant" (cf.: *San Francisco Examiner*, December 24, 1900: 2). It should be noted that previous scholars and researches have similarly, and erroneously, reported that either a total of 56 stayed in California (cf.: Medina 2001:90), or 49 (Carr 1989: 452-453), or proposed numbers as low as 40 (Sánchez Korrol 1994a: 285; Feldman 1978: 4).

However, a closer review of newspapers during the period from December 14, 1900 to December 26, 1900, identified a total of *at least* 64 Puerto Ricans, with three babies having been born in the United States (or in transit during the journey from Puerto Rico to California), of Puerto Rican parentage. The **at least** 64 cited persons *included* 14 children (i.e., under age 12), and 3 infants. As the 3 infants were born either in "transit", **or on American soil**, they became American Citizens, pursuant to the 14th Amendment of the U.S. Constitution. (See below: for the names of these *at least* 64 persons):

The Names of the "at least" 64 Immigrants that Stayed In California on December 14, 1900:

The Names Cited in the **San Francisco Examiner** (December 16, 1900 issue):

*Lola Dolores Marzan (16): the "sixteen-year old bride" who was seriously ill. She is the wife of Emilio Marzan (Marsan).

*Emelio Marzan: the husband of Lola Dolores Marzan. "Emilio Marsan was sent to a ranchita a few miles from Salinas [in Monterey County, CA]." "At the ranch of Mayor [of Salinas ?] R.F. Johnson, Emelio Marzan and wife [Lola Dolores Marzan] are pleasantly located." The newspaper articles did not identify what kind of work either Mr. Marzan, nor Mrs. Marzan, did. **Note:** Lola and Emelio were also cited in the *San Francisco Examiner's* December 15th and December 20th, 1900 editions.

*Senora Miguela and *Senora Guadaloupe: "they will remain with their **seven little tots** [one of which is] the twelve-day-old Miguela **baby** [who] is being well taken care of, and the mother is getting the most nourishing food.... They were at the Infant' Shelter." [**Note:** see the December 15, 1900 issue of the *San Francisco Examiner*, which has a photograph of these 7 children, page 2].

The Names Cited in the **San Francisco Examiner** (December 18, 1900 issue):

*Petronila Gimenez and *Serafin Gimenez, 4 ½ yr. old boy: House Servant; they were sent to: Diamond, in Alameda County. "The first person to find a comfortable home was Mrs. Petronila Gimenez, a young widow.... [with] a little boy, Serafin Gimenez."

*Santiago Panilla (14): he was sent to a home in [East] Oakland, at 764 East Fourteenth Street. He was the equivalent of being "adopted". "Santiago Panilla... found a home under very happy circumstances."

*Claudino Puty: he is nineteen. "The two found a refuge with Dr. Maritola's family last week and they have been right at home since."

[*Note*: The author determined that Santiago Panilla/Parnilla/Padilla is most likely the same person, especially since Dr. Carr wrote that Santiago Padilla was 12 or 14 years old (Carr 1989: 452). One newspaper reported that: Santiago Parrilla, was sent "to [the] Chicago Hotel."]

[*Note*: I determined from the following newspaper reference that Claudin Puez, was sent "to work in East Oakland," and is the same person as the 19 year old cited above, namely, Claudino Puty, or even Claudina Puez].

*Juan Perez (12): was to do "House errands". The December 16, 1900 issue of *The Examiner* wrote that "His parents were forced aboard the *Caroline* and the *Rio* [and sailed to Hawaii], and he was left behind [in San Francisco]." The December 16, 1900 edition of the *S.F. Examiner* indicated that Juan Perez "became separated from his parents and the kidnapers made no effort to find him. He is now in this city [San Francisco] and is being cared for by the '*Examiner*'." (Page 39) Juan went to the home of T.B. Carrington (The *San Francisco Examiner.* December 18, 1900).

The Names Cited in the **San Francisco Examiner** (December 19, 1900 issue):

"Joaquin Colon (14): taken in as a "foster son" and he was taken in by a "Spanish lady, Juanina Verales." He was "...adopted by Mrs. Verales, a widow, who lives at 428 Pacific Street [in Monterey, CA]." Joaquin was an "orphan boy."

*Juan Flores (15): an orphan boy, sent to: Berkeley (Hills), CA. Juan was taken in by "a lady of Cuban birth." "Juan Flores, the Porto Rican, who is living with Mr. and Mrs. B. W. Sturtevant in Berkeley, is well pleased with his new home. He is a bright lad fifteen years of age and he is learning very quickly."

The Names Cited in the **San Francisco Examiner** (December 20, 1900 issue):

*Ysidro Espiel (26): sent to Mayfield, Santa Clara County. "**Can read and write Spanish**. His home was about fifteen miles from San Juan. His object in leaving home was to better himself." "Ysidro Espiel, the young Porto Rican was fortunate enough to secure a comfortable home with the family of [Dr.] E. H. Samuels of this place, spent a most enjoyable Christmas...." (emphasis added)

*Nicomedes Pacheco (23): became the "new porter at the Chicago Hotel," which is located at 222 Pacific Street. He "has found a home with Nela Nelson, the landlord of the Chicago Hotel...."

*Carlos Barreto (16): taken by Mr. and Mrs. Frederick Raab of 44 India Avenue, Silver Heights, in the San Bruno road district of this city" "to a chicken ranch."

*Salvador Morales: sent to Salinas, CA, in Monterey County, to work for Dr. Gonzales as a Farm hand, on Dr. Gonzales' ranch. "Dr. Gonzalez is well known in Monterey County."

*Ramon Arbelo (22): "is to be taken in hand by the kind fathers of Santa Clara College, where he will be educated and be given an opportunity to become a good American citizen." "He **can read and write Spanish** and was a clerk in his father's store in San Juan.... Ramon will leave for Santa Clara, CA this morning." (emphasis added)

*Mateo Figueroa and his *wife [Maria]: were to be "given employment in a home in Las Palmas ranch." "Mateo Figueroa is with the family of [the Hon.] B. V. Sargent, while his wife [Maria Figueroa] is at the home of Horace W. Austin and wife, a block distant. Both had a Christmas dinner with Mrs. Austin."

*Ignosunty Heredia, *Francisco Torres, *Carmelia Billafana: all three were taken to Monterey [CA], to be sent to the San Francisquita ranch. As a result:

"In Monterey Ignosuntia Heridia is with J. P. Sargent; his companion, [Francisca?] Torres and the women Billafana being located in Salinas...."

"Carmelia was found a home in the San Carlos Mission house where she will be a cook and housekeeper for the rev. Father Ferrar." "Mrs. Alexander Chaboy and her two daughters have given Cermella Bellafano all the necessary clothing and a new dress for Sunday use...."

The Names Cited in the **San Francisco Examiner** (December 23, 1900 issue):

*Felix Miranda, left for Geyserville, in Oakland, CA, to a sheep ranch. He "entered the employ of J.T. Harlan of Oakland, who has a sheep ranch."

*Vicente Sanchez, left for Geyserville, in Oakland, CA, to a sheep ranch. He [also] "entered the employ of J.T. Harlan of Oakland, who has a sheep ranch."

*Manuel Valentin, the newspaper did not identify which city he left for, i.e., was "dispersed" to.

*Fabian Guez, "has entered the employ of Mrs. Arbeila at the Santa Clara Hotel in Santa Clara, CA...."

*Eusabia Lopez; the newspaper indicated that "Mrs. K. Foster has undertaken to provide for Eusabia Lopez, who will go to Folsom [CA] today." (cf.: Bib. #240).

*Sisto Soto and his *wife [wife's name was not identified] and their **five (5) children**: "have found a home." "... Sieto [*sic*] Soto, wife and five children are installed in a new and comfortable cottage on Lang [this is an unreadable word in the newspaper] ranch..." in Salinas, CA in Monterey County (See: immediately below under Ramon Ortez [*sic*]).

*Ramon Ortez, his *wife [wife's name was not identified], and their **baby**: "have found a home," in Salinas, CA [in Monterey County]. The *S.F. Examiner* newspaper indicated that "Ramon Ortiz, wife and child [child is unnamed], and Sieto Soto and [his] wife [Mr. Soto's wife's name was not identified] and **five children** were placed on the Gabilan ranch and are supplied with a complete outfit and food. Both Mr. Soto and Mr. Ortiz's occupation(s) were "woodchoppers." Mr. Ortiz was placed in Salinas, CA, in Monterey County, along with Mr. Soto and his family. [*Note*: this author was not able to determine from the newspaper articles whether this baby was one of the three (3) babies that were born "in transit", from Puerto Rico to San Francisco, CA.].

The newspaper article of December 24, 1900 (p. 2) went on to state that: "They were *the last* of the **fifty-six** [as opposed to the '*correct*' figure of at least **64**] Porto Ricans who escaped involuntary deportation to Hawaii on the 14th instant...." (emphasis added)

*Eduardo Reyes: went to Winters, CA. The newspaper identified his occupation as being a Woodchopper. "He has been taken care of by C.L. de Villiers, and is now in a good position."

*Victorian Cruz: worked at the Hotel Bardin as an assistant porter. "His duties will consist of cleaning woodwork, windows, etc., and making himself generally useful to his employer and the hotel guests." "He will be paid, after Feb. 1901, a regular salary of $10 a month." "Victorian Cruz ate the best dinner of his life at the Bardin house to-day. He is merry and cheerful."

*Ramon Martin and his *wife [not identified by name], have *"another son": and went to the Santa Lucia ranch. The newspaper did not identify which city they went to, or their respective occupations. "Ramon Martin, wife and **two children**, one of the latter but *three days old* [a Baby infant], spent their first Christmas in California at their house in the Santa Lucia hills." [*Note*: the 3 day old baby was born "in transit", on U.S. soil --- see the: December 26, 1900 edition]

Note that the newspapers list a Ramon Martin (the December 26, 1900 issue), as well as a Ramon Martel (the December 23, 1900 issue), however, this author believes that they are possibly one and the same, since the Dec. 23, 1900 newspaper edition wrote that: "...Ramon Martel and wife have another son. Mssrs. Lang and Dorn have one Porto Rican more than they expected on the Santa Lucia ranch."

The Names Cited in the **San Francisco Examiner** (December 26, 1900 edition):

*Ramon Santiago: "...the young Porto Rican who has found a home at Casa Juarez, near Napa." "He **wrote a letter** to his father in Porto Rico in the afternoon, the first that he has sent since arriving in this State [California]." [*Note*: Dr. Norma Carr in her dissertation cited two persons with the same name of Ramon Santiago, although she indicated the first was 19 years old, while the second Ramon Santiago has no age next to his name (Carr. 1989: 452). Therefore, it is not known whether these two names represent one and the same person]. (emphasis added)

*Juan Heresadia: "...is living in a perpetual sunshine of happiness at the Arguello home."

*Francisco Nunez: "... [is] located on the ranch belonging to Jesse D. Carr...."

*Francisco Trinoe: "... [is also] located on the ranch belonging to Jesse D. Carr...."

*Jose Agosto, "...at the home of Thomas Watson, Jose Agosto and *Pedro Rodriguez enjoyed a hearty Christmas dinner and spent the day in resting."

*Blanco Ignosund Berreto: "was supremely happy after his Christmas dinner."

*James Rodriguez: "... is with R. C. Sargent in Monterey, did nothing to-day except eat and rest."

*Louis Santiago: "the family of Louis Santiago [his *wife's name was not identified, nor the names of any of their children]," and the "Porto Ricans being provided for at ex-Supervisor J. S. Selby's ranch, had for their first Christmas spent in America a royal good dinner...in San Jose [CA]." "The ex-Supervisor had given **them** a pair of fine fat chickens and turned the ranch cellar over to **them**...." (This indicates *at least* two persons)

*Juan Medina: "who was given employment by Dr. Fred Gerlach, was also happy in his first Christmas experienced in America."

*Mateo Hernandes: "...was given employment with Edward Curran.... To-day on invitation, he took his Christmas dinner at the Tracy Hotel." [Dr. Carr cites his name as Mateo Hernandez (Carr 1989: 452)].

*Eugenia Volentico: "has a very comfortable home with the family of C. W. Armstrong, a druggist of this place, and is contented and happy."

*Gregoria Ribera: "has a very comfortable at $10 per month and board with William Spiers of the Calistoga and Clear Lake stage line, and seems to be perfectly contended."

*Jose Morales [18]: "who was placed with Supervisor A. Widemann, was given a holiday to-day and was delighted with his Christmas meal at the James Bardin ranch."

*De Soto, Aurelio (34), (see: Carr, 1989: 452).

In contrast to the *San Francisco Examiner* newspaper, the *San Francisco Chronicle* newspaper only cited one Puerto Rican immigrant by name, and that was in their December 15, 1900 edition, when it wrote the following: Jose Morales (18) was told that "... we could get plenty of work and make $2 or $3 a day." "Jose Morales, who was placed with Supervisor A. Widemann, was given a holiday to-day and was delighted with his Christmas meal at the James Bardin ranch."

It should be noted after a careful review of the following newspapers---the *San Francisco Call*, the *Los Angeles Times*, and the *San Francisco Chronicle*, that only one specific name was cited among the three, namely, Jose Morales (18)---therefore these three newspapers did not provide any "new", or additional name(s), to the *at least* 64 names provided by the *San Francisco Examiner*, since Jose Morales (18) was also cited by the *San Francisco Examiner* (see: above). [*Note*: see the **Bibliography** under the names of each of these separate newspapers, and for the names of each separate article].

It should be noted that I reviewed only English language newspapers as opposed to Spanish language newspapers from Puerto Rico, e.g., *La Correspondencia de Puerto Rico* (for 1900-1901). However, I

did read the "translations" of those articles which were reproduced in English from *La Correspondencia* and were included in the 1977 publication titled: *Documentos de la Migración Puertorriqueña (1879-1901) / Documents of the Puerto Rican Migration* (Centro de Estudios Puertorriqueños 1977: 13-18 20-31, 39-41). However, the emphasis of these articles from *La Correspondencia de Puerto Rico* were on immigrants going to Hawaii, and not relating to the *at least* 64 that stayed in California (cf.: *Ibid.*: 13-31ff.; Centro de Estudios Puertorriqueños 1981: 1-4, for a listing of 17 such articles covering the period from 1900-1901).

October 2016

For research purposes for additional articles reproduced from the *La Correspondencia* (San Juan, P.R.), newspaper, see the following publication: (Centro de Estudios Puertorriqueños (1981). *Preliminary Guide to Articles in Puerto Rican Newspapers Relating to Puerto Rican Migration Between 1900 and 1929,* (CENTRO de Estudios Puertorriqueños Publication)).

The Titles of these above referenced articles from the *La Correspondencia* newspaper, albeit a "selective sample", are as follows (**typed verbatim**):

"Los Tortoleños";

"Nota del Dia la Emigracion";

"Alerto Braceros";

"Braceros á las islas Haway";

"Por que no debe irse al Hawaii"

"La Emigración";

"Puertorriqueños que van á Hawaii"; and

"Para Hawaii".

CHAPTER 15

Norma Carr's Identification of 44 Puerto Rican Immigrants' Names, who were "voluntarily" left behind and subsequently "dispersed" in Northern California: December 14, 1900

It is important to acknowledge the seminal work of Norma Carr in her dissertation for the University of Hawaii when she ["really"] identified, by name, 44 out of the original [of the *at least* 64 who stayed in California] Puerto Rican immigrants to California who arrived in December 1900 (Carr 1989: 452-453, 105), and Nitza C. Medina identified a total of 20 specific names in her review of the newspaper articles from December 1900 for those persons that stayed in California as of December 14, 1900 (Medina. 2001). Note, however, that while Dr. Carr wrote in her 1989 dissertation that: "Forty-three **persons [i.e., Puerto Ricans]** were distributed to seventeen separate locations in California" (See **her**: "Appendix C"), she cited a total of 44 persons, [when you **include** the six children---"all under 6", and two babies.], and plus one additional person, Juan Perez (Carr 1989: 105, 452-453, her "Appendix C"; see: below). However, Dr. Carr did cite two persons with the same name, namely, Ramon Santiago, and although she indicated that one was 19 years old, there was no age for the second Ramon Santiago (cf.: Exhibits 12 and 13); however, I believe that they are the same person, since her "Appendix C" states that "young men interviewed by Livernash", and therefore, she actually cited a total of 44, if you include the two listings for the name of Ramon Santiago as one person.

Carr also listed two other persons with the same surnames, and although she listed each of these two with a different spelling (though very similar), namely, Orlagario Rodriguez and Eulagario Rodriguez, however, I determined that they are the same person since she referenced that Olagario Rodriquez namely, Orlagario Rodriguez and Eulagario Rodriguez, however, [or Eulagario Rodriguez] was a "young [man] interviewed by Livernash" (Ibid.: 452).

It should be noted that while Norma Carr listed a total of 43 names in her "Appendix C", on page 452, she also listed one person on her page 453, namely Juan Perez (12 years old), whom she cited as: "[he] later joined parents on Maui", therefore he was one of the at least 64 immigrants who were "dispersed" throughout Northern California (Carr. 1989: 452, 453). Thus, Juan Perez makes the 44th person whom Carr had listed.

However, a careful review of the San Francisco area newspapers confirmed the specific names of these same *at least* 64 persons (which included several unnamed wives); and included specific references to the Sieto Soto family having five (unnamed) children, the Ramon Ortez family having one (unnamed) baby, and finally, the Ramon Martel family having had two (unnamed) children. The San Francisco newspapers of the time wrote that these immigrants were then "dispersed" (to use Dr. Carr's word), to 17 different cities in 12 different Counties, throughout Northern California, including the San Francisco Bay area (see: Carr.1989).

Prior to their arrival in California on December 14, 1900, *The New York Times* reported the following on the Puerto Ricans immigrant's journey from New Orleans to San Francisco via train:

> "To avoid affording them any opportunity for **escape**, the [recruiting] agents had the cars side-tracked at a station in the great desert, 300 miles east of this point, and remained there three days, so as to reach San Francisco in time to make perfect connections with the ship…. They said they were decoyed from their homes aboard a ship ostensibly to land on the other side of their island. The ship took them to New Orleans, where they were hustled aboard a train and dispatched westward under close guard" (*The New York Times*. December 7, 1900: 1; see: *San Francisco Examiner*. December 7, 1900: 1, (Bib. #337)). (emphasis added) These immigrants were referred to by the newspapers of the day, as *[the so-called]* **"escapees,"** (cf.: Carr 1989: 452; Medina 2001: 88).

Medina posits that these Puerto Rican immigrants, who remained in California, were the individuals that started California's first Puerto Rican enclaves (*colonias*), or communities (Medina 2001: 88).

Importantly, Carr (1989: 452-453) identified the different Cities in Northern California which these 44 Puerto Rican immigrants were "dispersed" to during the last two weeks of December 1900. For example, she wrote that they were "dispersed" to the following Cities (and I then inserted the Counties in which these cities were/are located), namely:

One to Dixon (in Solano County); two to Diamond (Alameda County); one to San Francisco (San Francisco County); two to Monterey (Monterey County); one to Mayfield (Santa Clara County); eight to Salinas (Monterey County); one to Tulare (Tulare County); two to Folsom (Sacramento County); one to King City (Monterey County); two to San Jose (Santa Clara County); one to Winters (Yolo County); one to Tracy (San Joaquin County); one to Santa Clara (Santa Clara County); two to Gonzalez (Monterey County); one to Napa (Napa County); two to Calistoga (Napa County); and one to Antioch (Contra Costa County). Carr did not identify which County Juan Perez (12 yrs. old) was "dispersed" to, nor did she identify which County Sisto Soto, his wife, and their five children were "dispersed" to, nor the dispersal location for the four remaining Puerto Rican immigrants which she had cited. (Carr. 1989: 452-453).

CHAPTER 16

The 1900 Federal Census and California's Puerto Rican Immigrants: The Census Data

Since the City of San Francisco had, by far, the largest population of Puerto Rican immigrants, the decision was made to focus on the Puerto Rican immigrants that were living in San Francisco as of the census for 1910. Thus, the 1910 Census at AncestryInstitution.com provides a list of 151 Puerto Rican immigrants who lived in San Francisco (Lists of: 31 + 120), of which 21 were born in "Porto Rico," or "Puerto Rico", and having immigrated to the United States in **1900** (the "Year of Immigration" on the Census Form) (see: Exhibit 11). It is noteworthy that the **1900** Census Form did **not** identify which state, or city, a particular person may have initially immigrated to. The Census Form simply indicated that the person had immigrated to the United States in either 1900, or in 1901 (or after the 1900 Enumeration date). Therefore, a number of Puerto Rican immigrants had initially immigrated to the United States in either 1900, or in 1901, and then subsequently had migrated to California.

It should be noted that according to *Ancestry.com* the State of California had a total of 27 Puerto Ricans (i.e., those that Ancestry.com listed as being born in "Porto Rico"; including the 21 persons from San Francisco) who immigrated to the continental United States in 1900. *Note*: This total group of 151 does *not* include Santos and Nellie Santiago, both of whom immigrated in 1900, but did not appear on either list (see: below). Unfortunately, the Census Form itself did **not** list the specific State(s) each of these 151 persons had initially immigrated to.

The 1910 Census did provide a wealth of information, such as each individual's name, their age, their marital status, their "***Year of Immigration***", and where their "Home in 1910" was located, while the Ancestry's index provides their "Estimated year of birth." Thus, the Census evidence shows that all 29 (if you also include Santos and Nellie Santiago) of the following persons had immigrated to the continental United States **in the year 1900**, and who resided in California in 1910 (along with their respective occupations). They are as follows (their Names are in alphabetical order) [**Note:** San Francisco, CA will be abbreviated below as simply: S.F.]:

*Thomas Barreto (23; Single; born "abt 1887"), occupation: Laborer-Odd Jobs, Monterey, CA;

*Rosa Colon (22; wife; born "abt 1888"), occupation: "none", District 45, S.F.;

*Angel Colondre (25; Married, born "1885"), occupation: "none", S.F. District 45;

*Giacento Colondre (20 [30]; Married; born "abt 1890" ["abt 1880"]), Sailor-Steamer, S.F.;

*Manuel Colon (30; Married; born "abt 1880"), Fisherman, S.F. Assembly District 45;

*Maximina Elmgren (31; Married; born "abt 1879"), occupation: "none", Solano, CA;

*Ramona R. Farrell (19; Married; born "abt 1891"), occupation: "none", S.F. District 45;

*Charles Fernander [Charles Fernandez] (30; born "abt 1880"), occupation: ?, Los Angeles, CA;

*Olimpia Forne [Olimpia Tarus] (25; Married; born "abt 1885), occupation: left "Blank", S.F., CA;

*Dametria Garcia (34; Married; born "abt 1876"), occupation: "none", Eden, Alameda, CA;

*Frank Gonsales (25; Married; born "abt 1885"), Fisherman – Alaska Packers ?, S.F., CA;

*Mary Gonsales (18; Single; born "abt 1892"), Stripper-Tobacco Factory, District 45, S.F.,

*Tomasso Gonsales (28; Married; born "abt 1882"), Stripper-Tobacco Factory, Dist. 45, S.F., CA;

*Angelia Lugo (24; Married; born "abt 1886"), occupation: "none", S.F. District 33;

*Ramon Lugo (24; Married; born "abt 1886"), Leather Washer-Factory, S.F. District 33;

*Marie Mordecai (26; Married; born "abt 1884"), occupation: "none", S.F. District 45;

*Francesco Marcaro [Francesca Marcaro] (9; Single; born "abt 1901"), Pupil, District 32, S.F., CA;

*Marie Marcaro (15; Single; born "abt 1895"), Servant, S.F. Assembly District 32;

*Fela Ortiz (26; Married; "abt 1884"), Servant, S.F. Assembly District 41, S.F., CA;

*Joseph Pagan (26; Single; born "abt 1884"), occupation:? , S.F. Assembly District 39;

*Tony Perry (47; Single; born "abt 1863"), Laborer, San Jose, Santa Clara, CA;

*John B. Rodriguez (21; Single; born "abt 1889"), Farm Laborer – Hired Man, San Luis Obispo, CA;

*Ramon Roseris [Ramon Roserio] (35; Single; born "abt 1875"), Mattress Worker-Factory, S.F., CA;

*Nellie R. Santiago (20); Married; born "abt 1890"), occupation: "none", District 45; S.F.;

*Santos Santiago [Santoo Santiago] (23); born "abt 1887"), Laborer-Street Work, S.F.;

*Edwald Sarno (53; Married; born "abt 1857"), Fisherman-Sea Vessel, District 45, S.F.;

*John B. Veles (15; Single; born "abt 1895"), Laborer-Odd Jobs, S.F. Assembly District 32;

*Raymond Vales (21; Single; born "abt 1889"), Gardner-Vegetables, District 32, S.F., CA;

*Sarafin Veles (20; Single; "abt 1890"), Laborer-Farm, S.F. Assembly District 32, S.F.;

All 29 of these "California **Pioneros**" appear in the 1910 Census as being born in "Puerto Rico" (22 of them), or in "Porto Rico" (7 of them). This is my attempt to distinguish the "California *Pioneros*" from the New York City "*Pioneros*" (see: Matos-Rodríguez and Juan Hernández 2001; López 2009b: 3-4). In short, the New York City "Pioneros" were, "those Puerto Rican migrants [immigrants] who established themselves in New York City between the 1890s and the end of World War II….", (Matos-Rodríguez and Pedro Juan Hernández 2001: see the "Back Page of this Book").

Further, among these 29 persons, 23 lived in the following five (5) San Francisco Census District(s): 32, 33, 39, 41, and 45; and with part of their address appearing as: "San Francisco Assembly, District 32", District 33, etc. Six of these 29 California *Pioneros* had "non-San Francisco" related addresses. In other words, this suggests that many of the first Puerto Rican immigrants (**after** the initial Group of *at least* 64 immigrants) to California tended to stay and live in the City of San Francisco, as opposed to moving to other Northern California areas, such as Santa Clara, Marin, Monterey, and Sacramento Counties (cf.: U.S. Bureau of the Census. 1913c: 149, 144, 148). Therefore, the foregoing clearly shows the beginnings of the evolution of the Puerto Rican enclaves and communities (*colonias*) in California, and specifically within the San Francisco Bay Area.

Puerto Rican Deaths in San Francisco, 1903 (of only: "Surnames from A –D"):

While the name of Cruz Candelaro does not appear in the 1900 Federal Census of California, his name does appear in the book entitled *San Francisco Deaths 1865-1905: Abstracts from Surviving Civil Records. Volume I, Surnames Starting with A – D*, (California Genealogical Society & Library. 2010: 222, (Bib. #357); *CaliforniaAncestors.org*). This book listed Mr. Candelaro as being 23 years of age at the time that he died in San Francisco in 1903, after having been born in Puerto Rico. Similarly, this book also lists a Valentine Cuotodis as having died in San Francisco in 1903, at the age of 40, and having also been born in Puerto Rico. The book did not provide the respective cause as to how either of them died (Ibid.: 359).

Finally, this aforementioned book (i.e., Volume I), consists of a:

"four volume set of books, with over 96,000 records, [and] provides an index to all civil records of death known to have survived the San Francisco earthquake and fire of [April 18] 1906…most records contain a wealth of genealogical information: sex, age (often in years, months and days), occupation, place of birth… Readers should also remember that the original records were handwritten and legibility therefore varied considerably. It was often difficult, for instance, to distinguish among the capitals L, S and T. A researcher might find Simmons rather than Timmons or Landers/Sanders…" ("Introduction", page V).

Further research needs to be done to review the other three volumes of this set which lists thousands of names, although the surnames **are** alphabetized. Since the set of these four books lists 96,000 names, thus, "on average", each book has approximately 24,000 names!

CHAPTER 17

1901: The "Year of Immigration" for the California Puerto Ricans in the San Francisco Bay Area

In addition to the aforementioned 29 Puerto Ricans that initially immigrated to the U.S. and settled in California in 1900, at least 27 other immigrants went to the United States throughout the calendar year of **1901**. Although 18 of them stayed in the immediate San Francisco Bay Area, the remaining 9 were distributed outside the San Francisco Bay Area, while still staying in California.

The 11th (and the last Group), to go to Hawaii from Puerto Rico first arrived in California in October 1901 (cf.: Rosario-Rivera. 2000; Camacho Souza 1984; Carr 1989: 145). Consider, however, that the newspapers, beginning as of January 1901 and up through October, 1901, may not have published articles as to how many "Puerto Ricans" actually stayed in California, or had not gone on to Hawaii during this time period. Dr. Carr identified this 11th, and last journey from Porto Rico as being "Group XI," which was the "final group recruited the first year" (Carr 1989: 91, 145ff.).

A review of the Census evidence left me with a combined list of 151 confirmed Puerto Rican immigrants living in San Francisco (120 + 31= 151) by 1910. They began establishing new roots within the larger San Francisco community, which in turn began California's, and the San Francisco Bay Area's, first Puerto Rican enclaves and communities.

The names of the 27 persons that immigrated to the United States and settled in California during the calendar year of 1901, and their respective occupations (if listed), as well as the City and County where they each lived, are as follows:

*Frank Ayalas (25; Married; born "abt 1885"), occupation: Laborer-Farm, S.F. District 32;

*Mercedes Ayalas (25; Married; born "abt 1885"), occupation: "none", S.F. District 32;

*Andrew Baros [Andrew Baror] (24; born "abt 1886"), Laborer-Merchant Vessel, S.F., CA;

*Josie Baros [Josie Baror] (23; "abt 1887"), Laborer-Merchant, S.F. District 45, S.F., CA;

*Angela Carras (50; born "abt 1860"), Laborer-Merchant, wife, District 32, S.F., CA;

*Antonia Carras [Antonia Careas] (16; "abt 1894"), occupation: "none", Roomer, S.F., CA;

*Dolores Cootes [Dolores Coates] (30, born "abt 1880"), occupation: "none", Alameda Cty., CA;

*Philip Cootes [Philip Coates] (26, born "abt 1884"), Laborer-Farm, Alameda County, CA;

*Genara Cruz (33; born "abt 1877"), occupation: "Blank", District 41, S. F., CA;

*Leonardo Cruz (23; born "abt 1887"), Laborer-Brick Layer [?], District 41, S.F., CA;

*Segunda Cruz (33 [45]; born "abt 1877"?), occupation: "Blank", District 41, S.F., CA;

*Thomas Keda [Thomas Peda] (22; born "abt 1888"), Laborer-on Farm, in Oneal, San Joaquin, CA;

*Anna Lopetoguis (25; born "abt 1885"), occupation: "none", District 45, S.F., CA;

*Mateo Lopetoguis (28; born "abt 1882"), Stevedor–Steamer, District 45, S.F., CA;

*Emilio Mascia (41; born "abt 1869"), Laborer-Farm Work, Monterey, CA;

*Raymond E. Milan (29 [28], born "abt 1881" ["abt 1882"]), ? , Maker-Factory, S.F., CA;

*Julis Molcado [Julio Melcado] (22; born "abt 1888"), Laborer, San Rafael, Marin, CA;

*Delfin Ortiz (35; born "abt 1875"), occupation: "Odd Jobs"-Laborer, District 41, S.F., CA;

*Mercedes Tuvarsi [Mercedes Tuzarri] (31; born "abt 1879"), Laborer-Street Work, S.F., CA;

*Gregoria Quinney [Quinonez] (24, born "abt 1886"), occupation: "none", wife, Santa Clara, CA;

*Vidal Quinney [Vidal Quinonez] (47, born "abt 1863"), Laborer-General, Santa Clara, CA;

*Tomas Quinones (27; born "abt 1883"), Laborer-Factory, Assembly District 41, S.F., CA;

*Victoria Quinones (23; born "abt 1887"), occupation: "Blank" here, District 41, S.F., CA;

*Mary A. Reid (10; born "abt 1900"), occupation: "none", S. F. Assembly District 41;

*Ramon Rodriguez (28; "abt 1882"), Shipscaler-Shipyard, S. F. Assembly District 37;

*Celia Waldnado [Celia Waldnado] (25; born "abt 1885"), occupation: "none", S.F., CA;

*Manuel Waldnads [Manuel Waldnado] (29; born "abt 1881"), Chair Worker – Factory, S.F., CA;

[Note: Waldnado is probably the name for: Maldonado]

CHAPTER 18

The infants and children of the first California Puerto Rican Immigrants of 1900-1901: The First and Second Generations

Related and Relevant Quote: An insightful quote from Edna Acosta-Belén and Carlos E. Santiago directly relates to those children of the first Puerto Rican immigrants from 1900 to 1910 that were born in either California, or Hawaii, and which is still relevant today, 112 years after December 1900:

"…the right question to ask would not be who is a Puerto Rican, but what does it mean to be Puerto Rican on the island and in the United States? What are the contextual historical, ethnic, racial, social, and cultural factors that shape the different identity constructions of Puerto Ricanness, and what function does identity play for marginalized individuals and groups, such as Puerto Ricans, in their relationship to the wider U.S. society? And last, what are the differences, including generational ones, and similarities in the ways Puerto Ricans from 'here and there' negotiate, construct, and assert their respective identities, both in relation to US society and the panethnic US Latino population?" (Acosta-Belén and Carlos E. Santiago 2006: 220-221).

Note that according to the 1910 Federal Census definition, children of Puerto Rican immigrants that were not born in Porto Rico were **not** listed in the U.S. Federal Census of California's figures as being Puerto Rican, i.e., they were not identified as being Puerto Rican, back in 1910. Notwithstanding this 1910 Census defined technicality, it is still noteworthy that in addition to the aforementioned 151 (120 + 31) names of the San Francisco County Puerto Rican immigrants, the Census data also listed several California born Puerto Rican babies and infants, i.e., the first children born to the very first California immigrants that arrived *en masse* from 1900-1901. These children constitute the emergence of **the beginnings of the first and second Generation.** (See: Exhibits 12, and 13).

The first baby to be born to these newly immigrated Puerto Ricans was actually born, *in transit*, on the way to San Francisco, a mere "twelve days old" before the December 14, 1900 arrival to San Francisco by the "Group I" Immigrants (See: *San Francisco Examiner*, December 15, 1900, the hand-drawn picture and the caption on page 2, (See also: Bib. #344). In fact, the *San Francisco Examiner* in its December 15, 1900 issue reported on the new Puerto Rican arrivals into San Francisco, and the caption underneath the drawing read (cf.: Exhibit 12):

"In a blinding rainstorm the fifty-two [i.e., *at least* 64] Porto Ricans who escaped from the slave drivers started on the long walk from Port Costa to Oakland…. Babies in arms---one of them a wee mite only twelve days old---were cuddled against their mothers' bosoms and given what shelter the few rags worn by the women could afford" (*San Francisco Examiner*, December 15, 1900: 2). [*Note*: Once again a newspaper gives *different numbers* for the number of Puerto Rican immigrants].

The unnamed baby, "was born on United States soil while crossing the continent," while his mother [Señora Guadeloupe] was in transit to California. Another column from this December 15, 1900 issue of the *San Francisco Examiner*, noted as follows:

"But the babies! Poor, pitiful, helpless, silent little children. One of the women had five of them, and the five didn't have clothes that would have sufficed to keep them warm.... An infant in arms, but a few days old, was wrapped chiefly in shreds and ends of the mother's clothes" (*San Francisco Examiner,* December 15, 1900: 2).

This same issue of the *San Francisco Examiner* reported that:

"Down at the Infant's Shelter on Minna street...is a delicate creature named Senora Miguela, is about to become a mother, and has a baby boy of two years. The other, Senora Guadeloupe, is the mother of five children, the youngest a babe of twelve days.... [Dr. E. Calderon stated that] Seven of the children were quite anemic and emaciated, suffering from intestinal disturbances, no doubt due to bad food---especially so in the case of the infants." [The newspaper article, unfortunately, did not identify the baby, either by gender or by its first name] (*San Francisco Examiner*. December 15, 1900: 6).

October 2016

A mid-20th Century description, i.e., "definition", of Puerto Rican "migrants" to the United States, as well a description of "2nd generation" Puerto Ricans within the United States, at least as of 1968, was put forth in an article wherein it indicated that:

"The term 'Puerto Rican migrants' is here used to mean persons born in Puerto Rico who are now living in the continental United States. These people, of course, are native American citizens [as of 1917]. Similarly, persons born in the continental United States with one or both parents born in Puerto Rico are referred to here as 'the second generation,' but are no more and no less 'a second generation' than are native Californians whose parents were born in New York," (Kantrowitz, Nathan, (1968). "Social Mobility of Puerto Ricans: Education, Occupation, and Income Changes Among Children of Migrants, New York, 1950-1960", *International Migration Review*, Vol. 2, No. 2, "The Puerto Rican Experience on the United States Mainland," (Spring, 1968: 53-72)). (see: http://www.jstor.org/stable/3092041) (Published by: The Center for Migration Studies of New York, Inc.). (accessed: 02/04/2010)

NOTE: For historical comparison purposes, see page 57 of the 1st Edition of my book here, for a description of Porto Rican/Puerto Rican immigrants (and migrants) in 1910 versus in 1968.

CHAPTER 19

Children and young adults of Puerto Rican Immigrants, who were born in Puerto Rico and also cited in the 1910 Federal Census for California – (Alphabetized by Surname)

Children Born in Puerto Rico and who Immigrated to California at an Early Age:

Note: All ages cited below, are from the 1910 Census enumeration date (April 15, 1910). Also, *Ancestry.com* listed the following persons as being born in either "Porto Rico", or in Puerto Rico---therefore, the two different spellings of the island will be maintained here (cf.: Exhibit 11):

*Thomas Baley (5), was born in Porto Rico "abt 1905," and lived with his mother, Irene Baley (21), who appeared to have immigrated in 1906 [The Census date was difficult to read]. They lived in "Eden Township, San Leandro City, Alameda County, California."

*Bollan Family: Luteria Bollan (7) was born in Puerto Rico "abt 1903." Antonio Bollan (7), was born in Puerto Rico "abt 1903," and they lived with their mother, Maltina (46), and with their older siblings, Bomitila (15) [Domitila?], and three others (but their names were illegible), and they all lived in San Francisco District 45. They immigrated in 1907.

*Miguel A. Cardona (13), born in Puerto Rico "abt 1897"; Erminnio Cardona (12), born in Puerto Rico "abt 1898"; Francisco Gonzalez (3) was born in Hawaii "abt 1907"; all three of these children were listed as the "Stepson" of Armando Rivera (40) and Maria Rivera (32). They all lived in San Francisco Assembly District 33. Armando immigrated in 1902, while Maria in 1907. They also lived with their "Brother in Law", Domingo Palmieri (19), and with their "Sister in Law", Lahenia Palmieri (18). Armando, Maria, Domingo and Lahenia all were born in Puerto Rico. Armando's "Occupation" was simply cited as: Factory.

*Angelina Contreras (12), was born in Puerto Rico "abt 1898", and lived with her parents, Julia S. Contreras [Julio S. Contreras] (56), and Carmen Contreras (50), in San Francisco Assembly District 45. Mr. Contreras was born in "So Am" [South America], and Carmen Contreras was born in Puerto Rico, and all three immigrated in 1904.

*F Corti (Age: un) ["baby Corti"]. The Census lists the baby "F Corti's" "Age in 1910" as being: "un" [unknown], although *Ancestry.com* also lists his "Estimated birth year" as being "abt 1910" and notes that the male "baby Corti" was born in Porto Rico, to unnamed Puerto Rican parents, and was living on Grant Street [avenue?], in San Francisco Assembly District 44, and "Relation to Head of Household" was Lodger.

*Estrada Family: Joe Estrada (10); Angel (9); Bernita (8); Justo (6); Ramond (3); Bernito (1year and 2months old), and all six were born in Porto Rico, and all lived with their parents, George Estrada (44), and Geniba Estrada (34), in Huntington Beach, Orange County, California, and both parents had immigrated in 1910. Two older siblings also lived with the Estrada Family, namely, Abel (18), and Amelia (16). Geniba was apparently born in: "Sp – Spanish" [presumably Spain?], while George Estrada (44), was born in Puerto Rico.

*Francesco Marcaro [Francesca Marcaro] (9), was born in Puerto Rico "abt 1901", and she lived in "San Francisco Assembly District 32", however, neither of her parents' names appears in the 1910 Census. It also shows that she lived with presumably her sister, Marie Marcaro (15), was listed as being a Servant, and had immigrated earlier in 1900. The census showed that Francesco was a Pupil at the Roman Catholic Orphan Asylum. (**Note:** Since they are orphans, they were not living with their parents and as such the parents' names were not listed).

*Irene Martori (10), born in Porto Rico "abt 1900", and lived with her parents, James (45) [also appears as: James Marton] and Jennie (42) [Jennie Marton], in San Francisco District 45. Both parents were born in Puerto Rico.

*William L. Pillon (9), was born in Puerto Rico "abt 1901", and lived with his parents, Arthur Pillon (43) and Carmen Pillon (26), in San Francisco Assembly District 33, and his parents immigrated in 1905. Carmen Pillon was born in Porto Rico while Arthur Pillon was not, while they both immigrated in 1905.

*Mary A. Reid (10), was born in Puerto Rico "abt 1900", and she lived with her mother, Annie C. Reid, in San Francisco District 41. The Census identified Mary A. Reid as being a "Stepdaughter." The census indicates that Mary A. Reid immigrated in 1901.

*Eveline A. Wharton (6), was born in Puerto Rico "abt 1904", and lived with her parents, Harold J. Wharton (36), and Alice A. Wharton (36), with both parents born in England. They all lived in "Redondo Township, Los Angeles County, Los Angeles, California." Eveline (6) also lived with her other siblings, namely, Harold (13), and two older brothers (whose names are illegible), and with a sister, Ellana L. (11), all of whom were **not** born in Puerto Rico.

CHAPTER 20

The names of infants and children, born in California of Puerto Rican Immigrant Parents, from 1900-1910: The Second Generation

Note: Unless otherwise noted, the race noted for children in the census were listed as white, i.e., with a "W". The 1910 Census, under the "Personal Description" column(s), had the enumerator list the "color or race" for *each* individual person.

*Maria Ayalas (4), was born in California "abt 1906" and she lived with her parents, Frank (25) and Mercedes (25), in San Francisco District 32. Both parents were born in Porto Rico, and they immigrated to the U.S. in 1901.

*Rosie Baros [Rosie Baror] (1 [year] 11/12 months old), was born in California "abt 1908" and lived with her parents, Andrew and Josie, in San Francisco District 45, both Andrew (24) and Josie (23) were born in Porto Rico. The Census identified Rosie's "Race" as: "Mulatto." The parents immigrated in 1901.

*Camilla Colon (2), was born in California "abt 1908" and lived with her parents, Manuel Colon (30) and Rosa Colon (22), in San Francisco District 45. Both of her parents were born in Porto Rico, and both parents immigrated in 1900.

*Colondre Family: Santiago Colondre (6), was born in California "abt 1904." Jesus Colondre (4), was born "abt 1906." They both lived with their parents, Giacento (20 [30]) and Angel (25), in San Francisco District 45, and their parents immigrated in 1900.

*Josie Comocha (1 [year] 5/12 mos. old), was born in California "abt 1908" and lived with her parents, Joe (27) and Francis (26), in San Francisco District 45.

*Farell Family: Manuel Farrell, Jr. (7/12 mos. old), was born in California "abt 1909." Elena Farrell (1 [year] 8/12 mos. old), was born in California "abt 1908", and they both lived with their parents, Manuel C. Farrell (29) and Ramona R. Farrell (19), in San Francisco District 45, with both parents having immigrated in 1900.

*Clara Gomez (1 ½ years old), was born in California "abt 1908" and she lived with her mother, Maria Gomez (23), in San Francisco District 41, with Maria (23) having emigrated in 1902 from Puerto Rico. Maria is married, and a "Lodger", while the census did not list the name of any husband; only Maria's and Clara's names were listed. Maria's "Occupation" was cited as being a: "Domestic/Servant."

*Mary Lopetoguis (5), was born in California "abt 1905" and lived with her parents, Mateo (28) and Anna (25), in "San Francisco Assembly District 45", and the parents immigrated in 1901.

*Lugo Family: Antonio Lugo (1 ½ years old) was born in California "abt 1908"; Carlos Lugo (5) was born in Hawaii "abt" 1905; Moncerret Lugo (3) was born in California "abt 1907," and they all lived with their parents, Ramon Lugo (24) and Angelia Lugo (24), who had immigrated in 1900, (see also under: "Babies Born in Hawaii", for Carlos Lugo (5) in this book).

*Martinez Family: Rosando Martinez (3) was born in California "abt 1907." Sengen Martinez (1) was born in California "abt 1909", and they both lived with their parents, Raymon Martinez (22) and Margareth Martinez (25), in San Francisco District 45; Raymon immigrated in 1902; Margareth was born in Mexico, and had immigrated in 1900.

*Medina Family: D Medina (5), R Medina (1 [year] 8/12 months old), and E Medina (4/12 months old) [This is how The Census cited all three children], and all lived with their parents, A Medina (33), and M Medina (27) [again, the Census names], in "San Francisco Assembly, District 45, San Francisco, California." Both parents were born in Puerto Rico; with "Year of Immigration: Un" [Unknown]. The "Race" for each member of the Medina Family was listed as: "Mulatto."

*Mendoza Family: Matilde Mendoza (1 [year] 3/12 mos. old), was born in California "abt 1909," while Ines Mendoza (5), was born in Porto Rico, "abt 1905." Angelina Mendoza was born in Porto Rico "abt 1906", and they all lived with their parents, Fresto Mendoza (30) and Necolora Mendoza (26), in San Francisco District 32 (Precinct 25), and both parents immigrated in 1900.

*Milan Family: Herminia Milan (4), was born in California "abt 1906." Laura Milan (2), was born in California "abt 1908," and they both lived with their parents, Raymond E. Milan (29 and Cecelia Milan, in San Francisco District 33. The parents immigrated in 1901.

*Modecai Family: Julia Mordecai (9), was born in "abt 1901"; Viviane Mordecai (6), was born "abt 1904"; Violet Mordecai (5), was born "abt 1905"; Bernice Mordecai (3), was born "abt 1907"; and Nanette Mordecai (1 ½ years old), was born "abt 1908," and all five (5) were born in California, and all lived with their parents, Robert (31) and Marie (26) Modecai, in San Francisco District 45. Marie Mordecai (26) had immigrated in 1900, and was born in Puerto Rico in 1884, while Robert was born in Scotland, and he immigrated in 1910.

*George Narez (3), was born "abt 1907", in California, and he lived with his father (who was born in Puerto Rico), and his mother, who was born in Mexico.

*Quinones Family: Narsisa Quinones (2), was born in California "abt 1908." Tomas Quinones (9/12 mos. old), was born in California "abt 1909" and they both lived with their parents, Thomas (27) and Victoria (23). The parents immigrated in 1901. [*Note:* that Elisa Quinones (5), was born in Honolulu [Hawaii] "abt 1905," (see also below: Elisa Quinones, under the "Hawaiian Born Babies" section)].

*Rein Family: Josephine Rein (2), was born in California "abt 1908" and lived with her stepmother, Mary Gusselo [Mary Gusario] (40), and stepfather, Philis [?] Gusselo [Phelix Gusarlo] (28). Rosalina Rein (1 [year] 3/12 mos. old), was born in California "abt 1909". Fredds Rein (0), was born in California "abt 1910". They all lived with their stepparents, in San Francisco District 32. Mary immigrated in 1902, and Philis [Phelix] in 1907.

*Rico Family: John Rico (1 [year] 4/12 months old), was born in California, and Arrelio Rico (7), was born in Hawaii "abt 1903", and they both lived with their parents, Joe Rico (24), and Josel Rico (34), in San Francisco Assembly District 45, (see below under: the "Hawaii Born Babies" section).

*Rivera Family: Armando Rivera (1 [year] 9/12 mos. old), was born in California "abt 1908." Amelia Rivera (6/12 mos. old), was born in California "abt 1909" and they both lived with their parents, Armando Rivera (40) and Maria Rivera (32), in San Francisco District 33. Armando immigrated in 1902, while Maria immigrated in 1907.

*Sanchez Family: Dolors?? Sanchez (2) [This is how her name appears], was born in California "abt 1908." Louise Sanchez (2), was born in California "abt 1908" and they both lived with their parents, Balenteni (25) and Maria (20), in Eden, Alameda, California.

*"**Baby Silva**" [This is how she is identified] (2/12 mos. old), was born in California "abt 1910" and lived with her parents, John L. Silva (35) and Jennie L. Silva (20), in San Jose, Santa Clara, California. Jennie was born in Porto Rico, and immigrated in 1904; while John Silva was born in Portugal.

October 2016:

In the book titled, *Immigrant Ships Transcribers Guild: SS Alameda*, Honolulu to San Francisco, April 28, 1908, it cites the following two passengers as being, Santiago Colondre (age 11, Male, Puerto Rican), "where Alien entered Insular Possession" and the Time entering Insular Possession", namely, in 1901, (accessed: 5/14/2010), (http://www.immigrantships.net/1900/alameda19080428.html), and Sarinto Colondre (age 65, Male, Puerto Rican), also arriving in 1901, (pp. 1-2). (cf.: page 105 of this Book, for the "Colondre Family" name).

NOTE: The "Transcriber's Notes" indicated that, "The spelling of these Spanish and Portuguese names is questionable in many cases", (page 2).

CHAPTER 21

The names of Hawaiian born children of
Puerto Rican Immigrants who lived in California in 1910

Background Information:

In some circles there has been some historical debate as to whether or not the Puerto Rican immigrants, who arrived in San Francisco from Puerto Rico in December 1900, were in fact "contract laborers". In short, a contract laborer is an individual whereby "the act made it lawful for any person over twenty years of age to bind himself 'by written contract to serve another in any... employment' for up to five years" (Schmitt. 1995: 3). Also, in an article regarding the Puerto Rican immigrants the *San Francisco Examiner* of December 24, 1900, definitely made it clear that they were in fact contract laborers, when it indicated that:

"Now, annexation caried [sic] over the sea our Thirteenth Amendment, the Geary Act and our laws against the importation of paupers and **contract-labor** dependents" (*San Francisco Examiner*, December 24, 1900: 2).

Consequently, it was the children of the initial Group --- there were 11 such Groups---of Puerto Rican "contract laborers" born in Hawaii, and whose parents then migrated from Hawaii, and then resided in California as of the April 1910 Federal California Census enumeration date.

Edwin Maldonado suggested that there was a direct relationship between the Puerto Ricans who were hired as contract laborers for Hawaii in 1900 and the eventual evolution of California's Puerto Rican enclave (and communities):

"For the study of Puerto Rican communities in the United States its [i.e., contract labor's] importance lies in the fact that it was through the contract labor system that Puerto Ricans were made aware of opportunities in the urban areas outside New York [such as the San Francisco Bay Area, and California in general]. The Hawaiian recruitment in the early part of the century resulted in the creation of Puerto Rican enclaves in California, the second largest state for Puerto Rican settlement from 1910 to 1950" (Maldonado 1979: 115).

Mr. Maldonado also insightfully pointed out that:

"...the pioneers who established these communities were contract laborers hired to work in the United States. These agricultural and industrial workers provided the base from which sprang the Puerto Rican communities on the mainland" (Maldonado 1979: 103).

It is important to note, according to Physician Herbert Gunn, M.D., that by December 1910, a total of *at least* 100 Puerto Rican immigrants had left the Hawaiian Islands plantations to return to California, and to the City of San Francisco, where Dr. Gunn's practice was located. Many of these families had children who were born in the Hawaiian Islands. Thus, Dr. Gunn, writing in the *California State Journal of Medicine* in 1910, pointed out that, "...These conclusions [about his medical examinations of the

Puerto Rican immigrants to San Francisco, CA] were reached after the examination of over 100 Porto Ricans who had taken up residence in California after leaving the Hawaiian Islands" (cf.: Gunn, 1910: 410; Gunn. 1906).

Further, according to the **1920 Census** publication in its chapter entitled "Porto Rico", cites 1910 Census "Native Population" figures for Hawaii. It listed a total of 17 persons whose Place of Birth was Hawaii (then considered an "outlying possession," of the U.S. along with Puerto Rico). Also, the 1920 Census listed a total of 192 persons of Puerto Rican parents who were born in Hawaii as of 1920 (U.S. Bureau of the Census. 1922: 1196, 1197; U.S. Bureau of the Census. 1913d: 23, Bib. #284).

Thus, the following names are of those babies and children who were cited in the 1910 Federal Census (for California) as having been born in Hawaii, of Puerto *Rican parents:*

*Marine Appacko [Marino Appacho] (8), was born in Hawaii "abt 1902," with both of his "unlisted" parents having been born in Puerto Rico. His "Relation to Head of House" was listed as: "Inmate," and the census page, completed by the local enumerator, had shown him as one of 50 "Inmates" of the following Institution: "St. Vincent's Roman Catholic Orphan Asylum of San Francisco for Boys," in San Rafael, Marin, California; and he is able to speak English.

*Carlos Lugo (5) was born in Hawaii "abt 1905", and his parents, Ramon and Angelia, had immigrated to the United States in 1900, and in 1910, Carlos lived in San Francisco District 33, (see: the Lugo Family, above).

*Bracela Malinos (7), was born in Hawaii "abt 1903," and lived with her parents, Bertro (24) and Bracela (24), in San Francisco Assembly District 45, with both parents having immigrated in 1910.

*Angelo Munise (4), was born in Hawaii "abt 1906." However, Frank Munise (2), was born in California "abt 1908". Alexander Munise (1 [year] 5/12 yrs. old), was born in California, and all three children (apparently) lived with Maltina Bollan (46), Oruagin Bollan (26), and with Bonice Bollan (22), in San Francisco District 45. [The census page did not identify the children's "biological parents"]. (*Note*: From a review of the census page it appears that the Munise children lived with the Bollan Family members, although this is not 100% certain).

*Pompella Ortiz (5), was born in Honolulu [Hawaii] "abt 1905," and she lived with her parents, Delfin Ortiz (35) and Fela Ortiz (26), in San Francisco District 41. Fela immigrated in 1900, while her husband, Delfin, immigrated a year later, in 1901.

*Elisa Quinones (5), was born in Honolulu "abt 1905," and she lived with her parents, Thomas and Victoria, in San Francisco District 41, (see above: "Quinones Family").

*Arrelio Rico (7), was born in Hawaii "abt" 1903," and lived with his parents, Joe Rico (24) and Josel Rico (34); with his younger brother John Rico (1 [year] 4/12 months old), born in California. (See above under the "Rico Family", in Chapter 20).

*Veles Family: Ramon Veles (4), born "abt 1906"; Ramona Veles (3), born "abt 1907"; and Teresa Veles (2), born "abt 1908", and all three were born in Hawaii and all lived with their father, Raymond Veles (21) and their grandmother, Natalia B. Veles (40) and widowed, in San Francisco District 32, with the parents having immigrated in 1900. They also lived with two older relatives, John B. Veles (15), and Sarafin Veles (20), both the brothers of Raymond Veles.

In contrast, the **1910 Federal California Census** listed a total of 17 persons who were born in Hawaii, and were also residing in Puerto Rico in 1910 (U.S. Bureau of the Census. 1913a: 585, Bib. #281).

CHAPTER 22

The "Racialization" of the San Francisco and California Puerto Rican Immigrants: 1900-1910

It should be noted that Hawaiian born babies of Puerto Rican immigrants, who were then living in California, also faced a potentially daunting future in that the level of **anti-immigrant** vitriol (oftentimes, race-related) in Hawaii was as bad, and perhaps more so, than it was in California, and the San Francisco Bay Area in particular. Specifically, in regards to Puerto Ricans, it is what Professor Victor M. Rodríguez identified as being the beginning of the negative, historic and race based, "Racialization of Puerto Ricans" during the very beginning of the 20th century (cf.: Rodríguez, Victor M. 2005; Rodríguez, Victor M. 1997: 233-273; Duany 2005: 535-544). **8/**

Anthropologist Jorge Duany, of the University of Puerto Rico, quotes writer Howard Winant for a definition of this "Racialization process" as:

"Racialization signifies the extension of racial meaning to a previously racially unclassified relationship, social practice, or group...." (Duany 2005: 535).

Professor Duany goes on to add that:

"More specifically, it ["Racialization"] involves imputing a heredity origin to certain intellectual, emotional, or behavioral characteristics of an individual based on group membership.... Such traits are supposed to be natural, involuntary, and fixed.... Racialization often entails minimizing historical, cultural, and linguistic differences among peoples from [for example] Latin America" (Duany 2005: 535).

Victor M. Rodríguez points out that during the first two decades of the 20th Century, the "process of Racialization" of Puerto Ricans in the continental United States became a reality (cf.: Rodríguez, Victor M. 2005: 71). Importantly, Dr. Victor M. Rodríguez suggested the connection between early Puerto Rican immigration to the United States and the "Racialization" of the Puerto Rican immigrants when he wrote:

"While America is a nation of immigrants, immigrants have been **racialized**, eulogized, and despised.... Historically, in this country, race, culture, and immigration have walked through overlapping paths. Racialization---that social and historical process by which individuals and groups are assigned a racial identity and status---has hinged on the interrelationship of ideas and practices about race, culture, and imagination" (Rodríguez, Victor M. 2009: 264). (emphasis added)

In contrast to the Puerto Ricans, albeit more than a half century after the initial arrival of the Irish to America, the Irish eventually became "white", (cf.: *How The Irish Became White*, by Noel Ignatiev, 1965: 59. Routledge: New York). Mr. Ignatiev writes that: "In this chapter I have tried to suggest that, while the white skin made the Irish eligible for membership in the white race, it did not guarantee their admission; they had to earn it."

Finally, Victor M. Rodríguez therefore posited that Puerto Ricans in the United States became, "'racialized' (treated as other than white)...." (Rodríguez, Victor M. 1997: 267, n. 10.).

A concrete historical example of the racialization of the new Puerto Rican immigrants is represented in a newspaper column from 1900. Reporting from Los Angeles on December 13, 1900, or just one day *before* the Puerto Rican immigrants arrived in San Francisco, CA on December 14, 1900, the article in the *San Francisco Chronicle* contained the following "racialized" description of the coming Puerto Rican immigrants in its article, "Porto Ricans Take Flight...", in that:

"The Porto Ricans arrived in Los Angeles this afternoon en route to their destination in Hawaii. They are an unpresuming [illegible] looking lot. In **color** they range from a sallow yellow to jet black, some with straight hair and others with the **kinky wool of the full-blooded African**" (*San Francisco Chronicle*, Dec. 14, 1900: 4, 1). (emphasis added)

Another "racialized" example appeared in the *San Francisco Examiner* on December 14, 1900:

"Be they slaves or free men, the 114 Porto Ricans that arrived in Los Angeles this afternoon en route to their destination...are a disreputable lot. Through Don Nicolo Queirolo as interpreter the 'Record' learned some facts from the **dark people** [i.e., the Puerto Ricans]" (*San Francisco Examiner*, December 14, 1900: 1). (emphasis added)

Not only were the Puerto Rican immigrants racialized in California, but within just two days of their arrival in **Hawaii** on December 23, 1900, *The Honolulu Republican* (Honolulu, T.H.), described the most recent immigrants in a rather derogatory, and racialized, manner. For example, this newspaper reported that:

"The addition to Hawaii's population of these illiterate and degraded people is a menace to the future of the Territory. Hawaii wants thousands of settlers to come here and come as quickly as possible, but with the **mixed races** already here what she needs now is intelligent American laborers. The Porto Ricans are as undesirable a class as could be scraped up any where [*sic*] on the face of the earth and yet they are among the best from that [country?]. Being of **mixed Indian, Negro and Spanish blood** they constitute about the worst element of society ever introduced to these Islands, and God knows some pretty bad specimens were introduced under the old contract labor system" (*The Honolulu Republican*. December 25, 1900b: 4). (emphasis added)

Another example appeared in a dispatch column from San Francisco in the Hawaiian published newspaper, *The Pacific Commercial Advertiser*, which began to ascribe negative characteristics to those Puerto Ricans that decided to stay in San Francisco, and not continue their long and arduous journey to work in the plantations in Hawaii. Thus, they reported that:

"Some of the Porto Ricans who arrived in San Francisco Friday in a destitute condition, after having [been] prevailed upon to refuse to go to the Hawaiian Islands to work on the sugar plantations, were taken to the Almshouse yesterday, where they will receive temporary care....and they have become **public charges**" (*Pacific Commercial Advertiser*. December 27, 1900: 3).

The *Advertiser* went on to report on the letter written "by one of the most influential men in sugar plantation circles...Lorrin A. Thurston, ex-Judge and ex-Attorney-General of the Hawaiian Islands" wherein Mr. Thurston wrote:

"...the Porto Ricans, who were being imported for work on the sugar plantations of Hawaii...that the Porto Ricans were to be offered by R. A. MacFie, in behalf of the Hawaiian planters, the following inducements to leave their homes and settle in Hawaii: Free passage to Hawaii for themselves and families, $20 a month wages with free residence, fuel, water and medical assistance for three years or any portion thereof that they might Work" (*Pacific Commercial Advertiser*. December 27, 1900: 3).

The Puerto Ricans continued to be racialized in the Hawaiian newspapers, even though they had been working on the plantations for less than one year. For example, the *Advertiser* reported that, "the recruiting agents have orders to enlist no Spaniards and no pure black people are taken, the idea being, presumably, to have the men marry Hawaiian women and thus lose their identity with Porto Rico" (*Pacific Commercial Advertiser*. April 19, 1901: 5).

Also, the *Pacific Commercial Advertiser*, reporting in their August 12, 1901 issue referencing a Colonel Lake, wrote that:

"There is one thing, however, that employers of Porto Ricans should bear in mind. The customs of the people there were, until the United States assumed control, the opposite to the customs in any well regulated community of **white**; their moral standard was far below ebb and if employers will remember that discipline was not in their curriculum at home and that they must be brought up to a realization of it by degrees, the result will be more satisfactory. In other words, until the Porto Rican gets accustomed to his surroundings ***he must be treated like a child***" (Pacific Commercial Advertiser. August 12, 1901: 1; *cited in*: Arroyo. 1977: 85-86). (emphasis added)

The March 1903 issue of the *Pacific Commercial Advertiser* newspaper probably encapsulated the racial animus that was being perpetuated by some of the newspapers of the day (the "mass media of their day") when they emphasized, and perpetuated, the "fear factor" of the Puerto Rican immigrant, by reporting the following:

"In fact, when any crime is committed now whose author is at all in doubt, the police begin by instinct to *look for the Porto Ricans*. The story, therefore, is one--- that has two sides to it---and the side of the Porto Ricans is probably not the most injured side" (*Pacific Commercial Advertiser*. March 8, 1903: 1). (emphasis added)

A latter example came from the *San Francisco Call* newspaper of August 16, 1906, which had an article relating the "anti-immigrant" comments of a judge in Honolulu, Hawaii, when it reported on the Judge's inflammatory and "race-related" language, in that the:

"Hon. W.J. Robinson, Third Judge of the First Circuit Court of Hawaii, and formerly of Oakland [CA], is in trouble through a criticism made of the immigration policy that has been in force here, in which he characterized the Portuguese, **Porto Ricans**, Koreans and Molokans as 'alien pauper laborers', in many instances social pariahs, moral lepers and religious fanatics in the country from which they hail, reared and fostered in lands and under governments to which the American form of government is an anomaly, possessing no intellectuality and but little intelligence'" (*San Francisco Call*. August 16, 1906: 1). (emphasis added)

Maybe this quote begins to partially explain why a number of Puerto Rican immigrants that initially emigrated from Puerto Rico during the first decade of the 20th Century (1900-1910), decided to leave Hawaii, and return back to California, from where they departed for Hawaii initially. Further research may be needed here.

It should be noted that the historical Hawaiian concerns regarding the ever increasing influx of **foreign**

immigrants to the then Kingdom was expressed, at least as early as 1882, in the publication entitled *Biennial Report of the Attorney General to the Legislative Assembly 1882,* when it reported that:

"Owing to the large increase of the foreign population and the growth of the material interests of the Kingdom....there have been 13,274 arrests made during the past two years. Permit me to call the attention of Your Excellency [Reign of His Majesty Kalakaua] to the large increase of the foreign element in our midst. The increase from 1872 to 1881, as per Custom House Statistics, is no less than 19,333. These are of different **nationalities**, and most of them are of the laboring class, and to control these people and keep them in subjection to the laws of the Kingdom requires a Police Force of men who are to be depended upon in every emergency" (Hawaii Attorney General. 1882: 12, 13).

Similarly, the 1884 *Biennial Report of the Attorney General* expressed their concerns with the ever increasing numbers of Chinese immigrants to the Kingdom when it reported that:

"The Chinese: Another matter of Paramount importance is the influx and status of an element of residents on these [Hawaiian] islands whose presence has been a political anomaly everywhere on [the] globe except in their own country, the Chinese. There is no necessity for eulogizing the industry and thrift of some nor condemning the vice and lawlessness of others. From a purely political and dispassionate view it can be safely said that they do not form an element of residents much less citizens which strengthen the Kingdom internally or outwardly.... They are among us, an alien colony and no more. They carry their Chinese wall with them to every place which they overrun" (Hawaii *Attorney General*. 1884: 3, 4).

Note that this above cited 1884 *Biennial Report* provided a Table wherein it identified the number of men that were employed on several Sugar Plantations among the different nationalities which had been recruited earlier to the Kingdom of Hawaii as of the early 1880s. Thus, this Report identified the nationality numbers for the plantation laborers for: Hawaiians; Portuguese; Norwegians; Germans; South Sea Islanders; Chinese; American; British; and for Other Nationalities (Hawaii Attorney General. 1884: 14).

Additionally, the racialization of the Puerto Rican immigrant continued to be an ongoing historical process. For example, at least as early as 1905, West coast newspapers published articles equating the Puerto Rican immigrants to the spread of hookworm disease in the San Francisco Bay area, while failing to acknowledge and emphasize this economically-caused and related health condition (cf.: Bib. #316, p. 123). In June 1905, the *Los Angeles Times* had the sensational headline: "Porto Ricans Are Menace. Bringing Disease Into California via Hawaii." The article went on to indicate that:

"At a meeting of the State Board of Health today Dr. Martin Regensburger of San Francisco, the [State Board's] president, called attention to the fact that a large number of Porto Ricans are coming to this State [California] via Honolulu, bringing with them a disease scientifically known as uncinariasis. It is commonly known as 'hook worm' disease, and a report read to the board showed that 80 per cent of the population of Porto Rico is afflicted with it. The Porto Ricans were engaged in work on the sugar plantations of Hawaii **and over 1000 of them have come to California by way of Honolulu** during the past two years. Nearly all of them have the disease, which is contagious" (*Los Angeles Times*. June 25, 1905: 13**).** (emphasis added)

Finally, Physician Herbert Gunn, M.D., equated an economically-related health condition [i.e., it is more usually found in "economically poorer countries", and people from the tropics], namely, hookworm, among the Puerto Rican immigrants, to their "race" in an article that appeared in the *San Francisco Chronicle* newspaper in November 1906, which had the rather disturbing and damaging [for the

Puerto Ricans immigrants] headline: "Porto Ricans Menace Health: Dr. Gunn Recommends Isolation of the Race in Other Camp Localities," when Dr. Gunn informed the *San Francisco Chronicle* that:

"[Dr. Gunn is] …strongly recommending the concentration of Porto Ricans, who are scattered throughout the various camps of the city [in San Francisco]…. Dr. Gunn gives the main reason for his recommendation the matter of sanitation, stating that these people [Porto Ricans] are largely diseased and a menace to the **white people** within camps [i.e., this is *after* the April 1906 San Francisco earthquake], and finally to the city….water and air can become contaminated by their presence…it is strongly advisable to have these people isolated…. About 500 Porto Ricans are living in the city, 200 of whom are at Lobos square" (*San Francisco Chronicle.* 11/17/1906: 7; Bib. #321, #323, #353).

Vázquez pointed out that *Uncinariasis* ("hookworm disease") was the seventh leading cause of death **in Puerto Rico** in 1907, out of the top ten causes, and **not** among the top ten causes in 1913, with 919 deaths in 1913 (Vázquez. 1964: 253, Table 112, 113).

A Health-related Explanation for the Racially-tinged
Belief of "Laziness" Toward the Puerto Rican Laborers:

Importantly, and ironically, only one year later in 1907, the U.S. Department of Labor, in their report entitled *Commercial Porto Rico in 1906*, reported why the Puerto Rican laborer in Puerto Rico [and by extension, in Hawaii and in California], was oftentimes cited for "laziness", but that this "laziness" was directly caused by a wide-spread, and serious, **health problem** on the Island, and that this condition was now known in 1907:

"… that the 'laziness' of which the Porto Rican population was accused is mostly due to conditions of health. Ninety per cent of the laborers [in Puerto Rico] were until recently infected with a parasite called '**Uncinaria Americana**,' the most prominent effect of which is a profound anaemia, leading to a general depression and inability to bear exertion. This discovery was made by Dr. Bailey K. Ashford, assistant surgeon, United States Army, while he was post surgeon in Ponce, shortly after the hurricane in 1899."

This 1907 *Report* went on to point out that:

"As the disease had previously been studied in **Europe**, the means for its prevention and cure were well known, and were applied in Porto Rico with such signal success that practically all the cases treated were cured. The success attained by Doctor Ashford led to the appropriation of $5,000 by the insular legislature in 1904 for an 'Anemia commission'…. The commission had ample opportunity *to disprove the alleged laziness of the Porto Rican laborer, for they frequently found men working in the fields who in other countries would have been considered unable to perform labor.…* The legislature is disposed to be generous to this work [the eradication of this dreaded, and debilitating] disease, for it means nothing less than the physical regeneration of a million people" (see: U.S. Department of Commerce and Labor. 1907: 10). (emphasis added)

However, notwithstanding the scientific evidence for the medically-based so-called "Puerto Rican laziness", the "racialization of Puerto Ricans" in Hawaii continued in 1906 as evidenced by the *New York Times* article, in their Sunday edition, of February 18, 1906, which reported [incorrectly] that "…10,000 Porto Ricans, [were] imported [to Hawaii]", and that "the Porto Ricans have been scarcely less vagrant, and morally are worse than the Japanese. American negroes [Negroes] cannot be imported because of the strong social antipathy with which the native Hawaiians regard them" (*New York Times.* February 18, 1906: 1). [Talk about the historical tactic of "pitting" one "ethnic/racial group" against another!]

A further example as to how some newspapers of the day "racialized" Puerto Ricans (along with what would be called today, the other "non-white ethnic groups", and/or "people of color") was epitomized by a major full two-page article in their June 1907 issue with the condescending, and "racialized" headline of: "Under Our Flag: Throughout The World – Uncle Sam's White, Brown, and Black Children" (*San Francisco Call*. June 30, 1907: 4-5), and it went on to report that (cf.: Bib. #164):

"The vanishing race which once populated the Hawaiian Islands will soon be replaced by a type made up of a conglomeration of Chinese, Japanese (natives) and **Porto Ricans**, thousands of a low class of these peoples having immigrated to these delightful islands as laborers on the sugar plantations, with the inevitable result of leaving permanent traces of their presence in the generation now growing to manhood."

This June 30, 1907 article went on to report that:

"The people indigenous to **Porto Rico** and Cuba to all intents and purposes form an integral part of the United States and are, nominally at least under its protection. In both islands the native population is a mixture of every race, slave or free, from the Carib to the African, who ever set foot on their shores. They are the lowest in the scale of civilization and, in the opinion of United States army officers, inferior to the American negro [Negro] in every attribute [once again an example of pitting one "race" against another!].... Anemic, without ambition, brutish in habit and morals, degraded by a common admixture of degenerate races, there appears to be no future for the native of these productive islands. What civilization can do remains to be proved" (the *San Francisco Call*. June 30, 1907: 4-5). (emphasis added)

Finally, at least as late as 1910, the *Los Angeles Times* newspaper published another article, again with a rather sensational headline of "Death Lurks In Soil", regarding Porto Rican immigrants when it reported that:

"In an examination we have been making of some **1500 Porto Ricans** that live around San Francisco Bay, over 50 per cent are found to have the disease [hookworm disease].... It is primarily a rural disease and is transmitted by contact with the soil by those who go barefooted or have holes in their shoes [namely, the economically poor in society]" (*Los Angeles Times*. April 21, 1910: 15; see also: *New York Times*. June 24, 1905 and the *New York Times*. December 27, 1910 - or in the "Bibliography Addendum" section, Bib. #323, and #324).

June 2016: For an historical analysis, and connection, between "white European", and "non-white" immigrants (or what is today oftentimes referred to as: "people of color") to the United States covering well over a 100 year period, see a 2015 article, namely: "A Call for the Racialization of Immigration Studies: On the Transition of Ethnic Immigrants to Racialized Immigrants", (by Rogelio Saenz and Karen Manges Douglas, *Sociology of Race and Ethnicity*, Vol. I(I): 166-180). In short, and relevant for this chapter is as follows:

"That Jews, Italians, and Poles eventually came to be defined as white does not mitigate their racialization for immigration purposes. Garland (2014) points out that scholars are undecided about when Southern and Eastern Europeans officially became 'white.' What is clear, however, is that over time, the color line between nonwhites---Asians, blacks, and Mexicans [oftentimes Puerto Ricans]---and whites became more important than the division between old and new European immigrants," (page 168). "...Over the last half century we have seen the increasing racialization of immigrants, especially Mexicans [and probably Puerto Ricans, as well] and other Latinos, but also after 9-11 Middle Eastern people as well," (page 176).

CHAPTER 23

San Francisco County and the Puerto Rican Population: "Pre" and "Post" 1906 San Francisco Earthquake Relief

Pre-1906 San Francisco Earthquake and Puerto Ricans:

No sooner had the Puerto Ricans arrived in Hawaii on December 23, 1900 when one Hawaiian newspaper represented them in a most negative, if not "racist" manner (at least by today's standards). The newspaper *The Honolulu Republican* on December 25, 1900, in their column titled: "Stop Such Methods", reported that [Note: see immediately below - Here I am going to repeat a quote which I earlier used in Chapter 22]:

"The addition to Hawaii's population of these illiterate [it was referring to the new Puerto Rican immigrants!] and degraded people is [*sic*] a menace to the future of the [Hawaiian] territory. Hawaii wants thousands of settlers to come here and come as quickly as possible, but with the mixed races already here what she needs now is intelligent American laborers. The Porto Ricans are an undesirable a class as could be scraped up where any where [*sic*] on the face of the earth and yet they are among the best from that Land. Being of mixed Indian, Negro and Spanish blood they constitute about the worst element of society ever introduced to these [Hawaiian] islands, and God knows some pretty bad specimens were introduced under the old contract labor system." (*The Honolulu Republican*. December 25, 1900b: 4).

It should be noted that as of December 1902, the Puerto Ricans who arrived in Hawaii exactly two years earlier, in a meeting conducted in Honolulu, began to formally complain of their dissatisfaction with their working conditions in Hawaii. For example, the *San Francisco Chronicle* had the following headline, "Porto Ricans Anxious to Leave for Home. Will request President and Congress to Arrange Transportation from Hawaii." The newspaper reported that:

"...many were in favor of demanding that the [Hawaiian Sugar] planters who had brought them here return them to their native land. It was finally decided to ask the United States to provide transportation for all Porto Ricans who want to go back to Porto Rico.... It is said that a majority of the Porto Ricans here would like to go back to Porto Rico." (*San Francisco Chronicle*. December 9, 1902: 3).

It should also be noted that oftentimes newspaper articles, or dispatches, which were reported in the Hawaiian published newspapers, would also at the same time be reported in several of the San Francisco newspapers as well, and vice versa.

Similarly, the *New York Times* in an earlier article of August 1902, reported on the adverse conditions that the Puerto Rican immigrants in Hawaii suffered from:

"In a letter to a newspaper here the rev. S. E. Bishop, one of the oldest American settlers in Honolulu, gives **a pitiful account** of the fate of **thousands** of Porto Ricans who were shipped to Hawaii in the last year or two to supply labor on sugar plantations. The Porto Ricans are said to be extremely anxious to return to their old home [Puerto Rico]. They complain of **ill-treatment** by the overseers of the Plantations and the conditions under which they are made to labor" (*New York Times.* August 30, 1902: 8). (emphasis added)

The *Los Angeles Times* of December 15, 1904, in a news dispatch directly from San Francisco, had the rather sensational and disturbing article titled, "Porto Ricans Destitute. Five Hundred Helpless in San Francisco," which reported that there were 500 Puerto Ricans who were "destitute and near starvation", in the narrow streets of Telegraph Hill, in San Francisco. This article went on to indicate that soon San Francisco [if not the San Francisco Bay area] will have "5,000 helpless people in a strange land."

This December 1904 *Los Angeles Times* newspaper article further reported that these Puerto Ricans were:

"…from the sugar plantations of Hawaii, where three years ago, 5000 Porto Ricans were taken **under contract** [Labor] to sugar planters. The **contracts** have expired, and the forlorn exiles have drifted back to this city [of San Francisco] without money or means of support" (see: *Los Angeles Times.* December 15, 1904: 3). (emphasis added)

Less than a year later, in 1905, another Bay Area newspaper, the *San Francisco Call*, published an article with the intriguing title of, "Porto Rican Colony Of This City". This article pointed out that, "there are in San Francisco to-day 600 native Porto Ricans still waiting. Crowded together in a district of not more than five blocks radius…" [i.e., in a Colony, or a *Colonia*; cf.: Sánchez Korral 1994b] (See also: the *San Francisco Call.* May 28, 1905: 1).

Also, at least as early as 1905, the Puerto Ricans that had initially immigrated to Hawaii began to leave Hawaii due to their dissatisfaction with their employment situation(s) in Hawaii and then began to migrate to California in general, and to the San Francisco Bay area in particular. Thus, during the Eighth Annual Convention of the Nurses' Associated Alumnae of the United States, held on May 4th and 5th, 1905, it was reported to the Convention that:

"Since last October Miss Kane's energy has been used in the care of the Porto Ricans. A large colony of these people was imported from Porto Rico by the sugar planters of the Hawaiian Islands. The contract to pay the Porto Ricans a fair amount of wages for their labor was never kept, so with the hope of bettering themselves they keep coming from Hawaii to our city [*i.e.,* to San Francisco]" (The Proceedings of the Eighth Annual Convention (of the: Nurses' Associated Alumnae of the United States). 1905: 762). (see: Google books)

Of the 342 Puerto Ricans that resided in California as of the 1910 Census, further research needs to be conducted to determine how many of these 342 had migrated from Hawaii to California, and how many initially came directly to California and stayed to live in California **without** ever going to Hawaii **initially** (if any); unfortunately these figures did not appear in the following *primary sources* which this author reviewed:

"Demographic Statistics of Hawaii: 1778-1965" (1968); *"Historical Statistics of Hawaii: 1778-1962"* (1962); "Hawaiian *Almanac and Annual For 1921"* (1920); *"Report of The Governor of Hawaii to the Secretary of the Interior 1921"*, U.S. Dept. of the Interior, (1921); *"Thirteenth Census of the United States Taken in the Year 1910: Statistics For Hawaii-Containing Statistics of Population…"* (U.S. Bureau of the Census. 1913d), and the *Eight* and the T*hirteenth Annual Report of the Hawaiian*

Historical Society (Hawaiian Historical Society. The 1900, 1906 editions, respectively).

However, this author has been able to obtain data/ figures regarding the number of Puerto Ricans that had resided in Hawaii, who then "departed" from Hawaii, to the [presumably West] "Coast", and they appeared in the 1916 publication entitled *Labor Conditions In Hawaii: Letter From the Secretary of Labor*, which listed that from 1911-1915 (to June 1915), there were a total of 267 "Departures" of Puerto Ricans from Honolulu, Hawaii, of which 267 males, 63 females, and 92 children, departed for the [West] Coast, for a total of 442 Puerto Ricans who had immigrated to the Coast [with most, if not all, probably migrating to California] (U.S. Bureau of Labor Statistics:1916: 64).

It should be noted that while this cited Table covered the time period from July 1, 1900 to June 30, 1915, it did not list any possible Puerto Rican "departures" to the West Coast during the time period of July 1, 1900 to 1910. Thus, this cited Table showed that there was in fact a decrease in *immigration* of the Puerto Rican population to Hawaii, with a corresponding increase in the *migration* of Puerto Ricans out of Hawaii during the overall period from 1900 to June 30, 1915 (*ibid.*).

***Post-**1906 San Francisco Earthquake and Puerto Ricans:*

All immigrants, including "non-European ethnic immigrants", like the Chinese and the Puerto Ricans (who were considered "non-white") and whom were living in San Francisco during this time, were affected by the April 18, 1906 San Francisco Earthquake which devastated the city in general. The great fire that resulted from the earthquake took out much of the downtown area, "destroying 490 city blocks" (House and Bradley Steffens 1989: 42, 14-15). However, it is noteworthy that the **Relief Corporation** set up in San Francisco to help and assist the people of San Francisco after this earthquake, specifically identified the Puerto Rican colony (or enclave) as being in particularly dire straits. Thus, the October 20, 1906 edition of the *San Francisco Call*, in their article, "Porto Ricans In Need," noted the following:

"The Relief Corporation finds itself with a Porto Rican problem on its hands. The Porto Ricans among the refugees have proved particularly helpless and hard to handle, so when an opportunity [was] offered to send a large number to their old home the corporation jumped at the chance. It now develops that those given transportation were in the main husbands and fathers, bread-winners of families. The women and children have been left behind. It is now up to the corporation to provide for the women and children, a job that presents many difficulties" (*San Francisco Call*. October 20, 1906: 3, 1; see also: Russell Sage Foundation. 1913).

What is noteworthy, relative to the size of the Puerto Rican population and community immediately after the April 18, 1906 San Francisco Earthquake is the fact that the weekly journal of the organization known as Philanthropy and Social Advance, dated October 6, 1906, reported that **only** one (1) Puerto Rican person (or possibly family) left San Francisco and returned to Puerto Rico after the earthquake (Brandt. 1906: 32). Thus, it appears that the Puerto Rican population continued to stay in California, despite the April 1906 earthquake. (**Note:** It should be noted that the 1913 publication by the Russell Sage Foundation (1913: 304, 67, Table 14), or seven *additional* years after the Brandt's 1906 article, listed 13 departures from San Francisco back to Puerto Rico in October 1906 (see the following page for a further description of this)).

Also, an article in a 1923 issue of JAMA: *The Journal of the American Medical Association,* written by J.W. Kimberlin, *M.D., (Nov. 17, 1923: 1685-1687)(Vol. 81, No. 20),* also referenced the Puerto Rican colony in San Francisco after the 1906 Earthquake:

"**After** the great fire [in 1906], a large colony of Porto Ricans were brought here to help the labor problem, and they were quartered on Telegraph Hill. Their social and medical problem was solved by the Associated Charities, and solved chiefly through the Fruit and Flower Mission Clinic" (Kimberlin, J.W., M.D. 1923: 1686). [**Note:** Unfortunately, Dr. Kimberlin did not mention from where the Puerto Ricans came from, nor how many were there.] (emphasis added)

Interestingly, the publication titled *San Francisco Relief Survey: The Organization and Methods of Relief Used After the Earthquake and Fire of April 18, 1906*, (Russell Sage Foundation. 1913: 223), listed a total of 27 Puerto Rican Applicants ("Foreign born applicants of each specified nationality") that received housing shelter via the Camp Cottages which were dispersed to at least the following nationalities: American (Native Born), 193; Irish, 127; Italian, 73; German, 55; Mexican, 52; English, 34; **Porto Rican, 27**; French, 15; "Other Nationalities", 66 (Total: 449). (cf.: This publication is available on google.books.com, or google books) [emphasis added]

Future researches may want to check out the following resource: "Minutes of Executive Committee San Francisco Relief and Red Cross Funds," San Francisco, Cal. November 16th, 1906, wherein it is reported that:

"A communication from **Dr. Herbert Gunn**, in regard to **Porto Ricans** living in various parts of the city [i.e., San Francisco], was received. Upon motion, it was referred to the Chairman of Department 'D' for investigation and report." [**Note:** A transcription of this resource is on the Bancroft Library's webpage. The Bancroft Library is at the University of California, Berkeley, CA 94720-6000. I obtained this brief reference via personal communication. See James D. Phelan papers: Committees, Clubs and Organizations; Oct. 2-Dec. 18, 1906; San Francisco Relief & red Cross Funds: Executive Committee. Local Call Number: BANC MSS C-B 800, Carton 13:03. (<http://bancroft.berkeley.edu/>)]. (emphasis added)

Also, the *San Francisco Chronicle* newspaper issue of December 19, 1907, made a brief reference to the Puerto Ricans still residing in San Francisco **post**-earthquake, when it reported that:

"These [Relief Corporation] cottages which have been stealing away south and north and west at the rate of sixty a day, represent many curious home adventures and new fortunes.... All races and conditions of people are in this migration, and the movement is not all to the suburban hills. From the northern ["refugee"] camps where Mexicans, **Porto Ricans**, Italians and Chinese have lived since the earthquake, the breaking up of this modern Babel has turned the alien people in many currents." (San Francisco Chronicle. August 19, 1907: 5). (emphasis added)

Importantly, the publication by the Russell Sage Foundation entitled *San Francisco Relief Survey* reported in 1913 that after the earthquake of April, 1906, "the **Porto Ricans** and the Russians lead in the number of those who had come to San Francisco after the fire, and these are followed in point of number by the Mexicans and the Spanish." (emphasis added)

This Relief organization also provided a Table entitled, "Persons Sent from San Francisco, by Period and by General Destination, April 26th, 1906, to June 1908" (Table 14), which listed a total of 13 Puerto Ricans in October, and 52 in November 1906, whom departed from San Francisco and returned to **Puerto Rico** (Russell Sage Foundation. 1913: 304, 67). (emphasis added)

Finally, of the total of 87 persons who were sent (back) to "Other Foreign Points", 65 of these persons were sent to Porto Rico (Russell Sage Foundation. 1913: 67).

CHAPTER 24

San Francisco, California: the 1910 Federal Census population figures for Puerto Ricans

Background Information: In 1954, Clarence Senior of the University of Puerto Rico wrote:

"...that Puerto Ricans were found in all but nine states in the 1910 census (North and South Dakota, Kentucky, Alabama, Mississippi, Idaho, New Mexico, Arizona and Utah). By 1920, Utah, Nevada, and Wyoming, were the only states without Puerto Ricans. The 1930 and succeeding censuses report Puerto Rican-born persons in all 48 states" (Senior. 1954: 94).

Dr. Senior illustrated the historical importance of California for Puerto Rican immigration and as a population center for Puerto Ricans for the first half of the 20th Century, when he wrote that:

"...the second largest state of Puerto Rican settlement from 1910 to 1950 was **California**... [with] **San Francisco** [being] rated second to New York as a residence for Puerto Ricans, in the 1910 to 1950 census counts.... The original settlers in San Francisco had been on their way to Hawaii.... To these [figures] were added those who went on to Hawaii and then returned to settle in San Francisco, Oakland and on farms in California" (Senior. 1954: 95). (emphasis added) **9/**

Several years later, in 1966, Clarence Senior and Donald O. Watkins summarized how the process of the development of the Puerto Rican community emerged during the first decade of the 20th Century in San Francisco when they wrote that: "The San Francisco community, the second largest in the Nation until 1950, also grew out of the Hawaiian [contract laborer] recruitment" (Senior and Donald O. Watkins 1966: 716).

As a result, the Puerto Rican immigrants who had initially gone to work in Hawaii, for whatever reason(s), oftentimes, would then migrate to San Francisco to seek employment there. Some scholars have suggested that many, if not most, became disenchanted with the working conditions (and possible promises that may have been made to them) in Hawaii [cf.: *San Francisco Chronicle.* Dec. 9, 1902: 3; *San Francisco Chronicle.* March 17, 1903: 3).

San Francisco County and the 1910 Federal Census:

San Francisco County only consists of The City of San Francisco itself. According to *AncestryInstitution. com* the 1910 Federal Census [database on-line] listed a total of 120 Puerto Ricans who were "confirmed and verified" by their respective name(s), and who were identified in the census as having been born in "Puerto Rico," and who were also living in the City of San Francisco, CA (cf.: Exhibit 11).

Importantly, *AncestryInstitution.com* also listed a total of 31 additional names that I confirmed and verified of persons listed as born in "Porto Rico", and who were also living in San Francisco as of the 1910 Census. Therefore, I was able to identify, by name, a total of 151 (120 names + 31 names)

Puerto Ricans in San Francisco as of 1910 (out of a Federal Census listing of 213 persons, or 70.9% of the total 1910 Puerto Rican immigrant population in San Francisco). San Francisco's Puerto Rican population constituted 62.2% of California's total of 342 Puerto Ricans listed in the 1910 Census.

This made the city of San Francisco's Puerto Rican enclave (and later on, a community) literally four times larger than the next largest Puerto Rican enclave in California, namely, Alameda County, which included the City of Oakland, CA. Alameda County had a total of 31 Puerto Ricans as of the 1910 Census, (see below for more specific information relating to the San Francisco enclave and the very beginnings of the nascent, but ever-growing, San Francisco Bay area Puerto Rican community). (See: *AncestryInsitution.com*)

One definition of an ethnic enclave is provided in the encyclopedia *Immigration in U.S. History, Volumel I* (2006), by Carl L. Bankston and Antoinette Hidalgo, who provided a definition of an ethnic enclave as:

"Isolated ethnic communities, free from contact from the majority population that is usually intended to maintain customs and traditions that are under attack by outsiders.... Ethnic enclaves are territories inhabited by a distinct group of people who are separated from the dominant population by differences in language, religion, social class, or culture and who are frequently subjected to prejudice and discrimination. An ethnic group has a shared history based on a sense of difference from others resulting from several factors, including a unique set of experiences (among them defeated in a war), skin color or other physical differences (such as height, or geography)" (Bankston III and Danielle Antoinette Hidalgo, 2006: 219-220).

This software generated list of "120 Puerto Ricans", listed in The 1910 Census (which I extracted from *Ancestry.com*) by their individual name(s), and who were also living in San Francisco in 1910, cited an additional 14 identifying "fields", i.e., the social characteristics, for *each* of the 120 listed persons, (http://search.Ancestry institution.com/cgi-bin/sse.dll?l), (Accessed: April 22, 2010), namely:

"Name"; "Age in 1910"; "Estimated birth year"; "Relation to Head of House"; "Father's Birth Place"; "Mother's Birth Place"; "Spouse's name"; "Home in 1910"; "Marital Status"; "Race"; "Gender"; "Year of Immigration"; "Neighbors: view other on page"; "Household Members."

Consequently, the 1910 Federal Census allowed this author to identify, up to at least 14 separate "social characteristics/variables", for each of the 120, or more, Puerto Ricans which the Federal Census Enumerators entered on the census form itself.

AncestryInstitution.com provides a historical context and descriptive explanation about the 1910 United States Federal Census, as follows:

"This database is an every name index to individuals enumerated in the 1910 United States Federal Census, the *Thirteenth Census of the United States.* In addition, the names of those listed on the population schedule **are linked to actual images** of the 1910 Federal Census, copied from the National Archives and Records Administration microfilm, T624, 1.784 rolls...." This new index [was] (released June 2006) (AncestryInstitution.com.1910 United States Federal Census [database on-line])."

However, that for each of the 120 individuals in the 1910 census, this database, or index, included a separate link which identified "Household Members" associated with each of these same individuals. Therefore, in addition to the original tracking of these 120 persons, one would then click on the link for every separate "Household Member" connected to each of the already identified 120 Puerto Ricans, which may increase the number from 120 to a probably higher number.

Thus, this added task requires additional research to undertake, calculate, tabulate, verify and complete. Some of these 120 persons had listed under "Household Members", literally, as many as 20+ individuals and separate names, where one would then have to separately click on each name, i.e., on their own individual separate links. Thus, further research would be required to be able to obtain any additional potential Puerto Ricans (by name) that were living in California at the time of the 1910 Census, which would then include, "non-Heads of Households", as well as the children of the immigrants who were not born in Puerto Rico, but instead, were born in the United States.

For example, Clalio Burtardes (also cited as: Olalio Curtardio) literally had a total of 29 separately named individuals cited under the section of "Household Members" (although not necessarily family-related)! One would have to "click" on each individual name to ascertain whether or not any of these 29 individuals either were: born in Puerto Rico themselves, and/or had a Puerto Rican parent, notwithstanding the fact many of the last names were not "Spanish sounding" names, so to speak. This additional research task, in short, would require searching literally hundreds of these names for those persons of Puerto Rican heritage which would have been living within California, as well as within the city of San Francisco, and the Bay area in general, in 1910.

CHAPTER 25

**The beginnings of San Francisco's Puerto Rican Enclaves and *Colonias*:
1910 Census Districts and Beyond till 1925**

This research has revealed that the City of San Francisco developed the first Puerto Rican enclave, i.e., an "ethnic neighborhood" or *Colonia* (Colony), within California, at least as early as 1905. A careful review of the 1910 Federal Census allows one to identify their specific location(s) within the City itself (cf.: *San Francisco Call*, May 28, 1905: 1, "Porto Rican Colony Of This City").

For possible historical comparisons relating to other working class Puerto Rican labor immigrants, albeit from the East Coast, the web site for the Historical Society of Pennsylvania had an appropriate article titled, "Early Enclaves," which described the development of the "early enclaves" of Philadelphia during the late 19th Century, consisting of Spanish-speakers, including "Porto Ricans". Specifically, the author wrote that:

"These labor immigrants remained invested and involved in the political struggles of their homelands. As early as 1865, Cubans and **Puerto Ricans** in Philadelphia jointly organized a local chapter of the Republican Society of Cubans and Puerto Ricans.... Spaniards and Cubans were the largest Spanish-speaking groups in Philadelphia at this time, followed by Puerto Ricans and Mexicans....A survey of Philadelphia's 'Spanish-American colony' conducted for the catholic Archdiocese **in 1910** reported that there were roughly 2,000 Spanish-speakers dispersed throughout the city ...64 of these residents were **Puerto Rican-born**...." (see the web site for the: Historical Society of Pennsylvania (n.d.) [no date]: 1; no author cited for this article). (emphasis added) (<**http://www.hsp.org/default.aspx?id=361**>)

An "Operational Definition" of an Ethnic Enclave:

Writing in 1993, Ramón Borges-Mendez, writing about the emergence of the Puerto Rican community in Lowell, Lawrence, and Holyoke, Massachusetts, provided at least one concrete operational definition of an ethnic enclave, or *Colonia*, when he wrote that:

"During the early 1960's (1960-1963), the nuclei of the Puerto Rican *Colonias* in Lowell, Lawrence, and Holyoke were formed predominately by families that came directly from Puerto Rico. Most of them, no more than 12-20 families in each case, were poor families, that had a rural background with little or no experience in manufacturing, and had a low educational attainment. In 1960, according to the U.S. Census, there were 43 Puerto Ricans in Lowell, and 28, and 99 Puerto Ricans in Lawrence and Holyoke respectively" (Borges-Mendez 1993: 8). **10/** Consequently, utilizing Borges-Mendez' "operational definition" as a guideline, my research and the review of the 1910 census data, identified several likely "Puerto Rican enclaves" within the San Francisco Bay Area. For example, there were **at least 77 Puerto Ricans** who lived within "San Francisco Assembly **District 45**, San Francisco, California." San Francisco also had two other emerging Puerto Rican enclaves, since 26

Puerto Ricans lived in "San Francisco Assembly District 32", while 17 Puerto Ricans lived in "San Francisco Assembly District 41." **11/**

The 1910 Census listed a total of 22,206 persons that lived in **District 45** as of the 1910 Census date and 31,879 persons who lived in District 32, whereas San Francisco County's population was 416,912 in 1910 (U.S. Bureau of the Census. 1913c: 149).

The San Francisco City Blocks that Constituted Census District 45:

The One Step web page of Dr. Stephen P. Morse, *et al.*, entitled: "Obtaining Streets within EDs [Enumeration Districts] for the 1910 Census in One Step (Large Cities)", provided a listing of San Francisco's city streets that composed Census District 45, back in 1910. (cf.: Morse, Joel D. Weintraub and David R. Kehs, n.d. [no date], "Obtaining Streets within Eds for the 1910 Census in One Step (Large Cities)"; National Archives Trust Fund Board. 1982: vii, 1-2; National Archives and Records Administration [NARA] 2010: 1-12)) (cf.: Exhibit 11):

Names of the streets constituting **Census District 45** were as follows:

24th; 25th; Alabama; Balmy; Berkeley Ave.; Columbia Pl; Garfield Ave.; Gunnison Ave.; Harrison; Lucky; Treat Ave., and Yolo [Street].

Names of the streets constituting **Census District 32** were as follows:

16th; 17th; 18th; 19th; 20th; 7th; Center; Georgia; Illinois; Indiana; Iowa; Kentucky; Louisiana; Mariposa; Michigan; Minerva; Minnesota; Mississippi; Napa; Pennsylvania; Santa Clara; Solano; Tennessee; and Texas.

Names of the streets constituting **Census District 41** were as follows:

22nd; 23rd; Berkeley Ave; Bernal; Folsom; Gunnison; Harrison; Howard; Kennebec; Nevada; Shotwell; Treat Ave.

A close review of the streets of Census Districts 45 and 41 shows that several streets overlapped, or were the same, e.g., Berkeley Ave, Gunnison Ave, and Harrison streets, suggesting that at least these two Puerto Rican enclaves were in close proximity to each other.

Consequently, these above cited San Francisco Districts, with a relatively high concentration of Puerto Ricans within their respective District borders, constituted the beginnings of the Puerto Rican enclaves (*Colonias*), or were in fact an ethnic enclave itself, such as Census District 45. They will, over time, form the future basis of the San Francisco Puerto Rican community, if they were not already so. Of course, further research needs to be done to uncover the specific nature, and parameters, of these early Puerto Rican enclaves within the San Francisco Bay Area. (**Note:** To connect the past with the present, cf.: *Historic Walks in San Francisco: 18 Trails Through the City's Past* by Rand Richards, which "will take you back in time as you follow 18 self-guided walks down city streets", including the Mission District, etc.).

One concrete evidence of an emerging Puerto Rican *colonia*, or community, in San Francisco, was dramatically demonstrated by the formal beginning of the first Puerto Rican **organization** in California on February 25, **1912**, or just two years after the April 1910 Federal and California Census were finalized.

It was called (and *continues* to be called to this day, in 2013!) the **Club Puertorriqueño de San Francisco**.

Thus, it was incorporated 100 years ago and it was **formally organized** on July 13, 1912. **12/**

This fraternal organization produced the following document called: *Constitución, Leyes y Reglamento Del Club Puertorriqueño De San Francisco, Organizado en Febrero 25 de 1912 É Incorporado según la ley Estado de California en Julio 13 de 1912*, San Francisco, California (E.U. de A.), (Club Portorriqueño de San Francisco. 1912a).

The Club Puertorriqueño de San Francisco had their first formal meeting on February 25, 1912, wherein they produced the "minutes" of this meeting. The "minutes" from their first meeting were written as follows [translated from the Spanish by Rosario Camacho] (Copies of these "Minutes" were obtained from the Center for Puerto Rican Studies in N.Y., N.Y.):

"Puerto Rican Club of San Francisco: Patriotic-Social Association. PROGRESS-FRATERNITY. Ordinary Session. Minutes Number 1.

In San Francisco, California, on the 25th day of February of the year nineteen hundred twelve, on a special meeting called by the members on the left [there were a total of 16 persons' names on the first page of these minutes], they agreed to:

1. To organize as a progressive organization with the purpose of following and capturing for its members all the progress and advancements possible and to work by all means possible to promote and maintain the progress and good name of Puerto Rico, the native land of all its members.

2. The organization will be known with the name of **Club Puertorriqueño** (Puerto Rican *Club*). It will be called *"de San Francisco"* (of San Francisco), because there are other sister organizations in other cities in the United States of America, which have a similar title. The phrase "Agrupación Patriótico-Social" (Patriotic-Social Association) will be added because it is a representation of its purposes, and will also add the inspiring words **"Progreso, Fraternidad"** (Progress, Fraternity).

3. The organization would only have a limited number of members not to exceed fifty gentlemen. [Note: Consider the historical times, and context, in **1900**]....

The "minutes" went on to say, in relevant part:

"7. On a motion by the President on the first steps to take toward advancement, they agreed to:

I. Write to the honorable House of Legislature of Puerto Rico through the <u>speaker</u> and to the honorable resident representative of Puerto Rico in Washington, D.C. informing: a) That, as San Francisco celebrates a great world exposition in 1915, the organization **Club Puertorriqueño** would appreciate if the people of Puerto Rico would not be the last to vote for a decent amount to support this luxurious competition with the rest of the civilized world that would be in this great Californian metropolis." (Club Puertorriqueño de San Francisco. 1912b: 1; the "minutes" from their first meeting).

The names of the sixteen persons that were cited as attending this first meeting are as follows:

Dr. [Don?] Ramón E. Milán; Mercedes Irizarry; Marcelino Martínez; Asiscio Torres; Manuel Bonilla; Mario Aponte; Natalio Rivera; Eusebio Rivera; Ramón Lugo; Evaristo Berríos; Jorge Medina; Juan Berríos; Enrique Berríos; Santos Santiago; Luis Santiago; and Ramón Rodríguez. Ramón E. Milán was listed as the: Presidente. (*Ibid.*: 3).

Organizado en Febrero 25 de 1912 é Incorporado según la ley del Estado de California en Julio 13 de 1912.

The following are the original minutes (verbatim), in Spanish, for the Club Puertorriqueño De San Francisco:

Club Portorriqueño de San Francisco - Ogrupación Porríco-social –

Progreso – Fraternidad. Sesión Ordinaria. Acta No. I.

En San Francisco, California, el vigécimo quinto dia del mes de febrero y <u>añoro</u> <u>domini</u> mil novecientos doce, reunidos por convocatoria en convención especial los señores que á las margen se expresan, acordaron.... (Club Puertorriqueño De San Francisco. 1912b: 3, 3-10). [**Note:** these selected above cited **brief** notes are hand-written, therefore, some of the words/spellings are somewhat difficult to decipher].

Most impressively, this organization is still in existence today, and continues to meet in San Francisco. In fact, they just celebrated their 100th year Anniversary in February 2012. Their current web site is as follows: <www.clubpuertorriquenossf.com>.

Their address is: 3249A Mission Street, San Francisco, CA 94110 (415) 920-9606.

The Club Puertorriqueño de San Francisco also issued a hand-written document/notes entitled: (*Progreso – Fraternidas. Sesión Ordinaria. Acta No. 1)* ("Minutes of their Meetings" in February 1912). (Club Puertorriqueño de San Francisco. 1912b; cf.: for a copy of the Club's 1912 documents, see: the Archives of the Centro de Estudios Puertorriqueños/Center for Puerto Rican Studies. Hunter College. CUNY, New York City).

The *San Francisco Call* newspaper of May 23, 1913 reported that there were **1,200** Puerto Ricans residing in San Francisco at this time; thus the need for the *Club Portorriqueño de San Francisco* (San Francisco Call. 1913: 4):

Ten years later, on November 3, 1923, the Puerto Rican newspaper, *La Correspondencia*, published an article about the Puerto Rican colony (*colonia*) in their article entitled: "*La Colonia Puertorriqueña en California*" [Translated as: "The Porto Rican Colony in California"] (cited in: History Task Force. 1982: 176).

This 1923 article in *La Correspondencia* reported, and was translated for this author, in relevant part, as follows:

"According to the correspondence we recently received last October 20, in San Francisco, California, a social meeting/gathering was held by a group of Puerto Rican residents of that state [California], honoring Santiago Iglesias and Muñoz Marín, whom were there to research the Puerto Rican community's labor conditions. More than two hundred Puerto Rican families attended this important event. The majority of these families **had gone originally to Hawaii, but later had moved to San Francisco**. According to Mr. Iglesias, the Puerto Rican residents in San Francisco, around twelve hundred, were found in an enviable economic position, compared to many of our compatriots who have not left the island...." (emphasis added)

Additionally, *La Correspondencia* published an article on October 12, 1925 regarding the "Club Portorriqueño de San Francisco", as well as on a second Puerto Rican social organization, the "Liga Portorriqueña de California", titled: *"La Colonia Portorriqueña de California cuenta con dos grandes so-*

ciedades que trabajan por el mejoramiento de nuestros compatriotas residentes allí". The "sub-title" of this article is: "El 'Club Portorriqueño de San Francisco' y la 'Liga Portorriqueña de California', son dos agrupaciones que hacen honor a sus fundadores." (Cited in: History Task Force. 1982: 183-186). Thus, these two Puerto Rican social organizations were founded to address the social and economic concerns of the ever increasing Puerto Rican population, and community, in California in general, and the San Francisco Bay area in particular.

Summary of one of the major research goals of this book:

Finally, this book focused on the Puerto Rican immigrants to California, San Francisco and Hawaii. Until 1925, there was a relative paucity of resources that listed the number of Puerto Ricans that left (migrated from) Hawaii to the West Coast (very likely to California) during the period from 1901-1925.

However, one such example was the government publication titled *Labor Conditions in Hawaii: Letter From The Secretary of Labor...For The Year 1915*, which listed a total of 422 Puerto Ricans under "Departures", as opposed to those who arrived, from Hawaii to the "Coast" between 1911 to 1915 (U.S. Bureau of Labor Statistics. 1916: 64).

Also, while listing departures from Hawaii to the "coast" from 1900-1905, it included the Puerto Rican population along with Portuguese and Spanish populations, with all three populations being combined under the "Iberian category"--- therefore, there were no individual breakdowns for the number of Puerto Ricans who departed from Hawaii to the West Coast from 1906-1910. Puerto Ricans were not listed, at all, during the period from 1900-1905 (U.S. Bureau of Labor Statistics. 1916: 64, see Table 17: "Statistics of Immigration, Honolulu, July 1, 1900, to June 30, 1915", page 64).

Thus, these 422 Puerto Ricans from Hawaii contributed to the ever emerging and expanding Puerto Rican population in California, i.e., the "Coast", after 1910.

The population of Puerto Rico according to the 1920 U.S. Federal Census listed a total of 1,299,809 persons who were residing in Puerto Rico as of the 1920 enumeration date (U.S. Bureau of the Census. 1920: 1, 2, 4, 1ff.).

The 1920 State of California Census shows that the California Puerto Rican population, according to the *1920* U.S. Federal Census, listed a total of 935 persons who were born in Porto Rico and who were residing in California as well. Also, the 1920 Census identified the following California Puerto Rican communities' (*colonias*) populations as follows: San Francisco – 474; Oakland – 101; Los Angeles – 39; Sacramento – 12; San Diego – 9. In contrast to California, the New York Puerto Rican population in 1920 was listed as being at 7,719 (c.f.: Table 1 in this book; U.S. Bureau of the Census. 1922: 630, 635, 640, 678, 679; U.S. Bureau of the Census. 1923: 294-295). Further, the 1920 State of California Federal Census shows that there were a total of 73 persons who were listed as being born in Porto Rico and who were listed as also being the, "White Population of Foreign or Mixed Parentage born in Porto Rico", with 100 listed as being the, "Negro Population Born in Porto Rico" (pp. 650, 640). The 1930 U.S. Federal Census shows that California had 1,795 persons that were born in Puerto Rico. (U.S. Bureau of the Census. *Fifteenth Census of the United States : 1930 Population Volume II. General Report Statistics by Subjects*. 1933. Washington: GPO).

Additionally, the New York City (N.Y.C.) Puerto Rican population (i.e., born in Puerto Rico) in 1920 was listed as being at 7,364 (Ira Rosenwaike. *Population History Of New York City*. 1972. Syracuse, New York: Syracuse University Press. Page 102) [although "Puerto Ricans were separately tabulated for Assembly Districts, 16, 17, 18, and 19 in Manhattan; see: page 192]. The 1925 N.Y.C. Puerto Rican population was listed as being at 6,681 (History Task Force. *Labor Migration Under Capitalism: The Puerto Rican Experience*. Centro de Estudios Puertorriqueños. 1979. New York: Monthly Review Press. Page 192). Finally, the N.Y.C. Puerto Rican population in 1930 was listed as being at 44,908, while the United States had a total of 52,774 (Rosenwaike. 1972: 121). However, according to Sánchez-Korrol, "...the New York State Manuscript Census of 1925, was coded and computed for 7,322 Spanish-surnamed individuals living in Manhattan's" 16th, 17th, 18th and 19th Assembly Districts" (Sánchez-Korral. 1983 [1994]: 5).

Finally, the 1920 Census shows that Hawaii had a Puerto Rican population in 1910 of 4,890 (U.S. Bureau of the Census. 1922: 1173, Vol. III, *Composition and Characteristics of the Population*). Hawaii in 1920 had a total Puerto Rican population of 5,602, while in 1930 it was at 6,671 (U.S. Bureau of the Census. *Fifteenth Census of the United States: 1930. Outlying Territories and Possessions. Number and Distribution of inhabitants....* (1932), Wash. G.P.O.; Page 48); while the United States in 1930 had a total of 52,774 (see: Bibliography #366).

October 2016 - For a demographic and statistical population profile of Puerto Rico in 1930, see the: U.S. Bureau of the Census. *Fifteenth Census of the United States: 1930, Outlying Territories and Possessions: Number and Distribution of Inhabitants...*, (1932). See the Chapter titled: "Population – Puerto Rico", (pp. 123-250ff.). The following topics, among others, are provided for Puerto Rico, namely, the - "composition and characteristics of the Population; Gainful Workers by Industry Groups; Unemployment; Occupations; Color and Nativity of Gainful Workers..., (p. 119).

For example, the population of Puerto Rico in 1930 was at 1,543,913, and in 1920 it was at 1,299,809, (p. 123). The overall "Illiteracy of the Puerto Rican Population" in 1930 (i.e., persons "10 years and over") was at 41.4%, whereas in 1920 it was at 55.00%, (p. 141). Table 13 is titled, "Year of Immigration of the Foreign-Born Population, for Puerto Rico: 1930", (p. 146). Table 18 is titled, "Women 15 years old and over in selected occupations, by marital condition, with a distribution of the single and unknown and of the married by age, for San Juan: 1930", (p. 200). Table 19 is titled, "Number and proportion of children 10 to 15 years old gainfully occupied, by sex, for Puerto Rico and for San Juan, 1910 to 1930, and for cities of 25,000 to 100,00, 1930 and 1920", (p. 200).

Ira Rosenwaike's book, *Population History of New York City* (1972) provided the following New York City (N.Y.C.) Puerto Rican population figures (over several decades), for example, for 1950 it was at 187,586 ("Puerto Rican Birth"), and an additional 58,720 ("Puerto Rican Parentage"), for a total "Puerto Rican population in New York City...[at] 246,306 in 1950 (3.1% percent of the City's population) and 612,574 in 1960 (7.9%)." He goes on to write that by 1970, "the Puerto Rican population in New York was reported to have climbed to 811,843 constituting 10.2 percent of the City's residents", ("based on 15 percent sample"). (pp. 138, 139, 198)).

In 1955, Fernando Sierra Berdecia (Secretary of Labor), presented a paper entitled, "Puerto Rican Emigration: Reality and Public Policy" wherein he pointed out that,

"From January 1945 to October 1955, a total of 429,747 Puerto Ricans have moved themselves into the United States, but the number of residents proceeding from Puerto Rico, of the first and second generations, is estimated at more than 600,000," (p. 5). (A paper read on December 10, 1955 to the Ninth Convention on Social Orientation of Puerto Rico, University of Puerto Rico, CIDE, Centro De Investigacion Demografica, Edited by: Office of Industrial, Labor and Public Relations, Department of Labor, Commonwealth of Puerto Rico, San Juan, P.R.).

CHAPTER 26

The Book: *Exodo Puertorriqueño:*
(Las Emigraciones Al Caribe Y Hawaii: 1900-1915)

I was made aware of a Spanish language resource book by Dr. Victor M. Rodríguez, namely, Carmelo Rosario Natal's, *Exodo Puertorriqueño*: (*Las Emigraciones Al Caribe Y Hawaii: 1900-1915*). San Juan, Puerto Rico. 1983). [at: CUNY Graduate Ctr. – Interlibrary Loan]

I determined, by reviewing the book's Contenido (Table of Contents), that its focus was on Puerto Rican immigration **to** Hawaii (see: pages 58-86), as opposed to California. For example, Chapter 5 was entitled: "¡Al Hawaii! ¡Al Hawaii!---(a) Antes De La Salida, (b) La Ruta. Chapter 6: "El Trabajo Y La Vida En Hawaii"---(a) El Trabajo, (b) Vida Contidiana Y Problemas Sociales.

What is definitely important, especially for researches of the Puerto Rican *diaspora* to Hawaii, is Mr. Rosario Natal's Bibliography (pp. 130ff.), as well as his listings of various *Spanish language,* and several English, "Periódicos" [a total of 18 overall]. For example, Mr. Natal references the following *primary resources*:

- *Ataña, La*, 9 de Marzo 1902;
- *Boletín Mercantil, El,* años 1900-1903; numerous sueltos de otros años;
- *La Correspondencia, La*, años 1900-1903, numerous sueltos de otros años;
- *La Democracia, La*, años 1900-1903....;
- *Puerto Rico Eagle, The*, 12 de Nov. de 1909; *Puerto Rico Herald, The,* años 1901-1903, etc.

Additionally, Mr. Rosario Natal's Chapters, as they specifically deal with emigration to Hawaii, are as follows:

Chapter 5: "¡AL Hawaii! ¡AL Hawaii! (a) antes de la salida (b) la ruta (pages 58-86)

Chapter 6: "El TRABAJO Y LA Vida EN HAWAII (a) el trabajo (b) vida cotidiana y problemas sociales (pages 87-115)

See also: Chapter 8, Apendices: (a) La condición: la version official; Department of the Interior Superior Board of Health; San Juan, P.R., Jan. 21st, 1901, wherein the Secretary and Treasurer of the Superior Board of Health of Porto Rico (this person's name is not cited in the book), strongly contests, and denies, the existence of any "starvation", and therefore, of any famine, in Porto Rico. This stated position is/was in dramatically stark contrast to what had been represented in the English language press of San Francisco, CA, as well as what I have represented in this book (see pages: 122-124).

Austin Dias posits that:

"... Puerto Rican scholar, historian Carmelo Rosario Natal...emphasizes the exile aspect in writing about the Puerto Rican immigration to Hawaii. He calls the emigration a 'labor exile' *(exilio laboral)*; he further describes the Puerto Rico of this period as 'a land or perennial emigrants' *(una tierra de emigrantes perenes)*" (Dias. 2001: 102, Bib. #356).

October 2016:

"The most important paper [newspaper in Porto Rico] of this time was *La Correspondencia de Puerto Rico* (The Puerto Rican Correspondence, San Juan, 1890-1943). This newspaper is considered to be one of the oldest and most important Puerto Rican newspapers and crucial for studying the immigration of Puerto Rican workers to Hawaii and other places....", (*Handbook of Hispanic Cultures in the United States: Literature and Art*. (1993), Edited and introduced by Francisco Lomelí, (Instituto De Coopercion Ibero Americana)) (see the section titled, "Puerto Ricans and Their Press", pp. 370-371, 360ff.). (see also: "The Spanish-Language and Latino...Periodicals" Chapter, pp. 360ff.).

For a digitized "primary source" document(s) relating to "Foreigners" in Puerto Rico (Porto Rico), see:

The National Archives, National Archives and Records Service, General Services Administration. 1972. "*Extranjeros (Foreigners in Puerto Rico), CA. 1815-1845, Roll 14, Maumene, Juan - Mutrelle, luis*", (National Archives Microfilm Publications, Microfilm Publication T1170. (Washington: 1972). Note: I paid the National Archives around $125.00 to purchase this resource from them, which consists of well over 1,000 separate images/documents/pages!).

Selective Spanish language contemporaneous articles from the Puerto Rican (San Juan, P.R.) newspaper, *La Correspondencia*: all of these articles are reproduced in the publication titled, *Sources for the Study of Puerto Rican Migration - 1879-1930*, History Task Force, Center for Puerto Rican Studies, 1982), namely:

"*Braceros a las Islas Hawaii ó Sanchvvich*", 31 de Julio de 1900;
"*Por qué no debe irse al Hawaii*", 9 de agosto de 1900;
"*Puertorriqueños que van al Hawaii*", 17 de deciembre de 1900;
"*Competencia al Hawaii*", 27 de febrero de 1901;
"*Causa principal de la emigración*"; 26 de marzo de 1901;
Emigrantes en Colón. Puertorriqueños descontentos. No más emigracion", 26 de abril de 1901;
"*La colonia Puertorriqueña en California*", 3 de noviembre de 1923
"*La colonia Puertorriqueña de California cuenta con dos grandes sociedadess que trabajan por elmejoramiento de nuestros compatriotas residentes allí*", 12 de octubre de 1925

CHAPTER 27

NOTES (Footnotes)

1. **Note:** To minimize confusion, this book uses "Puerto Rico" except for quotes from publications of the time, when it appears as "Porto Rico", the name used by the U.S. government between 1898-1932. Thus, "Porto Rico" and Puerto Rico always refers to the same Island (country). See below: for a brief history of Puerto Rico's name change.

Clara E. Rodríguez pointed out that: "The name of the island was changed [in 1898] to 'Porto Rico,' which remained the official name until 1932, when Puerto Ricans succeeded in passing legislation to return it to its original spelling, Puerto Rico" (Rodríguez, Clara E. 2001: 225-226). As the Chief of the Bureau of Insular Affairs pointed out in 1932: "Public Resolution No. 20 restores to the island the official designation of 'Puerto Rico.' This is the name by which the island was known during its 300 years under Spanish sovereignty" (War Department, Annual Reports. 1932: 14, 28).

At least as early as 1834, the name of the island was still referred to as being **Puerto Rico** as evidenced by the book entitled, *An Account of the Present State of the Island of Puerto Rico*, by Colonel D. Flinter (1834: London: Longman, Rees, Orme, Brown, Green, and Longman, Paternoster Row).

For an historical context of the name change of the Island, the *Military Times: Your online resource for everything Military* newspaper (?) [Date unknown] reproduced a copy of the **Treaty of Paris** of December 1898 which identified it as being a: "Treaty of Peace Between the United States and Spain; December 10, 1898." Therefore, it appears that it was in the *Treaty of Paris* that the name of the island was "officially" changed from Puerto Rico to Porto Rico. The *Times* indicated that the Treaty had a total of XVII [17] Articles. The relevant Articles from this Treaty, relative to Puerto Rico's name change, and for purposes of this book, are as follows:

"Article II. Spain **cedes** to the United States the island of **Porto Rico** and other islands now under Spanish sovereignty in the West Indies...." (emphasis added)

"Article VIII. In conformity with the provisions of Articles I, II, and III of this treaty, Spain relinquishes in Cuba, and **cedes in Porto Rico** and the other islands in the West Indies...all the *buildings, wharves, barracks,* [etc.]..." (<http://www.homeofheroes.com/wallofhonor/ spanisham/18treaty.html>; Accessed: February 25, 2012).

However, at a later time, a distraught writer sent an eloquent and poignant "letter to the Editor", appropriately titled, "Status of Porto Ricans", published by the *New York Times* in March 1903, when he lamented the name change for the Island of Puerto Rico. He wrote:

"We [the Puerto Rican people] seldom complain or air our troubles. The name of the island Puerto Rico, was used over three hundred years ago, and without questioning how dear and sacred it is and was to the natives, how sweetly it has been immortalized by her poets, it was changed into a hybrid combination. We look at the many hundreds of Spanish-named cities...over the United States and can not understand why we should have been the ones to be deprived of our lovely name" (*New York Times*. March 25, 1903, signed simply as: Guarionex).

The **1910** U.S. Federal Census also identified the island as being called Porto Rico, *hence* the reference (name) to **Porto Ricans** (cf.: U.S. Bureau of the Census. 1913a: 185, 187; U.S. Bureau of the Census. 1910b. "Population of Counties and Equivalent Subdivisions": 25, 26). [**Note:** Although the 1910 U.S. Federal Census *Reports, Bulletins*, etc., continuously referred to the Island as "Porto Rico", the Census that was conducted in Puerto Rico in 1910, did refer to the Island as "Puerto Rico"---see: the Censo Décimotercero De Los Estados Unidos: 1910 – Población Puerto Rico"].

Finally, for a brief historical description of the name change for the Island of Puerto Rico in 1899 [1898], see (R. T. Hill, "Porto Rico or Puerto Rico?". *National Geographic Magazine*. 1899. Vol. X. pages 516-517. Washington). (Digitized by Google)

Note: While the newspapers in December 1900 reported that 114 Puerto Ricans departed Puerto Rico on November 22, 1900, my research revealed that the actual number **was *at least*** 120 (when you include young children of all ages).

Finally, and importantly, I made a concerted effort to obtain, and read, "**Primary sources**." According to the web site for the University of Oregon Libraries, primary sources are defined as follows:

"A primary source is a document, image, or artifact that provides evidence about the past. It is an original document created contemporaneously with the event under discussion. A direct quote from such a document is classified as a primary source. A secondary source is a book, article, film, or museum that displays primary sources selectively in order to interpret the past.… Primary sources enable the researcher to get as close as possible to what actually happened during a historical event or time period. A primary source reflects the individual viewpoint of a participant or observer.… Some examples of primary sources include: Books, magazines and newspaper articles published at the time…Records of government agencies…Records of organizations…Research data…." ("Primary Sources: What are Primary sources?" (Accesssed: April 30, 2012), (http://libweb.uoregon.edu/guides/history/primary.html).

2.   Note that for our purposes, in the years after 1910, the U.S. Bureau of the Census changed the "definition" for who is considered to be a "Porto Rican" ["Puerto Rican"], for official U.S. government purposes, namely, that:

"…Between 1910 and 1940, the available [census] figures refer to persons of Puerto Rican **birth** only; after 1950, they include persons of Puerto Rican **parentage** and, after 1970, they include all persons of Puerto Rican ***origin***" (see: Duany. 2003: 424, 427; "Table 1. Puerto Rican Population in the Continental United States, 1900-2000"). (emphasis added)

Additionally, certainly at least for the Census time periods covering 1900 through 1930, Lawrence R. Chenault pointed out in 1938 that any accounting for the Puerto Rican population figures had to consider the following methodological considerations:

"Since there is [was] no separate classification in the census covering the Puerto Rican people in the United States, we can only judge the total number of people of Puerto Rican origin by the number **born** in Puerto Rico and living in the continental United States.… In order to know the total number of persons of Puerto Rican origin residing in the United States, we should add to the number given in this table [Table 13] the number of people born of Puerto Rican **parentage** but not born in Puerto Rico" (Chenault. 1938: 53). (emphasis added)

3.   Clarence Senior provided a brief historical explanation of why Puerto Ricans, immigrating to the United States after December 1900, were in fact ***immigrants***, as opposed to simply being **mi-**

grants, when he wrote: "It should be noted that the terms immigrant and migrant are frequently misused. In the case of the Puerto Ricans, the term **immigrant** applies to those who came *before* 1917. The former should be used only in speaking of arriving aliens; the latter refers to citizens moving from one part of their own country to another" (Senior 1965: 70-71). (emphasis added)

Prior to December 1898, Puerto Ricans were citizens of Spain. Thus, in congressional hearings in 1912 regarding what was referred to at that time as "Porto Rican Citizenship", it was mentioned that:

"Historically, of course… the Porto Ricans, while they were under the Spanish rule, were citizens of Spain. They even had representation in the Cortez [the Spanish Legislature]. They had the feeling of being full-fledged citizens of the distant country to which they owed their allegiance…. The Porto Ricans came to the United States with the utmost loyalty and expressions of good will, and it has been a most loyal island ever since" (Committee on the Pacific Islands and Porto Rico. 1912: 4).

An early discussion, and debate, regarding whether to grant U.S. citizenship to the people of the Island of Puerto Rico was represented in the December 1900 issue of the *San Francisco Call*, when it reported that the Treaty of Paris [of December 1898] did not "grant", or allow, citizenship to the new territory (colony) of Puerto Rico. Thus, it reported that:

"We regard it as the settled conviction of a majority of the American people that the many millions of people under our jurisdiction by the Treaty of Paris [*sic*] shall not become citizens and, as such, be incorporated in the American Union. [Quoting Attorney General Griggs] 'It was the intention of the Treaty of Paris [*sic*] not to make the ceded islands a part of the United States, and not to make the inhabitants of those islands citizens'….The **Porto Ricans** and Filipinos cannot be citizens by the result of one election…" (*San Francisco Call.* December 20, 1900: 6; Schomburg. 1902: 8).

It should be noted that until 1917, the question of whether to offer citizenship to Puerto Ricans was continually debated. Thus, in 1912 (although originally written in 1905), during hearings before Congress regarding the question of Citizenship for Puerto Ricans, it was pointed out that (cf.: *San Francisco Examiner.* January 5, 1904; *Atlanta Constitution.* Jan. 5, 1904: 3).

"Under the Spanish regime Porto Ricans were classed as citizens of Spain, and it is naturally difficult for them to understand why citizenship of the sovereign country should be denied to them under the more free and liberal form of government in force in the United States. The granting of citizenship by Congress will greatly improve the feeling of loyalty with which the Porto Ricans regard the United States, and would greatly instill in them a healthy feeling of patriotism as being citizens of the country, and not merely citizens of a dependency of the country…." (Committee on Pacific Islands and Porto Rico. 1912: 31).

Thus, Puerto Ricans became U.S. Citizens in 1917. The 1918 *Report of the Governor of Porto Rico* pointed out that: "The new organic act which was approved by Congress on March 2, 1917, provided that all citizens of Porto Rico should become citizens of the United States unless they elected…to reject American citizenship… there were only 283 citizens of Porto Rico, out of more than a million, who availed themselves of this opportunity to reject American citizenship." (*Annual Reports*, War Department. 1918: 569, Volume III).

In 1938, Dr. Lawrence R. Chenault, then of Hunter College (N.Y.C.), presented a similar argument to Dr. Clarence Senior by identifying the every-day reality of Puerto Rican migrants [i.e., immigrants], once they had emigrated from Puerto Rico to America that the reality for them was that they were, in practical terms, truly functional immigrants, when he wrote:

"Since Porto Rico is a part of the United States and Puerto Ricans are citizens [beginning as of 1917], the movement in a technical sense is one of internal migration. Practically, however, it is much more like one of immigration than migration.... He is a citizen of the United States, but the adjustment required of him in New York [or in California, and in Hawaii] is in almost every way equivalent to that of a person who moves from a foreign county [e.g., like an early 20th Century European immigrant] to the United States" (Chenault 1938: 3, 4, "Preface").

Barry Moreno's book, *Encyclopedia of Ellis Island*, points out that Ellis Island in New York City opened on January 1, 1892, when it welcomed "the first immigrant, Annie Moore of Ireland." He also notes that Ellis Island reopened on December 17, 1900, "when 2,251 immigrants are examined." What is most relevant to the Puerto Rican immigrant experience to California was that the first Puerto Rican immigrants, **en masse** to California, arrived in San Francisco on December 14, 1900, or three days before Ellis Island was to be reopened (cf.: Moreno 2004: the "Chronology Section", p. xxiii).

In 1899, the U.S. War Department published a nine page bulletin describing Puerto Rico's "Immigration Rules" in: *Immigration Regulations For The Island of Porto Rico* (Washington: GPO. 1899). (Obtained from: Harvard Univ. Collection Dept., Widener Library, HCL).

Therefore, Puerto Ricans coming to the United States between 1900-1917 can accurately be identified *as immigrants*, and certainly in an every-day practical sense, similar to other immigrants who have similarly left their homeland/nation/culture, with all its attendant concerns, issues, adjustments, etc.

According to the web site entitled "1910 Census: Instructions to Enumerators", under the "Personal Description" section, number 108 reads: "*Column 6. Color or race.* –Write 'W' for white; 'B' for Black; 'Mu' for mulatto; 'Ch for Chinese; 'Jp' for Japanese; 'In' for Indian". (http://mail.aol.com/36216-111/aol-6/en-us/ Lite/MsgRead.aspx?folder= NewMail&uid = 298 ...) (Accessed: May 30, 2012).

4. For a **contemporary** "description" of a Puerto Rican, Anthropologist Jorge Duany, of the University of Puerto Rico, describes current alternate names for Puerto Ricans, as follows:

"Puerto Ricans are also known as Boricuas, a term derived from the island's indigenous name, Borinquen. Puerto Ricans in the United States are sometimes called Nuyoricans, a term used pejoratively on the island [although not necessarily so in New York City itself], implying that those living abroad are less Puerto Rican" (Duany 2004: 1055). [Note: For purposes of full disclosure, I am a "Nuyorican" who lived in the South Bronx, before and during my four years at De Witt Clinton H.S., Bronx, N.Y.].

A brief discussion of the important historical, as well as the contemporary meaning, of the word "Nuyorican" was presented by Acosta-Belén and Santiago when they wrote:

"The term 'Nuyorican' was adopted in the 1970s by New York-based Puerto Rican poets and artists.... Since the 1970s, the term 'Nuyorican' and 'Neorican' have been frequently used, especially by island Puerto Ricans, to refer to US Puerto Ricans. The term 'Diasporican' was introduced by poet Mariposa Hernández in her poem 'Ode to the Diasporican.' In some of the literature about Puerto Rican migration [and immigration] the terms 'mainland' and 'stateside' Puerto Ricans are used to distinguish the population living in the United States from that of the Island.... Whether hyphenated or not, the term 'Puerto Rican Americans' has been used by some North American scholars to describe the migrant populations.... This term, however, did not have much appeal within the community and it is rarely used today. [Finally] Some scholars argued that since Puerto Ricans are US citizens by birth the term is redundant. Others rejected it on political grounds as a sign of colonialism or cultural assimilation" (Acosta-Belén, Edna and Carlos E. Santiago 2006: 10, "Notes 9.").

5. Sociologist Clara E. Rodríguez of Fordham University (Bronx, New York) demonstrated how the *social* definitions of the concepts of "Race", and of "Ethnicity", have historically changed over time, since 1898. For example, Rodríguez provided the Table, "Dictionary Definitions of 'Race' and 'Ethnic,' 1898-1994," wherein she astutely identified at least a total of seven different substantive changes in the respective definitions for the social-historical concepts of Race and Ethnicity, as defined by Webster's Collegiate Dictionary over this almost 100 year time period (cf.: Rodríguez, Clara E. 2000: 44-45, Table 2.1, 42-45; see also: Reports of the Immigration Commission. 1911c. *Dictionary of Races Of Peoples*: 106).

A contemporary analysis of the important role and interconnectedness between how [some] 19th Century U.S. Congressmen viewed Puerto Rican immigrants' race, i.e., the "Racialization of Puerto Ricans", and their [the Puerto Ricans'] prospective citizenship issue, was made by Lorrin Thomas, when Thomas argued, in summary fashion, that:

"To a large extent, it was American lawmakers' perception of the **'mongrel'** Puerto Rican people, members of a **mixed and 'alien race'**, that had inspired many in the United States Congress to fight against offering them citizenship after the United States took control of the island in 1898, just two years after the *Plessy* decision.... The pragmatists in Congress... argued that America would have greater control over the island if the constitution 'followed the flag,' and they won out in 1917, conferring United States citizenship on a **mixed race people** already controlled by American law..." (Thomas. 2009: 9, 5-35; see also: Rodríguez, Victor M. 1997; 2005)). (emphasis added)

6. The "*AncestryInsititution.com*" Census pages web site was retrieved, reviewed, and obtained, over many months, at the San Diego Family History Center, The Church of Jesus Christ of Latter-Day Saints' Census and Genealogy library facility, in San Diego, CA. (http://search.ancestryinstitution.com/cgi-bin.....).

7. For the first-born children of the Puerto Rican immigrants from 1900 to 1910 would have to contend with the same, or similar issues, which for at least the next 112 years, thus far, all Puerto Ricans either born and/or raised in the United States as opposed to Puerto Rico, would contend with namely, what it really means to be "a Puerto Rican". Anthropologist Jorge Duany provided a portion of an insightful poem included at the start of one of his articles dealing with the ongoing issue of Puerto Rican identity (Duany 2009b: 1):

"Pride in being Boricua [Puerto Rican] has nothing to do with geography ... We are just as Puerto Rican as a Puerto Rican born on the Island. Being Boricua is a state of mind and a state of heart and a state of soul. And as far as I'm concerned, that's the only kind of state it's ever going to be." – María Teresa 'Mariposa' Fernández, author of the poem *'Ode to the Diasporican'*.

The Pew Research Center (Bib. #359), also pointed out, on May 26, 2011, that:

"An estimated 4.4 million Hispanics of Puerto Rican origin resided in the 50 U.S. states and the District of Columbia in 2009, according to the Census Bureau's American Community Survey. That is a slightly greater number than the population of Puerto Rico itself in 2009, which was 4.0 million. Puerto Ricans in this statistical profile are people who self-identified as Hispanics of Puerto Rican origin; this means either they themselves were born in Puerto Rico or they trace their family ancestry to Puerto Rico…. Puerto Ricans are the **second-largest population of Hispanic** origin living in the United States, accounting for 9.1% of the U.S. Hispanic population in 2009…." (Pew Research Center 2011: 1). (Emphasis added)

Finally, for a brief description of nineteenth century European immigration **to** Puerto Rico, as opposed to Puerto Rican emigration **out** of Puerto Rico, and therefore, the relative preponderance of "foreign sounding and looking names" (surnames), refer to the short book titled "Nineteenth-Century Puerto Rican Immigration and Slave Data". The pamphlet pointed out:

"…that Spanish authorities [from Spain] did not make a concerted effort to induce foreigners to settle in Puerto Rico until the issuance of the **Royal Decree** of August 10, 1815. This decree, usually referred to as the **Cédula de Gracias**, offered foreigners coming to live in Puerto Rico special inducements such as free grants of land, tax exemptions, and all the rights enjoyed by Spanish citizens…. It is estimated that this series contains about 3,000 names of immigrants…. In 1838 there were 2,833 naturalized foreigners living in Puerto Rico" [and as a result, the partial accounting for some of the many "non-Spanish" surnames of some Puerto Ricans] (cf.: National Archives and Records Service. 1973: 1, 2, 4, 5, 8, 9). (emphasis added)

Note: For an English translation of the **Royal Decree** of 1815, see the write-up which appeared in the 1902 publication of the then Military Governor of Puerto Rico, which included the full citations of the **26 Articles** which are cited within this August 15, 1815 dated **Decree** (Military Governor of Porto Rico on Civil Affairs. 1902: 366-369).

The publication, *Census of Porto Rico, 1899* reported that in 1900 "the number of foreign born returned by the [1899] census was 13,872 or about 1.5 per cent of the total [Puerto Rican] population" (U.S. War Department. 1900: 62).

Additionally, the *1920 Federal Census* showed that in 1910, Puerto Rico had a "total foreign born" population of 11,766, and in 1920, a "total foreign born" population of 8,167 (U.S. Bureau of the Census. 1922: 1196).

8. A compilation of newspaper articles, and of other publications, that presents many primary sources of the degree and type of *racism* that was presented in *some* of the newspapers of the day, and represented by some government officials during the first years of the 20th Century (1900-1903), were compiled in the publication *Documentos de la Migración Puertorriqueña (1879-1901) – Documents of the Puerto Rican Migration: Hawaii, Cuba, Santo Domingo, Ecuador*, (Centro de Estudios Puertorriqueños 1977: 1-51).

Another glaring example of racism exhibited by newspapers relating to their descriptions of Puerto Ricans [albeit on the East Coast], was described by a Puerto Rican immigrant [he arrived in New York in 1916], Bernardo Vega, who wrote of a prominent and influential 1902 New York newspaper:

"In November 1902 one of the widest circulation New York dailies, the *Morning-Sun*, published a series of articles on Puerto Rico. It has some fine things to say about Puerto Ricans, like 'these people are no more than savages who have replaced their bows and arrows with guns and knives'" (Vega 1984: 93).

In short, Vega summarized his observations in his essay "On diatribes and insults against Puerto Ricans", when he wrote that: "racism was rampant not only in newspapers…." (Vega 1984: 92ff).

Another example appeared in May 1, 1901 and was presented in an official government publication: *First Annual Report, Charles H. Allen, Governor of Porto Rico*. Allen was governor of Puerto Rico from 1900-1901. The Governor's report read as follows:

> "The movement in the population in the island of Porto Rico during the last year has been inconsiderable in proportion to numbers.... But particularly since the hurricane of *San Ciriaco* some of the poorer class of laborers have [*sic*] found it difficult to procure the means of a livelihood [in Puerto Rico].... Most of the *emigrants* are of the very poorest class of laborers, many of them without a box or a bundle or anything whatever more than the scanty apparel in which they stand upon the wharves. Very few of them have the least rudiments of education. In other words, these emigrants comprise the least desirable elements of this people.... Out of a population of nearly a million not more than 5,000 or 6,000 have emigrated---scarcely one-half of 1 per cent. *They will never be missed* in making up the census returns of the next decade. Porto Rico has plenty of laborers and poor people generally" (Allen. 1901: 74, 75; also cited in: *Documentos de la Migración Puertorriqueños (1879-1901)*, (Centro de Estudios Puertorriqueños. 1977: 10, 11)). (emphasis added)

9. For historical contrast, the **New York City** Puerto Rican population in 1910 was 554. Also, again for historical comparison and context, the New York City Puerto Rican population (i.e., those individuals born in Puerto Rico) in 1920 was 7,364, while the entire **State of New York** had a total of 7,719, and the **Continental United States** had a total Puerto Rican population in 1920 of 11,811. The 1950 Population Census listed the following New York State Puerto Rican population figures for each of the following census decades: 1910 – 641; 1920 – 7,719; 1930 - 45,973; and for the year 1950 – 191,305. (See: U.S. Bureau of the Census. 1953: 3D-4).

The New York City Puerto Rican populations were for the time periods of: 1910 – 554; 1920 – 7,364; 1930 ("Not Available"*); 1940 - 61,463; and for the year 1950 – 187,429 (U.S. Bureau of the Census. 1953: 3D-4). Further, social scientists Clarence Senior and Donald D. Watkins indicated that New York City had 429,710 Puerto Ricans in 1960 (Senior and Donald O. Watkins 1966: 705).

*Note: Marzán, *et. al.*, they cited that there were a total of 44,900 Puerto Ricans living in New York City in 1930 (Marzán, *et. al.*, 2008: 2).

In contrast to New York State, Dr. Senior indicated that in 1950 **California** had a total of 5,495 "Persons [that were] born in Puerto Rico", and 15,479 Puerto Ricans in 1960 (Senior. 1965: 77).

The Puerto Rican populations for the "Continental United States" were as follows: 1910 – 1,513; 1920 – 11,811; 1930 – 52,774; 1940 – 69,967; 1950 – 226,110 (cf.: U.S. Bureau of the Census. 1953: 3D-4).

Finally, social scientist, Father Joseph P. Fitzpatrick, then of Fordham University (Bronx, New York), presented a detailed Table (Table 2-1) "Persons of Puerto Rican Origin in Coterminous United States and New York City: 1920-80" (Fitzpatrick. 1987 [1971]: 15). His table of the Puerto Rican population figures was obtained from several U.S. Census sources. The Puerto Rican population in New York City for 1970 was 860,584, and in 1980 was 860,552 (i.e., Puerto Rican Birth combined with Puerto Rican Parentage, i.e., born in the U.S.), with 387,284 having been born in the U.S. (Fitzpatrick. 1987 [1971]: 15). Father Fitzpatrick's book is oftentimes cited, and referenced by scholars and researchers of the Puerto Rican *diaspora*. [**Note:** Ironically, although I have never met Father Fitzpatrick, nor was I aware of him as a High School student from 1966-1968, I graduated from the very first "Upward Bound Program" at Fordham University's Rose Hill Campus].

10. To connect the past with the present, according to the 2000 U.S. Federal Census, Holyoke, Massachusetts had the *highest concentrated presence* of Puerto Ricans among "Midsize US Cities", with 36.49% of its population being Puerto Rican. By contrast, in 2000, New York City's Puerto Rican population was 23.17% (cf.: Acosta-Belén and Carlos E. Santiago. 2006: 97, 96, Table 4.8, "Puerto Rican Presence in Midsize US Cities with Greatest Concentrations, 1980-2000").

Interestingly, the **2010** U.S. Census Bureau in their Table titled, "Hispanic or Latino by Type: 2010. 2010 Census Summary File 1," also listed Holyoke City, Hampden County, Massachusetts, as having a Puerto Rican population of 17,825, which represented 44.7% of its total population of 39,880 (see "Fact Finder" at the following web site: (http://factfinder2.census.gov/ faces/tableservices /jsf/pages/productiveview.xhtml? pid=Dec_10...)

11. The 1910 Federal Census (*The Thirteenth Census*) listed a total of 213 persons that were born in Puerto Rico (i.e., the "Native Population", or Puerto Ricans) and who also lived in San Francisco as of 1910 (U.S. Bureau of the Census. 1913b: 778, "Table 44"; see also: Teresa Whalen. 2005: 11).

Researchers should note that the annually published book, *California Cities, Towns & Counties: State and Municipal Profiles Series* (Information Publications, Inc. 2009), lists the Puerto Rican census population figures for California Cities; this book remains essentially the same from year to year [although the *specific year* of the book changes yearly] and lists the Puerto Rican census population figures for California Cities, Towns & Counties, citing the "Census Figures" from either the 2000 Decennial Census, the American Community Survey statistics, or the book *Almanac of the 50 States*, for each year. It also publishes the population figures for the State of California, as well as providing certain "ethnic groups" population figures, also on an annual basis.

The book, *California Cities, Towns, and Counties 2009* indicated that in 2007, California had a total Puerto Rican population of 164,460, with a total "Hispanic or Latino" population of 13,220,888, or almost a third of the state population of 36,553,215 (page 545). The **2010** U.S. Census' *Fact Finder* website listed the Puerto Rican population for California as **189,945 persons** (9/10/11), (http://factfinder2.census.gov/faces/tableservices /jsf/pages/productview.xhtm? pid=DEC_1...). (See also: Duany and Matos-Rodríguez. 2006: 8, especially "Table 1", Bib. #317).

12. A copy of this organizations "First Minutes", hand-written in Spanish from 1912, can **also be obtained**, via interlibrary loan (in microfilm fashion), through the Bancroft Library, University of California, Berkeley, California 94720-6000 (reference: BANC Film 3163, refer to: Reel No. 1, Vol. 1; February 25, 1912-February 3, 1916 Reel). Title: "Club Portorriqueño de San Francisco".

It is noteworthy that the above reference Reel 1 covers the "Minutes" of the Club Portorriqueño up till December 14, 1924 (page 113 in this Reel).

September 2016 - The historical importance of the role played by race in Porto Rican (Puerto Rican) history as it affected its relationship to the United States (at least up to 1925, and certainly thereafter), especially as it related to Porto Rico's ability for full self-governing, can be somewhat "summarized" in the following quote: "Race clearly defined the disabilities of excluded Chinese workers, Jim Crowed African Americans, American Indians confined to reservations, and Puerto Rican and Filipino subjects denied self-government," David R. Roediger, *Working Toward Whiteness: How America's Immigrants Became White, The Strange Journey From Ellis Island to the Suburbs*, (2005) (Amazon.com; Kindle Edition, pp. 14-16).

(see also: Bibliography #386, "The U.S. Census and the Contested Rules of Racial Classification...")

Exhibit 1

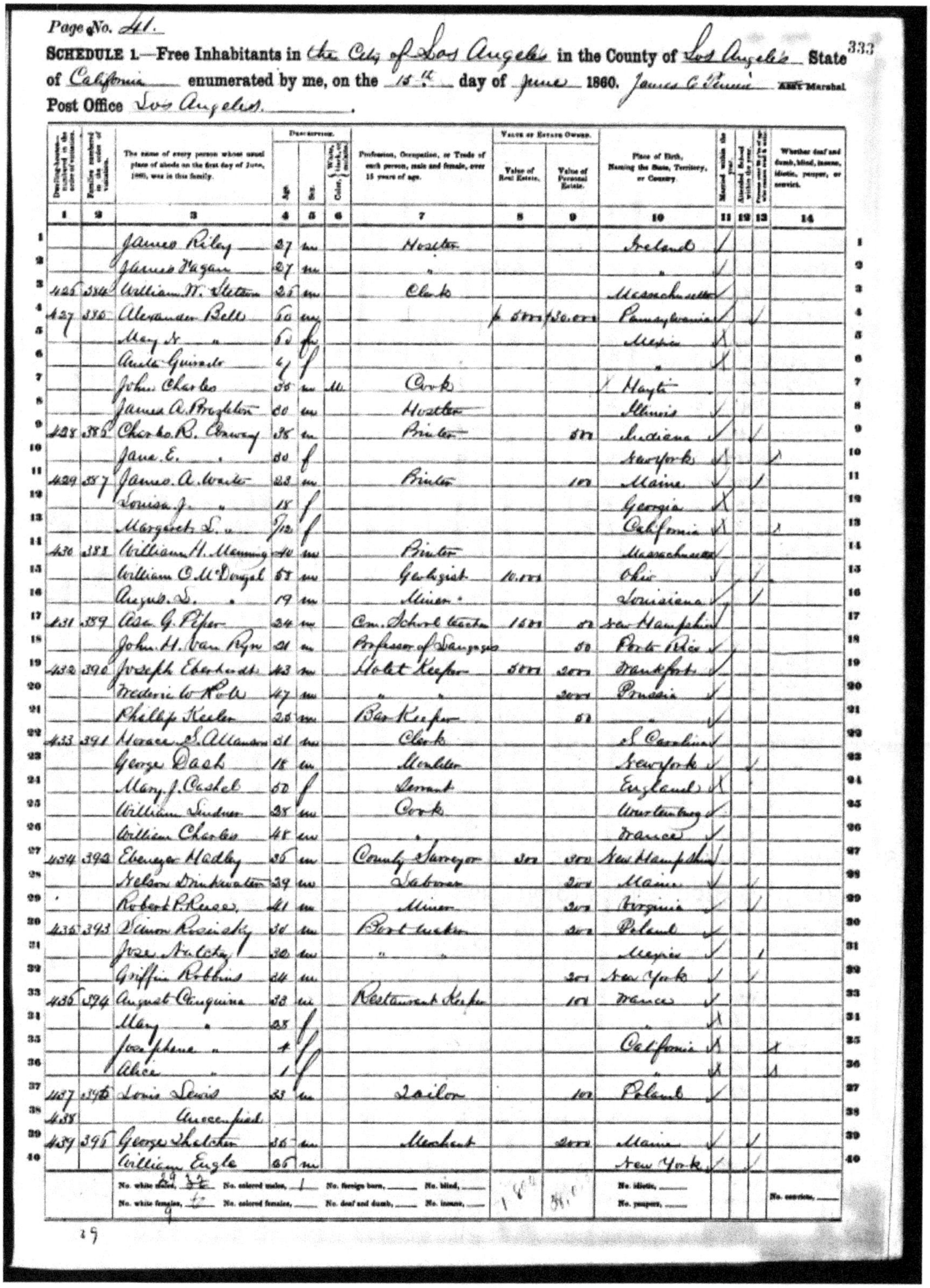

Page No. 41. 333

SCHEDULE 1.—Free Inhabitants in the City of Los Angeles in the County of Los Angeles State of California enumerated by me, on the 15th day of June 1860. James C. Pennie Ass't Marshal

Post Office Los Angeles.

	Dwelling-houses numbered in the order of visitation	Families numbered in the order of visitation	The name of every person whose usual place of abode on the first day of June, 1860, was in this family	Age	Sex	Color	Profession, Occupation, or Trade of each person, male and female, over 15 years of age	Value of Real Estate	Value of Personal Estate	Place of Birth, Naming the State, Territory, or Country	Married within the year	Attended School within the year	Persons over 20 y'rs of age who cannot read & write	Whether deaf and dumb, blind, insane, idiotic, pauper, or convict	
	1	2	3	4	5	6	7	8	9	10	11	12	13	14	
1			James Riley	27	m		Hostler			Ireland	✓				1
2			James Fagan	27	m		"			"	✓				2
3	425	384	William W. Stetson	25	m		Clerk			Massachusetts	✓				3
4	427	385	Alexander Bell	60	m			5000	30.000	Pennsylvania	✓		✓		4
5			Mary N. "	50	f					Mexico	X				5
6			Anita Guirado	4/	f					"	X				6
7			John Charles	35	m	M	Cook			Hayti					7
8			James A. Broughton	30	m		Hostler			Illinois	✓				8
9	428	386	Charles R. Conway	38	m		Printer		500	Indiana	✓		✓		9
10			Jane E. "	30	f					New York	X			✓	10
11	429	387	James A. Waite	23	m		Printer		100	Maine	✓		✓		11
12			Louisa J. "	18	f					Georgia	X				12
13			Margaret L. "	5/12	f					California	X			✓	13
14	430	388	William H. Manning	40	m		Printer			Massachusetts	✓				14
15			William O. McDougal	58	m		Geologist	10.000		Ohio	✓		✓		15
16			August L. "	19	m		Miner			Louisiana	✓		✓		16
17	431	389	Asa G. Piper	24	m		Com. School Teacher	1600	50	New Hampshire	✓				17
18			John M. Van Ryn	21	m		Professor of Languages		50	Porto Rico	✓				18
19	432	390	Joseph Eberhardt	43	m		Hotel Keeper	5000	2000	Frankfort	✓				19
20			Frederic W. Rolle	47	m		" "		2000	Prussia	✓				20
21			Phillip Keeler	26	m		Bar Keeper		50	"	✓				21
22	433	391	Horace S. Allanson	31	m		Clerk			S. Carolina	✓				22
23			George Dash	18	m		Moulder			New York	✓		✓		23
24			Mary J. Cashel	50	f		Servant			England	X				24
25			William Lindner	28	m		Cook			Wurtemberg	✓				25
26			William Charles	48	m		"			France	✓				26
27	434	392	Ebenezer Hadley	35	m		County Surveyor	300	300	New Hampshire	✓				27
28			Nelson Drinkwater	29	m		Laborer		200	Maine	✓		✓		28
29			Robert P. Reese	41	m		Miner		200	Virginia	✓		✓		29
30	435	393	Simon Rosinsky	30	m		Boot Maker		200	Poland	✓				30
31			Jose Nalchy	30	m		" "			Mexico	✓		✓		31
32			Griffin Robbins	34	m				200	New York	✓		✓		32
33	436	394	August Canguina	33	m		Restaurant Keeper		100	France	✓				33
34			Mary "	28	f					"	X				34
35			Josephine "	4	f					California	X			X	35
36			Alice "	1	f					"	X			X	36
37	437	395	Louis Lewis	33	m		Tailor		100	Poland	✓				37
38	438		Unoccupied												38
39	439	396	George Thatcher	36	m		Merchant		2000	Maine	✓		✓		39
40			William Engle	65	m					New York	✓		✓		40

No. white males, 32 (29) No. colored males, 1 No. foreign born, ___ No. blind, ___ No. idiotic, ___ No. convicts, ___

No. white females, 7 (9) No. colored females, ___ No. deaf and dumb, ___ No. insane, ___ No. paupers, ___

29

1860 CA Federal Census – John M. Vanryn (21 yrs. old) (Los Angeles, CA; Profession/ Occupation/Trade: Professor of Languages); Birthplace: **Porto Rico** (1839) [see: Line #18 above] (**Courtesy of Ancestry.com**)

Exhibit 2

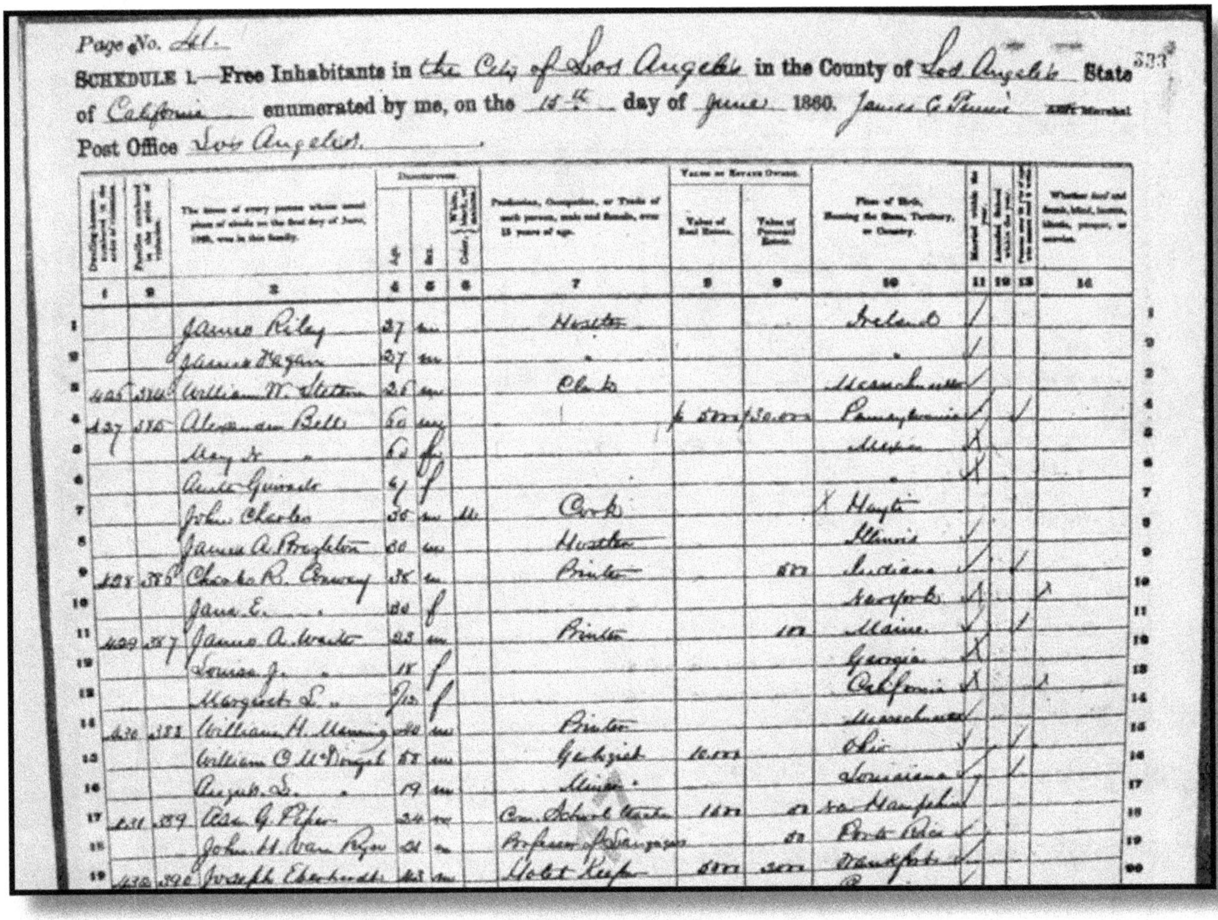

Page No. 41.
SCHEDULE 1.—Free Inhabitants in the City of Los Angeles in the County of Los Angeles State of California enumerated by me, on the 15th day of June 1860. James C. Pennie Ass't Marshal
Post Office Los Angeles.

	1	2	3	4	5	6	7	8	9	10	11	12	13	14
1			James Riley	27	m		Hostler			Ireland	/			
2			James Hagan	27	m		"			"	/			
3	425	384	William W. Stetton	26	m		Clerk			Massachusetts	/			
4	427	385	Alexander Bell	60	m			$5000	$30,000	Pennsylvania	/		/	
5			Mary "	62	f					Mexico	X			
6			Ante Guirado	41	f					"	X			
7			John Charles	36	m	M	Cook			X Hayti				
8			James A. Brazleton	30	m		Hostler			Illinois	/			
9	428	386	Charles R. Conway	38	m		Printer		500	Indiana	/		/	
10			Jane E. "	30	f					New York	X			/
11	429	387	James A. Waite	23	m		Printer		100	Maine	/		/	
12			Louisa J. "	18	f					Georgia	X			
13			Margaret L. "	7/12	f					California	X			/
14	430	388	William H. Manning	30	m		Printer			Massachusetts	/			
15			William C. McDougal	57	m		Geologist	10,000		Ohio	/		/	
16			August L. "	19	m		Miner			Louisiana	/		/	
17	431	389	Asa G. Piper	34	m		Com. School Master	1800	50	New Hampshire	/			
18			John M. Van Ryn	21	m		Professor of Languages		50	Porto Rico	/			
19	432	390	Joseph Eberhardt	43	m		Hotel Keeper	5000	3000	Frankfort	/			

1860 U.S. Federal Census (State of California) (enlarged size of this Page) for John M. Vanryn; born in **Porto Rico** (Line #18 on <u>this</u> Census Form page: see above) (**Courtesy of Ancestry.com**)

Exhibit 3

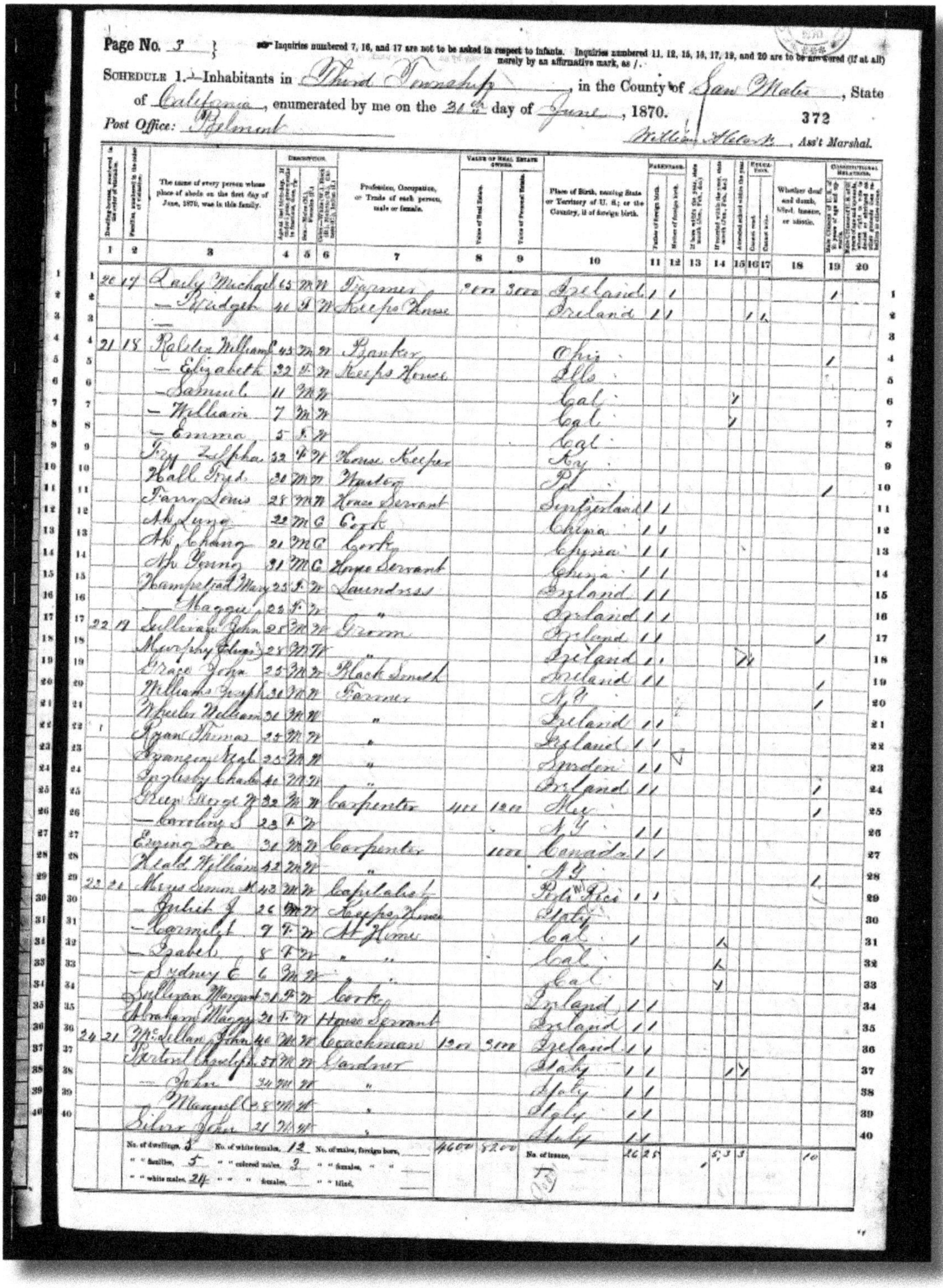

Page No. 3

☞ Inquiries numbered 7, 16, and 17 are not to be asked in respect to infants. Inquiries numbered 11, 12, 15, 16, 17, 19, and 20 are to be answered (if at all) merely by an affirmative mark, as /.

SCHEDULE 1.—Inhabitants in Third Township, in the County of San Mateo, State of California, enumerated by me on the 31st day of June, 1870.

Post Office: Belmont

372

William Hebert, Ass't Marshal.

1 Dwelling-houses, numbered in the order of visitation	2 Families, numbered in the order of visitation	3 The name of every person whose place of abode on the first day of June, 1870, was in this family	4 Age	5 Sex	6 Color	7 Profession, Occupation, or Trade of each person, male or female	8 Value of Real Estate	9 Value of Personal Estate	10 Place of Birth, naming State or Territory of U. S.; or the Country, if of foreign birth	11 Father of foreign birth	12 Mother of foreign birth	13	14	15 Attended school within the year	16 Cannot read	17 Cannot write	18 Whether deaf and dumb, blind, insane, or idiotic	19	20
20	17	Daily Michael	65	M	W	Farmer	2000	3000	Ireland	1	1							1	
		— Bridget	41	F	W	Keeps House			Ireland	1	1				1	1			
21	18	Ralston William C	45	M	W	Banker			Ohio									1	
		— Elizabeth	32	F	W	Keeps House			Ills										
		— Samuel	11	M	W				Cal					1					
		— William	7	M	W				Cal					1					
		— Emma	5	F	W				Cal										
		Fry Zilpha	32	F	W	House Keeper			Ky										
		Hall Fred	30	M	W	Waiter			Pa									1	
		Farr Louis	28	M	W	House Servant			Switzerland	1	1								
		Ah Lung	22	M	C	Cook			China	1	1								
		Ah Chang	21	M	C	Cook			China	1	1								
		Ah Yenny	31	M	C	House Servant			China	1	1								
		Hampstead Mary	25	F	W	Laundress			Ireland	1	1								
		— Maggie	23	F	W	"			Ireland	1	1								
22	19	Sullivan John	28	M	W	Groom			Ireland	1	1							1	
		Murphy Elias	28	M	W	"			Ireland	1	1		1/						
		Grace John	25	M	W	Black Smith			Ireland	1	1							1	
		Williams Joseph	30	M	W	Farmer			N.Y.									1	
		Wheeler William	31	M	W	"			Ireland	1	1								
		Ryan Thomas	25	M	W	"			Ireland	1	1								
		Franzen Neal	25	M	W	"			Sweden	1	1								
		Inglesby Charles	40	M	W	"			Ireland	1	1							1	
		Green George W	32	M	W	Carpenter	400	1200	Mex									1	
		— Caroline S	23	F	W				N.Y.	1	1								
		Ewing Ira	31	M	W	Carpenter		1000	Canada	1	1								
		Heald William	42	M	W	"			N.Y.										
23	20	Mezes Simon M	43	M	W	Capitalist			Porto Rico	1	1							1	
		— Juliet J	26	F	W	Keeps House			Italy										
		— Carmelita	9	F	W	At Home			Cal	1				1					
		— Isabel	8	F	W	" "			Cal					1					
		— Sydney E	6	M	W	" "			Cal					1					
		Sullivan Margaret	31	F	W	Cook			Ireland	1	1								
		Abraham Maggie	31	F	W	House Servant			Ireland	1	1								
24	21	McLellan John	40	M	W	Coachman	1200	3000	Ireland	1	1								
		Bertoni Christopher	57	M	W	Gardner			Italy	1	1		1	1					
		— John	34	M	W	"			Italy	1	1								
		Manuel C	28	M	W	"			Italy	1	1								
		Silvo John	21	M	W	"			Italy	1	1								
		No. of dwellings, 5; No. of white females, 12; No. of males, foreign born, —; " " families, 5; " " colored males, 3; " " females, " " —; " " white males, 24; " " " females, —; " " blind, —					4600	8200	No. of insane, —	26	25		1	5	3	3		10	

1870 CA Federal Census – Simon M. Mezes (43 yrs. old) San Mateo County, CA; Profession/ Occupation/ Trade: "Capitalist"; Birthplace: **Porto Rico** [see Line 29 above] (**Courtesy of Ancestry.com**)

Exhibit 4

Puerto Rican Population of the United States, the State of California, and San Francisco: 1900, 1910, and the 2000 Census Figures

	Year: 1900	Year: 1910	Year: 2000
California Total	7[1]	342[4]	140,570[4]
San Francisco	3[1]	213[9]	3,758[4]
New York City	300[2]	554[9]	789,200[2]
U.S. Total Puerto Rican population	678[3]	1,513[8]	3,406,178[6]
Puerto Rico	953,243[10]	1,118,012[5]	3,808,610[7]

1. **Notes: The smaller numbers next to the population figures (the superscript) are notated as follows** – The *1900 U.S. Federal Census* (for California) listed a total of **6** persons born in Puerto Rico as of April 1900, and who also resided in California at that time. However, *Ancestry.com* identified, by name, **7** persons who were born in Puerto Rico as of **April 1900**, and who resided in California at that time. For example, *Ancestry.com* identified the following seven (7) names: Ben Camacho; Charles Rodigez; Charles F. Benzon; Mcenty Portrico; Clara Blair; M O Munroe; and B L A Munroe.

For a contemporary description of the Puerto Rican diaspora within the United States from 1960-2000, which outlined the ever-changing geographic distribution of the Puerto Rican population, succinctly summarized in a Table format (see: Duany, Jorge and Matos-Rodríguez. 2006: 8, "Table 1", entitled "Geographic Distribution of the Puerto Rican Population in the United States, by State, 1960-2000 (Percentages in Parentheses); see also: Tables 3 and 4)." The Duany and Matos-Rodríguez article is referenced in this book under the "Bibliography Addendum" portion ---at the very end of the Bibliography section).

Also, this Duany, J. and Matos-Rodríguez's article provided another "Table", which represented the 2003 Puerto Rican population distribution within the top 10 Metropolitan Areas in the United States, see "Table 4" entitled: "Top Ten Metropolitan Areas with Puerto Rican Residents in the United States, 2003." (page 11)

For assistance in conducting Family genealogy, contact the Hispanic Genealogical Society of New York (HGSNY); and their "award-winning", and timely newsletter is called: **Nuestra Herencia.**

2. Marzán, Gilbert, *et. al.* (2008: 2).

3. Duany, Jorge. (2003: 426).

4. Teresa Whalen. (2005: 11, 32).

5. U.S. Dept. of Commerce & Labor. (1911: 22).

6. U.S. Bureau of the Census. (2001). "Profiles of General Demographic Characteristics 2000 – United States. 2000 Census of Population and Housing." (Issued: May 2001).

7. U.S. Bureau of the Census. (2002). "Census 2000 Data for Puerto Rico: The Population of Puerto Rico on April 1, 2000 was 3,808,610." Released 6/4/2002.

8. U.S. Bureau of the Census. (1913a: 185).

9. U.S. Bureau of the Census. (1913b: 778, 779).

10. U.S. Bureau of the Census. (1902: 7, 22).

NOTE: The above Table/Chart (i.e., Exhibit 4) was compiled, and prepared by this author based upon the various sources cited in the above **"Notes"**; for a more comprehensive presentation of the Puerto Rican population in selected Counties and Cities throughout the United States, covering the time periods of 1900, 1910, 1920 and 2000, refer to "Table 1" of this book (after "Exhibit 21"), entitled -

"Puerto Rican Population Figures for the United States, The State of California, and for selected California Counties and Cities and Years: 1900, 1910, 1920, 2000."

June 16, 2016: A more current statistical profile of the U.S. Puerto Rican population can be found in the Pew Research Center's (Washington, D.C.) Sept. 15, 2015 publication titled, "Hispanics of Puerto Rican Origin in the United States, 2013: Statistical Profile", by Gustavo López and Eileen Patten. They wrote that: "An estimated 5.1 million Hispanics of Puerto Rican origin resided in the U.S…in **2013.** That is a substantially greater number than the population of Puerto Rico itself, which was 3.6 million in 2013…", (p, 1). (emphasis added)

September 2016: The Pew Research Center's article titled, "PuertoRicans leave in record numbers for mainland U.S." (October 14, 2015, page 1) wherein it states as follows:

"As of 2013, there were more Puerto Ricans living in the U.S. mainland (5.1 million) than on the island itself (3.5) million…. The island's population isn't expected to rebound anytime soon. The Census Bureau projects the population of Puerto Rico will continue to shrink…falling to 3 million by 2050".

Exhibit 5

Simon M. Mezes (aka: S.M. Mazie): possibly the first *documented* Puerto Rican in California ---see the **1852 State of California Census**; he was born in Puerto Rico, "about 1828," and was reported to have arrived in San Francisco, CA, on February 22, 1850 (see: *Ancestry. com;* Millard. 1924a; Millard. 1924b).

Since one may not be able to read the "small print" in this *book*, this author hereby will write verbatim, what was written/presented on the cover page of the above referenced journal entitled: ***La Peninsula***: *Journal of the San Mateo County Historical Association.* Vol. XIV. May, 1967, No. 2, relating to Simon Montserrate Mezes:

"REDWOOD CITY CENTENNIAL EDITION"

"In this country's early years, Simon Montserrate Mezes was one of its most prominent citizens, yet we know very little about his personal history. One source, apparently reliable, records him as being **born in Puerto Rico** and educated in Spain." (emphasis added)

(***Courtesy of:*** San Mateo County Historical Association).

It has been written that Simon M. Mezes immigrated to San Francisco, California on February 22, 1850 (Millard. 1924a). The University of California's Bancroft Library's "Antonio María Osio Papers, 1823-1853" refers to Documents (arranged chronologically; Folder 18; under the name: Osio, Antonio María) which cites S. M. Mezes (aka: Simon M. Mezes) having been involved in a business transaction, as follows: "Contrata, Nov. 14, 1850, with S. Sterrett and S. M. Mezes re Santa Clara Mission orchard" (Antonio María Osio Papers, BANC MSS C-B 833, The Bancroft Library, University of California, Berkeley; via the *Online Archives of California (OAC)*; accessed: February 18, 2013, Bib. #363). Unfortunately, I have not as of yet, reviewed these papers, although I just recently placed my request to do so, upon just becoming aware of them.

Almost forty years after the 1880 Federal California Census was taken, a copy of a November 26, 1918 document corroborates that Simon M. Mezes was born in Puerto Rico, which further confirms that Mr. Mezes' 1880 Census Form page that listed him as having been born in Spain, was not "accurate." For example, the document obtained from *Ancestry.com*, and entitled "Application for Special Passport" (no. 481), had the following information on the top of the Form, namely:

"United States of America. Duplicate. [Edition of 1917.]. [Form For Native Citizen.]".

This application form was completed by Simon M. Mezes' **son**, Sidney Mezes [also cited as: Sydney E. Mezes], and date-stamped on Nov. 26, 1918. The completed form shows that Sidney Mezes was born in Belmont, California, on or about September 23, 1863, and that his father [who was by then deceased] was S. M. Mezes, and who "was born in **Porto Rico**…and is now deceased [as of 1884],… [and] who had emigrated to the United States…circa 1848; that he [Simon] resided 36 years, uninterruptedly, in the United States, from 1848 to 1884, at Belmont, California." [emphasis added] (see: Loosley.1927: 1-14, *Foreign Born Population of California, 1848-1920*).

In November 1918, Sidney Mezes cited his occupation as being: College President. Sidney graduated from Harvard University, where he also obtained his doctorate degree (PH.D.) in 1893 from Harvard. Therefore, he was obviously very well educated, and signed this Application when the Application was both sworn to, and signed by, Mr. Sidney Mezes. (accessed via: *Ancestry.com*). (**Note:** this Passport Application was forwarded to me by Tony Rivera Maldonado, Genealogical Researcher, see his website at: <www.derievra.com>.). (See Exhibit 5b on the next page)

Sidney Mezes' 1900 and 1910 U.S. Federal Census listed his Father's Place of birth (which is cited by the Enumerator) as: Porti Rico (i.e., Porto Rico) and Porto Rico (*Ancestry.com*).

[**NOTE:** Simon M. Mezes lived for over 20 years in Belmont, CA, thus, he resided in San Mateo County, California.]

2010: "Belmont, CA (population:26,000 today is situated half-way between San Francisco and San Jose, in San Mateo County" --- from the City of Belmont, CA web site)].

Redwood City is a California city in the San Francisco Peninsula in Northern California approximately 27 miles south of San Francisco. Today the city is known as the home of several technology companies such as Oracle and Electronic Arts. As of the 2010 census, the city had a total population of 76,815.

Exhibit 5b

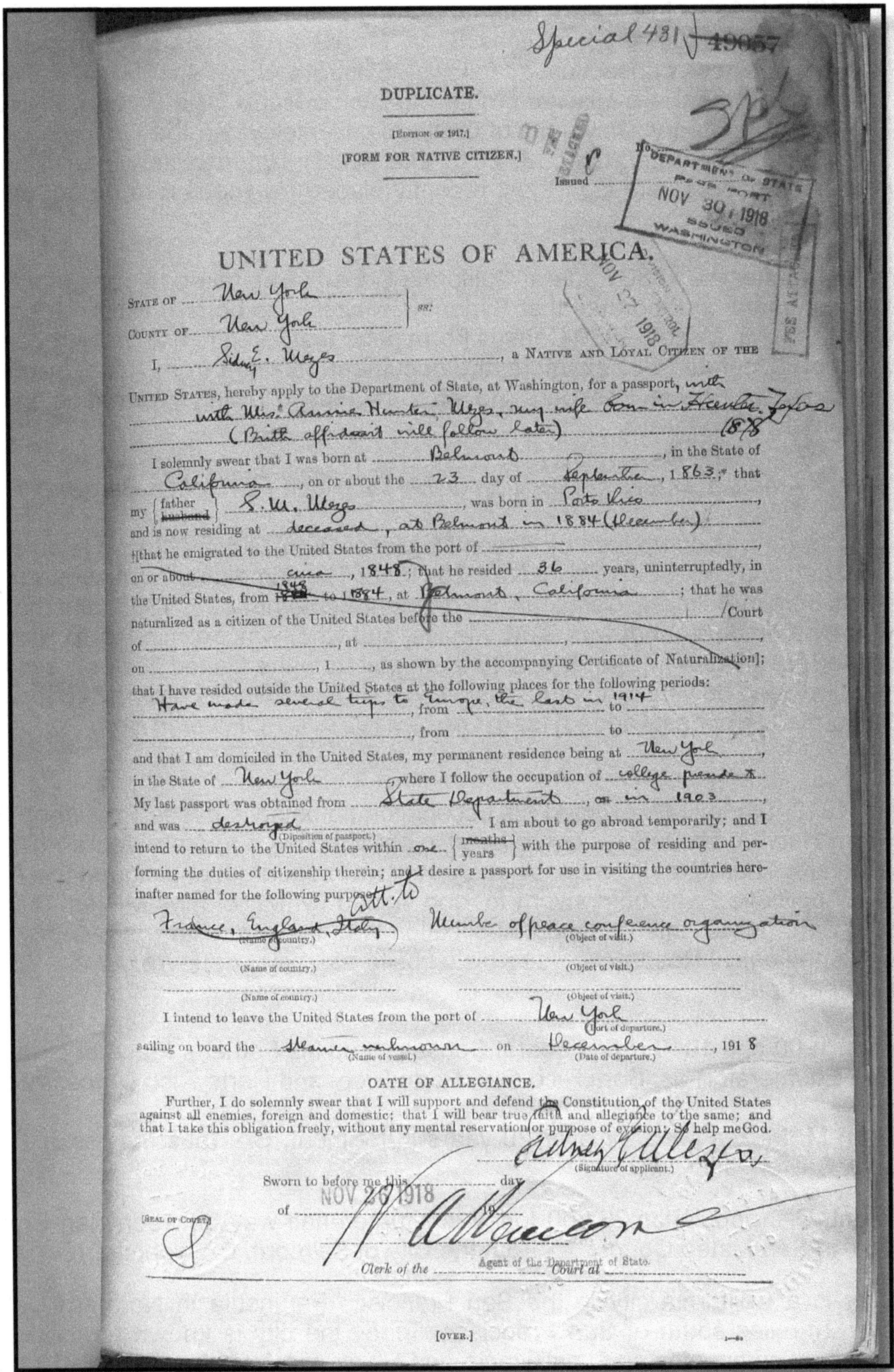

DUPLICATE.
[Edition of 1917.]
[FORM FOR NATIVE CITIZEN.]

Special 481 / 49057

No. ____ Issued ____

DEPARTMENT OF STATE
NOV 30 1918
ISSUED
WASHINGTON

UNITED STATES OF AMERICA.

STATE OF **New York**
COUNTY OF **New York** } ss:

I, **Sidney E. Meyes**, a NATIVE AND LOYAL CITIZEN OF THE UNITED STATES, hereby apply to the Department of State, at Washington, for a passport, with **Mrs. Annie Hunter Meyes, my wife born in Hunter, Texas 1878 (Birth affidavit will follow later)**

I solemnly swear that I was born at **Belmont**, in the State of **California**, on or about the **23** day of **September**, **1863**; that my father **S. M. Meyes**, was born in **Porto Rico**, and is now residing at **deceased, at Belmont in 1884 (December)**; [that he emigrated to the United States from the port of _____ on or about **circa**, 1848; that he resided **36** years, uninterruptedly, in the United States, from **1848** to **1884**, at **Belmont, California**; that he was naturalized as a citizen of the United States before the _____ Court of _____, at _____ on _____, I _____, as shown by the accompanying Certificate of Naturalization]; that I have resided outside the United States at the following places for the following periods: **Have made several trips to Europe, the last in 1914** from _____ to _____, from _____ to _____, and that I am domiciled in the United States, my permanent residence being at **New York**, in the State of **New York**, where I follow the occupation of **college president**. My last passport was obtained from **State Department**, on/in **1903**, and was **destroyed** (Disposition of passport.) I am about to go abroad temporarily; and I intend to return to the United States within **one** {months/**years**} with the purpose of residing and performing the duties of citizenship therein; and I desire a passport for use in visiting the countries hereinafter named for the following purposes, to wit: to

France, England, Italy / **Member of peace conference organization**
(Name of country.) / (Object of visit.)

_____ / _____
(Name of country.) / (Object of visit.)

_____ / _____
(Name of country.) / (Object of visit.)

I intend to leave the United States from the port of **New York** (Port of departure.) sailing on board the **steamer unknown** (Name of vessel.) on **December** (Date of departure.), 191**8**

OATH OF ALLEGIANCE.

Further, I do solemnly swear that I will support and defend the Constitution of the United States against all enemies, foreign and domestic; that I will bear true faith and allegiance to the same; and that I take this obligation freely, without any mental reservation or purpose of evasion: So help me God.

Sidney E. Meyes
(Signature of applicant.)

Sworn to before me this **NOV 26 1918** day of _____, 19____

[SEAL OF COURT]

_____
Clerk of the _____ Court at _____
Agent of the Department of State

[OVER.]

(Courtesy of *Ancestry.com*)

Exhibit 5c

(Courtesy of *Ancestry.com*)

Exhibit 6

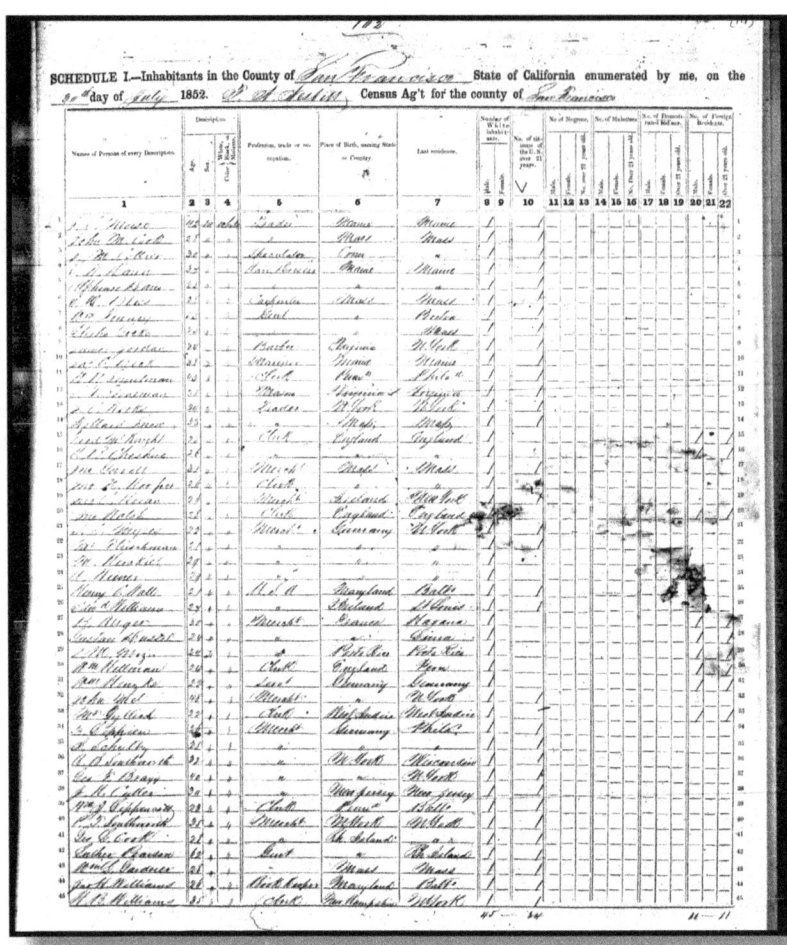

The following information below is "extracted", i.e., is being taken from "Exhibit 6" from the above page verbatim, which is from the *1852 State of California Census*, namely:

1852 State of California Census – S M Mazie; [AKA: S. N. Mazie; Simon M. Mazie; Simon M. Mezes; Simon Montserrate Mezes]; *Birth Place:* **Porto Rico**, "abt 1828"; Age: 24; Residence: San Francisco; Profession: "not readable":

Schedule I. – Inhabitants in the County of San Francisco State of California enumerated by me [the Enumerator], on the 30th day of July 1852. [Name of the Enumerator is "not readable"], Census Ag't for the county of San Francisco.

Column 1: Name – S M Mazie;
Column 2: Age – 24;
Column 3: Sex – Male;
Column 4: Color – White;
Column 5: Profession, trade or occupation [unreadable]
Column 6: Place of Birth, naming State or Country – "Porto Rico";
Column 7: Last residence – "Porto Rico";
Column 8: Number of white inhabitants – 1 White Male;
Column 10: No. of citizens of the U.S. over 21 yrs.: (Mr. Mazie was *not* a citizen);
Column 20: No. of Foreign Residents – 1 Male;
Column 22: No. of Foreign Residents – 1 over 21 yrs. Old
S. M. Mazie's name appears on **Line 29** above (on the Census page Form itself).

Mr. Mazie's "Profession", while listed on line 29, is "not readable" by this author. (See also Exhibit 18 of this book)

Source: Ancestry.com. *California State Census, 1852* [database on-line]. Provo, UT, USA: *Ancestry.com* Operations, Inc. 2010. Original data: California State Census of 1852 Sacramento, CA: California State Library. (**Courtesy of Ancestry.com**)

Exhibit 7

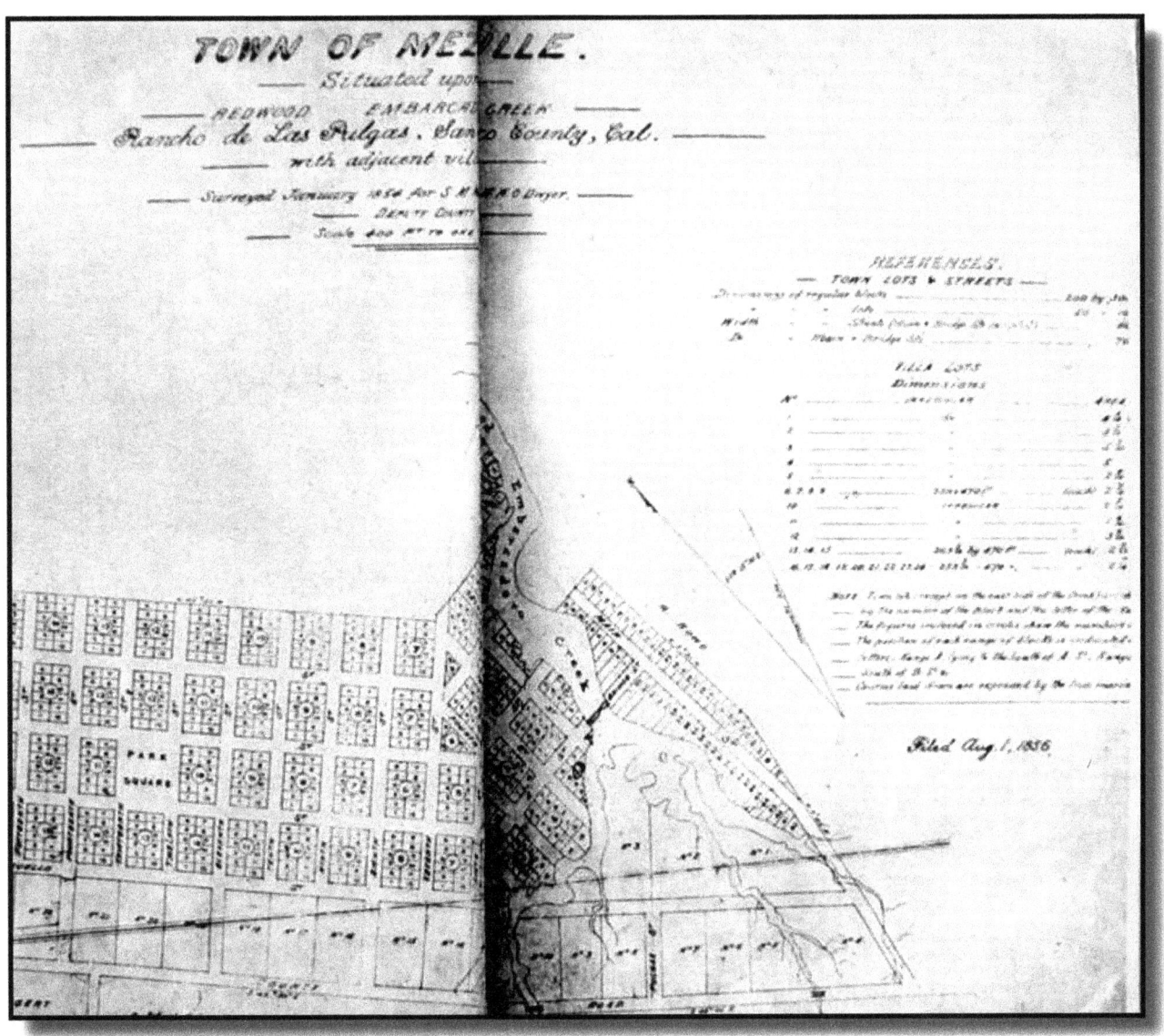

The map above was drawn by Simon M. Mezes, and was filed on Aug. 1, 1856 (refer to the lower right-hand side of this map) for the town that he founded, namely, Mezesville, CA (today known as: Redwood City, CA). [**Note:** I received *written permission* from the **San Mateo County Historical Association**, which published the May 1967 Centennial issue of the *La Peninsula:* Journal of the San Mateo County Historical Association, to use the above photo(s) of Mr. Mezes (see: Exhibit 5, above), and the above copy of the 1856 map (Exhibit 7), for this book].

Exhibit 8

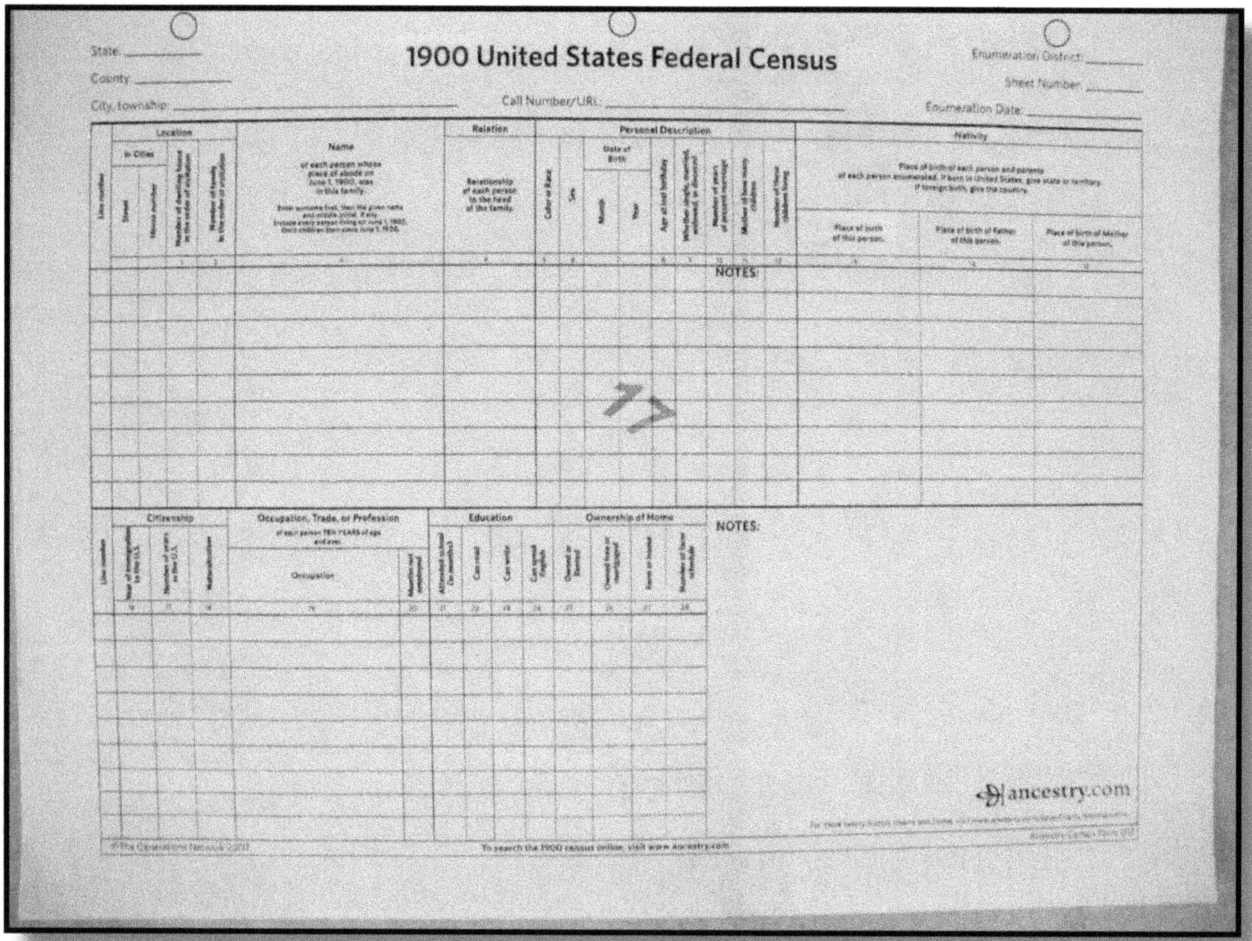

"**Blank copy**": (a non-completed "sample page") of the *1900 United States Federal Census* page, showing some selected columns from this Census: **Nativity column** (identified ones: "Name"; "Age"; the "place of birth of each person and parents of each person enumerated. If born in United States, give state or territory. If foreign birth, give the country"; the "Citizenship" column. (**Courtesy of Ancestry.com**)

Exhibit 9

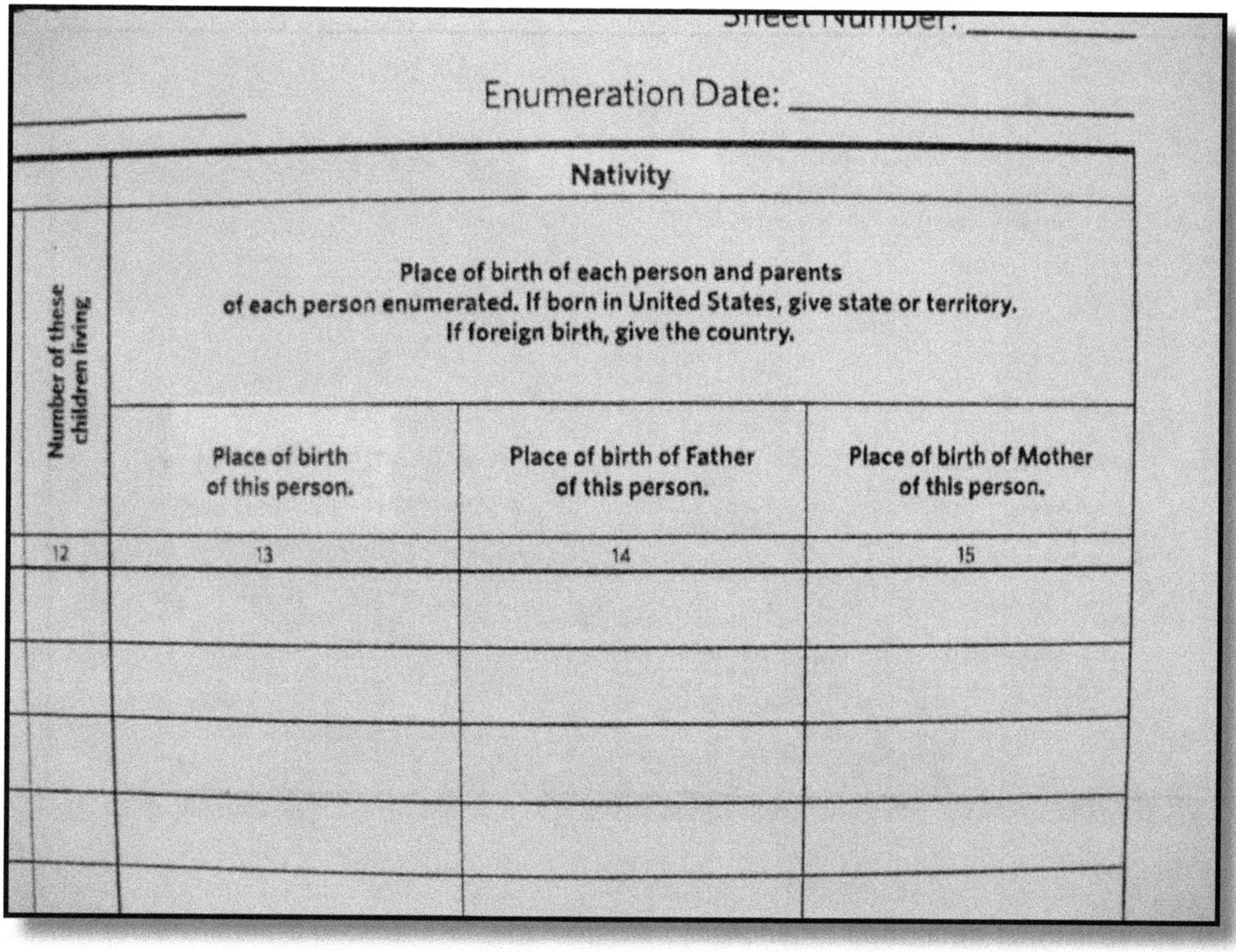

Number of these children living	Nativity		
	Place of birth of each person and parents of each person enumerated. If born in United States, give state or territory. If foreign birth, give the country.		
	Place of birth of this person.	Place of birth of Father of this person.	Place of birth of Mother of this person.
12	13	14	15

Sheet Number: _____

Enumeration Date: _____

"**Blank copy:** of the *1900 U.S. Federal Census* (enlarged copy of this page), showing the *"Nativity" column*, as well as showing the following sub-columns: "Place of birth of this person"; "Place of birth of Father of this person"; "Place of birth of Mother of this person." (**Courtesy of Ancestry.com**)

Exhibit 10

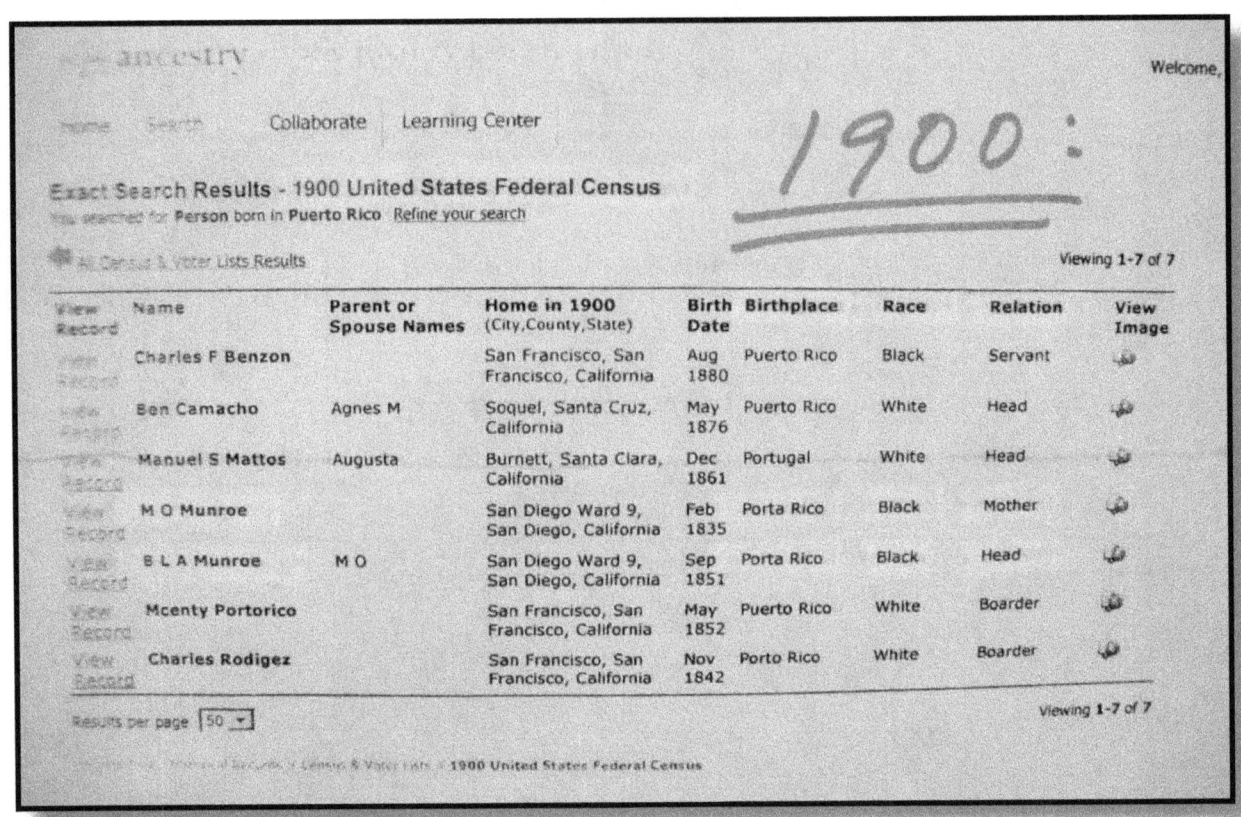

The above list was generated by *Ancestry.com* from the *1900 United States Federal Census* (for California) of those persons who were both **born in Puerto Rico (Porto Rico)** and who were also residing in San Francisco, CA according to the *1900 U.S. Federal Census* (California), including two (2) persons who were residing in San Diego, CA, namely: M O Munroe (Mother) and B L A Munroe (Head/[Son]) [cited and spelled this way on the 1900 Census Form page itself], both of whom were listed as having been born in "Porta Rico" (i.e., Puerto Rico)]. At the time of the *1900 U.S. Federal Census* (California), the Munroe's lived in San Diego Ward 9. (**Courtesy of Ancestry.com**)

Note: The 3rd name on the above list, Mr. Mattos, was born in Portugal, and therefore, he is *not* counted as having been born in Puerto Rico/Porto Rico.

Exhibit 11

Exact Search Results - 1910 United States Federal Census

You searched for **San Francisco District 45** born in **Puerto Rico** Refine your search

All Census & Voter Lists Results   Viewing 1-50 of 63 | Next »

View Record	Name	Parent or Spouse Names	Home in 1910 (City, County, State)	Birth Year	Birthplace	Relation	View Image
① View Record	Placida Anegro		San Francisco Assembly District 45, San Francisco, California	abt 1887	Puerto Rico	Lodger	
View Record	Joe Augustin		San Francisco Assembly District 45, San Francisco, California	abt 1882	Puerto Rico	Head	
View Record	Juana Balde	Ralph G	San Francisco Assembly District 45, San Francisco, California	abt 1884	Puerto Rico	Wife	
View Record	Joseph Bancco		San Francisco Assembly District 45, San Francisco, California	abt 1884	Puerto Rico	Lodger	
⑤ View Record	Maltina Bollan		San Francisco Assembly District 45, San Francisco, California	abt 1864	Puerto Rico	Head	
View Record	Oruagin Bollan	Maltina	San Francisco Assembly District 45, San Francisco, California	abt 1884	Puerto Rico	Son	
View Record	Bonice Bollan	Maltina	San Francisco Assembly District 45, San Francisco, California	abt 1888	Puerto Rico	Son	
View Record	German Bollan	Maltina	San Francisco Assembly District 45, San Francisco, California	abt 1890	Puerto Rico	Son	
View Record	Bomitila Bollan	Maltina	San Francisco Assembly District 45, San Francisco, California	abt 1895	Puerto Rico	Daughter	
⑩ View Record	Luteria Bollan	Maltina	San Francisco Assembly District 45, San Francisco, California	abt 1903	Puerto Rico	Daughter	
View Record	Antonio Bollan	Maltina	San Francisco Assembly District 45, San Francisco, California	abt 1903	Puerto Rico	Son	
View Record	Monseratte Colon	Lucas	San Francisco Assembly District 45, San Francisco, California	abt 1868	Puerto Rico	Wife	

The above list was generated by Ancestry.com from the *1910 United States Federal Census* (California) listing those persons who were **born** in Puerto Rico, and who also were residing in San Francisco, CA as of the *1910 Federal Census* (California) enumeration date. This list provided the following census data/information: Name; Parent or Spouse Names; Home in 1910 (City, County, State); Birth Year; Birthplace; Relation [to the "Head of Household"]. (**Courtesy of Ancestry.com**)

On June 14, 2010, I visually confirmed that all the names listed on this page (as well as on **all** of the other pages which I reviewed) were **born** in Puerto Rico (or which were also cited as being: "Porto Rico"), by looking at the individual Census Page Form(s) themselves, and which were also provided by *Ancestry.com*.

Exhibit 12

Source: The *San Francisco Examiner*, December 15, 1900 (page 2).

The <u>caption</u> from the *San Francisco Examiner* read:

"Seven of the ragged, half-starved little Porto Ricans who had escaped from a life of slavery on Hawaii's plantations were photographed by flashlight in *The Examiner* editorial rooms by Percy Dana, an *'Examiner'* Photographer. The little chap who sits third from the left side of the picture, holds in [her] arms the twelve days' old baby girl that was born on American soil while crossing the continent." (Italicize added)

(Written Permission obtained from the University of California (Berkeley, CA), the Bancroft Library, as well as a telecon with the *San Francisco Examiner* Editor). **(Courtesy of: the Bancroft Library)**

Exhibit 13

Source: The *San Francisco Examiner*, December 24, 1900 (page 2).

The <u>caption</u> from the *San Francisco Examiner* read as follows:

"Last of the stranded refugees leaving this city [San Francisco] yesterday morning, from the infants' shelter in Minna Street. They went to comfortable homes on Monterey Country Ranch."

(Written Permission obtained from the University of California, Bancroft Library) **(Courtesy of: the Bancroft Library)**

Exhibit 14

1890s life in Puerto Rico during the Spanish Colonial period.

The above photograph is from the 1899 book entitled:

Our Islands and Their People: As Seen With Camera and Pencil (Volume I), by José De Olivares, 1899. New York: N.D. Thompson Publishing Co. (page 268). Mr. Olivares is cited in the book as being: "The noted Author and War Correspondent."

Exhibit 15

1890s life in Puerto Rico during the Spanish Colonial period:

The above photograph is from the 1899 book entitled:

***Our Islands and Their People* (Volume I)**, by Jose De Olivares, 1899. New York: N.D. Thompson Publishing Co. (page 334).

Exhibit 16

1890s life in Puerto Rico during the Spanish Colonial period:

The above photograph is from the 1899 book entitled:

***Our Islands and Their People* (Volume I)**, by Jose De Olivares, 1899. New York: N.D. Thompson Publishing Co. (page 261).

Exhibit 17

Source: The *San Francisco Examiner*, December 15, 1900 (page 1).

This is an enlarged copy of the front page of the Dec. 15, 1900 issue of the *Examiner*. **Note:** The full <u>*caption*</u> was earlier identified (typed-out in full) by this author in the beginning section of this book titled: "The Cover Page Description of This Book".

(**NOTE:** Written permission, via e-mail correspondence, was obtained from the University of California's Bancroft Library, who are the current "owners" of this historic photograph from the *San Francisco Examiner* newspaper, i.e., the December 15, 1900 issue, and thereafter.)

(Courtesy of: the Bancroft Library)

Exhibit 18

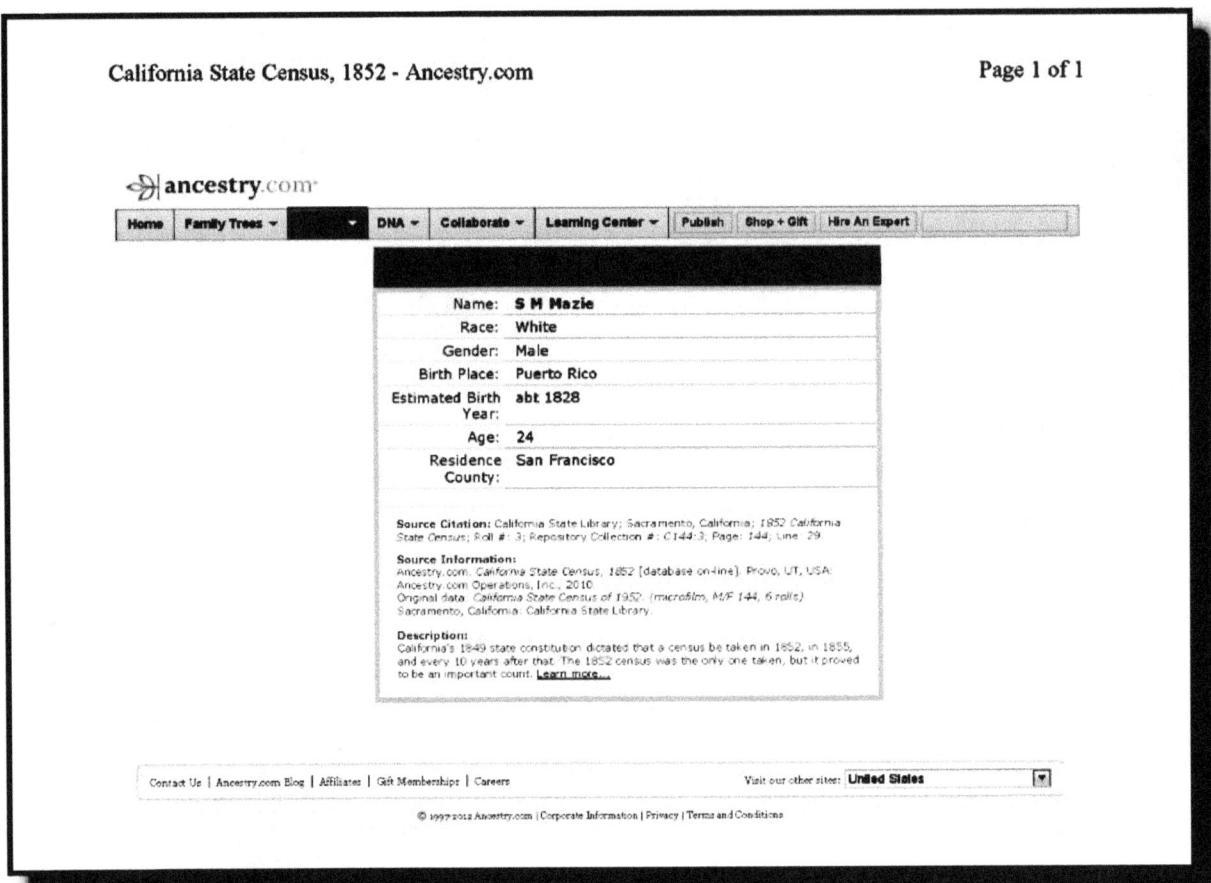

Exhibit 18: From the *California State Census, 1852 - Ancestry.com* - Name: S M Mazie [aka: S.M. Mezes; Simon M. Mezes];

Race: White;

Gender: Male;

Birth Place: Puerto Rico;

Estimated Birth Year: abt 1828;

Age: 24;

Residence County: San Francisco. (**Courtesy of: ancestry.com**)

U.S. Bureau of Labor

REPORT

OF THE

COMMISSIONER OF LABOR

ON

HAWAII.

1902.

WASHINGTON:
GOVERNMENT PRINTING OFFICE.
1903.

morally upset by their long travels and changed environment, and many could not acquire the new habits of life necessary to their new condition. So a considerable number became strollers and vagabonds, and, wherever possible, flocked into the towns.

The social regimen of the islands is strict. There is no extreme poverty, and begging is unknown. Any industrious and able-bodied man can always find employment in the country, and planters act upon the theory that a man who doesn't work is bound to steal. So a person without visible means of support is not allowed to remain on a plantation, and as the plantations cover nearly all the settled portion of the islands, it is exceedingly difficult for a man to follow a life of vagrancy with comfort. A certain number of Asiatics contrive to do so, but they live a sort of parasite existence upon their fellows, visiting from plantation to plantation among their more industrious brothers, and do not sink to the social rank or follow the methods of tramps or public beggars. Therefore Porto Ricans so disposed did not find conditions favorable to the *dolce far niente* existence so common among their own country population. They were confronted with the necessity of constant labor, and this was a new situation to most of them. A fair number are meeting the emergency with credit, and are acquiring habits of persistent industry that they might never have gained in their own country. But a certain proportion have failed to adapt themselves to any sort of an industrious life, and these have drifted from the plantations into the towns or their immediate vicinity and form a class of malcontents and petty criminals.

The Porto Ricans arrived in Hawaii in 11 expeditions, beginning in December, 1900, and continuing until October 19, 1901. There were about 450 in each party, the total number of immigrants being about 5,000, of whom 2,930 were men and the remainder women and children. The exact cost of recruiting and bringing them to Honolulu was $564,191.68, or more than $100 per capita—a sum amply sufficient to assure their comfortable transportation and entertainment while en route. An English translation of the notice in Spanish, posted by agents recruiting laborers in Porto Rico for the Hawaiian Planters' Association, and known as the "Contract under which the Porto Rican laborers went to Hawaii," follows:

AGREEMENT FOR THE EMPLOYMENT OF LABORERS FOR THE ISLANDS OF HAWAII.

The Planters' Association of the Hawaiian Islands needs laborers for the cultivation of cane and the manufacture of sugar, and therefore makes the following offer to working people and their families who will go to that country:

1. To furnish such laborers, their wives, children, and relatives free passage from Porto Rico to Honolulu, including subsistence and medical attendance during the journey.

2. To furnish such laborer upon his arrival with agricultural employment for the period of three years from the date of actually commencing work; also furnishing employment to his wife and elder children if they so desire.

CHAP. I.—GENERAL CONDITION OF LABOR AND INDUSTRY. 27

3. To guarantee the laborer the following wages for each month of 26 working days of actual labor:

	Per month.
During the first year	$15
During the second year	16
During the third year	17

and to pay his wife and elder children, if they wish to work, as follows:

	Per day.
Boys from 15 to 18 years of age	$0.50
Girls from 15 to 18 years of age	.35
Women from 18 to 40 years of age	.40

4. The laborer and his family will receive, free of cost, living apartments, fuel and water for domestic use, medical attendance, and medicines.

5. The laborer shall be exempt from personal taxes, he and his family will enjoy the full protection of the laws of the Territory of Hawaii, and his children under 14 years of age will be provided with primary instruction in the public schools.

6. At the conclusion of three years from the time of actually beginning work the planter will pay the laborer $72 bonus, providing always that the laborer shall have worked continually during this period upon the plantation to which he was assigned an average of not less than 20 days in each month.

Upon their arrival in Honolulu the workmen and their families will be instructed in the methods of cane culture followed upon the Hawaiian plantations.

Ten hours constitute a working day in the fields and 12 hours in the mill, it being understood that this work is not continuous, as the laborer is given time to eat his meals and rest from his work.

All overtime in excess of the hours stated will be paid for at the rate of 10 cents an hour; 26 working days constitute a month.

The journey will be made as follows: The laborers will embark upon comfortable steamers for New Orleans, a trip of 4 days; from there they will travel by rail to San Francisco, which will require about 4 days more, and from California they will embark in a Pacific liner, which will take them to Hawaii in 6 days more. The whole journey will occupy about 14 days.

The workmen and their families will be provided by the Planters' Association upon embarking with *clothing, underclothing, footwear, and blankets*, as follows:

For men and boys, 1 pair of shoes and stockings, 1 suit of underwear, 1 shirt, 1 pair of trousers, 1 hat, and 1 blanket. For women and girls, cloth for a dress and undergarments, stockings, shoes, a head cloth, and a blanket.

The climate of the Hawaiian islands is similar to that of Porto Rico, inasmuch as it lies in the 18th degree of latitude, and the temperature does not fall below 15° C. (59° F.) or rise above 25° C. (77° F), a less degree of heat than in Porto Rico.

The products of the islands are sugar, coffee, tobacco, pineapples, and all the fruits found in Porto Rico, such as bananas, yams, sweet potatoes, etc.

The inhabitants of the islands profess different religious faiths, among them the Roman Catholic, which denomination has many churches and priests there.

From cablegrams and letters received we know that the Porto Ricans, who have gone to Hawaii in the first five expeditions have been given satisfactory employment upon the plantations of the islands, as well as their wives and children. This is corroborated by letters which the emigrants have sent to their families in Porto Rico. Letters of a very satisfactory tenor have been received by several commercial establishments in Yauco for delivery to friends. These letters are on file at the Hawaiian agency, at the disposition of any who care to examine them.

Porto Rico, April 16, 1901.

R. A. MACFIE,
W. D. NOBLE,
The Agents, San Jaun, Ponce, Adjuntas.

Exhibit 20 - (courtesy of: Hayward Area Historical Society)

Exhibit 21 - (courtesy of: Hayward Area Historical Society)

HAYWARD AREA HISTORICAL SOCIETY
22701 MAIN STREET, HAYWARD, CA 94541 • (510) 581-0223

FOR IMMEDIATE RELEASE

July 13, 2002

Contact: Jim DeMersman, Director
510.581.0223
510.581.0217(fax)
jimdhahs@aol.com

(Historical Society Free Open House)

Hayward, CA—In conjunction with its current exhibition, *California Century: Puerto Ricans in the San Francisco Bay Area, 1900 – 2000*, the Hayward Area Historical Society will present a free public open house on July 18 from 5:30 – 8:30 p.m. During the open house, Kaleponi Ukulele Strings – a group of teen and adult students from Hollis Baker's Hayward Adult School classes – will perform from 6:00 – 7:30 p.m. Hollis Bakker is the co-founder of Hayward's Ukulele Festival with Puerto Rican-American John Ogao. At 7:30 p.m. renowned Puerto Rican/African-American poet and performer Aya de Leon will share some of her most well known poems, such as *Grito de Vieques*. Ms. de Leon is an award-winning member of the western regional poetry slam team and will be an artist-in-residence at Stanford University this year. This will also be a final chance to see the current exhibit before it closes on Saturday, July 20. The exhibit commemorates the 100th anniversary of the arrival of the first Puerto Ricans to the Bay Area (particularly the East Bay) and explores how this community has lived, worked and worshipped over the past century.

Puerto Ricans were hired as contract laborers to work in the sugar fields of Hawaii. Taken by ship and rail from Puerto Rico, some refused to continue the journey to Hawaii, while others did go to Hawaii and eventually doubled back to settle in the Bay Area. The exhibit was guest curated by scholar Aurora Levins Morales and included photographs of Barry Kleider.

MORE

Hayward Area Historical Society

Since the reader may not be able to read the above print (i.e., Exhibit 21) this author hereby will type type this July 13, 2002 **"Press Release"**, verbatim:

FOR IMMEDIATE RELEASE

July 13, 2002

Contact: Jim DeMersman, Director

(Historical Society Free Open House)

Hayward, CA---In conjunction with its current exhibitions, ***California Century: Puerto Ricans in the San Francisco Bay Area, 1900 – 2000***, the Hayward Area Historical Society will present a free public open house on July 18 from 5:30 – 8:30 p.m. During the open House, Kaleponi Ukulele Strings --- a group of teen and adult students from Hollis Baker's Hayward Adult School classes – will perform from 6:00 – 7:30 p.m. Hollis Baker is the co-founder of Hayward's Ukulele Festival with Puerto Rican-American John Ogao. At 7:30 p.m. renowned Puerto Rican/African-American poet and performer Aya de Leon will share some of her most well known poems, such as *Grito de Vieques*. Ms. De Leon is an award-winning member of the western regional poetry slam team and will be an artist-in-residence at Stanford University this year. This will also be a final chance to see the current exhibit before it closes on Saturday, July 20. The exhibit commemorates the 100th anniversary of the arrival of the first Puerto Ricans to the Bay Area (particularly the East Bay) and explores how this community has lived, worked and worshipped over the past Century. [emphasis added]

Puerto Ricans were hired as contract laborers to work in the sugar fields of Hawaii. Taken by ship and rail from Puerto Rico, some refused to continue the journey to Hawaii, while others did go to Hawaii and eventually doubled back to settle in the Bay area. The exhibit was guest curated by scholar Aurora Levins Morales and included photographs of Barry Kleider.

[**Note:** The Hayward Area Historical Society is a private, non-profit, educational organization located at 22701 Main Street in historic downtown Hayward, three blocks from the downtown Hayward BART station.]

(Courtesy of: the Hayward Area Historical Society)

TABLE 1

Puerto Rican Population Figures for the United States, The State of California, and for Selected California Counties, Cities and Years: 1900, 1910, 1920, 2000

City	Year 1900	Year 1910	Year 1920	Year 2000
California Total	7[a]	342[i]	935[f]	140,570[d]
San Francisco (San Francisco County)	3[a]	213[j]	474[f]	3,758[g]
Alameda County	1[a]	31[a]	-	10,186[g]
City of Oakland [In Alameda County]	0[a]	10[j]	101[f]	2,325[g]
City of Los Angeles	1[a]	10[j]	39[f]	13,427[g]
Los Angeles County	1[a]	-	-	37,862[g]
City of San Diego	2[a]	3[a]	9[f]	5,938[g]
San Diego County	2[a]	3[a]	11[a]	14,037[g]
New York City	300[b]	554[j]	7,364[f]	789,200[b]
United States Total Puerto Rican Population	678[c]	1,513[i]	11,811[f]	3,406,178[c]
Puerto Rico	953,243[k]	1,118,012[e]	1,299,809[e]	3,808,610[h]

Sources:

[a] AncestryInstitution.com.
[b] Marzan, *et. al.* (2008).
[c] Duany, Jorge. (2003);
[d] Teresa Whalen, Carmen. (2005).
[e] U.S. Bureau of the Census. (1975).
[f] U.S. Bureau of the Census. (1922: 679). Vol. II.
[g] Information Publications, Inc. (2009).
[h] U.S. Bureau of the Census. (2010). "Census 2000 Data for Puerto Rico".
[i] U.S. Bureau of the Census. (1913a: 185). 13th Census. "Abstract".
[j] U.S. Bureau of the Census. (1913b: 778, 779). 13th Census. "Population".
[k] U.S. Census Office. (1902: 7). "Abstract of 12th Census: 1900." "Table 1."

Note: See: the "Bibliography" for the *complete* citation for all of the sources referenced above, and below, as well.

Note: In his article, Dr. Jorge Duany points out that, "Between 1910 and 1940, the available figures refers to persons of Puerto Rican birth only; after 1950, they include persons of Puerto Rican parentage and, after 1970, they include all persons of Puerto Rican origin," (Duany 2003: Table 1- 3, p. 426, "Note").
Note: Information Publications, Inc. (2009: 553-555, 557, 560, 564, 587, 591, 598, 599).

Note: While the 1910 Census listed 10 Porto Ricans that resided in the City of Los Angeles, it did not provide the figures for Los Angeles County. AncestryInstitution.com listed the specific individual *name(s)* of a total of eight (8) Porto Ricans that resided in Los Angeles County in 1910.
Note: The author not able to locate the 1920 Porto Rican figures for either Alameda County nor for Los Angeles County.

Note: While the 1920 Federal Census identified 9 Porto Ricans in San Diego for 1920 (i.e., persons born in Porto Rico), however, Ancestry.com identified a total of 10. Dr. Chenault (1938: 57) indicated there were 7,719 Puerto Ricans in New York State, and California had 935, "persons [who were] born in Puerto Rico," in 1920 (U.S. Bureau of the Census. 1922: 630, 678).
Note: Figures are for Puerto Rican birth and parentage for the 2000 Census Figures. (Teresa Whalen 2005: 32).

Note: AncestryInstitution.com, *1910 United States Federal Census* [database on-line]. Provo, UT, USA: Ancestry. Com Operations Inc. 2006. AncestryInstitution.com listed **8** Puerto Ricans in the City of Oakland in 1910.

Note: The 1900 "Population [is] as of 1899", from the "Census of Puerto Rico," (Chenault 1938: 29, "Table 6"; next to the "Source," at the bottom of "Table 6," (U.S. Bureau of the Census 1975); Acosta-Belén, Edna (2010: 1).

Note: The 1900 Census listed six (6) persons who were born in Porto Rico, as well as a total of seven (7) Porto Ricans who were living in the "Western div." of the United States (U.S. Census Bureau. 1902. *Abstract of The Twelfth Census of The United States: 1900.* 7); as well as a total of 336 Porto Ricans living in New York State in 1900 (page 54).

(09/02/2010)

BIBLIOGRAPHY

1: Acosta Belén, Edna. 2010. "Puerto Rican Diaspora in the United States." *Puerto Rico Encyclopedia.* January 28, 2010. Retrieved on April 13, 2010. (<http://www. enciclopediapr.org/ing/printversion. cfm?ref=06082951>) (Fundación Puertorriqueña de las Humanidades).

2: Acosta-Belén, Edna and Carlos E. Santiago. 2006. *Puerto Ricans in the United States: A Contemporary Portrait.* Boulder, Colorado: Lynne Rienner Publishers, Inc.

3: Allen, Charles H., Governor. 1901. *First Annual Report of Governor of Porto Rico Covering the Period From May 1, 1900, to May 1, 1901.* May 1, 1901. Washington: Government Printing Office. (Accessed via: Google books)

4: *Amador Ledger, The.* (California) 1901. [Jackson, Amador County, California] "Foreign." July 5, 1901; [Newspaper].

5: American Federation of Labor, The. 1902. *Proceedings of the American Federation of Labor: 1902 – 1903.* Report of Proceedings of the Twenty-Second Annaul Convention. Held at New Orleans, Louisiana, November 13 to 22, 1902. Washington, D.C.: The Law Reporter Co.

6: Ames, Azel, M.D. 1901. "Labor Conditions In Porto Rico." *Bulletin of the Department of Labor.* May 1901, No. 34. (Accessed via: Google books)

7: *Ancestry.com. 1850* United States Federal Census [database on-line]. Provo, UT, USA; Ancestry. com Operations, Inc. 2009. Images reproduced by FamilySearch. Original data: Seventh Census of the United States; (National Archives Microfilm Publication M432, 1009 rolls); Records of the Bureau of the Census, Record Group 29; National Archives, Wash., D.C). Retrieved on: 04/23/10. (<http:// search. ancestry institution.com/search/db.aspx?dbid=8054.>).

8: *Ancestry.com*. California State Census 1852 [database on-line]; California State Library, Sacramento, California, Roll #3; Record URL is: (<http://search. ancestry.com/cgi-bin/sse.dll?h =01141&db=1852 californiastatecensus&rank=1&new=1>).

9: *Ancestry.com. 1860.* United States Federal Census [for: California] [database on-line]. Provo, UT, USA; Ancestry.com Operations, Inc., 2009. Images reproduced by FamilySearch. Original data: 1860 U.S. census, population schedule NARA microfilm publication M653, 1,438 rolls. Washington, D.C.: National Archives and Records Administration, n.d. Retrieved on April 24, 2010 (and thereafter). (<http://search.ancestryinstitution.com/search /db. aspx?dbid=7667>).

10: *Ancestry.com. 1870.* United States Federal Census [database on-line]. Provo, UT, USA: Ancestry.com Operations, Inc., 2009 Images reproduced by FamilySearch. Original data: 1870 U.S. Census, population schedules. NARA microfilm publication M593, 1,761 rolls. Washington, D.C.: National Archives and Records Administration, n.d. Retrieved on April 24, 2010. (<http://search. ancestryinstitution. com/ search/ db.aspx?dbid=7163>).

11: Ancestry.com. 1880. United States Federal Census. Source Citation: Year: 1880: Census Place: Belmont, San Mateo, California; Roll 80; Family History Film: 1254080; Page: 386D; Enumeration District: 237; Image: 0656. Source Information: Ancestry.com and The Church of Jesus Christ of Latter-day Saints. 1880 United States Federal Census [database on-line]. Provo, UT, USA: Ancestry. com Operations, Inc., 2010. Original data: *Tenth Census of the United States. 1880.* (NARA microfilm publication T9. 1,454 rolls). Records of the Bureau of the Census. Record Group 29. National Archives, Washington, D.C. Retrieved on June 3, 2010 (and thereafter). (<http://search.ancestry institution. com/cgi-bin/sse.d11?db= 1880usfedcen& indiv=try&h= 20637...>).

12: Ancestry.com. 1890. United States Federal Census: Fragment. The **California** portion of this Census was destroyed by fire. Accessed on April 22, 2010 (and thereafter). See: (<http://search.ancestryinstitution.com/search/db.aspx?dbid=5445>).

13: Ancestry.com. 1900. United States Federal Census [database on-line]. Provo, UT, USA: Ancestry.com Operations Inc. 2004. Original data: United States of America, Bureau of the Census. *Twelfth Census of the United States, 1900*. Washington, D.C.: National Archives and Records Administration, 1900. T623, 1854 rolls. Retrieved on April 22, 2010 (and thereafter). (<http://search.ancestryinstitution.com/search/db.aspx?dbid=7602>).

14: AncestryInsititution.com. 1910. United States Federal Census [database on-line]. Provo, UT, USA: ancestry.com Operations Inc, 2006. Retrieved on April 22, 2010, and for several months thereafter (April-July 2010). (http://search.ancestryinstitution.com/search/ db.aspx?dbid=7884).

15: Arroyo, Ronald. 1977. *Da Borinkees: The Puerto Ricans of Hawaii*. Ph.D. Dissertation, Union Graduate School: Cincinnati.

16: Atlanta Constitution, The. 1904. "Porto Ricans Are Not Aliens. Decision to That Effect by United States Supreme Court." January 5, 1904. [Newspaper]

17: Bankston III, Carl L. and Danielle Antoinette Hidalgo, Editors. 2006. "Ethnic Enclaves". In *Immigration in History. Volume 1*. Project Editor: R. Kent Rasmussen. Pasadena, CA: Salem Press, Inc.

18: Board of Immigration. 1907. *First Report of the Board of Immigration to the Governor of the Territory of Hawaii*. Honolulu: Bulletin Publishing Co., LTD.

19: _____. 1909. *Second Report of the Board of Immigration to the Governor of the Territory of Hawaii*. Honolulu: The Hawaiian Gazette Co., LTD.

20: Board of Supervisors. 1873. *San Francisco Municipal Reports For the Year 1872-73, Ending June 30th, 1873*. San Francisco: Spaulding & Barto, Printers, "Scientific Press" Job Printing Office. (Accessed via: Google books)

21: Borges-Mendez, Ramón. 1993. "Migration, Social Networks, Poverty and Regionalization of Puerto Rican Settlements: Barrio Formation in Lowell, Lawrence and Holyoke, Massachusetts." *Latino Studies Journal*. A Special Issue on Puerto Rican Migration and poverty, Guest Editor: Edwin Meléndez. May 1993, Vol. 4, No. 2. 3-21.

22: Brandt, Lilian. 1906. "Rehabilitation Work in San Francisco." *Charities And The Commons: A Weekly Journal of Philanthropy and Social Advance*. October 6, 1906. Vol. XVII, No. 1.

23: Bulletin of the Department of Labor. 1903a. "*Report of the Commissioner of Labor on Hawaii*." No. 47. July 1903. Washington. (Accessed via: Google books) (see: page 685ff.)

24: _____. 1903b. "Labor conditions in the sugar industry in Hawaii, California, Texas, Louisiana, Cuba, and Porto Rico." 1903. No.47. July 1903. *Report of the Commissioner of Labor on Hawaii*. Washington: Government Printing Office. (Accessed via: Google books) (see: pages 767-772)

25: _____. 1905. "Labor Conditions in Porto Rico," by Walter E. Weyl, Ph.D. No. 61. November 1905. Washington. (Accessed via Google books)

26: _____. 1905. Section titled: "Educational Opportunities of the Porto Rican Workman." No. 61. Washington. (Accessed via Google books)

27: _____. 1905. Section titled: "Competition of Porto Rican With Foreign Labor." No. 61. November 1905. Washington. (Accessed via Google books)

28: California State Library, California History Section. 1866-1898. *Great Registers, 1866-1898* [the record for: B L A Munroe]; Collection Number: 4–2A; CSL Roll Number: 20; FHL Roll Number: 977994. (Source Information): Ancestry.com. *California, Voter Registers, 1866-1898* [database on-line]. Provo, UT, USA: Ancestry.com Operations, Inc., 2011.

29: California. Unknown Date. *Vital Search-CA: Deaths – 7748. Bottom Frame-Search California Deaths: 1905-1929.* San Diego, CA: San Diego Genealogical Society. Accessed: May 27, 2010. (<http://www.vitalsearch-ca. com/picdata/CA/deaths/190/CA__de9...>).

30: Camacho Souza, Blasé. 1975. "The Puerto Ricans in Hawaii". In *A Legacy of Diversity: Contributions of the Hawaiians, Chinese, Japanese, Portuguese, Puerto Ricans, Koreans, Filipinos and Samoans in Hawaii.* Ethnic Resource Center for the Pacific College of Education, Educational Foundations, University of Hawaii. Honolulu: Hawaii.

31: _____. 1984. "Trabajo y Tristeza--'Work and Sorrow': The Puerto Ricans of Hawaii 1900-1902," *Hawaiian Journal of History.* Vol. 18. Honolulu: Hawaiian Historical Society, (URL: Unknown; Retrieved the article on-line).

32: Carr, Norma. 1980. *PUERTO RICAN: One Identity From a Multi-Ethnic Heritage.* (see: the "*Forward*" page, by Charles G. Clark, Superintendent of Education). University of Hawaii at Hilo Library.

33: _____. 1987. "Image: The Puerto Rican in Hawaii." In *Images and Identities: The Puerto Rican in Two World Contexts.* Edited by Asela Rodríguez de Laguna. Transaction Inc.: New Brunswick, N.J. (U.S.A.).

34: _____. 1989. *The Puerto Ricans in Hawaii: 1900-1958.* Ph.D. Dissertation, University of Hawaii. Department of American Studies. Ann Arbor, Michigan: UMI Dissertation Services.

35: Castanha, Anthony. 2004. *Adventures In Caribbean Indigeneity Centering on Resistance, Survival and Presence on Borikén (Puerto Rico).* University of Hawaii Ph.D. Dissertation. Department of Political Science. (Chapter 6, "Boricua Exodus to Hawaii", was e-mailed to me by Dr. Castanha).

36: Centro de Estudios Puertorriqueños. 1977. *Documentos de la Migración Puertorriqueña (1879-1901) – Documents of the Puerto Rican Migration: Hawaii, Cuba, Santo Domingo, Ecuador.* No.1., Bilingual Publication, Center for Puerto Rican Studies, The City University of New York.

37: _____. 1981. *Preliminary Guide to Articles in Puerto Rican Newspapers Relating to Puerto Rican Migration Between 1900 and 1929.* New York: Library of the Centro De Estudios Puertorriqueños (CUNY).

38: _____. History Task Force. 1982. "Manifestación." 14 de Julio de 1902. Fondo Fortaleza. Archivo General de Puerto Rico. Cited in: *Sources for the Study of Puerto Rican Migration – 1879-1930.* Hunter College of the City University of New York.

39: Chenault, Lawrence R. 1938. *The Puerto Rican Migrant in New York City.* New York: Columbia University Press; [Also reissued, Russell & Russell, 1970].

40: Club Puertorriqueño De San Francisco. 1912a. *Constitución, Leyes y Reglamento Del Club Puertorriqueño De San Francisco, Organizado en febrero 25 de 1912 é Incorporado según la ley Estado de California en Julio 13 de 1912*, San Francisco, California (E.U. de A.).

41: _____. 1912b. *Progreso – Fraternidas. Sesión Ordinaria. Acta No. 1* ("Minutes of their Meetings" in February 1912). Archives of the Centro de Estudios Puertorriqueños/Center for Puerto Rican Studies. Hunter College. CUNY, New York City. The Bancroft Library, University of California, Berkeley, has Vol. 1: Feb. 25, 1912; Feb. 3, 1916. (BANC Film 3163).

42: Committee on Immigration and Naturalization, The. 1921. "Labor Problems in Hawaii." *Hearings Before The Committee on Immigration and Naturalization.* Serial 7-Part 1. Wash.: Gov. Printing Off.

43: Committee on Pacific Islands and Porto Rico. 1912. "Citizenship of Porto Ricans." *Hearings Before The Committee on Pacific Islands and Porto Rico United States Senate.* Sixty-Second Congress. Second Session on H.R. 20048. May 7, 1912. Wash: Gov. Printing Off.

44: De Olivares, José. 1899. *Our Islands and Their People: As Seen With Camera and Pencil.* Introduced by Major-General Joseph Wheeler (U.S. Army), with Special Descriptive Matter and Narratives by José De Olivares. Volume I. St. Louis: N.D. Thompson Publishing Co. (In the author's private collection).

45: Dilts, Bryan Lee. 1984. *1860 California Census Index: Heads of Households and Other Surnames in Households Index.* Salt Lake City, UT: Index Publishing.

46: Dollarhide, William. 1999. *The Census Book: A Genealogist's Guide to Federal Census Facts, Schedules and Indexes.* Bountiful, Utah: Heritage Quest.

47: Duany, Jorge. 2003. "Nation, Migration, Identity: The Case of Puerto Ricans." *Latino Studies*, 1, Nov. 2003. 424-444. Retrieved on May 11, 2010). (<www.palgrave-journals.com/1st>).

48: _____. 2004. "Puerto Ricans in the United States." In *Encyclopedia of Diasporas: Immigrant and Refugee Cultures Around the World,* edited by Melvin Ember, Carol R. Ember, and Ian Skoggard, Vol. 2, pp. 1055-1068. New York: Kluwer/Plenum.

49: _____. 2005. "Race and Racialization." In *The Oxford Encyclopedia of Latinos and Latinas in the United States.* Editors in Chief, Suzanne Oboler and Deena J. González. Volume 3. New York: Oxford University Press.

50: _____. 2009a. "The Puerto Rican Diaspora To The United States: A Postcolonial Migration?" Research Seminar at the Centro de Estudios Puertorriqueños, February 13, 2009. Presenter: Jorge Duany, University of Puerto Rico, (URL: Unknown; Accessed February 6, 2010); cf.: <http://www. centropr. org/events. htm?event=32>. See: Dr. Duany's "Table 2", titled "Geographic Distribution of the Population of Puerto Rican Origin in the United States, by State, 1960-2007". See also: (<http:// graduados.uprrp.edu/ Sociologia/facultad/jorgeduany.htm>).

51: _____. 2009b. "The Nation in the Diaspora: The Multiple Repercussions of the Puerto Rican Emigration." Abridged and updated English version. *In Governance in the Non-Independent Caribbean: Challenges and Opportunities in the 21st Century,* edited by Peter Clegg and Emilio Pantojas-García, Kingston, Jamaica: Ian Randle Publishers, (URL: Unknown; Retrieved in 2010: Date Unknown).

52: _____. 2010a. "The Orlando Ricans: Overlapping Identity Discourses Among Middle-Class Puerto Rican Immigrants." *CENTRO: Journal of the Center for Puerto Rican Studies.* Spring 2010. Volume XXII, Number I.

53: _____. 2010b. "A Transnational Colonial Migration: Puerto Rico's Farm Labor Program." *New West Indian Guide.* Vol. 84, no. 3-4 (2010).

54: Duany, Jorge and Emilio Pantojas-García. 2006. "Fifty Years of Commonwealth: The Contradictions of Free Associated Statehood in Puerto Rico." Chapter 2. In *Extended Statehood in the Caribbean: Paradoxes of Quasi Colonialism, Local Autonomy, and Extended Statehood in the USA, French, Dutch, & British Caribbean*, ed. by Lammert de Jong and Dirk Krujit, pp. 21-58. Amsterdam: Rozenberg Publishers. (URL is Unknown; Accessed on May 11, 2010. 21-57); cf.: (<http://graduados.uprrp.edu/ Sociologia/facultad/ jorgeduany.htm>).

55: Duany, Jorge and Patricia Silver. 2010. "The 'Puerto Ricanization' of Florida: Historical Background and Current Status." Introduction Guest Editors. *CENTRO: Journal of the Center for Puerto Rican Studies*. Volume XXII, Number I, Spring 2010. 4-31.

56: Feldman, David. 1978. *The Puerto Ricans of California: A Minority Within a Minority*. Prepared by David Feldman, Ph.D. and Research Associates, San Diego, CA, June 1978.

57: Filion, Ron and Pamela Storm. 2003. "1870 Federal Census, San Mateo County, California, Page 372A, Third Township, Post Office Belmont," in San Mateo County Genealogy (SFgenealogy) web site. Retrieved June 3, 2010. (<http://sfgenealogy.com/sanmateo/1870 sm70372a.htm>).

58: Fitzpatrick, Joseph P. 1987 [1971]. *Puerto Rican Americans: The Meaning of Migration to the Mainland*. Englewood Cliffs, New Jersey: Prentice-Hall, Inc.

59: Fritz, Christian G. 1986. "Politics and the Courts: The Struggle Over Land in San Francisco 1846-1866." *Santa Clara Law Review*. Volume 26, No. 1 (Winter 1986).

60: Flores, Juan. 1984. "Translator's Preface." In *Memoirs of Bernardo Vega: A contribution to the history of the Puerto Rican community in New York*. edited by César Andreu Iglesias, translated by Juan Flores. New York: Monthly Review Press.

61: Gunn, Herbert, M.D. 1905. "Uncinariasis in California, Based on Observation of Sixty-Two Cases." *California State Journal of Medicine*. July, 1905, Vol. III, No. 7. 212-214. (URL: Unknown; Retrieved on May 19, 2010).

62: _____. 1906. "Bilharzia Disease: Report of Two Cases Observed Among Porto Ricans in San Francisco." *The Journal of the American Medical Association*. Vol. XLVI, No. 14, April 7, 1906. 1031-1032. Retrieved on May 19, 2010. (<http://jama/ama-assn.org/cgi/content/ summary/ XLVI/ 14 /1031>).

63: _____. 1910. "The Menace of Tropical Diseases to California." *California State Journal of Medicine*. Dec. 1910, Vol. III, No. 12. 409-411. Retrieved on May 19, 2010. (URL: Unknown).

64: Hawaii Attorney General. 1882. *Biennial Report of the Attorney General to the Legislative Assembly of 1882. [Reign of His Majesty Kalakaua – Ninth Year]*. Honolulu: Hawaiian Gazette Office.

65: _____. 1884. *Biennial Report of the Attorney General to the Legislative Assembly of 1884. [Reign of His Majesty Kalakaua – Eleventh Year]*. Honolulu: Hawaiian Gazette Print.

66: Hawaii Board of Health. 1905. *Report of the President of the Board of Health of the Territory of Hawaii for the Six Months Ending June 30, 1905*. Honolulu: The Bulletin Publishing Co., LTD.

67: Hawaiian Historical Society. 1900. *Eight Annual Report of the Hawaiian Historical Society*. Honolulu, H.T. 1900.

68: _____. 1906. *Thirteenth Annual Report of the Hawaiian Historical Society. with a Paper on the Development of Hawaiian Statute Law....* Honolulu: 1906.

69: **[Hawaiian Published Newspapers]** *The Democrat* (Honolulu, T.H.). 1910. "Importing A Population". November 1, 1910. [See: Library of Congress – Chronicling America web site; **Note:** All of the following Hawaiian newspapers obtained via this Library of Congress web site; (<http://chroniclingamerica.loc.gov 1ccn/sn8201 5415/1900-12-24/ed-1/seq-1/;words= Porto+...>)].

70: [Hawaiian] *Evening Bulletin*. 1900. "Porto Ricans are in the Poor House." December 26, 1900.

71: _____. 1902. "What Porto Ricans are Sending Home." November 14, 1902.

72: _____. 1902. "Porto Rican Complaints." November 14, 1902.

73: *Hawaiian Gazette*, The. 1900. "Laborers Coming. Porto Ricans Due to Reach Here Today. The Examiner's Usual Horror. The Yellow Journal Tries to Scare Them From Sailing." December 21, 1900. (Library of Congress, (<http://chronicliningamerica. loc.gov/lccn /sn83025121/1900-12-28/ed-1/seg-5>, Accessed: March 17, 2012)).

74: _____. 1900. "Laborers Are Here. Porto Ricans Came on The Rio. Only 56 of 134 Hired." December 26, 1900.

75: _____. 1900. "Porto Ricans are Public Charges. Condition Wrought By the Lying Examiner of San Francisco." December 28, 1900.

76: _____. 1901. "San Francisco, May 8" Dispatch. May 17, 1901.

77: *Hawaiian Star, The*. (Honolulu [Oahu]). 1900a. "Porto Ricans Arrive: Small Portion of Original Party Here. Nearly Ninety Induced by Deliberate Falsehoods to Desert Their Companions—To Work..." December 24, 1900.

78: _____. 1900b. "The Rio was in Danger...Porto Ricans Greatly Terrified by the Storm—Only One Pump Left in Working Order." December 24, 1900.

79: _____. 1900. "The Porto Ricans." December 26, 1900.

80: _____. 1901. "Some Sickly Laborers. 400 More Half-Starved Porto Ricans." January 16, 1901.

81: _____. 1901. "Porto Ricans." May 15, 1901.

82: *Honolulu Republican*. 1900."Herded in Cars Like Slaves in a Pen. Such the Position of Porto Ricans Coming Here. People of California Aroused. Action of Men in Charge of Train Vigorously Denounced. Deceit Practiced to induce Porto Ricans to embark on their Long Journey to Hawaii." December 22, 1900.

83: _____. 1900a. "Arrived Early Sunday Morning... Plantation Laborers Hurried Off to Spreckeisville—Large Number Deserted in California –Few Complaints from those Who Came." December 25, 1900.

84: _____. 1900b. "Stop Such Methods." December 25, 1900.

85: _____. 1900c. "Held For The Time As Real Prisoners. Porto Ricans Not Allowed a Minute On Shore. Arrived Early Sunday Morning. Steamer Lehua Brought Up Alongside Rio For Quick Embarkment". December 25, 1900.

86: _____. 1901. "Favors Porto Ricans For Hawaiian Islands. Ex-Governor General Davis Commends Planters' Course. Migration would be a great benefit to America's West Indian possession...." January 10, 1901.

87: _____. 1901. "More Porto Rican Laborers Arrive. Are a Half-Starved, Poverty-Stricken Lot. Poor Specimens of Humanity." January 17, 1901.

88: Hayward Area Historical Society. 2012. Various different separate documents, and "write-ups", from the: *California Century: Puerto Ricans in the San Francisco Bay Area, 1900-2000,* "Travelling Exhibit" that was "commemorating the 100th anniversary of the arrival of the first Puerto Ricans in the San Francisco area in 1900." Co-sponsored by the: California Puerto Rican Historical Society. Hayward Area Historical Society address: 22701 Main Street, Hayward, CA 94541. (510) 581-2424. Curated by: Aurora Levins Morales; photographs by Barry Kleider.

89: The Historical Society of Pennsylvania. (n.d.) [no date]. "Early Enclaves." Unknown Author. Retrieved on May 9, 2010. (<http://www.hsp.org/default.aspx?id=361>).

90: History Task Force. 1982. *Sources for the Study of Puerto Rican Migration, 1879-1930.* NY: CUNY, Centro de Estudios Puertorriqueños. Research Foundation of the City of New York.

91: House, James and Bradley Steffens. 1989. *The San Francisco Earthquake.* Illustrations by Maurie Manning. World Disasters Book. San Diego, CA: Lucent Books, Inc.

92: Ignatiev, Noel. 1965. *How The Irish Became White.* Routledge: New York.

93: Information Publications, Inc. 2009. *California Cities, Towns & Counties 2009: State & Municipal Profiles Series.* Woodside, CA: Information Publications, Inc.

94: Jackson, Ronald Vern and Gary Ronald Teeples. 1978. *California 1850 Census Index.* Bountiful, Utah: Accelerated Indexing Systems, Inc.

95: Lainhart, Ann S. 1992. *State Census Records.* Baltimore, MD: Genealogical Publishing Co., Inc.

96: La Peninsula. 1967. "Local History: Redwood City, CA – Simon M. Mezes." *La Peninsula: Journal of the San Mateo County Historical Association.* May 1967, vol. xiv, no. 2. Retrieved on June 3, 2010. (<http://www.ci.redwood-city.ca.us/about/local_history/exhibits/mezes/mezes.html>).

97: Lazú, Jacqueline and Marisol Negrón. 2000. "Language in Dialogue: Reflections on the 4th International Congress of the Puerto Rican Studies Association." *CENTRO Journal.* Volume XII, Number 1. Fall 2000. [Journal of the Center for Puerto Rican Studies. Hunter College, CUNY]

98: Leyland, R.C. 1980. *Puerto Ricans in the San Francisco Bay Area, California: An Historical and Cultural Geography.* Master's Thesis, Master of Arts in Geography, February 1980. California State University, Hayward.

99: López, Daniel M. 2009a. "Puerto Ricans Living in California as of 2007," *El Boricua* Newsletter, March/April 2009, pp. 4-5; (House of Puerto Rico-San Diego, San Diego, California).

100: _____ 2009b. "Pioneros: PRs in NYC", *El Boricua* Newsletter, January/February 2009, pp. 3-4; (House of Puerto Rico-San Diego, San Diego, California).

101: López, Iris and David Forbes. 2001. "Borinki Identity in Hawai'i: Present and Future." *CENTRO: Journal of the Center for Puerto Rican Studies.* Spring 2001. Vol. XIII, No. I.

102: *Los Angeles City Directory. 1892*. Retrieved on October 13, 2010, page 856, from "*footnote.com." [currently known as: Fold3.com] (<www.footnote.com/ image/226208895>).

103: _____. 1894. Retrieved on October 13, 2010, page 1347, from "*footnote. com." [Note: currently known as: Fold3.com]

104: *Los Angeles Herald*. 1909. "Japanese Strike Appears Broken. Many Laborers Are Hired To Take Places. Hawaiians Are Determined To Replace Orientals. Two Fires Break Out on Plantation, but Are Not Believed to Have Been of Incendiary Origin." May 16, 1909. [Newspaper]

105: _____. 1909. "Hawaiian Immigration Board to Help Needy. Destitute Spaniards and Porto Ricans at San Francisco to Be Taken Back." June 26, 1909.

106: *Los Angeles Times.* 1900. "Progress Of Porto Rican Pilgrims: Peons Pass Through City En Route To Hawaii." December 14, 1900. [Aka: Los Angeles Daily Times] [Newspaper]

107: _____. 1900. "Porto Ricans Refuse to Go. Only Seventy of the 'Slaves' Sail." December 15, 1900.

108: _____. 1904. "Porto Ricans Destitute: Five Hundred Helpless in San Francisco." December 15, 1904. [ProQuest Historical Newspapers].

109: _____. 1905. "Porto Ricans Are Menace: Bringing Disease Into California via Honolulu." June 25, 1905.

110: _____. 1910. "Death Lurks In Soil: California State Medical Society is Warned That Hookworm Disease is Entering State." April 21, 1910.

111: Maldonado, Edwin. 1979. "Contract Labor and the Origins of Puerto Rican Communities in the United States." *International Migration Review*. Spring 1979. Vol. 13, No. 1. 103-121.

112: Maldonado-Denis, Manuel. 1980. *The Emigration Dialectic: Puerto Rico and the USA*. Translated by Roberto Simón Crespi. New York: International Publishers.

113: Martinez, Robert A. 1984. "The Emergence of Imperialist Capitalism and Puerto Rican Emigration, 1879-1901." *Journal of American Ethnic History.* Vol. 3, No. 2 (Spring 1984). (Published by the University of Illinois Press on behalf of the Immigration & Ethnic History Society). (http://www.jstor.org/stable/27500318).

114: Marzán, Gilberto, Andrés Torres, and Andrew Luecke. 2008. "Puerto Rican Outmigration from New York City: 1995-2000," Policy Report, Vol. 2, No. 2, Fall 2008. New York: Centro de Estudios Puertorriqueños, Hunter College, (CUNY).

115: Matos-Rodríguez, Félix V. and Pedro Juan Hernández. 2001. "Introduction" in *Pioneros: Puerto Ricans in New York City 1896-1948,* Bilingual Edition, Images of America Series, Charleston, SC: Arcadia Publishing.

116: Medina, Nitza C. 2001. "Rebellion in the Bay: California's First Puerto Ricans," *CENTRO: Journal of the Center for Puerto Rican Studies*, (Spring 2001) Vol. XIII, Num. 1.

117: Military Governor of Porto Rico on Civil Affairs. 1902. *Annual Reports of the War Department for the Fiscal Year Ended June 30, 1900. Part 13. Military Governor Of Porto Rico On Civil Affairs.* [AKA: Report of the Military Governor of Porto Rico on Civil Affairs; Puerto Rico, Military Governor, John Rutter Brooke [1898], Guy Vernor Henry [1898-1899], Division of Insular Affairs]. Washington: Government Printing Office.

118: Millard, Bailey. 1924a. "The San Francisco Bay Region. S.M. Mezes." Vo. 3. 382-383. Published by The American Historical Society, Inc. (Transcribed by Elaine Sturdevant). Retrieved on May 21, 2010. (<http://free pages.genealogy.rootsweb.ancestry.com/ ~npmelton/smbmez.htm>).

119: _____. 1924b. *History of the San Francisco Bay.* The American Historical Society, Inc. San Francisco, [Volumes I, II, and III].

120: Moreno, Barry. 2004. *Encyclopedia of Ellis Island.* Westport, Connecticut: Greenwood Press.

121: Morse, Stephen P., Joel D. Weintraub, and David R. Kehs. (n.d.) [no date]. "Obtaining Streets within EDs for the 1910 Census in One Step (Large Cities). [Enumeration Districts]." Retrieved on June 20, 2010. (http://stevemorse.org/census/index.html?ed2street=1).

122: National Archives, The. 2009. *The United States Constitution and Other American Documents.* New York: Fall River Press.

123: National Archives and Records Administration [NARA]. 2010. *1910 Federal Population Census.* College Park, Maryland. [Section on: "Enumeration Districts (Eds).")] Retrieved on May 23, 2010. (<http://www. archives.gov /pulications/ microfilm-catalogs/census /1910/ general-info.html>)

124: National Archives and Records Service. 1973. *Nineteenth-Century Puerto Rican Immigration and Slave Data.* By George S. Ulibarri. Reference Information Paper No. 64. Washington: General Services Administration.

125: National Archives Trust Fund Board. 1982. *The 1910 Federal* Population *Census: A Catalog of Microfilm Copies of the Schedules.* Washington, DC: National Archives Trust Fund Board.

126: *New York Times.* 1900. "Porto Rican Relief." May 5, 1900.

127: _____. 1900. "Porto Ricans for Hawaii." August 3, 1900.

128: _____. 1900. "Porto Ricans Go To Hawaii. Men Say They Were Kidnapped for the Spreckels Sugar Plantation-Closely Guarded on Train." December 7, 1900.

129: _____. 1901. "The Porto Rican Exodus. Men and Women Anxious to Leave the Island for Hawaii. Best Laborers Flee from the Distress Said to Exist in their Native Land." April 4, 1901.

130: _____. 1901. "Porto Ricans in Hawaii. Immigrants So Weak from Lack of Food that They Cannot Go to Work." May 29, 1901.

131: _____. 1901. "Good Traits of the Porto Ricans." August 4, 1901.

132: _____. 1902. "Porto Ricans in Hawaii. Those Shipped to Work on Sugar Plantations Declared to be Anxious to Return Home." August 30, 1902.

133: _____. 1903. "Status of Porto Ricans". ("to the Editor of *The New York Times").* March 25, 1903: (the page number is not known). [Possibly: March 29, 1903].

134: _____. 1906. "Sunshine and Shadows of Hawaii: A Bird's Eye View of America's Blighted Paradise." Part Three, First Magazine Section. February 18, 1906.

135: North San Diego County Genealogical Society and The Carlsbad City Library. 1981. *San Diego County CALIFORNIA CENSUS INDEX: 1900.* Evelyn Jean White, Editor. (Genealogy Reference. Chula Vista City Library, Chula Vista, California). (Ref Family Research 312 White).

136: *Pacific Commercial Advertiser* [Honolulu, Hawaii]. 1900. "To Enter Hawaii. Porto Ricans May Come and Go. An Important Ruling." December 10, 1900. [Newspaper]

137: _____. 1900. "Porto Ricans are Public Charges: Conditions Wrought By the Lying Examiner of San Francisco." December 27, 1900.

138: _____. 1900. ["No Title to this section/column"]. December 27, 1900.

139: _____. 1901. "Ship Caputred [sic] by Porto Ricans…Immigrants are Poor Looking Lot. Four Hundred Go to Other Islands…Pitiful Scenes Among Them." January 17, 1901.

140: _____. 1901. "The Coming Porto Ricans. Eight Hundred and Thirty-Nine in the California Steerage." April 19, 1901.

141: _____. 1901. "New Idea in 'Help' Porto Rican Girls for Domestic Work. Waialua is Experimenting." May 2, 1901.

142: _____. 1901. "*The Colon* Arrives With Porto Ricans." May 14, 1901.

143: _____. 1901. "Labor of Porto Rico. Its Surplus Needs a Chance in Hawaii. We Can Take About 12,000." May 17, 1901.

144: _____.1901. "Many Glad They Came. Porto Ricans Feel Satisfied With Work. Conditions on Maui Estates. Some of the Newcomers Who Will do Nothing But Beg or Steal." August 6, 1901.

145: _____. 1901. "Chinese Needed. Best Laborers for Our Sugar Farms. Hawaii Needs Many of Them…." August 12, 1901.

146: _____. 1901. "A Traveling Ananias." August 12, 1901.

147: _____. 1901. "How Hawaii Helps To Re-Distribute The Population." August 23, 1901.

148: _____. 1901. "A Test Of White Men. An Old-Time Labor Experiment on Maui. The Colony of Lincolnville. It Started in for Ten Years and Did Not Last Two---The Reasons." September 2, 1901.

149: _____. 1901. "A Labor Invasion. 25,000 Porto Ricans Intended for Hawaii. So Says A New Orleans Dispatch. A Local Planter Doubts that Contract Was Made But Admits Many Are to Come." October 7, 1901.

150: _____. 1902. "Vagrants Must Get To Work. Can Field or the Rock Pile in Sight. High Sheriff Plans Crusade. Porto Ricans Who Try to Live Without Work to be Corralled at Once." January 17, 1902.

151: _____. 1902. "Porto Ricans Effective." February 25, 1902.

152: _____. 1902. "No Right To Vote. Porto Ricans Not Citizens, says Dole." February 26, 1902.

153: _____. 1902. "Ask Help For Porto Ricans." November 24, 1902.

154: _____. 1902. "The Labor Issue In The Islands.... A Careful Review of an Economic Problem Which Presents Many Phases of Special Interest to Statesmen in Washington." December 11, 1902.

155: _____. 1903. "Porto Ricans Are Kicking. Make Complaint to Government at Washington. Testimony of Laborers Is Being Taken Here. This is a Long Story that Has Two Sides to it." March 8, 1903.

156: *Pacific Rural Press and California Fruit Bulletin* (San Francisco, CA) [Newspaper]. 1909. "More About Hawaii." May 22, 1909.

157: Pattison, Robert E. 1900. "Robert E. Pattison Describes How Imperialism Has Made Porto Rico A Land of Horror... Pennsylvania's Former Governor Visits the Island for the Journal and Reports on the Disastrous Results of Our Colonial Policy". *New York Journal and Advertiser.* October 7, 1900.

158: Pew Research Center. 2011. "Hispanics of Puerto Rican Origin in the United States, 2009." Statistical Profile. May 26, 2011. Washington, D.C.: Pew Research Center.

159: Platt, Lyman D. 1998. *Census Records for Latin America and the Hispanic United States.* Baltimore, MD: Genealogical Publishing Co., Inc.

160: Porto Rico, Executive Secretary. 1905. *Register of Porto Rico for 1905 Compiled by The Secretary of Porto Rico December 1905.* Bureau of Printing and Supplies: San Juan, Porto Rico.

161: *Redwood City (Cal.) Tribune.* 1951. "So We Shall Always Remember." (Photograph). November 29, 1951. [Newspaper]

162: *Redwood City Tribune* (Cal.). *1978. "Mezesville: ghost of Redwood City past." June 3, 1978.* [Newspaper]

163: _____. 1978. "Mezesville map." June 3, 1978. (cf.: Bib. #358).

164: Reimers, David M. 1999. *Teaching Immigration of People of Color to the United States.* Washington, D.C.: American Historical Association.

165: Report of the Commissioner of Labor on Hawaii - 1902. (1903). "Labor Conditions in the Sugar Industry in Hawaii, California, Texas, Louisiana, Cuba, and Porto Rico." Washington: Government Printing Office. (Accessed via: Google books)

166: Report of the Commissioner of Labor. *Fourth Report of the Commissioner of Labor on* Hawaii - 1910. (1911). Washington. (Accessed via: Goggle books)

167: Reports of the Immigration Commission. 1911a. *Abstracts of Reports of the Immigration Commission. With Conclusions and Recommendations and Views of the Minority.* In Two Volumes. (In Two Volumes: Volume I). [aka: The Dillingham Commission]. 61st Congress, 3rd Session. Senate. Document No. 747. Washington: Government Printing Office. (Referred to as: the Committee on Immigration).

168: _____. 1911b. *Abstracts of Reports of the Immigration Commission. With Conclusions and Recommendations and Views of the Minority. (In Two Volumes: Volume II).* [The Dillingham Commission]. Document No. 747. Washington: Government Printing Office.

169: _____. 1911c. *Dictionary Of Races Or Peoples*. Presented By Mr. Dillingham. Referred to the Committee on Immigration. December 5, 1910. Document No. 662. Washington: Government Printing Office.

170: _____. 1911d. *Immigrants In Industries. Part 25: Japanese and Other Immigrant Races in the Pacific Coast and Rocky Mountain States*. (In Three Volumes: Vol. III) – Diversified Industries. Document No. 633. Washington: Government Printing Office.

171: _____. 1911e. *Emigration Conditions In Europe*. Washington: Government Printing Office. Document No. 748.

172: Richards, Rand. *Historic Walks in San Francisco: 18 Trails Through the City's Past*. San Francisco: Heritage House Publishers.

173: Rodríguez, Clara. 1974. *The Ethnic Queue in the U.S.: The Case of Puerto Ricans*. San Francisco, CA: R and E Research Associates.

174: _____. (c. 1989). "Puerto Ricans: Immigrants and Migrants–A Historical Perspective." (Americans All. A National Education Program). 1-10. Retrieved in 2010. (URL: Unknown).

175: _____. 2000. *Changing Race: Latinos, the Census, and the History of Ethnicity in the United States*. New York: New York University Press.

176: _____. 2001. "Puerto Ricans in Historical and Social Science Research." In *Handbook of Research on Multicultural Education*. James A. Banks (Ed.) and Cherry A. McGee Banks (Associate Editor). San Francisco, CA: Jossey-Bass.

177: _____. 2005. "Census." *The Oxford Encyclopedia of Latinos and Latinas in the United States*, Suzanne Oboler and Deena J. González, Editors in Chief, Volume 1, New York: Oxford University Press.

178: Rodríguez, Victor M. 1997. "The Racialization of Puerto Rican Ethnicity in the United States." In *Ethnicity, Race and Nationality in the Caribbean*. Juan Manuel Carrión, Editor. Institute of Caribbean Studies. University of Puerto Rico. UPR Station. San Juan: Puerto Rico.

179: _____. 2005. "The Racialization of Mexican Americans and Puerto Ricans: 1890s-1930s," *CENTRO: Journal of the Center for Puerto Rican Studies*. Spring 2005. Vol. XVII, No. I.

180: _____. 2009. Book Review: "America Beyond Black and White: How Immigrants and Fusions are Helping US Overcome the Racial Divide," by Ronald Fernandez. Ann Arbor: The University of Michigan Press, 2007. *CENTRO: Journal of the Center for Puerto Rican Studies*. Spring 2009. Volume XXI, Number I.

181: Rosario-Rivera, Raquel. 2000. "Pasaporte A La Angustia: Sufrimientos de los emigrados y familiars con destino a Hawaii (Incluye registro de emigrados hasta ahora localizadis)." Tomado de la *Revista de la Pontificia Universidad Católica de Puerto Rico*. Ponce, Octubre 2000, Año XLIV, Num. 87 [Journal of the Catholic University of Puerto Rico]. She references the: A.G.P.R. Fondo Oficina Del Gobernador: Correspondencia General, Caja 17; see: "*Registro de los emigrados que se fueron para Hawaii*." [This article was e-mailed to me as a PDF file by a Professional Genealogist].

182: Ruiz, Vicki L. 2006. "*Nuestra América*: Latino History as United States History." *The Journal of American History*. December 2006. Vol. 93, No. 3.

183: _____ . 2009. "Why Latino History Matters to U.S. History." *The Japanese Journal of American Studies.* No. 20 (2009).

184: Russell Sage Foundation. 1913. *San Francisco Relief Survey: The Organization and Methods of Relief Used After the Earthquake and Fire of April 18, 1906.* Compiled from Studies by Charles J. O'Connor, *et. al.*, New York: Survey Associates. (Available via: books.google.com)

185: *Sacramento Daily Record-Union.* 1884. "Overdose of Chloral Hydrate." December 9, 1884. [Newspaper]

186: _____. 1899. "Dissatisfaction in Porto Rico. Complaint Among Lower Class of Natives. That the Cost of Living has Increased Since the Americans Occupied the Island." April 6, 1899.

187: _____. 1899. "Suffering Porto Ricans. Californians Appealed To For Help." *Sacramento Daily Union.* August 26, 1899.

188: Sanabria, Carlos. 1985. "Labor Migration from Puerto Rico 1900-1930 and the origins of the Puerto Rican community in New York City." (Master's Thesis. History Dept., Hunter College, The City University of New York. New York New York; Interlibrary Loans).

189: Sánchez Korrol, Virginia. 1994a. "In Their Own Right: A History of Puerto Ricans in the U.S.A." In *Handbook of Hispanic Cultures in the United States: History.* Editors. Alfredo Jiménez, Nicolás Kanellos and Claudio Esteva Fabregat. Houston, TX: Arte Público Press.

190: _____.1994b [1983]. *From Colonia to Community: The History of Puerto Ricans in New York City.* Berkeley and Los Angeles, CA: University of California Press.

191: _____. 1999. *Teaching U.S. Puerto Rican History.* Washington, D.C.: American Historical Association.

192: _____. 2005. "Bridging the Caribbean: Puerto Rican Roots in Nineteenth Century America." Immigration Issue Three. (History Now: American History Online–The Historian's Perspective). 1-4. Retrieved on May 12, 2010. (<http://www.gilderlehrman.org/ historynow/03_2005/ historian4.php>).

193: San Diego City. 1868-1915. *Index to Obituaries and Death Notices in the San Diego Union (1868-1915) and the San Diego Herald (1851-1860).* San Diego, California: San Diego Genealogical Society. Accessed: June 2, 2010.

194: San Diego City. 1893-1894. *Directory of San Diego City and County For 1893-94.* San Diego, California: Retrieved on May 27, 2010. Obtained at the San Diego Genealogical Society. [This author reviewed a digitized copy of this book].

195: _____. 1895. *San Diego City and County Directory: 1895.* Retrieved on May 27, 2010.

196: San Diego County. 1894. *The Great Register of San Diego County for 1894: An Alphabetical list of registered voters in San Diego County, California 1894.* Book Owned by the : San Diego Public Library. Accessed: May 27, 2010 at the San Diego Genealogical Society, San Diego, California.

197: San Diego Genealogical Society. 2010. *Index to Obituaries and Death Notices in the San Diego Union (1868-1915) and the San Diego Herald (1851-1860).* [Database] (Accessed on: June 2, 2010).

198: *San Francisco Call*. 1900. "Porto Ricans Pass Through Los Angeles: Look Forward to a Happy Future in Hawaiian Islands." December 14, 1900. Retrieved on April 6, 2010. (California Digital **Newspaper** Collection, Center for Bibliographic Studies Research, University of California, Riverside), accessed over several different months, via: (http://cdnc.ucr.edu); (http://cdnc.ucr.edu/ newsucr/cgi-bin/ newsucr?a=d&d =SFC19001214.236 &c1=search& srpos...).

199: _____. 1900. "Learn Too Late They Are Dupes. Thirty Destitute Porto Ricans Are New Objects of Charity...." December 16, 1900.

200: _____. 1900. "The Court And The Colonies." December 20, 1900.

201: _____. 1901. "Porto Ricans Reach Hawaii. Secretary of the Planters' Association Speaks of the Experiment." January 2, 1901.

202: _____. 1901. "Makes Paupers of Porto Ricans. Yellow Journalism's Recent Achievement Bears Fruit. Santa Clara County is Asked to Care for Islanders Who Were Offered Homes in Hawaii." March 7, 1901.

203: _____. 1901. "Porto Ricans Die on the Way to Hawaii." April 9, 1901.

204: _____. 1901. "Porto Rican Laborers Sail For The Islands. *Zealandia* Starts for Hawaii With Nearly One Thousand." April 14, 1901.

205: _____. 1901. "Destitution Exists Among Porto Ricans: Federation of Labor in the Island Sends Petition to the President at Washington." April 16, 1901.

206: _____. 1901. "Porto Ricans Deceived by False Promises: Stone Masons Lured to Honolulu on Promise of Being Paid $5 a Day." November 13, 1901.

207: _____. 1905. "Porto Rican Colony Of This City." May 28, 1905.

208: _____. 1906. "Hawaiian Jurist Stirs Portuguese. Classes Them With the Pariahs and Lepers of Humanity. Conditions in Islands Said to Give the Lie to Critic." August 16, 1906.

209: _____. 1906. "Porto Ricans in Need. Men Sent Away and Women and Children Left. [Relief Board To Auction Autos]." October 20, 1906.

210: _____. 1907. "Under Our Flag: Throughout The World – Uncle Sam's White, Brown, and Black Children." June 30, 1907. (Has article and Illustrations)

211: _____. 1907. "A People Without Nationality" November 17, 1907.

212: _____. 1909. "Government May Deport Porto Rican Families. Many Laborers From Hawaii Stranded in This City." June 6, 1909.

213: _____. 1910. "Orientals Outnumber Others by 105,000 to 85,000." November 16, 1910.

214: _____. 1913. "Site Dedicated For Porto Rico At Exposition." May 23, 1913.

215: *San Francisco Chronicle*. 1900. "Ocean and Water Front. Steamship Acapulco Here From Panama." July 2, 1900. [Newspaper]

216: _____. 1900. "Porto Ricans on the Way to Hawaii. Railroad Man Says the Islanders are the Most Miserable People He Ever Saw." December 2, 1900.

217: _____. 1900. "Porto Ricans Prisoners in Railway Cars: Pitiable Plight of Islanders on the Way to the Plantations of Hawaii." December 7, 1900.

218: _____. 1900. "Porto Ricans Take Flight: Twenty-five Leave the Train by Stealth Just South of Pomona." December 14, 1900.

219: _____. 1900. "Frightened At Slavery: The Porto Ricans Arrive on Their Way to the Hawaiian Islands." December 15, 1900.

220: _____. 1900. "Porto Ricans Are Now In The Almshouse. The New Additions to the City's Population Have Become Public Charges." December 16, 1900.

221: _____. 1900. "Famine's Rule In Porto Rico. Army Surgeon's Report on Conditions Existing in the Island. Sickness and Death Due to Starvation. Declares That the Situation at Adjuntas is Most Appalling. Fifty Succumb Each Week for Want of Food." December 23, 1900.

222: _____. 1901a. "Laborers for the Hawaiian Plantations. Porto Ricans and Portuguese Arrive in Honolulu—Number of Negroes Expected Soon." January 2, 1901.

223: _____. 1901b. "To Work in Sugar Fields. More Porto Ricans Soon to Reach New Orleans En Route to Hawaii. Agent of the Planters Ready to Meet Them. Seeking to Guard Against the Mishaps that Befell the First Party. Declares the Conditions in the Pacific Group are far Ahead of Those in Their Former Homes." January 2, 1901.

224: _____. 1902. "Porto Ricans Not Citizens. An Important Decision by United States Judge of New York." October 9, 1902.

225: _____. 1902. "Porto Ricans Anxious To Leave For Home. Will Request President and Congress to Arrange Transportation From Hawaii." December 9, 1902.

226: _____. 1903. "Porto Ricans Secure An Investigation. Government to Inquire Into the Treatment Accorded Them in Hawaii." March 17, 1903.

227: _____. 1904. "Doors Open to Porto Ricans. The Supreme Court Holds That They Are Not Aliens in the Meaning of the Statutes. Decision in Case of Gonzales Woman. Tribunal Refused to Consider Broard Question of Status of the Residents, as Only One Point Was Involved." January 5, 1904.

228: _____. 1906. "Porto Ricans Menace Health: Dr. Gunn Recommends Isolation of the Race in Other Camp Localities." November 17, 1906.

229: _____. 1907. "Naturalization Laws Are Strict: Seventy-Five Per Cent of the Applicants Refused on Examination." February 1, 1907.

230: _____. 1907. "One-Third of Refugees Gone: San Francisco's Experiment in Paternalism is Slowly Dissolving. Many Left On Last Day. Procession of Moving Homes Seeks Mainly Southern Districts." August 19, 1907.

231: _____. 1909. "Ruin Came With American Rule: Porto Ricans Claim the Island Was Better Ruled by Spain." March 26, 1909.

232: *San Francisco City Directory.1852* (September 1852). (accessed at several different times) (<www.archive.org/stream/awmorgancossanfr1852/ awmorgancossanfr1852awm...>). (Digitizing sponsor: the San Francisco Public Library).

233: *San Francisco Examiner*. 1900. "Dash For Liberty By Porto Ricans: Locomotive Is Pressed Into Service in the Chase After the Fugitives." December 14, 1900; [Newspaper].

234: _____. 1900. "Threats And Force Put 66 Porto Ricans on Rio, But Fifty Others Escape." December 15, 1900.

235: _____. 1900. "Planters Growing Disposed To Grant Now Assurances Porto Ricans Asked At Indio: San Franciscans Nobly Rally to Make the Exiles Comfortable." December 16, 1900.

236: _____. 1900. "Successful Efforts of 'The Examiner' In Finding Homes For Porto Ricans: Three Children and One Women Happily Placed With Residents Across the Bay and in This City." December 18, 1900.

237: _____. 1900. "Porto Ricans Are Finding Work At Salinas." December 19, 1900.

238: _____. 1900. "Finding Homes On Ranches And Haciendas. Seven Porto Ricans Welcomed in Salinas and an Eight at Mayfield, While More Will Follow Them." December 20, 1900.

239: _____. 1900. "All Porto Ricans In New Homes." December 23, 1900.

240: _____. 1900. "Porto Ricans Are All In Homes; Lesson Taught The Planters." December 24, 1900.

241: _____. 1900. "Christmas of the Exiled Porto Ricans." December 26, 1900.

242: _____. 1901. November 13, 1901.

243: *San Mateo County Gazette*. 1859. Description: General Transcription. "Married". December 24, 1859. (<http:// www.newspaperabstracts.com/link.php?action=detail &catid=595&orderid=119>); [Redwood City, San Mateo County, CA]. Retrieved on June 3, 2010; "submitted: July 2, 2005"). [Newspaper]

244: *San Mateo Times – County Fair Supplement*. 1976. "The Acquisitive Instinct." July 23, 1976 (by John Horgan).

245: *Sausalito News* [Marine County, CA]. 1910. "Pithy Resume Of Events Of Entire World." February 5, 1910; [Newspaper].

246: Schmitt, Robert C. *Firsts and Almost Firsts*. 1995. Edited by Ronn Ronck. University of Hawaii Press.

247: _____. *Historical Statistics of Hawaii*. 1977. Honolulu: The University Press of Hawaii.

248: Schnack, George F. 1940. *Subjective Factors in the Migration of Spanish From Hawaii To California*. Master's Thesis. Department of Economics, Division of Sociology. Leland Stanford Junior University [better known today as: Stanford University].

249: Schomburg, Arthur A. 1902. "Questions By A Porto Rican." To the Editor of the *New York Times*. August 9, 1902. (AKA: Arturo Alfonso Schomburg)

250: Seabury, Joseph B. 1908. *The World and Its People - Porto Rico: The Land of the Rich Port.* New York: Silver, Burdett And Company.

251: Secretary of the Interior. 1872a. *Ninth Census-Volume I. The Statistics of the United States, Embracing the Tables of Race, Nationality, Sex, Selected Ages, and Occupations....* Wash.: Government Printing Office.

252: _____. 1872b. *A Compendium of The Ninth Census (June 1, 1870). Compiled Pursuant to a Concurrent Resolution of Congress, and Under the Direction of the Secretary of Labor.* Washington: Government Printing Office.

253: _____. 1900. *Report of the Governor of Hawaii to the Secretary of the Interior. 1900.* Wash.: Government Printing Office.

254: _____. 1901. *Report of the Governor of Hawaii to the Secretary of the Interior. 1901.* Wash.: Government Printing Office.

255: _____. 1902. *Report of the Governor of the Territory of Hawaii to the Secretary of the Interior.* Washington: Gov. Printing Off.

256: _____. 1905. *Report of the Governor of the Territory of Hawaii to the Secretary of the Interior. 1905.* Washington: Gov. Printing Off.

257: _____. 1906. *Report of the Governor of the Territory of Hawaii to the Secretary of the Interior. 1906.* Washington: Gov. Printing Off.

258: _____. 1914. *Report of the Governor of Hawaii to the Secretary of the Interior For the Fiscal Year Ended June 30, 1914.* Wash.: Gov. Printing Off.

259: _____. 1916. *Report of the Governor of Hawaii to the Secretary of the Interior For the Fiscal Year Ended June 30, 1916.* Wash.: Gov. Printing Off.

260: _____. 1919. *Report of the Governor of Hawaii to the Secretary of the Interior. 1919.* Wash.: Government Printing Office.

261: _____. 1920. *Report of the Governor of Hawaii to the Secretary of the Interior. 1920.* Wash.: Government Printing Office.

262: _____. 1921. *Report of the Governor of Hawaii to the Secretary of the Interior.* Wash.: Gov. Printing Office.

263: _____. 1922. *Report of the Governor of Hawaii to the Secretary of the Interior.* Wash.: Gov. Printing Office.

264: _____. 1923. *Report of the Governor of Hawaii to the Secretary of the Interior.* Wash.: Gov. Printing Office.

265: _____. 1924. *Report of the Governor of Hawaii to the Secretary of the Interior for the Fiscal Year Ended June 30, 1924.* Wash.: Gov. Printing Off.

266: _____. 1925. *Report of the Governor of Hawaii to the Secretary of the Interior 1925.* Washinton: Gov. Printing Off.

267: _____. 1926. *Report of the Governor of Hawaii to the Secretary of the Interior 1926.* Washinton: Gov. Printing Off.

268: Senior, Clarence. 1947. *Puerto Rican Emigration.* Social Science Research Center. University of Puerto Rico, Rio Piedras.

269: _____. 1954. "Patterns of Puerto Rican Dispersion in the Continental United States." *Social Problems.* October 1954. Vol. 2, No. 2.

270: _____. 1965. *Our Citizens from the Caribbean.* New York: McGraw-Hill Book Company, Webster Division.

271: Senior, Clarence and Donald O. Watkins. 1966. "Toward A Balance Sheet of Puerto Rican Migration." In *U.S.-P.R. Commission on Status of Puerto Rico: Selected Background Studies.* [Online version: URL is unknown, pages 689ff.]. U.S. Department of Health, Education & Welfare Office of Education. Washington, D.C.: Government Printing Office.

272: Silver, Patricia and Carlos Vargas-Ramos. 2012. "Demographic Transitions: Research Brief". Center for Puerto Rican Studies. Hunter College, CUNY. centropr.hunter.edu. 695 Park Ave., New York, N.Y. Issued: November 2012. (Accessed: December 2, 2012)

273: Silvestrini-Pacheco, Blanca and María de los Angeles Castro Arroyo. 1981. "Sources For The Study of Puerto Rican History: A Challenge to the Historian's Imagination." *Latin American Research Review.* Vol. 16, No. 2. 156-171. See also: (<http://www. jstor.org/ stable /503130>). (Accessed: June 29, 2010).

274: Teresa Whalen, Carmen. 2005. "Colonialism, Citizenship, and the Making of the Puerto Rican Diaspora: An Introduction." *The Puerto Rican Diaspora: Historical Perspectives.* Edited by Carmen Teresa Whalen and Victor Vázquez-Hernández. Philadelphia: Temple University Press.

275: Thomas, Lorrin. 2009. "Resisting the Racial Binary? Puerto Ricans' Encounter With Race in Depression-Era New York City." *CENTRO: Journal of the Center for Puerto Rican Studies.* Spring 2009. Volume XXI, No. I.

276: United States Census Office. 1901. *Twelfth Census of the United States, Taken in the Year 1900.* Census Reports Volume I. "Population Part I". Table 25, "Native Population, Distributed According to State Or Territory of Birth, By States and Territories: 1900." Washington: Census Office.

277: U.S. Bureau of the Census. 1902. *Abstract of The Twelfth Census of the United States: 1900.* Washington: Government Printing Office.

278: _____. 1904. *Abstract of The Twelfth Census of the United States: 1900.* Third Edition. Washington, D.C.: Government Printing Office. (Digitized by Google – Google Books). Retrieved on Aug. 6, 2010. (http://books.google.com/books?id= pzcPAAAAYAAJ&oe =UTF-8). (cf.: (<http://books. Google.com/>); for "the full text of this book on the web.").

279: _____. 1910a. *Thirteenth Census of the United States: 1910 Bulletin.* "Population: United States. Abstract – State of Birth of Native population." Retrieved on July 27, 2010. (<http://www.archive .org/ bookreader/print.php?id=thirteenthcensus03unit& server = ia311042...>). (The "digitized version" of the 1910 Bulletin).

280: _____. 1910b. *Thirteenth Census of the United States: 1910 Bulletin.* "Population: United States. Population of Counties and Equivalent Subdivisions." Retrieved on July 7, 2012.

281: _____. 1913a. *Thirteenth Census of the United States Taken in the Year 1910: Abstract of the Census, Statistics of Population, Agriculture, Manufactures and Mining for the United States, the States, and Principal Cities. Supplement For Porto Rico....* Washington: G.P.O.

282: _____. 1913b. *Thirteenth Census of the United States Taken in the Year 1910: Population 1910, General Report and Analysis. Volume I.* Washington: Government Printing Office.

283: _____. 1913c. *Thirteenth Census of the United States Taken in the Year 1910: Population 1910, Reports by States, with Statistics for Counties, Cities and Other Civil Divisions. Alabama-Montana. Volume II.* Washington: Government Printing Office.

284: _____. 1913d. *Thirteenth Census of the United States Taken in the Year 1910: Statistics for Hawaii. Containing Statistics of Population…Cities.* Washington: GPO. [see also: Thirteenth Census of the U.S. Taken in the Year 1910: Statistics For Porto Rico: Containing… Population…. (1913)].

285: _____. 1914. *Thirteenth Census of the United States Taken in the Year 1910: Population 1910, Occupation Statistics. Volume IV.* Washington: Government Printing Office.

286: _____. 1920 [?]. *Fourteenth Census of the United States: 1920 Bulletin. Population: Porto Rico – Number of Inhabitants, By Municipalities And Minor Civil Divisions.* (Dept. of Commerce). Washington: Government Printing Office.

287: _____. 1922. *Fourteenth Census of the United States Taken in the Year 1920: Population. 1920. Composition and Characteristics of the Population by States. Volume III.* Washington: Government Printing Office.

288: _____. 1922. *Fourteenth Census of the United States Taken in the Year 1920. General Report and Analytical Tables. Volume II.* Washington: Government Printing Office.

289: U.S. Bureau of the Census. 1923. *Abstract of the Fourteenth Census of the United States 1920.* Washington: Government Printing Office.

290: _____. 1953. *United States Census of Population: 1950. Bureau of the Census.* "Special Reports: Puerto Ricans in Continental United States. 1950 Population Census Report P-E No. 3D Preprint of Volume IV, Part 3, Chapter D." Washington, D.C.: U.S. Govt. Printing Office.

291: _____. 1975. *Historical Statistics of the United States, Colonial Times to 1970, Bicentennial Edition, Part 2.* "Population of the United States and Outlying Areas: 1880 to 1970." Table: Series A 9-22. Page 9. Washington, D.C.: U.S. Government Printing Office.

292: _____. 1999. "Nativity of the Population and Place of Birth of the Native Population: 1850 to 1990. Table 1." U.S. Census Bureau, Population Division, by Campbell Gibson and Emily Lennon. Internet Release date: March 9, 1999. Retrieved on July 28, 2010. (<http://www.census.gov/population/ www/documentation/twps0029/tab01.html>).

293: _____. 2001. "Profiles of General Demographic Characteristics 2000 – United States. 2000 Census of Population and Housing." (Issued: May 2001).

294: _____. 2010. *1910 United States Federal Census,* [Original data: Thirteenth Census of the United States, 1910 (NARA microfilm production T624, 1,178 rolls); Records of the Bureau of the Census, Record Group 29. National Archives, Washington, D.C.]. (Source Information: Ancestry.com.1910 United States Federal Census [database on-line]. Provo, UT, USA: Ancestry.com Operations Inc, 2006). (The 1910 Federal Census, via Ancestry.com and AncestryInstitution.com).

295: U.S. Bureau of Labor. 1902. *Report of the Commissioner Of Labor On Hawaii. 1901.* Wash.: Government Printing Office.

296: _____. 1903. *Report of the Commissioner Of Labor On Hawaii. 1902.* Wash.: Government Printing Office.

297: _____. 1916. Labor Conditions in Hawaii. *Letter from the Secretary of Labor Transmitting the Fifth Annual Report of the Commissioner of labor Statistics on Labor Conditions in the Territory of Hawaii for the Year 1915.* Washington: Government Printing Office.

298: U.S. Census Bureau. 2002. "Census 2000 Data for Puerto Rico. The Population of Puerto Rico on April 1, 2000 was 3,808,610." Released on 6/4/2002. (<http://www.census.gov/census2000/states/pr.html>).

299: U.S. Civil Rights Commission. 1980. *Puerto Ricans in California.* (A Staff Report of The Western Regional Office, United States Commission on Civil Rights, January 1980). Washington, D.C.: U.S. Government Printing Office.

300: U.S. Department of Commerce. 1931. *Statistical Abstract of the United States 1931.* Fifty-Third Number. Wash.: Government Printing Office.

301: U.S. Department of Commerce and Labor. 1906. *Third Report of the Commissioner of Labor on Hawaii. 1905.* Wash.: Government Printing Office.

302: _____. 1907. *Commercial Porto Rico in 1906. Showing Commerce, Production, Finances… Population, and Details of Trade with the United States….* Wash.: Government Printing Office.

303: _____. 1911. *Statistical Abstract of the United States: 1910.* Thirty-Third Number. Bureau of Statistics. Washington: Government Printing Office.

304: U.S. Department of Labor. Off. of the Secretary. 1919. *Labor Conditions in Porto Rico. Report by Joseph Marcus, Special Agent, U.S. Employment Service.* Wash.: Government Printing Office.

305: U.S. War Department. 1900. Office Director Census of Porto Rico. 1900. *Report on the Census of Porto Rico, 1899.* Washington: Government Printing Office.

306: Vega, Bernardo. 1984. *Memoirs of Bernardo Vega: A contribution to the history of the Puerto Rican community in New York.* ed., César Andreau Iglesias. Juan Flores, trans. New York: Monthly Review Press.

307: Varela-Lago, Ana M. 2008. *Conquerors, immigration, Exiles: The Spanish Diaspora in the United States (1848-1948).* Ph.D. dissertation in History. University of California, San Diego. (see the section titled: "Andalusian farmers in Hawaii and California").

308: Vázquez, José L. 1964. *The Demographic Evolution of Puerto Rico.* Ph.D. Dissertation. University of Chicago.

309: Vázquez Calzada, José L. 1968. "Las Causas Y Efectos De La Emigracion Puertorriqueña." Universidad De Puerto Rico. Escuela De Medicina. Departamento de Medicina Preventiva y Salud Pública Sección de Estudios Demográficos. (Mimeografiado) (Octubre, 1968). Accessed on: Aug. 21, 2012 from Dr. Vázquez Calzada's web site.

310: _____. 1978. *La Población de Puerto Rico Y Su Trayectoria Historia.* Julio de 1978. University of Iowa Libraries. Obtained via an: "Interlibrary Loan." (Catedratico Asociado Escuela De Salud Publica Recinto De Ciencias Medicas Universidad De Puerto Rico).

311: _____. 1990. "La Historia De Los Censos En Puerto Rico." CIDE. 1990 AGO; Núm. XIII. [CIDE: UPR, Centro De Investigaciones Demograficas]. Accessed on August 21, 2012 from the web page of Dr. José Luis Vázquez Calzada, presented on: 4 de Abril de 1990. (<http://demografia. rcm.upr.edu/new_page_19.htm>).

312: Vázquez Calzada, José L. and Zoraida Morales del Valle. [Undated]. "Los Movimientos Migratorios Entre Puerto Rico Y El Exterior." Programa Graduado de Demografía. (Mimeografiado). Accessed on: August 21, 2012 from the web site of Dr. Vázquez Calzada; see above: for the full URL citation.

313: War Department, Annual Reports. 1932. *Annual Report of the Chief of the Bureau of Insular Affairs. 1932.* Washington: Government Printing Office.

314: War Department, U.S.A. 1900. *Census of Porto Rico, The Direction of the War Department, U.S.A.* Bulletin No. 1, Bulletin No. II, Bulletin No. III. Total Population By Departments, Municipal Districts, Cities, And Wards. Washington: Government Printing Office.

315: Washington, Government Printing Office. 1864. *Population of The United States in 1860; Compiled From the Original Returns of The Eight Census.* (Available on books.google.com).

Bibliography Addendum:

316: Colbert, John W., M.D. 1913. "Railway Surgeons. Hookworm Disease, and Its Importation into California." *California State Journal of Medicine.* March 1913; page 123.

317: Duany and Felix V. Matos- Rodríguez. 2006. "Puerto Ricans in Orlando and Central Florida." Policy Report, Vol. I, No. I (Spring 2006). Cento de Estudios Puertorriqueños. CUNY.

318: *The Hawaiian Gazette.* 1900. "Laborers Coming. Porto Ricans Due to Reach Here Today. The Yellow Journal Tries To Scare Them From Sailing." December 21, 1900

319: *The Hawaiian Star.* 1910. "Good Riddance Bothers California." May 4, 1910. Second Edition.

320: *Los Angeles Herald.* 1904. "Porto Ricans are Deserting Hawaii: San Francisco now has Five Hundred in Destitute Condition and Five Thousand More are Coming Soon." December 15, 1904.

321: *The Medical News.* A Weekly Journal of Medical Science. 1905. "Uncinariasis in California." Vol. 87. Aug. 5, 1905.

322: *New York Times.* 1900. "Progress of Porto Rican Pilgrims. Peons Pass Through City En Route To Hawaii. Report That Twenty-five of the Party Escaped—No Signs of Ill Treatment of Emigrants in Evidence—Dissatisfaction Caused by Mexicans." December 14, 1900. (See: Bib. #106)

323: _____. 1905. "An Epidemic of Laziness. A Whole Region in Porto Rico Afflicted with the Lazy Worm. June 24, 1905.

324: _____. 1910. "Porto Rico Checks Hookworm Ravages. Major Bailey K. Ashford Tells of the Successful Fight Against the Parasite. Death Rate Much Reduced. Only 426 Deaths in Five Years Out of Thousands Treated—Cost of the Fight $154,191." December 27, 1910.

325: _____. 1917. "Contract Labor in Hawaii. Evil Conditions Due to Evasion of Immigration Laws." March 21, 1917.

326: *San Francisco Call, The.* 1900. "More Porto Ricans Coming." December 31, 1900.

327: _____. 1901. "Those Porto Ricans." May 24, 1901.

328: _____. 1902. "Filipinos are Aliens in Eye of the Law: Immigration Regulations Applied to Them as Well as Porto Ricans." August 12, 1902.

329: _____. 1904. "Porto Ricans Not Aliens At United States Ports. Chief Justice of the Federal Supreme Court who has Handed Down an Opinion that Porto Ricans Cannot be Classified as Aliens at American Ports." January 5, 1904.

330: _____. 1904. "Board to Care for Porto Rican Pupils. Will Set Aside Two Rooms in Le Conte School for the Nation's Dusky Wards." December 2, 1904.

331: _____. 1909. "Stranded in This City." June 6, 1909.

332: _____. 1909. "Teachers Laugh at California Woman's Word. Miss Mart Shirley Boldly Champions Cause of Suffrage at Denver Meeting. San Francisco is Chosen as the Place for Holding 1910 Convention." July 9, 1909.

333: _____. 1909. "Hawaiian Planters Dissatisfied With Japanese." July 27, 1909.

334: _____. 1910. "Spread of Hookworm in California." November 26, 1910.

335: _____. 1911. "Fruit Men Seek Labor in Hawaii. One Thousand Filipinos and Porto Ricans Secured for Coastal Canneries." April 5, 1911.

336: *San Francisco Chronicle*. 1912. "City Physician Gunn Provides Nurse and Policeman for Porto Rican's Home." July 12, 1912.

337: *San Francisco Examiner*. 1900. "Kidnaping Slaves From Porto Rico: One Hundred and Fourteen Men and Women Held Prisoners on a Southern Pacific Train in Texas…Being Taken to Hawaiian Plantations. Several Have Tried to Escape, but Were Pursued, Recaptured and Turned Over to Their Guards Again." December 7, 1900.

338: _____. 1900. "Liberty of Porto Rican Laborers…Being Hurried to Hawaiian Islands. It is Alleged They Were Procured by a New York Emigration Agent. Americans are Said to be Employed to Guard the Men and They are not Allowed to Talk of Their Troubles." December 8, 1900.

339: _____. 1900. "Government Blind to Trade in Labor." December 9, 1900.

340: _____. 1900. "Bullets Used to Coerce a Boy Laborer. Guarding the Porto Ricans Who are Coming Westward, Bound for the Cane Fields of Hawaii. Tales Told the Simple-Minded Blacks Were the Same Used to Lure the Galicians Into a Condition of Slavery." December 10, 1900.

341: _____. 1900. "Porto Ricans Are Prepared to Resist. They Declare They Will Not Go Aboard the Ship Here to be Transported to Sugar Plantations of Hawaii…. Contracts Were Entered Into Verbally in Porto Rico Which Have Not Been Fulfilled in Any Measure." December 12, 1900.

342: _____. 1900. "Record-Breaking Run To Be Made By Exile Train. Porto Ricans to be Rushed from Indio to Oakland on 'Flyer' [sic] Time in Order to Connect With the Steamship Rio de Janeiro, Which is Booked to Sail for Honolulu next Friday Afternoon. It is Evident it is the Intention of the Contractors to Get the Laborers Out on the Ocean Before They Know What is Happening to Them. Their Childish Dispositions, They Will Hustle Them Aboard Before They Can Resist." December 13, 1900. (Written by: Edward J. Livernash)

343: _____. 1900. "Nearly Half the Charges of the Slave-Drivers Make at Port Costa a Successful Break for Liberty. Their Companions in Exile Rushed Aboard Ship Against Their Will, and Weeping and Protesting, Sail for Hawaii." December 15, 1900. (written by: Edward J. Livernash)

344: _____. 1900. "The Involuntary Departure of Forlorn, Unhappy Porto Ricans, and Plight of the Friendless Escapes, Marked by Great Pathos." December 15, 1900.

345: _____. 1900. "Planters Relenting. They May Talk Things Over With the Porto Ricans." December 16, 1900.

346: _____. 1900. "Will Protect Porto Ricans. 'The Examiner' to Provide for the Exiles Until All Obtain Good Homes. Southern Pacific Company and Hawaiian Planters Basely Desert Their Victims." December 17, 1900.

347: _____. 1900. "Southern Pacific Company and Planters' Association Squirming Under The Blame." December 18, 1900.

348: _____. 1900. "Salinas Providing For Porto Ricans." December 20, 1900.

349: _____. 1900. "Good Position Found For One At Tracy." Dec. 20, 1900.

350: _____. 1900. "Contended and Happy in Salinas Homes." Dec. 23, 1900.

351: _____. 1900. "Alameda Gave Best of Cheer. The Strangers Excellently Treated Across the Bay." December 26, 1900.

352: _____. 1900. "All Satisfied in Monterey County." December 26, 1900.

353: Smith, Claude A. 1905. "Further Remarks on the Mode of Infection in Uncinariasis." *Transactions of the Section on Practice of Medicine of the American Medical Association*. Fifty-sixth Annual Session, held at Portland, Ore., July 11 to 14, 1905 (pages 293-301).

354: Stead, Alfred. 1902. "The Labor Question In Hawaii: An Object Lesson To American Statesmen." *Collier's Weekly*. Nov. 29, 1902. (Vol. 30, No. Nine).

355: Morín, José Luis. "Indigenous Hawaiians Under Statehood: Lessons for Puerto Rico." *CENTRO: Journal of the Center for Puerto Rican Studies*. Spring 2000. Vol. XI, No. 2.

356: Dias, Austin. 2001. "Carlo Mario Fraticelli: A Puerto Rican Poet on the Sugar Plantations of Hawai'i." *CENTRO: Journal of the Center for Puerto Rican Studies*. Spring 2001. Vol. XIII, No. 1.

357: California Genealogical Society. 2010. *San Francisco Deaths 1865-1905: Abstracts from Surviving Civil Records. Volume I, Surnames Starting with A – D*. (Compiled by Barbara Ross Close and Vernon A. Deubler). California Genealogical Society & Library. Oakland, California. CaliforniaAncestors.org.

358: City of Redwood City, (Redwood City, California). 2010. "Mezesville Map, 1856." (http:// www.redwoodcity.org/phed/econdev/redevelopment/downtown/history/mezesville.h...). Redwood City Redevelopment – Downtown Yesterday. Accessed: March 30, 2011. (cf.: Bib. #163).

359: Pew Research Center. 2013. "Statistical Portrait of Hispanics in the United States, 2011." By Seth Motel and Eileen Patten. Released: February 15, 2013. Accessed: February 13, 2013. (http://www.pewhispanic.org/2013/02/15/Statistical-portraait-of-hispanic...).

360: *New York Times*. 1902. "Questions By A Porto Rican." August 9, 1902. [Note: This article is earlier cited/referenced under the author's name in this Bibliography, namely under: Schomburg, Arthur A., page 8 of the *Times*] (See: Bib. #249).

361: _____. 1904. "Porto Ricans Not Aliens. Federal Supreme Court Renders Decision in Gonzales Case. Citizenship Not Decided, Says Justice, Simply That Residents, of Porto Rico Are Not Immigrants." January 5, 1904.

362: _____. 1922. "Spanish-American War Seen From Porto Rico." December 17, 1922.

363: *Antonio María Osio Papers,* BANC MSS C-8 833, The Bancroft Library, University of California, Berkeley; via the OAC (Online Archives of California); accessed: February 18, 2013). (http://www.oac.cdlib.org/findaid/ark:/13030/tf5000048n/entire_text/).

364: Looseley, Allyn Campbell. 1927. *Foreign Born Population of California, 1848-1920.* (A Thesis, University of California. (R & E Research Associates, 1971. Call no.: F870.A1L61971)). (Accessed at the: San Diego State University, The Love Library).

365: Camacho Souza, Blasé and Alfred P. Souza. *De Borinquen A Hawaii Nuestra Historia:* From Puerto Rico to Hawaii. 1985. Puerto Rican Heritage Society. Honolulu, Hawaii.

366: Gibson, Campbell and Emily Lennon. 1999. *Historical Census Statistics on the Foreign-Born Population of the United States: 1850 to 1990.* Population Division. Working Paper No. 29. U.S. Bureau of the Census. February 1999. Washington, D.C. (Digitized by Google)

367: Oral History Task Force. Centro de Estudios Puertorriqueños. 1985. *Extended Roots' From Hawaii to New York: Migraciones Puertorriqueñas a los Estados Unidos.* Hunter College, City University of New York. Second Edition, 1998. New York, NY.

Note: The 2nd Edition's Bibliography #368 - #423 begins on page 239 ff.

Note: The 2nd Edition portion of this book begins on the next page, page 195.

EPILOGUE

EPILOGUE (*documentation* of Simon M. Mezes having been born in Puerto Rico)   6/14/16

With the advantage of three plus years having passed since the printing of the 1st Edition of this book in March 2013, I have conducted further research on the history (biography) of one of the first recorded, if not the first person, that was born in Porto Rico (Puerto Rico) and who emigrated from Porto Rico to California, namely, Simon M. Mezes (aka: S. M. Mezes) (see: Chapter 12 of this book). One of his "main" biographers, Bailey Millard, (Bib. #118, #119), wrote in 1924 that Mr. Mezes arrived in San Francisco, CA on February 22, 1850, (see: p. 81 of this book, see: Bib. #119, Vol. III, p. 382). A biography of Mr. Millard listed him as being the author of the three volume set titled, "History of the San Francisco Bay Region" (1924). He was also an editor for several different newspapers during his lifetime, including among others, and most relevant for this book, the *San Francisco Chronicle*, the *San Francisco Call*, the *San Francisco Examiner*, *San Francisco Evening* Bulletin, and the *Los Angeles Examiner,* (Bib. #119, Volume II, p. 373).

However, additional research since 2013 has unequivocally shown that Mr. Millard's statement above was not correct. For example, a newspaper at the time, the *Alta California (Weekly)*, had an advertisement displayed in its December 29, 1849 issue (page 3), which cited the firm of *Henrichson, Reincke & Co.* (General Merchants, San Francisco, corner of Sacramento and Kearny streets), with the following partners/employees, namely, O.F. Cipriani, H.W. Hinrichson, R. Reincke, and **S. M. Mezes** (emphasis added) (page 3, column 2, of the newspaper, Volume 1, Number 52, Dec. 29, 1849). It should be noted that, "Ottavio Cipriani [aka: O.F. Cipriani]---Listed in San Francisco Directories from 1850 to 1859…from 1852 to 1854 with the [above referenced Mezes firm] of Hinrichsen, Reincke & Co., commission merchants [i.e., "real estate operators"] (see: Ottavio Cipriani's cousin's book, *California and Overland Diaries of Count Leonetto Cipriani from 1853 Through 1871....*, *cited* below, pp. 3, 18, 30 (Footnote 11), 59, 65, 68-69, 70, 71, 94). (cf.: p. 198; Exhibit 22, p. 246) (Bib. #421).

Note that the 1850 *San Francisco City Directory* (by Charles P. Kimball, September 1, 1850, page 26) listed the firm [company] of: Cipnani [*sic*], C.F., f. Henrickson, Remick & Co., Mont [Montgomery] b [between] Sac & Cal. (pages 58). This same 1850 *Directory* also listed the company as Reinicke, H. f. Hinrickson, R & Co., on Mont b [between] Sac and Cal [Sacramento and California Streets?], (p. 93). The 1850 *Directory* also listed the *Alta California* (Daily and Weekly) newspaper "in the city" (of San Francisco), among the other newspapers (pages 26, 127). Page 58 listed the company as being: Hinrickson, Reinecke & Co. (com merchts [merchants], Mont b [between] Sac and Cal [Streets], (pages 58, Preface). The commonality for the three separate citations in this cited 1850 *San Francisco City Directory* is that the address for all three are the same, notwithstanding that the spellings of these respective company names are spelled differently---all three are one and the same company. Sometimes proper names of people, and companies, were not spelled correctly, and/or were consistently the same, in this *Directory*.

Also important is the fact that Mr. Millard wrote that S. M. Mezes was "born of pure Spanish lineage… having come to Porto Rico while a boy…" suggesting that Mr. Mezes was born in Spain, rather than in Porto Rico (Puerto Rico), (see: Bib. #119, Vol. III, p. 382). Once again, Mr. Millard is "incorrect" (see: below), in the sense that to say that S.M. Mezes was born in Spain, and not in Porto Rico (Puerto Rico) can be historically explained, such as the 1880 U.S. Census indicated.

As genealogist, Tony Rivera Maldonado astutely pointed out in his December 2013 *Report* (revised Sept. 25, 2015), that: "While, at first blush there appears to be a conflict between the two places cited as Simon's [S.M. Mezes'] place of birth, there is in fact no such conflict. Most of these documents [in his *Report*] clearly indicate that Simon was born in 'Porto Rico' and since Puerto Rico was either a Spanish territory (as of 1493) or Province (as of 1897) until it fell into American hands (in 1898) as a result of the Spanish-American War of 1898, it's fairly easy to see that being born in 'Spain' does not exclude the possibility of being born in Puerto Rico", (see: Bib. #400, p. 1).

Research conducted after the 1st Edition of this book was printed shows that there existed a "primary source" document that confirms that Mr. Mezes' was born in Mayagüez, Puerto Rico (Porto Rico). For example, a recently obtained copy of a baptismal record titled, "**CERTIFICADO DE PARTIDA DE BAUTISMO**" (Baptismal Certificate), dated January 25, 1824 sheds new light on this very question. The rite of baptism was conducted by the Rev. Manuel G. Casuela. This Catholic Church document states that a child named Simón Meces [aka: S.M. Mezes] was born on December 25, 1823, in Mayagüez, Puerto Rico (Porto Rico), and that his father was, Juan Simón Meces, and his mother was Maria del Carmen Moreno [she was born in Venezuela]. A certified copy of this baptismal record was obtained from the church in which it was conducted, *Nuestra Señora de la Candelaria*, and is dated April 14, 2015. I was also later able to secure a digital photograph, from an independent source, of the page from the original sacramental book in Puerto Rico (Porto Rico) where it was recorded (see: p. 248). (Exhibit 24, p. 248; Bib. #400: 1, 2, 18, 19, 21, 22, 6).

It should be noted that since after the 1st Edition of my book was printed there continued to be some discussion and debate as to whether S.M. Mezes was actually born in Spain, or in Puerto Rico (Porto Rico). While it was clear to me that he was in fact born in Puerto Rico, I then retained the professional services of Puerto Rican genealogist, Tony Rivera Maldonado. As a result, much of the above subsequent research was conducted by Tony Rivera Maldonado (Member, APG [Association of Professional Genealogists]), who specializes in "the Genealogy of Puerto Rico". His company is called: **de Ribera Researchers**, at: www.derivera.com. His documents, analysis and findings were first presented in his report titled, "Preliminary Research Results into The Birth Place of Simon Mezes of Belmont, California, December 16, 2013 (*Revised* September 25, 2015") (18 pages, hereinafter cited as the *Report, Bib. #400*), (cf.: page 198 for the Library of Congress article).

With respect to S.M. Mezes' father's immigration to Puerto Rico in the early 1800s, it should be noted that Tony Rivera Maldonado's *Report* had additional "primary documents", which both historians and genealogists would find helpful in helping to confirm that S.M. Mezes was born in Puerto Rico. Dr. Raquel Rosario Rivera's book, *La Real Cédula de Gracias de 1815 y sus primeros efectos en Puerto Rico: Incluye Registro de Emigrados*, (1995, San Juan, P.R.), includes a chart/table titled the "Registro de emigrados: 1815-1820", which lists S.M. Mezes' father as having immigrated to Puerto Rico. For example, the list reads as follows: Juan Simon Mesas, arrived in Puerto Rico from New Orleans, Louisiana to the town of Mayagüez, Puerto Rico in 1811, (pages 208-209, 269). For the historical and genealogical description, and <u>connection</u>, between the spellings of the names of S.M. Mezes and that of his father, Juan Simon Mesas, [aka: Meces or Meses] refer to the above referenced *Report* of professional genealogist, Tony Rivera Maldonado, (Bib. #400).

Similarly, Puerto Rican historian Estela Cifre De Loubriel, in her book appropriately titled, *Catálogo De Extranjeros Residentes En Puerto Rico En El Siglo XIX* (1962, page 34), wrote about S.M. Mezes' father that: "*Messes o Nesses, Juan* Simón. *Natural [born] de Nueva Orleáns. Estados Unidos; reside en Puerto Rico desde el 1811; obtiene carta de naturalización en junio de 1816 al amparo de la Cédula de Gracias. A.G.I.* [Archivo General de Indias de Sevilla, Spain]*, Aud. Sto. Dgo., Leg. 2421*," (page XX; Bib. #373).

Specifically, among the primary, and secondary *documents*, provided in the above cited *Report* by Tony Rivera Maldonado (Genealogist, APG) which unequivocally shows that S.M. Mezes was born in Puerto Rico (Porto Rico), and <u>not</u> in Spain, are as follows:

1) Juan Simon Messes, Immigration to Puerto Rico from Louisiana, 1811; 2) Juan Simon & Maria del Carmen Moreno, Marriage 05/29/1822 [these are S.M. Mezes' parents], *Nuestra Señora de Calendaria, Mayagüez, Puerto Rico;* 3) Simon Meces [aka: Simon Mezes], Baptism 01/31/1824, *Nuestra Señora de Candelaria,* Mayagüez, Puerto Rico ; 4) George C. Jackson, "Some Louisiana Immigrants to Puerto Rico" (1977, *New Orleans Genesis*, Genealogical Research Society of New Orleans, vol. 36: 142, April 1977); 5) U.S. and Canada, Passenger and Immigration Lists Index, 1500s-1900s, Name: Juan Simon Messes, Arrival Year: 1811, Arrival: Puerto Rico, Source Publication Code: 347625, Annotation: Date and place of receipt of letter of citizenship or date and place of first mention of residence in the New World. Place of origin and other genealogical information are also provided (cf.: Cifre De Loubriel, 1964: LXXX, Bib. #374; Rivera Maldonado: 2013 and 2015, Bib. #400).

Another researched primary source document which was provided by Tony Maldonado Rivera in a December 14, 2015 *e-mail* to me, with the subject of S.M. Mezes' father, namely: "Juan Simon Mezes – Record from Archivo de Indias", "Attachments: Mezes, Juan Simon – *Cedula de Gracias* – 27 June 1815, Puerto Rico". His *e-mail* to me also stated as follows: "Attached is a copy of the record I was able to obtain from the researcher in **Spain**. Mezes' name is the last one mentioned on the bottom of page 3. It says he filed a petition for Spanish citizenship on June 27, 1816 after residing... [for] five years in Puerto Rico and that he was born in New Orleans". The first page of this document reads as follows: "Relacíon de los Colonos establecidos en la Isla de S.n Juan Baut. De Puerto Rico, á consequencia de la *Real Cedula 10 de Agosto de 1815*" (note: this is the best that I was able to read this hand-written document, and loosely translated to: Records of Colonists who settled on the Island of Puerto Rico...). ([Original] Source: AGI, Santo Domingo, 2421, pages 250, 251, along with three other pages, which I could not read their respective page numbers), (see: Exhibit 26, p. 250).

Conclusions regarding S.M. Mezes being Born in Puerto Rico:

The *Report* of Genealogist Tony Rivera Maldonado (see: Bib. #400) concluded that:

"After reviewing the various documents cited herein, especially the several references to 'Simon Mezes' being born in Puerto Rico, it's fairly clear to me that the 'Simon Meces' baptized in Mayagüez, Puerto Rico in 1824 is the one and same as the 'Simon Mezes' of Belmont, San Mateo County, California fame. Particularly convincing is the reference, in the 1880 U.S. Census for Belmont San Mateo County, California, that Simon Mezes father was born in 'France' and his mother was born in 'Venezuela'. The marriage record for 'Juan Simon Meses' and 'Maria del Carmen Moreno' clearly states that Juan Simon was born in 'Nuevo Orleans' [present day New Orleans, Louisiana] (see Item 14), which was French territory during the period 1682 to 1762, which after it was ceded to Spain, and was again French from 1800 to 1803, and that Maria del Carmen was from Venezuela."

"While, Juan Simon Mezes [S.M. Mezes' father] was most likely born during the period of Spanish rule, it is easy to see, given the above historical facts, how someone years later, say at the time of the 1880 census, could err in thinking that because Simon's father was born in New Orleans that it meant he was born in France as that was from whom Louisiana had been purchased in 1803 by the United States. Most people would know or remember that Louisiana was purchased from the French thereby making anyone born in New Orleans French", (Rivera Maldonado, 2015: 2, Bib. #400).

Finally, the above cited 2015 *Report* posited that:

"The variations in the spelling of the last name [of Mezes] can easily be accounted for by it being written down **phonetically** by the recorder, based on what he heard. I believe that no matter how it was written, Mezes, Messes, Meces, Meses, [Mesas] the pronunciation was, and is essentially, the same and it would be hard to confuse it with any other surname. So, it's fair to say that in my opinion the 'Simon Mezes' of Belmont fame and 'Simon Meces' baptized in Mayagüez, Puerto Rico are one and the same. Additionally, his father, 'Juan Simon Meces', is the same 'Juan Simon Messes' who traveled from Louisiana to Puerto Rico in 1811 as supported by his 1822 marriage record. And, while the baptismal record for Simon does not state where he was born, we do know his parents were married in Mayagüez about 1-1/2 years before his birth, and being baptized in the same place shortly after his birth the odds of Simon having been born somewhere else other than in Puerto Rico is extremely highly unlikely", (*Ibid.*: 2).

Newspaper **Accounts**:

Finally, aside from the earliest known newspaper citation that I am aware of, of the name of S.M. Mezes (*Alta California*, Dec. 29, 1849), in California (San Francisco area), the earliest known book reference, that I am aware of, relating to S. M. Mezes appeared in a diary which was written by one of S.M. Mezes' contemporaries, Count Leonetto Cipriani, with the exceedingly long, though **relevant**, title of:

California and Overland Diaries of Count Leonetto Cipriani From 1853 Through 1871...*the assembling of his elegant prefabricated home in Belmont* [California], *the first consequence on the San Francisco peninsula, later to become the Ralston Mansion*, (Translated and edited by Ernest Falbo, Published by: The Champoeg Press, Portland, Oregon) (MCMLXII) [1962?], (see: pages 65, 70, 12, 30, 71, 94; Bib. #421). (emphasis added)

While my research has not discovered as to how, and as to what mode of transportation that S.M. Mezes arrived in California (i.e., San Francisco) at least as early as December 1849, the above cited diary of Count Leonetto Cipriani (who was a contemporary and who "knew" S.M. Mezes personally as evidence by having specifically cited Mr. Mezes' in his *Diaries*), gives us a clue as to how Mr. Mezes arrived in California. For example, in Mr. Cipriani's *Diaries*, it pointed out Mr. Cipriani's, "… first journey to California in 1851, a second in 1853… [and that] his first journey to California was by sea and the Panama route in 1851-52, the second by covered wagon and horse from Missouri in 1853, and the last in 1871… [by] Pullman car", (p. 1, of Cipriani's book).

It is noteworthy that Count Leonetto Cipriani actually sailed to **Puerto Rico**, in that, "in 1835, he sailed for Trinidad, Saint Thomas, and Puerto Rico to protect his investments threatened by an English law emancipating the slaves in all British colonies," (page 12); thus, this is another "direct connection" between S.M. Mezes, the Cipriani's', and Puerto Rico. Count Cipriani (apparently first) arrived in California "... in October 1853," (p. 129).

It should be noted that Count Leonetto Cipriani, in his *Diary*, indicated that: "In 1853, I crossed the American continent from St. Louis to San Francisco with a covered wagon train. It took six months to cross 2,500 miles of unsettled country which had neither roads nor bridges", (page 137).

Finally. the name of C.F. Cipnani appears in "The San Francisco City Directory" in 1850 (by Charles P. Kimball. September 1, 1850) (San Francisco, 1850) [he is a possible relative of Count L. Cipriani?]. This firms' address is cited as being: "F Henrickson, Remick & Co., Mont b Sac & CAL", (page 26).

(see: "*French Immigrants to Louisiana 1796-1800. Settlements of Bastrop....*", Univ. of Texas Libraries, Austin, Texas, (by Luis Marino Pérez, (1907 ?) (Call #: 975 S088 V. 11 1907)).

(Library of Congress. (undated), *"Louisiana: European Explorations and the Louisiana Purchase: A Special Presentation from the Geography and Map Division of the Library of Congress"*) discussing the role(s) played by Spain, France and by the U.S. relating to Louisiana's historical developements (including New Orleans, in particular) (provided by Genealogist, Tony Rivera Maldonado (8/13/16)).

NOTE: **see the next page for the comprehensive INDEX for this book.**

INDEX

10/18/16

Note: a) immediately after the "source citation" is the page number(s) within the book. Thereafter is the Bibliography source; b) f*or brevity sake, and where it applies, I have abbreviated the words for California (as: CA), and for Bibliography (as: Bib.). Thus, for example, Bib. #3 stands for Bibliography #3, (cf.: Allen, Charles H. Governor. 1901, on page 171 in the* **BIBLIOGRAPHY** *of this book); and c)* "**Porto Rico**" (*as opposed to* **Puerto Rico** *and where applicable) is used since the Island was officially called, and was referred to, as "Porto Rico" from 1898-1932. Finally, and again where applicable, the* name *Porto Rico is abbreviated as being: "P.R."*.

Selected Published Primary Sources:

I) *The Census: Federal and State* – The *Ancestry.com* web site for a 1910 description of itself is as follows: "This database is an index to the head of households enumerated in the 1910 United States Federal Census [as being one example]…. Each indexed name is linked to actual images from the 1910 Federal census. The information recorded in the census includes: name, relationship to head of family, age at last birthday, sex, color or race, whether single, married, widowed, or divorced, birthplace, birthplace of father, and mother, and more…."

Ancestry.*com* 1852 **California State Census**, 15, 79-80, 146, 150, 162; (Bibliography: #8)

*Ancestry.*com 1850 U.S. Federal Census, 59, 79, 80; (Bib. #7, #94)

Ancestry.com 1860 U.S. Federal Census (for CA), 59, 81, 141-142 (Exhibits 1; 2); (Bib. #9)

Ancestry.com 1870 U.S. Federal Census (for CA), 59, 82-83, 143; (Bib. #10, see: Bib. #57)

Ancestry.com 1880 U.S. Federal Census (for CA), 59, 79, 83, 147; (Bib. #11)

Ancestry.com 1890 U.S. Federal Census (for CA), 59, 83; (Bib. #12)

Ancestry.com 1900 U.S. Federal Census (for CA), 59, 61, 63, 79, 80, 83, 95, 97, 144-145, 147, 152-154 (Exhibit 8, Exhibit 9, Exhibit 10), (see: 169-170); (Bib. #13, #276 - #278)

Ancestry.com 1910 U.S. Federal Census (for CA), 53-54, 59, 61-63, 85, 95-97, 101, 103-104, 105-107, 110, 118, 121-123, 125-126, 140, 145, 147, 155, 169-170; (Bib. #14, cf.: #279 - #285, #294)

California 1850 Census Index (1978) (by Ronald V. Jackson and Gary R. Teeples; Bountiful, Utah), 81; (Bib. #94)

1860 California Census Index: Heads of Households and Other Surnames in Household Index (1984) (by Bryan Lee Dilts; Salt Lake City, UT), 81; (Bib. #45) (AncestryInstitution.com 1910)

II) *Note* – The following Censuses are the "*printed* Federal Census books", which were published by the U.S. Bureau of the Census, Wash., D.C.; (Bib. #276 - #290, #294, #315, #366):

- See also: *the above cited* **Censuses** *which are also identified in* this *book under: Ancestry.com. For example, the* **Bibliography** *(pp. 171-172, in this book) cites the* following *(as an example): Ancestry.com 1850 (United States Federal Census), (cf.: Bib. #7, #8 - #14).*

These Censuses, obtained via the *Ancestry.com* software, is a digitized copy of the "original" Federal Census Forms taken in 1850, 1860, 1870, etc., which lists the social characteristics, i.e., "social variables", which were asked by the Federal Government, e.g., Name, Nativity, Date of Birth, Occupation/Profession, etc. Over the years the specific type of social data requested changed.

U.S. Federal Census (the <u>printed</u> versions from Washington, D.C.):

Note: The following ***<u>printed</u>*** Census sources were published by the U.S. Bureau of the Census (pp. 188-189, 191) or from the Secretary of the Interior (p. 187), and contained collective and aggregate data and Tables, and not the individual person's names, births, etc., like what is included among the *Ancestry.com* Census sources.

U.S. Federal Census (**1850**), 7, 19, 59, 79-80; (Bib. #7, #94, #95, #292))

U.S. Federal Census (**1860**), *Population of the United States in 1860: Compiled From the Original Returns of the Eight Census*, (1864), *80,* 81; (Bib. #45, #315)

U.S. Federal Census (**1870**), *A Compendium of the Ninth Census (June 1, 1870)…* (1872b), *79,* 82-83; (Bib. #252; see: Bib. #57, Bib. #251)

U.S. Federal Census (**1870**), *Ninth Census-Volume I. The Statistics of the United States, Embracing the Tables of Race, Nationality, Sex, Selected Ages, and Occupations…* (1872), 82-83; (cf.: Bib. #251, cf.: Bib. #57, Bib. #252)

U.S. Federal Census [**1899**] of ***Porto Rico***, *Report of the Census of Porto Rico, **1899***. (By the: U.S. War Department) (Published in: 1900), 10, 12, 34, 61, 68, 72, 138 (Footnote 7); (Bib. #305, #314)

U.S. Federal Census (**1900**), 17, 61, 72, 152-154; (Bib. #276 - #278; cf.: #292, #366)

U.S. Federal Census (**1910**), 17, 61-62, 97, 126, 140; (Bib. #279 - #285, #294)

U.S. Federal Census (**1920**), 53, 75, 110, 129, 130, 138 (Footnote 7); (Bib. #286 – #289)

U.S. Federal Census, (**1930**), *Fifteenth Census of the United States: 1930. Outlying Territories and Possessions. Number and Distribution of Inhabitants.* (1932), (U.S. Bureau of the Census), 130; (cf.: Bib. #366)

U.S. Federal Census, (**1930**), Fifteenth *Census of the United States: 1930 Population Vol. II…* (1933), (U.S. Bureau of the Census), *130;* (Bib. #366))

U.S. Federal Census, (**1950**), *United States Census of Population. 1950. Bureau of the Census.* (1953) "Special Reports: Puerto Ricans in the Continental United States", 139 (Footnote #9); (Bib. #290; cf.: #291 - #292)

Washington, GPO. *Population of The United States in 1860: Compiled From the Original Returns of the Eight Census.* (1864), 80, 81; (Bib. #315; cf.: Bib. #45) (see: above)

War Department, U.S.A. *Census of Porto Rico, The Direction of the War Department, U.S.A. Bulletin No. 1.* Total Population By Departments, Municipal Districts…. (1900), 72; (Bib. #314)

III) ***<u>Note</u>:***

*1910 Federal Population Census. (*2010), (National Archives and Records Administration [NARA], 126; (Bib. #123)

The 1910 Federal Population Census: A Catalog of Microfilm Copies of the Schedules. (1982); 126; (Bib. #125)

Historical Census Statistics on the Foreign-Born Population of the United States: 1850 to 1990. (1999), (Bureau of the Census), (by C. Gibson and E. Lennon), 57; (Bib. #366)

Statistical Abstract of the United States: 1910. (1911), 43, 79, 145 (Footnote #5); (Bib. #303)

Statistical Abstract of the United States 1931 (1931), 50; (Bib. #300)

The United States Constitution and Other American Documents, (National Archives, 2009) (N.Y.: Fall River Press); 15, 16, (cf.: 137, Footnote 5)); (Bib. #122)

IV) **_Note:_** *Special Publications (**non**-Federal Govt. Publications); plus Genealogical Sources –*

American Federation of Labor, The. (1902), *Proceedings of the American Federation of Labor: 1902 – 1903.* (Report of the Proceedings of the Twenty-Second Annual Convention. Held in New Orleans, LA, Nov. 13 to 22, 1902, Washington, D.C.; 38, 42; (Bib. #5)

Antonio Maria Osio Papers, 1823-1853. (Accessed on: Feb. 18, 2013, online) (The Bancroft Library, Univ. of California, Berkeley), 147; (Bib. #363)

Board of Supervisors. (1873), *San Francisco Municipal Reports For the Year 1872-73. Ending June 30th, 1873;* 80; *(Bib. #20)*

California (*California Voter Registration (1866-1898)* (aka: *Great Registers, 1866-1898*), 84; (Bib. #28) (see: below)

California Genealogical Society. (2010), *San Francisco Deaths 1865-1905: Abstracts from Surviving Civil Records. Volume I, Surnames Starting with A – D*; 97; (Bib. #357)

California State Library, California History Section. (1866-1898), *Great Registers, 1866-1898*, 84; (Bib. #28) (see: above)

California, (Unknown Date). *California Deaths: 1905-1929. Vital Search-CA: Deaths – 7748. Bottom Frame-Search* [**microfiche**], 83; (Bib. #29)

*Eight Annual Report of the Hawaiian Historical Society. (*1900), Hawaiian Historical Society (Honolulu, H.T.), 118-119; (Bib. #67)

Hayward Area Historical Society. (2012), various different separate documents, and "write-ups" from the: *California Century: Puerto Ricans in the San Francisco Bay Area, 1900-2000, "Traveling Exhibit"* (Curated by: Aurora Levins Morales); 6, 7, 31, 167, 168; (see: Bib. #88)

Russell Sage Foundation. (1913), *San Francisco Relief Survey: The Organization and Methods of Relief Used After the Earthquake and Fire of April 8, 1906.* (1913), 120; (Bib. #184)

San Diego City. (1868-1915), *Index to Obituaries and Death Notices in the San Diego Union (1868-1915) and the San Diego Herald (1851-1860)*; 83, 84; (Bib. #193) (SD Genealogical Soc.)

San Diego City. (1893-1894), *Directory of San Diego City and County For 1893-94*; 83; (Bib. #194)

San Diego City. (1895), *San Diego City and County Directory: 1895*, 83; (Bib. #195)

San Diego County. (1894), *The Great Register of San Diego County for 1894: An Alphabetical list of registered voters in San Diego County, California 1894*, 83; *(Bib. #196)*

San Diego Genealogical Society. (2010), *Index to Obituaries and Death Notices in the San Diego Union (1868-1915) and the San Diego Herald (1851-1860).* [Database], 83; (Bib. #197)

Thirteenth Annual Report of the Hawaiian Historical Society with a paper on the Development of Hawaiian Statute Law.... (1906), Hawaiian Historical Society (Honolulu, H.T.), 118-119; (Bib. #68)

V) *Newspapers (Primary Sources):*

Amador Ledger, The (California) (1901), 24, 60; (Bib. #4)

Atlanta Constitution, The (1904), 135; (Bib. #16)

The Democrat [Honolulu, T.H. (Territory of Hawaii)] (1910), 43; (Bib. #69)

El Problema (Puerto Rico) (in Spanish) newspaper, 27, 28, 33 [article is cited in Bib. #38]

[Hawaiian] *Evening Bulletin (Oahu, Hawaii)* (1902), *9, 41, 59;* (Bib. #70-72)

The Hawaiian Gazette, 8, 39, 41, 59, 176, 191; (Bib. #73-76; Bib. #318)

The Hawaiian Star (Honolulu [Oahu]), 8, 9, 21, 39, 41, 59, 176, 191; (Bib. #77-81, Bib. #319) (see: Bib. #34, p. 66, 83, 114, 129, 154, 161, 217, 228, 256)

Honolulu Republican, 8, 9, 37, 38, 59, 112, 117; (Bib. #82 - #87)

La Correspondencia (San Juan, Porto Rico), 40-41, 72-73, 91, 92, 128-129, 131, 183-186; (Bib #34, p. 216) (cf.: Bib. #90, pp. 16-20, 22-25, 28-29, 37 of the Centro's book)

La Democrata (Caguas, Porto Rico), 41; (Bib. #81 (this P.R. newspaper cited in this article))

Los Angeles Daily Times [aka: *Los Angeles Times*], 63; (Bib. #106 - #110)

Los Angeles Herald, 25, 59, 178; (Bib. #104, #105); (Bib. #320)

Los Angeles Times, 59, 63, 69, 91, 114, 116, 118; (Bib. #106 - #110)

Louisiana Planter and Sugar Manufacturer, A Weekly *newspaper, The* (1903), 73-74; (Bib. #410)

New York Journal and Advertiser (1900); (Bib. #157)

New York Times, The, 26-27, 39-40, 60, 68, 69, 93-94, 115, 117-118, 133; (Bib. #126-#134, #249, #322-325, #360-362) (Bib. #34, p. 98, 130, 134, 163, 167)

Pacific Commercial Advertiser (Honolulu, Hawaii), 33, 35-42, 59, 67, 112-113; (Bib. #136-#155), (note: inadvertently also cited as: *Pacific Coast Advertiser*, 28, 37, in the March 2013 First Edition of this book) (Bib. #34, p. 83-84, 98, 113, 163)

Pacific Rural Press and California Fruit Bulletin, (San Francisco, CA) (1909), 18; (Bib. #156)

Puerto Rico Herald, 131; (Bib. #34, p. 154, 168-169, 256)

Redwood City (Cal.) Tribune (1951), 82; (Bib. #161)

Redwood City Tribune (Cal.) (1978), 82; (Bib. #162-#163)

Sacramento Daily Record-Union (1884), 59-60, 82; (Bib. #185-#186)

Sacramento Daily Union (1899), 25-26; (Bib. #187)

San Juan News (San Juan, Porto Rico) (1902), 41

San Francisco Call, 9, 12, 13, 25, 28, 33, 36, 38, 39, 41, 42, 52, 57, 59, 64, 69, 91, 113, 116, 118, 119, 125, 128, 135; (Bib. #198-#214, #326-#335)

San Francisco Chronicle, 7, 9, 12, 16, 27, 37, 38, 59, 64, 67, 69, 81, 86, 87, 91, 112, 114, 115, 117, 120, 121; (Bib. #215-231, #336)

San Francisco Examiner, 7, 13, 14, 41, 52, 59, 72, 87, 88, 89, 90, 91, 101, 102, 109, 112, 135 (Footnote 3), 156 (Exhibit 12), 157 (Exhibit 13), 161 (Exhibit 17); (Bib. #233-#242, #337-#352)

San Mateo County Gazette (1859) (Redwood City, Cal.), 60, 81; (Bib. #243)

San Mateo Times County Fair Supplement (Cal.) (1976), 82; (Bib. #244)

Sausalito News (1910) (Marine County, Cal.), 42-43, 60; (Bib. #245)

VI) *U.S. Government Reports, Hearings, Bulletins and Directories (Primary Sources)*:

Abstract of the Twelfth Census of the United States: 1900. (1902); 61, 63, 68, 77; (Bib. #277)

Abstract of the Twelfth Census of the United States. 1900. U.S. Bureau of the Census (1904); 61; (Bib. #278)

Los Angeles City Directory, (1892), 80; (Bib. #102)

Los Angeles City Directory, (1894), 80; (Bib. #103)

Reports of the Immigration Commission. (1911a), "*Abstracts of Reports of the Immigration Commission. With Conclusions and Recommendation and Views...*", (Vol. I), 43, 44; (Bib. #167)

Reports of the Immigration Commission. (1911b), "*Abstracts of Reports of the Immigration Commission. With Conclusions and Recommendations and views of the Minority*", (Vol. II), 44; (Bib. #168)

Reports of the Immigration Commission, (1911c), "*Dictionary of Races Or Peoples*", (Presented by Mr. Dillingham. Referred to the Committee on Immigration), 137 (Footnote 5); (Bib. #169)

Reports of the Immigration Commission, (1911d), "*Immigrants In Industries.....*", 86; (Bib. #170)

Reports of the Immigration Commission, (1911e), "*Emigration Conditions in Europe*", 51; (Bib. #171)

San Francisco City Directory. 1852 (Sept. 1852). San Francisco Public Library. (Digitizing sponsor: the San Francisco Library), 80; (Bib. #232)

Twelfth Census of the United States, Taken in the Year 1900. U.S. Census Office (1901), 63; (Bib. #276; see also: Bib. #277, #278)

U.S. Bureau of the Census, there are seven (7) different publications of the *Thirteenth Census of the United States: 1910*, all <u>printed</u> from 1910 to 1914; (see: Bib. #279 - #285)

U.S. Bureau of the Census, there are four (4) separate publications on the *Fourteenth Census of the United States: 1920*, all <u>printed</u> from 1920 [?] to 1923; (see: Bib. #286 - #289)

U.S. Bureau of the Census, five (5) other different publications printed, (see: Bib. #290 - #294)

War Department, Annual Reports. *Annual Report of the Chief of the Bureau of Insular Affairs*. (1932), 133 (Footnote 1); (Bib. #313)

VII. Selected *Publications relating to the* **Territory** *of Hawaii and also the Kingdom of Hawaii:*

Board of Immigration. (1907), *First Report of the Board of Immigration to the Governor of the Territory of Hawaii For the period from April 29, 1905 to January 31, 1907*; 64; (Bib. #18)

Board of Immigration. (1909), *Second Report of the Board of Immigration to the Governor of the Territory of Hawaii* For the period from December 31, 1906 to February 18, 1909; 64; (Bib. #19)

Bulletin of the Department of Labor. (1903a), R*eport of the* Commissioner *of Labor on Hawaii.* (No. 47, July 1903) (see the section titled: "Agreement for the Employment of Laborers for the Islands of Hawaii", i.e., the "Hawaiian Porto Rican Plantation Contract") (see: pages 702, 703-704, of this *Bulletin*), 27, 34, 44-45; (Bib. #23; cf.: Bib. #6))

Bulletin of the Department of Labor. (1903b) *Report of the Commissioner of Labor in Hawaii.* (No. 47 – July 1903), (see the section titled: "Labor Conditions in the sugar industry in Hawaii, California, Texas, Louisiana, Cuba, and Porto Rico", (see: pp. 767-772, of this *Bulletin*), 27, 44; (Bib. #24)

Committee on Immigration and Naturalization. (1921), *"Labor Problems in Hawaii", Hearings Before The Committee on Immigration and Naturalization,* 21, 22, 48; (Bib. #42)

Eight Annual Report of the Hawaiian Historical Society. (1900), 118-119; (Bib. #67)

Firsts and Almost Firsts. (1995), (by Robert C. Schmitt; Univ. of Hawaii Press), 8, 109; (Bib. #246)

Hawaii Attorney General, *Biennial Report of the Attorney General to the [Legislative] Assembly of 1882. [Reign of His Majesty Kalakaua – Ninth Year]*, (1882); 114, (Bib. #64)

Hawaii Attorney General, *Biennial Report of the Attorney General to the Legislative Assembly of 1884. [Reign of His Majesty Kalakaua – Eleventh Year]*, (1884); 114, (Bib. #65)

Historical Statistics of Hawaii. (1977), (by Robert C. Schmitt), 69; (Bib. #247)

Report of the Commissioner *of Labor on Hawaii – 1902.* (1903), (see: "Labor conditions in the Sugar Industry in Hawaii, California, Texas, Louisiana, Cuba, and Porto Rico", see: pages 7-120 "Introduction", 26-27, 29, 50, 90-95), 27, 86; (Bib. #296)

Report of the Commissioner of Labor. (1911), "*Fourth Report of the Commissioner of Labor on Hawaii – 1910*", (see section titled: "Labor Conditions in Hawaii", etc.); 46, 69; (Bib. #166)

Report of the President of the Board of Health of the Territory of Hawaii for the Six Months Ending June 30, 1905. (1905), 42; (Bib. #66)

Secretary of the Interior, *Report of the Governor of Hawaii to the Secretary of the Interior.* GPO, (**covering the** following **years**: 1900-1902; 1905-1906; 1914; 1916; 1919-1926). A total of 15 separate *Reports*, 11, 13, 22-24, 34, 40, 48, 49, 50, 59, 64, 85; (Bib. #253 - #267)

Thirteenth Annual Report of the Hawaiian Historical Society.... (1906), 118-119; (Bib. #68)

Thirteenth Census of the United States Taken in the Year 1910: Statistics for Hawaii-Containing Statistics for Hawaii. Containing Statistics of Population…Cities. (U.S. Bureau of the Census, 1913d), 118; (Bib. #284)

U.S. Bureau of Labor. (1902), *Report of the Commissioner of Labor on Hawaii. 1901*, (U.S. Senate document) (Table: "Number and Nationality of Unskilled Plantation Laborers", (Document No. 169), 11; (Bib. #295)

_____. (1903), *Report of the Commissioner of Labor on Hawaii. 1902*, (cf.: the "Agreement for the Employment of Laborers for the Islands of Hawaii" contract (April 16, 1901) and the ("General Conditions of Labor and Industry" sections), 44, 86; (Bib. #296)

U.S. Bureau of Labor. (1916), *Labor Conditions in Hawaii. Letter from the Secretary of Labor Transmitting the Fifth Annual* Report *of the Commissioner of Labor Statistics on Labor Conditions in the Territory of Hawaii for the Year 1915; 46, pp. 47, 119, 129*; (Bib. #297, see: the *many* detailed and comprehensive "Tables" relating to the Sugar Plantations and the Laborers)

U.S. Department of Commerce and Labor, (1906), *Third Report of the Commissioner of Labor on Hawaii - 1905, pp. 24-25;* (Bib. #301)

Additional "Hawaiian-based" Primary Sources reviewed by the Author, were cited in the book, but which were NOT cited in the Bibliography of this Book:

Demographic Statistics of Hawaii: 1778-1965 (1968), 118

Hawaiian Almanac and Annual for 1921 (1920), 118

Historical Statistics of Hawaii: 1778-1962 (1962), 118

Report of the Governor of Hawaii to the Secretary of the Interior 1921 (1920) (U.S. Dept. of the Interior (1921)), 118

VIII. Selected Publications relating to *Porto Rico/Porto Ricans, and Puerto Rico/Puerto Ricans:*

*Note: Most of the above citations of the sources which are listed **immediately under "Section VI"** for Hawaii include references to the **Porto Rican** (Puerto Rican) **plantation laborers** and workers within these sources. The reason being is that as of October 1901, there were well over 5,000 Porto Rican Immigrants (laborers) working on the Hawaiian Plantations by this time.*

*Thus, most of the Hawaiian-based Government **Reports** and **Bulletins** which were published contained Porto Rican statistical, population, economic and employment data and information relating to them, as well as also containing this information for the many other "nationalities" which had been similarly recruited to also work on the 50+ Hawaiian Plantations, beginning with the Chinese immigrants in the early 1800s, etc., as well. Thus, a researcher should look at the above cited sources to obtain the available data/information relating to the **Porto Ricans** laborers in Hawaii beginning from December 23, 1900 to 1925 (and thereafter).*

Bulletin of the Department of Labor. (1901), *Labor Conditions in Porto Rico*, (No. 34) (written by: Azel Ames, M.D.), (No. 34, May 1901), pages 377ff.), 26, 34; (Bib. #6)

Committee on Pacific Islands and Porto Rico. (1912), *Hearings Before The Committee on Pacific Islands and Porto Rico…*, "Citizenship of Porto Ricans", 135 (Footnote 3); (Bib. #43)

Military Governor of Porto Rico on Civil Affairs. (1902) *Annual Reports of the War Department for the Fiscal Year Ended June 30, 1900. Part 13;* 10-11, 138 (Footnote 7); (Bib. #117, p. 210ff., Chapter XX, "Hurricane Relief"; p. 455, APPENDIX I. "Hurricane Relief", and "the central Porto Rican relief committee") (Puerto Rico, Military Governor, John Rutter Brooke)

Nineteenth-Century Puerto Rican Immigration and Slave Data. (1973), (National Archives and Records Services), 138 (Footnote 7); (Bib. #124)

Register of Porto Rico for 1905 Compiled by The Secretary of Porto Rico December 1905. (1905), (Executive Secretary Porto Rico), 68; (Bib. #160)

U.S. Census Bureau. (2002), *Census 2000 Data for Puerto Rico. The Population of Puerto Rico on April 1, 2000 was 3,808,610.* (Released on 6/4/2002), 145; (Bib. #298)

U.S. Civil Rights Commission. (1980), *Puerto Ricans in California,* 71; (Bib. #299)

U.S. Department of Commerce and Labor. (1907), *Commercial Porto Rico in 1906. Showing Commerce, Production, Finances, Area, Population, and Details of Trade with the United States and Foreign Countries during a Term of Years,* 115; *(Bib. #302)*

U.S. Department of Labor. Office of the Secretary. (1919), *Labor Conditions in Porto Rico.* (Report by: Joseph Marcus, Special Agent, U.S. Employment Service), 10, 47; (Bib. #304)

U.S. War Department. Office Director Census of Porto Rico. (1900). *Report on the Census of Porto Rico, 1899.* (Wash.: GPO), 10, 12, 34, 61, 63, 68, 72, 138 (Footnote 7), 200, 206; (Bib. #305)

War Department. (1932). *Annual Report of the Chief of the Bureau of Insular Affairs.* ("…restores to the island the official designation of 'Puerto Rico'", p. 14), 133; (Bib. #313)

War Department, U.S.A. (1900) *Census of Porto Rico, The Direction of the War Department, U.S.A.* Bulletin No. 1 "Total Population By Departments…", (see: No. 1, No. 2, No. 3), 72; (Bib. #314)

NOTE:

The 2nd Edition's "TOPICAL INDEX" portion of this book begins on the next page, page 207.

TOPICAL INDEX

Agents, labor recruiting (Hawaiian Planter's Association) (Recruiting Puerto Rican laborers/ workers), 8, 12, 22, 23, 26, 33, 42, 44, 93, 94, 113; (Bib. #221, #223, #394, pp. 23, 139-144)

Agricultural population of Porto Rico in 1899, numerically and percentage, 34; (Bib. #302, page 11)

Alameda County, CA, 65, 88, 94, 96, 99, 103, 107, 122, 169 (Table 1), 170; (Bib. #351)

Alameda County, CA (Puerto Rican population in 1900, 1910, 1920, in 2000), 65, 88, 94, 99, 103, 122, 169 (Table 1), 170; (Bib. #351)

Aliens admitted to and departing from the Territory of Hawaii between the years 1910 and 1921, inclusive, pp. 12-13, 16, 18, 135; (Bib. #16, #42, page 546, (Table), "Aliens admitted to and departing from the Territory of Hawaii between the years 1910 and 1921, inclusive"; Bib. #227, #328, #329, #361) (cf.: Bib. #6, pp. 1007-1008, "Employment of Aliens", Porto Rico, 1901)

Allen, Charles U., (Governor of Porto Rico, 1900-1901), 68, 74, 139; (Bib. #3)

American Federation of Labor (and Porto Rican labor conditions in Hawaii), 38, 42; (Bib. #5)

Ames, Azel, M.D., 26, 34; (Bib. #6)

An "Operational Definition" of an Ethnic Enclave, 125-129; (Bib. #21)

Appalling and onerous working conditions in Hawaii (according to the American Federation of Labor), 38, 42, 215; (Bib. #5, #205, Bib. #377, cf.: page 5)

Arcadia (ship cited by the *San Francisco Chronicle* newspaper (December 1, 1900, p. 1; Bib. #402), although the correct spelling of the name is the *Arkadia*), 67; (see: Bib. #34, p. 90, 158; Bib. #326) (see: immediately below)

Arkadia (ship also previously cited as: *Arradia*; *Arcadia*) (the 1st ship which took the Porto Rican immigrants to New Orleans, LA, to their final destination of Hawaii in Dec. 1900), 2, 67; (Bib. #34, pp. 90, 92-93, 98, 108-109, 114, 138, 157, 158, 331; Bib. #136, #326) (see also: *New York Times*. "Status of Porto Ricans. Arrival of Contract Laborers at New Orleans En Route for Hawaii Will Bring Up the Question", (Nov. 25, 1900: 1)). (see also: *New York Tribune (Metropolitan Holiday Supplement)*, Part IV, p. 10; December 24, 1898, Four Parts). Cites the: New York and Porto Rico Line and the ***Arkadia*** steamship, aka the *SS Arkadia*. (see: the *Gaceta de Puerto Rico. Periodico Official Del Gobierno*. Año 1897, Viernes 1." De Enero. Número 1. Page 1.); (#376, pp. 1, 2; #384, #389, #390) (accessed 04/10/16: Chronicling America – The Library of Congress)

Arradia [*sic*] (the correct name of this steamship was/is: Arkadia) (see: above), 67; (Bib. #136)

Arrests (in Hawaii in 1882, of 13,274 arrests of the "foreign population"), 114; (Bib. #64)

Arroyo, Ronald (*De Borinkees: The Puerto Ricans of Hawaii*), (1977), (Ph.D. Dissertation), 33, 40, 113; (Bib. #15)

Ashford, Bailey K., M.D. (Assistant Surgeon, U. S. Army, while he was post surgeon in Ponce, Porto Rico, after the August 1899 hurricane in P.R., and wrote about the Porto Rican laborer in P.R., and effects of the parasite called "*Uncinaria Americana*"), 115; (Bib. #324, see: #304, p. 10, 15; #302, p. 10; Dr. Ashford and Dr. Gutierrez, Institute of Tropical Medicine & Hygiene in P.R.)

Bancroft Library (University of California, Berkeley) (regarding the *Antonio Maria Osio Papers*), 120, 140, 147, 156, 157, 161, 201; (Bib. #41; #363; #423)

Banks and banking (and Simon M. Mezes as a Banker), 80-82; (Bib. #118)

Bay Area (San Francisco, CA , Alameda County and Oakland, CA)), 3-4, 6-9, 13-15, 17, 21, 31-33, 46, 57, 59, 64, 67-69, 77, 80, 82, 86, 88, 93, 97, 99, 103, 101, 107, 109, 111, 113-114, 118, 121-122, 125-129, 132, 136, 140, 144, 146-147, 150, 154, 157, 162, 166-170, 195, 201, 207, 216, 221, 229, 226, 234, 246; (Bib. #20, #22, #40, #88, #96, #98, #198 - #245, #326-#352, #357-#358, #364, #396)

Board of Immigration (*First Report of the Board of Immigration*), 64; (Bib. #18, #19)

Brief description of why the Puerto Ricans Immigrated to Hawaii, 21-22

Bureau of Insular Affairs (BIA), *Annual Report of the Chief of the Bureau of Insular Affairs.* (1932) (War Department, Annual Reports, 1932), 133; (Bib. #313)

Calderon, E., M.D. (Doctor), 102

California (beginnings and evolution of the California and San Francisco Porto Rican Population/ *colonias*, 1900-1910), 4, 8, 15, 17, 77, 86, 93-107, 109, 117-120, 125ff., 208

California (beginnings of the San Francisco Porto Rican enclaves/*colonias*: 1910 and beyond till 1925), 4, 7, 8, 13-14, 17, 19, 21, 77, 85-86, 109-110, 121-123, 125-130; (Bib. #17, #21, #89)

    -Deaths (and Porto Ricans), 82-84, 97; (Bib. #29, #185, #357)

    -Genealogical Society (CA), (2010), *San Francisco Deaths 1865-1905: Abstracts from Surviving Civil Records. Vol. I, Surnames Starting with A – D,* (Bib. #357), 97, see: 5, 7

    -*Pioneros* (as opposed to the New York City Porto Rican *Pioneros*), 96-97; (Bib. #100, #115)

    -(Porto Rican migration from Hawaii to CA), 6, 7, 8, 13-15, 17, 21, 26, 48-50, 64, 85-86, 118, 119; (Bib. # 36-#38)

    -Porto Ricans ("where did they all come from", 1900 to at least 1940), 64-65

    -(Puerto Rican population in 1900, 1910, 1920, 2000), 169 (Table 1), cf. 144 (Exhibit 4)

    -(Puerto Rican CA population in 1950 was at 5,495; in 1960 at 15,479), 139 (Footnote 9)

    -(San Francisco City, CA), (The 1900 and 1910 Porto Rican Census Figures), 64, 71, 77, 82, 85, 86, 95-110, 121-123, 125-130, 144-145, 169-170, 208, 227

    -(San Francisco County and the Porto Rican Population: "Pre" and "Post" 1906 population figures; as well as the San Francisco Earthquake Relief Corporation and its *Survey*), 4, 8, 64, 85, 117-120, 121ff., 126, 208, 227; (Bib. #184)

    -(selected Counties and Cities' Porto Rican population in 1900, 1910, 1920, 2000), 169, (Table 1), 169-170, see also: 144-145 (Exhibit 4)

    -*California State Journal of Medicine* (in 1905, 1910, and 1913 issues), 109, 208, 210, 216; (Bib. #61, #63, #316)

    -California State Library, CA History Section (on Porto Rican, B L A Munroe), 84, 150, 171, 173, 201, 209, 210; (Bib. #28) (note: aka as B L A Monroe)

-(State of CA) (Puerto Rican Population in 1900 and in 2000), 64, 77, 144 (Exhibit 4), 169 (Table 1), 170 (see: the "Footnote Sources")

-(State of CA) (Puerto Rican Population from 1900-2000), 144 (Exhibit 4), 169 (Table 1)

-(the First Porto Ricans which arrived on Dec. 14, 1900, and then stayed in California), 3, 6, 7, 14, 15, 21, 67-69, 77, 86, 87-92, 93-94, 156-157, 161, 168; (see the following newspaper articles from 1900-1901: Bib. #88, #107, #116, #199, #219, #220, #234 - #241, #344 - #346, #348 - #352, #416)

-(the "Original Porto Ricans", and/or Puerto Ricans, from 1850-1900 in CA), 77, 79-84

-(The "Racialization" of Porto Ricans, 1900-1910, in both California and in Hawaii), 4, 15, 43, 111-116, 137 (Footnote 5), 209, 225; (Bib. #49, #178, #179, #180)

California's Puerto Rican Enclaves and Communities (U.S. Federal Census Population figures for 1900, 1910 and 1925), 77, 109, 125-130

Camacho Souza, Blase, 18-19, 21-22, 27-28, 45, 60, 99; (Bib. #30, #31, #365)

Candelaro, Cruz (Porto Rican's name appears in the book *San Francisco Deaths 1865-1905: Abstracts from Surviving Civil Records. Vol. I. Surnames Starting with A – D* (published: 2010)), 97; (Bib. #357)

Carr, Norma, 3, 7, 9, 11, 13, 17, 18, 22, 28-30, 31, 32, 40, 43, 48-49, 50, 69, 71-72, 74, 75, 87, 88, 90, 91, 93-94, 99, 173, 211, 215, 224, 232, 233, 238, 244, 245; (Bib. #32-#34); and (her citations of the Names of Puerto Rican Immigrants to Hawaii from 1900-1925), 28-30; (Bib. #34)

Caruso, Stephen (Member, House of Puerto Rico-San Diego and his comments on this Book), 16

Castanha, Anthony, 27, 37, 38; (Bib. #35)

Cédula de Gracias (Royal Decree of 1815) (it allowed Immigration *into* Porto Rico), 138; (Bib. #124)

Census Column in the 1910 Census ("1910 Census: Instructions to Enumerators", under the "Personal Description" section...), 136 (Footnote 3)

-in Puerto Rico ("*La Historia De Los Censos En Puerto Rico*"), (Bib. #311); (cf.: p. 12)

Center For Puerto Rican Studies (the CENTRO), CUNY, (cf.: El Centro de Estudios Puertorriqueños) (cf.: immediately below)

Centro de Estudios Puertorriqueños (Centro) (CUNY), 6, 30, 73, 127-128; (Bib. #36-38, #40, #41, #52, #55, #97, #101, #116, #179, #180, #272, #275, #355, #356)

Charities And The Commons: A Weekly Journal of Philanthropy and Social Advance, "Rehabilitation Work in San Francisco", (October 6, 1906), 119; (Bib. #22) (By: Lilian Brandt)

Chenault, Lawrence R., 53, 63, 65, 134 (Footnote 2), 135 (Footnote 3)

Childbirth and births by Porto Ricans (in transit to Hawaii), 90, 93, 101-102, 109-110

-born in Puerto Rico and who immigrated to California at an early age, 103-104

Chinese laborer's immigration to Hawaii, and their population figures (in 1823, 1852 and in 1886, and years thereafter), 11, 18, 22-23, 25, 36, 37, 45, 52, 64, 114, 116, 119, 120, 136, 205, 218; (Bib. #30, #145)

Citizenship (Column) on the 1900 U.S. Federal Census page, (152, Exhibit 8); (Bib. #43)

-(U.S.) and Hawaiian Porto Ricans and the struggle for U.S. Citizenship, 12, 30-31, 135; (Bib. #152)

-(U.S.) (Citizenship as well as challenges to Puerto Rican Citizenship), 52-53, 135-136 (Footnote 3), 137 (Footnote #5); (Bib. #43, #152, #227, #249, #274, #360) (cf.: Bib. #117, pp. 366-369 (in 1900), ROYAL DECREE, also known as "Cédula of Grace", Aug. 15, 1815)

-(U.S.) (citizenship granted to Porto Rico and Porto Ricans, 1917), 12, 30-31, 52-53, 135-136 (Footnote 3), 137 (Footnote #5); (Bib. #274) (cf.: pp. 15-16 regarding the United States Constitution, the 14th Amendment and U.S. Citizenship relationship)

Citizens of Spain (Porto Ricans as), and therefore, they are no longer "colonial subjects" of Spain, according to the new 1812 Spanish Constitution, 135; (see: Bib. #34, p. 21-22)

Civil Servants (the first Porto Rican Civil Servant in California, Emilio Avilés, when he began working for the Post Office in 1906), 32

Club Puertorriqueño de San Francisco (Puerto Rican Club of San Francisco) (1912), 126-129, 140 (Footnote #12); (Bib. #40, #41)

Colbert, John W., M.D. ("Railway Surgeons. Hookworm Disease, and Its Importation into California"), (published in the: *California State Journal of Medicine*), (1913); (Bib. #316)

Colon, The (steamship) (to Hawaii in May 1901); (Bib. #142) (Bib. #34, p.132, 135-136, 144-145)

Concentration of wealth and land in Puerto Rico (see the: U.S. Dept. of Labor *Report*, 1919), 47; (Bib. #304)

Connections between Immigrants versus Migrants as it related to Porto Ricans/Puerto Ricans, 134-136; (Bib. #270)

-between Porto Rican Hawaiian Contract Workers and the beginnings of the California Porto Rican enclaves, 109-110; (Bib. #111)

Contracts (i.e., contract labor) (a *photo copy* of the Porto Rican laborers' **First** Contract in/to Hawaii, April 16, 1901), 8, 9, 21, 26, 31, 32, 33, 38, 44-45, 48, 63, 67, 109, 163-165; (cf.: Bib. #34, pp. 83, 85, 93, 99-100, 102, 186, 193-194, 202-203, 227, 253, 333-334, 343-344, 364-365, 367) (Bib. #149, #199, #325, #341)

Cost of living for the general population (in San Francisco in 1904), 86

-(in Hawaii, 1901), 24, 86; (see: Bib. #295, pp. 99-112, 241-245, Table V. "Cost of living- Description of the family"); (Bib. #24, "Wages and cost of living upon plantations [in Hawaii]", pp. 756-766) (Bib. #34, pp. ix, 242-243, 334)

-(in Porto Rico), (the increasing and the high cost), 9-10, 25; (Bib. #6, pp. 413-424, #25, pp. 757, 764-765, 776ff. (for 1901), Bib. #186)

De Borinquen A Hawaii Nuestra Historia: From Puerto Rico to Hawaii (1985), 60; (Bib. #365)

De Olivares, José, 174 (*Our Islands and Their People: As Seen With Camera and Pencil*), (1899), (Volume I, Introduced by Major-General Joseph Wheeler (U.S. Army)), 17; (Bib. #44)

Deaths (infant mortality rate of Porto Ricans in Hawaii in 1925), 50

-(Porto Rican deaths and births in California and in Hawaii), 28, 33, 49, 50, 83-84, 85, 97; (Bib. #29, #261, pp. 72-73 (for 1920), #324; #357) (Bib. #34, pp. 108-109, 126, 235)

-(Porto Rican deaths in San Francisco in 1903), 97, 209

-in Porto Rico (due to the devastating *San Ciriaco* hurricane, of nearly 3,000 Porto Ricans, on August 8, 1899), 10-11, 26, 27, 39, 139 (Footnote 8)

-(in Porto Rico in 1905 and 1910 due to Hookworm Disease), 114; (Bib. #110, #323, #324)

-(in Porto Rico in 1907 and in 1913), 115; (Bib. #324)

-of Porto Ricans in Hawaii (due to the 1918 "influenza epidemic"), 49

-of Porto Ricans (in transit by steamship to Hawaii), 33; (Bib. #203)

"Definition"/Description (a "description" of a Porto Rican in the early 1900s), 3, 57, 59, 61-62, 101, 134 (Footnote 2), 137 (Footnote 5), 138-139 (Footnote 8)

-("definition" of a Puerto Rican, **Boricua**, and/or Nuyorican, in the 21st Century), 136-137, 137 (Footnote 7); (cf.: pp. 53, 54); (Bib. #51)

Demographic Evolution of Puerto Rico, The (Ph.D. Dissertation) (1964), 12; (Bib. #308)

Departures (13 "Departures" from San Francisco, CA to Porto Rico in 1906), 119; (Bib. #320) (cf.: Bib. #34, p. 131-132, 210-212, 234)

Devastation caused by the August 8, 1899 *San Ciriaco Hurricane* in Puerto Rico, 10-11, 12, 25-26, 27, 34, 37, 39, 52, 139

Dias, Austin ("Carlo Mario Fraticelli: A Puerto Rican Poet on the Sugar Plantations of Hawaii"), 30, 132; (Bib. #356)

Dictionary, *Webster's Collegiate Dictionary* (Definitions of 'Race' and 'Ethnic', 1898-1994, in a Table provided by Sociologist Clara E. Rodríguez, and the socio-historical concepts of Race and Ethnicity), 137 (Footnote 5); (Bib. #175)

Disease in California, Hawaii and Porto Rico (Porto Ricans as carriers of disease, i.e., Hookworm Disease), 114-116, 119-120; (see also: Bib. #61 - #63, #109, #110; see also: Bib. #34, p. 285, 356)

Dispersion (of Porto Rican immigrants in Northern California Cities and Counties during December 1900), 3, 87, 89, 93-94, (Carr: 1989: 452-453 (Table)) (cf.: Bib. #269)

Disputed figures of the number of Puerto Rican Immigrants to Hawaii (1900-1901), 27-28

Dollarhide, William (*The Census Book: A Genealogist's Guide to Federal Census Facts, Schedules and Indexes*), 79; (Bib. #46)

Duany, Jorge, 11-12, 54, 57, 63, 77, 111, 134, 136 (Footnote 4), 137 (Footnote 7), 140, 144, 145; (Bib. #47- #55, #317)

Education in Porto Rico in 1899, including school attendance and literacy, 10, 72, 139; (Bib. #26, #302, page 12; #305, pages 72ff.) (cf.: Bib. #34, pp. 247, 380)

Educational Opportunities of the Porto Rican Workman, (Bulletin of the Department of Labor), (1905), (No. 61) (this subject is only a "Section" of this *Bulletin*); (Bib. #26; see also: #314, *Census of Porto Rico taken under the Direction of the War Department, U.S.A., Bulletin III.* 1900, "Citizenship, Literacy, and Education"; see: p. 72 in this book)

Emigration (a comparison of mileage traveled between Porto Rican versus European emigration in the late1880s and the early 1900s, to California and then to Hawaii (by the Porto Ricans), and to New York City (by the Europeans)), 43-44, (cf.: 138 (Footnote 7)); (Bib. #303)

-(from Puerto Rico to Hawaii and/or to CA), 2, 5, 6, 8, 10, 11-12, 15, 16, 33, 35-37, 39, 45, 47, 51, 52, 67, 68, 74, 86, 131, 132, 138; (Bib. #51, #112 - #113; cf.: #111, #171, #268, #338)

-(the names of several Porto Ricans who joined the 1st Expedition to Hawaii on Dec. 23, 1900), 31, 32, 33

Encyclopedia of Ellis Island (book by Barry Moreno in 2004), (Ellis Island and its relationship to the first Porto Rican immigrants to S.F. California, ***en masse***, of Dec. 14, 1900), 136; (Bib. #120)

Europe (comparison between the hookworm disease in Europe and its subsequent prevention attempts in Porto Rico), 115

European Immigrant's Journey in miles traveled to the U.S. (in comparison to the miles traveled by the Porto Rican's Immigrant's Journey traveling to Hawaii), 43-44; (Bib. #303)

-immigration to the U.S. compared to Porto Rican immigration to Hawaii, 46, 51-52, 53, 57

Ewa Plantation near Honolulu (Hawaii), 31; (Bib. #34, p. 82, 243, 336-337, 339, 450)

Expeditions, ship (return from Hawaii, and/or from CA, to Porto Rico), 86; (Bib. #56)

-(the first 11 expeditions from Porto Rico to Hawaii, from December 1900 through October 1901), 27-28, 31, 45

Exports of Principal Articles from Porto Rico from 1871-1897 and 1901-1906 (Statistical Table), including sugar, coffee, Tobacco (unmanufactured), cotton, cigars, etc.; (Bib. #302, page 54)

Feldman, David (*The Puerto Ricans of California: A Minority Within a Minority*), (June 1978), 71, 86, 87; (Bib. #56)

Females (non-employment in Porto Rico in 1899) (two thirds of women [whom] "have no employment whatever"), 10

-(5 Porto Rican), ("Foremen and Bosses" as Cigar Workers in San Francisco, 1910), 86

-(21 Porto Rican) (it cited workers in the manufacturing of Cigars in San Francisco, 1910, among the eight establishments which the Commission had investigated in S.F.), 86

-(175 Porto Rican) (Field Hands on Hawaiian Sugar Plantations in 1902), 24

-(Porto Ricans as Domestic Servants in Hawaii in 1901), 35; (Bib. #141)

-(Porto Rican Field Hands in the 1902 Hawaiian Sugar Plantations, with 175 Females (and 1,679 males, and they worked 6 days per week)), (Bib. #296, p. 162)

-(Porto Ricans departing from Hawaii to the West Coast, likely to California, 1911-1915), 48, 49, 119; (Bib. #297)

-(772 "unskilled" Porto Rican male and 48 "unskilled" female Laborers on the Hawaiian Sugar Plantations in 1920), 48

First Porto Rican Ministers in the Pentecostal Mission in Hawaii, 29; (Bib. #34, p. 209-210)

Fitzpatrick, Father Joseph P. (with Fordham University, Bronx, N.Y.), 139 (Footnote 9); (Bib. #58)

Flinter, Colonel D. (1834) (author: *An Account of the Present State of the Island of Puerto Rico*), 133

Fordham University (Bronx, N.Y.), 137 (Footnote 5), 139 (Footnote 9)

Fourquet Batiz, Charlie (of the Hispanic Genealogical Society of New York (HGSNY)), 16, (cf.: see also his "Review" of this Book, i.e., on the "Back page" of this Book)

Fritz, Christian G. "Politics and the Courts: The Struggle Over Land in San Francisco 1846-1866", in the (*Santa Clara Law Review*, 1986), 81-82; (Bib. #59)

General W. Davis (military Governor of Porto Rico who investigated both wages and the labor question in Porto Rico, and recommended emigration from Porto Rico in 1901), 10, 35; (Bib. #86)

Gibson, Campbell, and Emily Lennon, (*Historical Census Statistics on the Foreign-Born population of the united states: 1850 to 1990*), (1999); (Bib. #366, #292))

Grillo-López, Antonio J., M.D. (Director, Museum of the House of Puerto Rico-San Diego), and his comments relating to this Book, ("Back page" of this author's Book)). Served as Consultant of clinical research and regulatory stategy to the National Cancer Institute (NCI); several biotechnology Co.

Gunn, Herbert, M.D. (Doctor), 63-64, 109-110, 114-115, 120; (Bib. #61, #62, #63, #228, #336)

Harvard University Collection Dept. (Widener Library, HCL), 136

-(Sidney E. Mezes, the son of Puerto Rican Immigrant in 1850 to San Francisco, CA, i.e., Simon M. Mezes. Sidney earned his Ph.D. Degree from Harvard Univ. in 1893), 147, 148; (University President; Peace Conference Official for World War I (WWI); Author)

Hawaii Attorney General (regarding arrests in Hawaii of different nationalities and of the laboring class in 1882), 113-114, 207

-Board of Health (*Report of the President of the Board of Health of the* Territory *of Hawaii for the Six Months Ending June 30, 1905*), (1905), 42; (Bib. #66)

-(First Porto Ricans to arrive in Hawaii on Dec. 23, 1900), 8-9; (Bib. #74, #77, #79, #83, #85, #137, #201, #222, #223, #326))

-(Hilo), (The Plantations on Hilo), 41

-(list of Porto Rican population and Plantation Laborers and "skilled employees" from 1904 through 1915, and for 1920), 46, 48

-(list of Porto Rican population and sugar Plantation workers in 1915 and their 41 varied occupational positions which they held), 46, 47

-(list of Porto Rican school attendance (Public/Private) listed from 1901-1925), 48

-National Guard in 1925 (consisted of 1,486 members with 74 Puerto Ricans (.049%)), 50

-(Porto Rican "Departures" from Hawaii to the "[West] Coast" from 1911 to 1919, most likely to California), 48-50, 64, 85, 119, 129; (Bib. #320)

-(The State of) (Hawaii's Puerto Rican Population in 2010 as being at 44,116), 5

-(The Territory of Hawaii) (International labor request needs, 1852-1899), 22-23

-(The Territory of) (Porto Rican "Departures" from Hawaii to the [West] "Coast"), 48-50, 64, 85; (Bib. #258, #260, #263, #264, #266)

-(The Territory of) (the Porto Rican Population and Plantation Laborers from 1901-1925), 48, 49

-(The Territory of) (the Porto Rican population on December 23, 1900 was at 56), 8

-Hawaii (The Territory of) (the Porto Rican Population in 1910 was at 4,890), 42, 69, 85, 130

-(The Territory of) (the Porto Rican Population in 1919 was at 5,400), 85

-(The Territory of) (the Porto Rican Population in 1920 was at: 5,602), 130

-(The Territory of) (the Porto Rican Population in 1925 was at: 6,382), 48

-(The Territory of) (the Porto Rican Population in 1930 was at: 6,671), 130

-(Waialula) (on the Island of O'ahu) (The Waialula Sugar Mill Plantation), 35

Hawaiian Historical Society (1900, 1906, 1984, and 1986), 19, 118-119; (Bib. #31, #67, #68)

Hawaiian-based Newspaper articles, i.e., "Primary Sources", relating to the Porto Rican Immigrants, (cf.: Bib. #69 - #87, #136 - #155, #318 - #319)

Hawaiian Puerto Ricans and U.S. Citizenship (the historical role played by Manuel Olivieri Sanchez in Hawaii for Porto Ricans acquiring U.S. Citizenship), 30-31

-Sugar Plantations, 8, 9, 15, 17, 18, 19, 21, 22, 24, 25, 26, 27, 30-32, 35, 42, 47, 86, 118

-Hawaiian Sugar Planters Association (HSPA) (i.e., the Planters), 8, 9, 11, 18, 21-22, 24-25, 27, 36-37, 39, 42-46, 49, 63, 75, 113, 117-118; (Bib. #86, #149, #201, #223, #235, #240, #345, #346, #347)

-(**List** of names of Hawaiian born children of Porto Rican parents who lived in California as of the 1910 Census enumeration date), 109-110

Hayward Area Historical Society and Archives, 31-33 (in Haywood, CA); (Bib. #88, #98)

Hayward, CA, 6, 7, 14, 31-33, 166-168 ("Exhibit 20", "Exhibit 21", "Hayward Area Historical Society"); (Bib. #88)

Health-related explanation for the racially-tinged belief of "Laziness" toward the Puerto Rican laborers, 115-116

Hernandez, Rafael (he was born on "Puerto Rico Island", he lived in San Francisco, CA, and was cited in the 1880 Federal Census for/of California), 83

Hilo, Hawaii and its various plantations and Porto Ricans in 1901, 41; (Bib. #34, p. 185, 205, 217-220, 237, 256, 450)

Historical context of Hawaii's International Labor request needs (1852-1899), 22-23

-context of Puerto Rican Migration to Hawaii, 17-18

How far traveling was the Puerto Rican Immigrant's journey and how did it compare to that of European Immigrants?, 43-44

How the Irish Became White (book by Noel Ignatiev, 1965), 52, 111-112, (Bib. #92), (cf.: pages 111-116, for comparison(s) to how Porto Ricans were viewed and treated)

Hurricane (*San Ciriaco* in 1899, in Porto Rico, and the devastating effects on agriculture, and the laborers of Porto Rico, as well as on their everyday lives / and Relief), 10, 11-12, 25-27, 34, 37, 39, 52, 139; (Bib. #34, pp. 5, 48, 463; Bib. #117, p. 210ff., "Hurricane Relief", pp. 455-466)

Iglesias, Santiago (Representative of: Federation of Labor in Porto Rico; Gen. Org., American Federation of Labor), 25, 42, 128; (Bib. #5, pp. 15, 87, 88, 155, 216; #90, p. 71, 112-114, 131-134, 176; #377) [AKA: Santiago Iglesias Pantín] (see also: "Samuel Gompers and the American Federation of Labor in Puerto Rico", *Centro Journal* (Spring 2005, vol. XVII, no. 1, by Carlos Sanabria, p. 141) (See also: *Harper's Weekly.* (1905), "We Should do Something for Porto Rico At Once", (September 30, 1905, Vol. XLIX, No. 2545)) [Mr. Iglesias] "...averred that 600 Porto-Ricans died monthly from starvation [in Porto Rico]." (see: Bib. #410, p. 367)

Illiteracy (Porto Rican) (contributing to mass poverty in 1899 Porto Rico), 10, 72, 139; (cf.: Bib. #34, p. 247, 380)

Immigration into Porto Rico as of 1899 (the number of "foreign born"); (Bib. #302, page 10ff.)

-*Immigration Regulations For The Island of Porto Rico* (a nine page bulletin, published in 1899, by the U.S. War Department), 136; (cf.: Bib. #328)

-to Hawaii (Porto Rican), 11-13, 15, 18, 21ff., 24, 36, 38, 42, 50-52, 55, 57, 64, 67-69, 72, 99, 109, 113, 119, 121; (Bib. #18, p. 24; #19, Table titled "Statistics of Immigration"; #297, p. 64, Table 17, "Statistics of Immigration, Honolulu..., July 1, 1900 to June 30, 1915")

Interviews (personal) cited in Dr. Norma Carr's 1989 Dissertation (and conducted by Dr. Carr), 32; (Bib. #34, pp. 216, 258-259, 291-292, 319). Note: Dr. Carr conducted over 75 interviews, consisting of over 1,800 transcribed pages, during the early 1970s, (Bib. #34, pp. xiii-xiv)

JAMA (The Journal of the American Medical Association articles of 1906 and 1923 relating to Porto Ricans in San Francisco, California, from Herbert Gunn, M.D., and J.W. Kimberlin, M.D., regarding the *Uncinariasis* disease affecting Porto Ricans), 109-110, 119-120; (Bib. #62)

Japanese laborer's immigration to Hawaii, 18

Jones Act, The (1917) (aka: Jones-Shafroth Act of 1917), (and Hawaiian Porto Ricans and U.S. Citizenship), 30-31; (Bib. #34, p. 235-238, 256, 463) (cf.: Bib. #117, p. 34 (Oct. 18, 1898))

Kohala district (Hawaii), "There are few American Negroes in Hawaii… About a dozen were brought…in the spring of 1901, and some 100 men and their families were imported from Louisiana and Alabama by Maui planters under a contract…"; (Bib. #296, page 24)

La Correspondencia de Puerto Rico (newspaper), 40, 72, 91-92, 128, 131; (cf.: Bib. #36, 37)

"Labor Conditions in Porto Rico" (1901), (*Report* by Azel Ames, M.D.), 26, 34; (Bib. #6)

"Labor Conditions in Porto Rico" (1905), (*Report* by Walter E. Weyl); (Bib. #25)

Labor Conditions in Porto Rico (1919), (*Report* by Joseph Marcus)) 10; (Bib. #304)

Labor in Hawaii ("The Labor Question in Hawaii" in 1902); (Bib. #354)

Labor Report, (a *Table* entitled "Labor Report of 42 plantations of the Hawaiian Sugar Planter's Association for the month of 1925, by racial classification, listed that there were a total of 1,088 Puerto Ricans who were 'employees on pay roll'…."), 49; (Bib. #266)

Laborers in Hawaii from 1901-1925 (Porto Rican), 23-30, 37-38, 40-43, 46-47, 49-50, 115, 129; (Bib. #24, #87, #204, #326, #327, #338)

-In Hawaii (Historical context of Hawaii's International Labor Request needs for immigrant laborers, 1852-1899), 22-23

-in Hawaii (Porto Rican) (the appalling conditions for the Porto Rican workers in Hawaii according to the *Proceedings of the American Federation of Labor, 1902-1903* publication (printed in 1902), 42; (Bib. #5))

Lahaina Porto Ricans, 9; (Bib. #34, p. 89, 106, 161, 163)

Landless farmers (in Porto Rico), "between 1899 and 1910 the number of landless farmers increased considerably as the number of farms smaller than [19] acres fell from 87.8% to 72% of all the farms...", 26, 47, (cf.: Bib. #304, pp. 12-14)

Leyland, R.C. (*Puerto* Ricans *in the San Francisco Bay Area, California: An Historical and Cultural Geography*), (1980) (a Master's Thesis), 71, 86; (Bib. #98)

List: (*Medical* Journals and *Medical*-related publications reviewed relating to health-medical related issues affecting Porto Ricans/Porto Rico; Note: some were not cited in the 1st Edition of this book):

-California State Board of Health: Weekly Bulletin. (1925), "Migration and the Spread of Disease", (Walter M. Dickie, M.D., Secretary and Executive Director), (January 31, 1925, Vol. III, No. 51, page 1ff.), 228, 238 [Not cited in the 1st Edition "*Bibliography*" of this book] (This is an extract from an address at Stanford University Medical School, January 23, 1925.)

-*California State Journal of Medicine*, (issues published in 1905, 1910, 1913), 63-64, 109; (Bib. #61, #63, #110, #316)

-Hawaii Board of Health (1905), (*Report of the President of the Board of Health…"*), 42; (Bib. #66)

-*JAMA: The* Journal *of the American Medical Association* (1906), "Report of Two Cases Observed Among Porto Ricans in San Francisco", 109-110, 119-120; (Bib. #62))

-Los Angeles Times. (1910), "Death Lurks in Soil: California State Medical Society is Warned that Hookworm Disease is Entering State", (April 21, 1910), 116; (Bib. #110)

-The Medical News: A Weekly Journal of Medical Science (Aug. 5, 1905, Vol. 87, page 227), (The American Medical Association), "Uncinariasis in California"; (Bib. #321)

-The Post-Graduate: A Monthly Journal of Medicine and Surgery (July 1906, Vol. XXI, No. 10, page 1015), "Bilharzia Disease Amongst Porto Ricans in San Francisco", (*note:* this article was originally published in the *Journal of Tropical Medicine*, July 16, 1906, p. 224), [*not* cited in the 1st Edition "*Bibliography*" of this book]

-Transactions of the Section on Practice of Medicine of the American Medical Association. (1905), "Further remarks on the Mode of Infection in Uncinariasis", (pages 293-301); (Bib. # 353)

Lists *(Different types of Lists relating to Porto Rican Immigrants, and their children);*

-List (names of babies and children, cited in the 1910 Federal Census for CA, being born in Hawaii, of Porto Rican immigrants [parents]), 109-110

-List (names of children born in Porto Rico and who immigrated to CA at an early age), 103-104

-List (names of infants and children, born in CA of Porto Rican immigrants parents, 1900-1910: The Second Generation), 105-107

-List (names of Puerto Ricans/Porto Ricans in CA, 1852-1900, cited in these Censuses), 79-84

-List (names of the "at least" 64 Porto Rican immigrants that stayed in San Francisco, California on December 14, 1900, and who did **not** immigrate to the Hawaiian Territory), 87-92; (see also: below in the newly added "**Topical INDEX**" Section of this book)

-List (27 names of Porto Ricans that immigrated to the United States and whom resided in California during calendar 1901, according to the Federal Census), 99-100

-List (29 names of Porto Ricans who had immigrated to the United States during calendar year 1900, and whom also resided in CA in 1910, according to the Federal Census), 95-97

List: "Nationalities" of *laborer's* (on the Hawaiian Plantations over time as well as in Porto Rico), (in Alphabetical Order, with page numbers) (cf.: p. 51, for nationalities in S.F., CA; (Bib. #171 for a "Nationality Beakdown" of 29 groups of immigrants by "Race Break" in U.S., 1908-1909, p. 59)):

-"American Negroes"/"Colored" [how cited in the original source(s)], 11, 69, 72, 112, 115, 116, 117, 118, 129, 216, 217, 218, 219, 220, 221; (Bib. #222; Bib. #253, pp. 4, 64, 99; Bib. #296, pp. 24, 84, 85, 156 (in 1902 Hawaiian Sugar Plantations), 208; (see: Bib. #405). [*Note:* The 1962 publication titled, *Historical Statistics of Hawaii: 1778-1962* (Dept. of Planning & Research) in its Table called, "Ethnic Stock: 1853 To 1960" (page 8), cited several different *immigrant* "Ethnic Groups", including the Puerto Ricans, and *"Negro"* [name in the original source], however, they were "combined numerically", with the other "Ethnic Groups", namely, Korean, Samoan, American Indian…therefore, no exact [numerical] figure could be determined]; (see: #6, 383-384; Bib. #34, pp. 96, 102, 139-141, 145) (In 1901, there were 55

["American Negroes"/"Colored" **continued**] "Negro" laborers among the 58 Hawaiian sugar plantations; #6, pp. 383, 384; #42, pp. 530, 539, 545; #262, p. 28; #266, pp.105 (1925); #296, pp. 8, 24, 84, 85, 91, 156, 208; #304; #305, pp. 30, 32, 34-35, 40, 55-56, 93-95, 187; #314, p. 5, "Colored population"/ "Negroes in Porto Rico" 1899 Census, No. III, Table); #304, pp. 10, 11, "Introduction of negro Slaves [in Porto Rico]"; [NOTE: Bib. #42, immediately below, has a "Part 1" and a "Part 2" - in two parts]

-Americans, 5-6, 9, 11, 12, 19, 23, 25, 36-38, 42, 47, 48, 52, 55, 57, 62, 67, 81, 87, 112-117, 119-120, 135-137, 156, 183, 185, 215-218, 223, 230, 242; (Bib. #5; #58; #118-#119; #186; #191; #42 (Part 2), pp. 539-540, 542 (Table); #231; #253, p. 19 (in 1896), p. 16; #266, p. 40, 66, 88; #295, p. 19, 131ff.; #297, pp. 7, 18, 19, 78); #329; #338, p. 1; #353, #362

-Australians (or Australia), 23, 47; Bib. #253, p. 16 (in 1899); #295, p. 27

-British [i.e., English] (or Great Britain), 11, 23, 43, 47, 52, 114, 119, 120, 230; (Bib. #42, p. 546 (Table); #253, pp. 16, 19; #266, pp. 40, 66, 88, 90; #295, pp. 18, 27, 131ff.; #371, p. 680)

-Chinese, 11, 18, 22-23, 25, 36-37, 45, 52, 64, 114, 116, 120, 136, 205, 210; (Bib. #30, #42, pp. 533, 536, 539, 542, 546 (Table); #145); (Bib. #262, p. 38; #295, #296, p. 208)

-Filipinos and Samoans, 13, 45, 51, 135; (Bib. #30; #296; #297; #328; #335; #407; #411)

-Galicians, 23, (Bib. #42, pages 539, 542; #340)

-Germans (or Germany), 11, 23, 42, 43, 47, 52, 114, 120; (Bib. #42, see: pages 533, 539, 542 546; #266, p. 40, 88; # 295, p. 19, 27, 131ff.; #296, p. 208); (#253, pp. 16 (in 1896), 19)

-Hawaiians, 11, 23, 25, 29, 45, 48, 113, 114, 115; (Bib. #30; #42, pp. 542; #104, #262, pp. 38, 87; #296, p. 208; #253, pp. 16, 19 (in 1896); #295, pp. 19, 368, 381; #355; #371, p. 675)

-Italians (or Italy), 9, 18, 47, 51, 52, 116, 120; (Bib. #42, see: pages 533, 546 (Table); #266, p. 66; #296, p. 208; #401, p. 168)

-Japanese, 9, 11, 18, 21, 22-25, 36-37, 45, 52, 64, 115-116, 136 (Footnote 3), 215, 229; (Bib. #30, #42, pp. 533, 536, 540, 542, 546); #104, #170; #262, p. 38; #253, pp. 16, 19 (in 1896); #295, pp.27, 125, 131ff., 368, 381; #296, p. 208; #333; #371, p. 674; #407, pp. 345, 347)

-Koreans, 18, 45, 64, 69, 113, 217; (Bib. #30; #42, p. 533, 540, 546; #262, p. 38; #371)

-Mexicans (Mexico), 15, 81, 106, 116, 120, 125, 229; (Bib. #42, p. 546 (Table); (#170, pp. 409-411, 414, 416; #179; #295, p. 27; #322; #401, pp. 168, 172)

-Negro (Labor) in Hawaii, 11, 69, 112, 115, 116, 118, 129, 216, 217-218, 219, 220, 221; (Bib. #42, pages 219, 533, 539, 545); #296, p. 84, 85, see: "Distribution of Labor on Hawaiian Sugar Plantations, By Groups of Occupations and Nationality" (Table); #34, 158; #222); (#262, p. 32; #266, pp. 39, 66; #267, p. 38; #295, pp. 19, 125; #371, p. 675-676; #405)

-Norwegians, 23, 114, (Bib. #42, p. 542); #253, p. 19 (in 1896); (#266; #295. p. 27)

-**"Other Nationalities"**, and/or **"All Others"** (Laborers on the Hawaiian Plantations), 11, 23, 114, 120, 241; (Bib. #42, p. 219; #392)

-Polish/Poles (Hawaii), 116, 120; (Bib. #42, pp. 545, 546; #167, p. 106; #171, p. 59; #266, p. 66; # 296, p. 208; #401, p. 168) (Polish/Poles in Porto Rico, Bib. #109; #254, p. 4)

-Porto Ricans, 5, 6-8, 13-15, 17, 21, 42, 47, 90, 93, 101, 110, 113-115, 117-120, 125ff., 133, 156, 174, 176, 195-198, 205-256; (Bib. #69 - #87; #105 - #110; #126 - #134; #136 - #157; #173 - #181; #186 - #192; #198 - # 231; #233 - #245; #249 - #250; #253 - #271; #273 - #274; #290; #295 - #305; **#314**; #266, pp. 39-41, 66, 71, 86, 88, 90, 105; #316; #318 - #354; #358 - # 362; #365; #367; #407, pp. 345, 348; #371, pp. 676, 680, 687, 724; #410, p. 367); (see: #30; #42, p .545; #90, p. 30-33 (1901); #262, p. 38); (#296, pp. 162, 208ff.; **#305**, pp. 78, 92-95, 187, see the Table: "Negro Slaves in Puerto Rico: 1765-1860") (In 1902 Hawaiian Sugar Plantations had 1,679 Porto Rican males, and 175 Porto Rican females as Field Hands)

-Portuguese (or Portugal), 9, 11, 18, 19, 23, 25, 29, 45, 47, 48, 64, 107, 113, 114, 129, 154, 244; (Bib. #30, #41, pp. 533, 539, 546; #42, pp. 535, 537, 540, 542, 544, 546 (Table); #208, #222, #253, pp. 16, 19; #262, p. 38; #296, p. 208; #371, p. 674; #407, p. 345, #417)

-Russians (or Russia), 43, 47, 48, 51, 120, (Bib. #42, see: pages 533, 542, 544, 545, 546; #262, p. 38; #266, pp. 40, 41, 66, 88; #371, p. 687, 724; #407, p. 348)

-Scandinavians/Scotch/or Sweden, 23, 106; (Bib. #42, see: pp. 533, 537, 546 (Table); #253, pp. 16, 20-22; #257, p. 73; #266, p. 66; #295, p. 27, 131ff.; #371, p. 680)

-Spaniards (or Spain), 2, 6, 9, 11, 12, 18, 25, 30, 37, 40, 42, 43, 46, 47, 48, 52, 53, 57, 61, 67, 81, 82, 83, 84, 104, 112, 113, 117,120, 125, 129, 133, 135, 138, 146, 147, 158-160, 195, 196, 197, 210, 222, 224, 228; (Bib. #42, pp. 533, 540, 545, 546); #105, #231, #248, #267, p. 39; #295, #307, #362, #371, p. 724; #375, #407)

-South Sea Islanders, 11, 23, 114; see: (Bib. #42, pp. 533, 534, 535, 536, 539, 542; #296, p. 208; #253, pp. 16, 19 (in 1896)); (#295, pp. 19, 125; #371, p. 675)

-List ("sample" list of the names of some of the Porto Rican immigrants to Hawaii in 1901), 60

-List (persons born in Porto Rico/Puerto Rico, who also lived in California between **1850-1900**), Simon M. Mezes; R V Spence; Clara Blair; Edward Dufish; John M. Vanryn; William Tate; Rafael Hernandez; Charles F. Benzon; Ben Camacho; O Munroe [this is the Census spelling of this name]; B L A Munroe [the census spelling]; Mcenty Portorico [the Census spelling]; Charles Rodigez [the Census spelling]. *NOTE:* these names were cited in the U.S. Federal Census (Censuses), and they all lived in California at various times between 1850-1900], 79-83

Literacy (in Porto Rico in 1899, 212, 218, 219, 220; (Bib. #305, see: pages 78ff.);(Bib. #314, Bulletin III, pp. 1, 6) (cf.: for "illiteracy", see: pages 10, 21, 215, in this book)

Looseley, Allyn Campbell (*Foreign Born population of California, 1848-1920*), (A Thesis, University of California) (1971), 82; (Bib. #364)

López, Daniel M., 5 (Author's "Biography"), 5, 13, 16, 54, 96, 139 (Footnote 9); (Bib. #99, #100)

Los Angeles Area newspapers, 25, 59, 63, 69, 91, 114, 116, 118; (Bib. #104-110, #320)

Los Angeles City (Puerto Rican population in 1900, 1910, 1920, in 2000), 169 (Table 1), 170

-County (Puerto Rican population in 1900, 1910, 1920, in 2000), 169 (Table 1), 170

Los Angeles (The City), 29, 33, 38, 64, 69, 77, 84, 86, 104, 112, 129

Makawali Plantation (Hawaii), where a riot by Porto Ricans was reported in 1901, where they demanded a pay raise which was denied, (Bib. #34, p. 185)

Maldonado, Edwin, 26, 109; (Bib. #111)

Maldonado-Denis, Manuel (*The Emigration Dialectic: Puerto Rico and the USA*) (1980), (Translated by Roberto Simón Crespi), 16; (Bib. #112)

Martinez, Robert A. ("The Emergence of Imperialist Capitalism and Puerto Rican Emigration, 1879-1901" in the *Journal of American Ethnic History*) (Spring 1984), 36; (Bib. #113)

Massachusetts (the Porto Rican Population in the 1990s and in the 2000 Census for Lowell, Lawrence, and Holyoke, Massachusetts), 125, 140 (Footnote 10); (Bib. #21)

Maui (Hawaii) (Porto Rican laborers in Dec. 1900, and in Sept. 1901), 31, 36, 93; (see: Bib. #34, pp. 106, 113, 133, 163-167, 218, 220, 228, 319, 450, 453; Bib. #296, p. 24)

McBryde Plantation (Hawaii), and Porto Ricans; (Bib. #34, p. 185, 451)

Medina, Nitza C. ("Rebellion in the Bay: California's First Puerto Ricans"), (2001), 71; (Bib. #116)

Methodology (the Author's Research Methodology, etc., "Proceeded as Follows"), 13, 14, 19, 59-60, 79, 122, 123

Mezesville Map (1856), (made/drawn by: Simon M. Mezes, on Aug. 1, 1856, of the "Town of Mezesville, CA", later changed to: Redwood City, CA), 151, 149; (Bib. #162, #163, #358)

Migration to California (Porto Rican immigration, CA and Hawaii), 6, 8, 11-17, 21, 26, 28, 32, 33, 35, 37, 43, 45, 48, 50-55, 57, 64, 67-69, 71, 79-81, 85-110, 120, 121, 122, 130, 136, 138, 208, 212, 213, 215-216, 223-224, 229, 233; (Bib. #18, #19, #34, #36, #37, #42, #56, #86, #90, #98, #105, #111, #113, #116, #167, #268, #328, #338, #385, #394, #402, #405, #407, #413)

Military Governor of Porto Rico on Civil Affairs (1902) (*Annual Reports of the War Department For The Fiscal Year Ended June 30, 1900*), 10-11, 138 (Footnote 7); (Bib. #117) (pp. 206, 213, 239)

Military Times: Your online resource for everything Military publication, (it reproduced on-line a digitized copy of the **Treaty of Paris** of December 10, 1898), 133

Miranda Case, The; (Bib. #34, pp. 203-208)

Moreno, Barry (*Encyclopedia of Ellis Island*), (2004), 136 (Footnote 3); (Bib. #120)

Morse, Stephen P., *et. al.*, ("Obtaining Streets within Eds for the 1910 Census in One Step (Large Cities) [Enumeration Districts])". (Retrieved on June 20, 2010), 126; (Bib. #121)

Municipal (Census) Districts, Cities and Wards (in Porto Rico in 1900), 60; (Bib. #314)

Municipalities, towns and villages' names (in Porto Rico, where many of the Immigrants first emigrated from Porto Rico to Hawaii), 60; (Bib. #314, #365)

Names of the Immigrants and the Newspaper's descriptions of the "First Group" of Immigrants (*en masse*) of Puerto Ricans that stayed in California on December 14, 1900: "Group 1", 87-92

Negroes (percentage of the population **in Porto Rico**, 1899), (Bib. #302, p. 10; #314, *Census of Porto Rico...Bulletin II.* (1900), "Population by Age, Sex, Race, Nativity, Conjugal Condition, and Literacy"; #304, p. 10 "Introduction of Negro Slaves"; #305, *Report on the Census of Porto Rico, 1899.* (1900), "Negroes", pp. 30-32, 93-94, 187ff.); see: *Report of the Commissioner of Labor on Hawaii. 1902* (1903), (Bib. #296, p. 24) (cf.: Bib. #34, 101-102) [*note*: In 1899 Porto Rico, the

Census used the term "Colored"] (Bib. #6, p. 384 "Negro Slaves in Porto Rico, 1765 to 1860"), ("Negro Labor" in Hawaii, Bib. #42, p. 539 (in 1921))

New York City Assembly Districts (Porto Rican Census Population Districts in 1925), 129-130

   -New York City Porto Rican population (in 1910 it was 554; in 1920 it was 7,364; in 1940 it was 61,463); in 1950 it was 187,429; 139 (Footnote 9)

   -(Puerto Rican population in 1900, 1910, 1920, in 2000), 139, 169 (Table 1), 170

New York State Manuscript Census of 1925, 130

New York State (Porto Rican population in 1910 it was 641; in 1920 it was 7,719; in 1930 it was 45,973; and in 1950 it was 191,305), 77, 139 (Footnote 9)

New York Times, The (articles relating to Porto Ricans and Porto Rico from 1900–1922), 26, 27, 39, 40, 60, 68, 69, 94, 115, 116, 117, 118, 133, 202, 207, 224; (Bib. #126 - #134, #249, #322 - #325, #360 - #362, #389, #390; (cf.: Bib. #157))

Newspapers (negative and "racialized" descriptions of the Porto Rican immigrants, 1900-1910, both in California, as well as in Hawaii), 111-116

Non-Spanish "sounding" [spelled] surnames in Porto Rico, as well as in Hawaii, 61-62

Number of laborers employed in the sugar industry from 1900-1920; (Bib. #42, see: page 296)

Nuyorican(s) (a contemporary meaning), 5, 136-137 (Footnote 4)

Oahu, Hawaii (Plantation), 8, 9, 32, 39, 42, 202 (Oahu Insane Asylum---different nationalities were placed in), 226; (Bib. #34, p. 87, regarding plantation on Oahu) (for Oahu, Hawaii see: Bib. #34, pp. 75, 87, 192, 216, 229, 236-239, 253, 258, 261, 266, 291, 319, 450; #77ff.; #397)

Oakland, CA (The City), 5, 7, 65, 77, 88-89, 101, 113, 121-122, 129, 208, 226; (Bib. #342, #357)

   -(Puerto Rican population in 1900, 1910, 1920, in 2000), 169 (Table 1), 170

Ookala Plantation (Hawaii), where in 1901 Porto Ricans walked off the job, 29, 233; (Bib. #34, p. 185)

Olowalu Plantation (near Lahaina, Hawaii) [possibly had 22 Porto Rican Laborers in 1904], 21; (Bib. #34, p. 285, 450)

Our Islands and Their People: As Seen with Camera and Pencil (book by José De Olivares, 1899), 17, (Bib. #44)

Paauilo Plantation (Hawaii), 73; see also: (Bib. #90, p. 52, 51-53; Bib. #417)

Pauuilo Plantation (Hamakua, Hawaii) and the July 1902 grievance complaint; (Bib. #34, p. 193)

Parentage (Porto Rican) (as defined in the U.S. Federal Census from 1910-1950, as well as from 1960-2000), 57

Pennsylvania Historical Society (aka: Historical Society of Pennsylvania), 125; (Bib. #89)

Pentecostal Church and Mission (Porto Ricans in California, Hawaii and in Porto Rico), 29, 32, 213,

[Pentecostal Church and Mission continued] 221, 222; (Bib. #34, pp. 209-210)

Per Capita Wealth (in Porto Rico) in 1919 (and/or "lack thereof", in comparison to 14 other Countries in the world, including the United States, Spain, Great Britain, etc.), 47

Pew Research Center (Washington, D.C.), 137-138; (Bib. #158, #359)

Photos (1890s life in Puerto Rico during the Spanish Colonial period), 158-160

Pioneer Mill Plantation (Lahaina, Maui, Hawaii), 9, 21, 22, 229; (Bib. #34, p. 106, 161, 163, 450)

Pioneros (distinguishes between the "California *Pioneros*" versus the New York City *Pioneros*", 96, 97; (Bib. #100, #115)

Plantation Laborers (in Hawaii in 1899 and beyond), 11, 22, 23, 25, 42, 48, 114, 205, 213, 214, 222, 229, 230; (Bib. #83)

- Laborers (in Hawaii in 1905 and other years), 24; (Bib. #34, p. ix, 81, 82, 100, 103 450)

Plantations (in Hawaii), 7-9, 15, 17-18, 21-27, 32, 35-37, 39-43, 45-49, 63, 67, 73-74, 86, 109, 112-114, 116, 118, 156, 205, 217, 218, 224; (Bib. #42 (page 219), #217, #222, #337, #341, #356)

-(in Porto Rico), 9, 10, 26, 27, 37

Population of Porto Ricans (in San Francisco, CA, in 1910, was listed at 213), 140 (Footnote 11)

-of Porto Ricans in the Continental United States in: 1910 – 1,513; 1920 – 11,811; 1930 – 52,774; 1940 – 69,967; 1950 – 226,110), 139 (Footnote 9)

Porto Rican Colony (*colonia*) of San Francisco, 4, 8, 15, 17, 33, 64-72, 77, 85-110, 117-129, 208; (Bib. #380, #385; cf. #190)

Porto Rican "Departures", and/or "Desertions" from Hawaii, 48-50, 64, 85, 119, 129, 211, 214, 225; (Bib. #320, p. 1, "Porto Ricans Are Deserting Hawaii..." (Dec. 1904))

-(*grievances* and *complaint* letters among the plantation laborers in Hawaii), 38, 40-42, 45, 72-74, 86, 118, 221; see also: (Bib. #34, p. 187; #72,#83, #90, p. 51-53; Bib. #181); see: *Islanders in the Empire: Filipino and Puerto Rican Laborers in Hawaii* (2014), by Joanna Poblete, Chapters 1, 3, and 6, especially, pp. 34-40, (see: the INDEX section for the full reference citation for this book), (Bib. #394)

-(Historical Census *undercounting* of the population), 64; (cf.: Bib. #175)

Porto Rican immigrant's mileage (to Hawaii compared to the mileage of the European immigrant's mileage to the United States (i.e., N.Y.) in the early 1900s, and before), 43

-laborers in Porto Rico in 1901 ("with over three-fourths of the *breadwinners* of the island engaged in agriculture, and of the total number of the *breadwinners, four-fifths* [were] laborers...."), 34; (cf.: p. 44)

-Pentecostal Ministers in Hawaii (some of their names: Rev. Juan (Juanito) Feliciano; the Rev. Ramon Quinones; Rev. Jose Pagan; Rev. Juan Castro), 29

-Plantation Employees in Hawaii in 1901 was at 2,095 (5.5%), 11, 23, 40, 48; (Bib. #166, p. 23)

-Population (in California in 1910), 44, 63

-Population (in New York City, and in New York State, in 1910), 63

-Population (in the United States in 1910), 63

-("surplus labor") (the Porto Rican emigrants to both California and to Hawaii represented "surplus labor", i.e., "working class" laborers….), 2, 15, 17, 35, 36, 224, 229

Porto Rican laborers Riot at the Makawali Plantation on Kauai (Hawaii), 219; (Bib. #34, p. 185)

Porto Ricans costs (by the Hawaiian Sugar Planters' Association of recruiting and bringing them to Hawaii), 43, 164 (Exhibit 19)

-on the Island of Kauai (preached to by the Salvation Army), 29

Porto Ricans (Puerto Ricans) (a positive book describing the contributions which Porto Ricans (Puerto Ricans) made to Hawaiian Society and culture (published in: 1975)), 45

Porto Ricans (the First Porto Ricans' arrival in Hawaii on December 23, 1900), 8-9, 45

-(283 rejected U.S. Citizenship in 1917, "out of a total of more than a million, who availed themselves of this opportunity to reject American citizenship"), 135

Porto Rico (agriculture in Porto Rico in 1899 was: "… 78.6 percent of the entire population is practically rural and essentially agricultural…."), 34; (cf.: "Porto Rico's" name, Bib. #313, p. 14)

-(the coffee crop and the coffee plantations destroyed in 1899 by the hurricane and its effects on the Island's economy and its people), 10-11

-(*1899 Porto Rican Census* data; printed in 1900), 10, 68, (Bib. #250, #305, see: #304)

(Porto Ricans claim ruin came with "American Rule"), 37; (Bib. #231)

-Porto Rico Census, 1899 (*Census of Porto Rico, The Direction of the War Department*), 63; ((Bib.: #250, #314) (This publication is a pamphlet)

-Porto Rico Census, 1899 (*Report on the Census of Porto Rico, 1899*) (published in: 1900), 10, 12, 34, 61, 63, 68, 72, 138 (Footnote 7), 206; (Bib. #305)

Porto Rico *Cities, Townes and Villages* (*selected communities in Porto Rico of emigration to California and to* Hawaii):

Adjuntas (P.R.), 27, 31-32, 44, 60, 165 (Exhibit 19), 185 (Bib. #34: 87, 109; Bib. #221);

Aguadilla (P.R.), 60; (Bib. #34, p. 87; Bib. #277, p. 95; Bib. #379, p. 6);

Aguas Blanca (P.R.), 60;

Arecibo (P.R.), 32, 60, 231; (Bib. #34, p. 87; Bib. #277, p. 95);

Caguas (P.R.), (cited by *The Hawaiian Star* newspaper incorrectly as being, Carguas [*sic*]), 41, 202, 231;

Guayanilla (P.R.), 60;

Juan Diaz (P.R.), 60;

Lares (P.R.), 27, 32, 60; (Bib.#240);

Maricao (P.R.), 27;

Mayagüez (P.R.), 27, 60, 84, 196, 197, 198; (Bib. #34, p. 87; #117, p. 16; #277; #398. #419, #420);

Peñuelas (P.R.), 32-33, 60;

Ponce (P.R.), 5, 27, 32, 42, 43, 44, 60, 74, 115, 165, 207; (Bib. #34, p. 87, 119; #117, p. 16 (Date which American Forces occupied the principal port of Ponce, July1898); #181, #277, p. 95; #376);

Quebradillas (P.R.), 60;

San Juan (P.R.), 2, 41, 43, 44, 60, 89, 131 165, 202-3, 240-241; (Bib. #34; #160, #178, #379, #398);

Utuado (P.R.), 27;

Yauco (P.R.), 27, 30-32, 60, 233, 239.

Porto Rico (labor conditions in Porto Rico in 1899-1900, and in 1905), 68; (Bib. #25, p. 723ff.)

-(labor conditions in the Sugar industry in Porto Rico, Hawaii, and California, etc., in 1903), 24; (Bib. #24)

-Population Census Figures (from 1900-2000), 77, 144 (Exhibit 4), 169 (Table 1), 170

-(Porto Rican emigrants to Hawaii in 1901) (Norma Carr wrote as follows: that the area in Porto Rico "called Pina, near the neighborhoods known as Vegas, Naranjo and Rubias, which sent many laborers" ["to the Hawaiian plantations"]), 32, see: (Carr, 1989, p. 229)

-("Puerto Rico in a Very Brief Historical Context"), 11-13

-Porto Rico or Puerto Rico?, *National Geographic Magazine.* (1899), Vol. X, 134 (Footnote 1); (cf. 133 (Footnote 1) wherein this person (i.e., Mr. Guarionex lamented Puerto Rico's name change to Porto Rico), (cf.: 134 (Footnote 1)); (see: Bib. 133)

-(the concentration of wealth and land), 11, 26, 47, 210; (Bib. #304)

-(the number of Professional men on the Island in 1899 (physicians, lawyers, and teachers, was at "only about 2200 men on the Island"), out of a population of 953,243), 10, 144

-(the "Spanish-American War Seen From Porto Rico", from *The New York Times*, December 17, 1922), (cf.: pp. 11-13, 125 (cf.: pp. 196, 228)); (Bib. #362)

-(under Spanish [Spain] rule, and being "citizens of Spain"), 135; (Bib. #117, pp. 30-37)

Porto Rico's (low wages for Laborers from 1899 to 1906), 9-10

-("Official") Name Change (1898-1932) from Puerto Rico, 133, 134 (Footnote 1)

Porto Rican (immigration to Hawaii and the role played by "surplus labor", and labor strikes), 36

Porto Rican Studies and Scholarship (or "lack thereof") (compared to American Studies), 55

Porto Ricans (the Salvation Army preaching to Porto Ricans on the Island of Kauai), 29

Post-1906 San Francisco Earthquake and Puerto Ricans, 119-120

Pre-1906 San Francisco Earthquake and Puerto Ricans, 117-119

Primary Sources (defined, and with examples presented), 1, 4, 5, 6, 52, 59, 72, 75, 84, 118, 134 (Footnote 1), 138 (Footnote 8)

Public Health and Sanitation in Porto Rico in 1899; (Bib. #302, page 11)

Puerto Rican (Population Figures in CA for 1920 and 1930 was 935, and 1,795, respectively), 65

-"Departures" from Hawaii to the [West] "Coast", 48-50

-Hawaii plantation laborer, and Field Hands, figures, 46-47, (Bib. #296, see: the following "Tables", pages 84, 85, 152, 156, 158, 162, 208; see also: Bib. #297, see: the "Tables")

-Historical context for immigrating to Hawaii, 23-27

-Immigration to Hawaii and Hawaii's continuing need for International Labor for their Sugar Plantations, 22

-Plantation labor in Hawaii, June 1901, 40-43

-(Population Figures for U.S., for CA, etc.: 1900, 1910, 1920, 2000), 144, 169 (Table 1)

-Parentage (and of Puerto Rican origin, between 1910 and 1940; 1950 and after 1970, they include all persons of Puerto Rican origin), 134; (Bib. #47)

Puerto Ricans (are the second-largest population of Hispanic origin living in the United States, accounting for 9.1% of the U.S. Hispanic population in 2009), 138; (Bib. #158)

Puerto Rico (Population on the Island in 1900, 1910, 1920, in 2000), 169 (Table 1), (see also: 144 (Exhibit 4))

Race and racial and ethnic issues (Porto Ricans and Puerto Ricans), 2, 4, 15, 23, 35-37, 43, 49-50, 53, 101, 111-116, 137 (Footnote 5); (Bib. #49, #178–180, #275) (cf.: Bib. #34, p. viii, 77-78, 139, 149, 225, 340, 347, 353, 358, 363-364, 374, 378, 382, 398, 436, 457, 477; #49)

Racialization of Porto Ricans (in California and in Hawaii), 2, 4, 15, 43, 111-116, 137, 209, 226 ; (Bib. #34, pp. 101, 148-152, 162, 167; #49; #178, #179, cf.: #148) (see also: above)

Ramon Vandrel, José (hired in March 1901 for a period of three months to write letters for the [Porto Ricans] and articles for publication in newspapers back on the island [Porto Rico]), 72

Recruitment of European laborers (by the Hawaiian Sugar Planters Association), 18, 46

Recruitment of laborers to Hawaii (Puerto Rican) (by the Hawaiian Sugar Planters Association (HSPA)), 2, 8-9, 17-18, 21-26, 27, 29, 33, 34, 36, 43, 46, 99, 109, 121, 205. 240, 241

Regensburger, Dr. Martin (of San Francisco [State Board of Health]) (his comments regarding hookworm disease and Porto Ricans in San Francisco in 1905), 114

Relief Corporation, The (and Porto Ricans during the 1906 San Francisco Earthquake), 119

Relief Survey [San Francisco]: The Organization and Methods of Relief Used After the Earthquake and Fire of April 18, 1906 (and 27 Puerto Rican applicants for relief of a housing shelter, along with [continued]: eight other cited "nationalities") (1913), (Russell Sage Foundation), 120

Report of the Governor of Hawaii to the Secretary of the Interior (1900-1926), 59, 204; (Bib. #253-#267)

Rio de Janeiro (the steamer) (the 1st ship, i.e., the "1st Expedition", which took the Porto Rican immigrants to Hawaii on December 23, 1900), 8-9, 13, 38, 87, 88; (Bib. #34, p. 90, 94, 100, 103-104, 106; Bib. #73, #74, #78, #85, #107, #201, #234, #342)

Robinson, Hon. W. J. (Third Judge of the First Circuit Court of Hawaii and formerly of Oakland, CA, quoted as having said "racial-oriented" comments in the *San Francisco Call* newspaper against Porto Ricans, and against "other ethnic groups", or "nationalities", in 1906), 113

Rodríguez, Clara E., 53, 55, 57, 61, 133, 137 (Footnote 5); (Bib. #173-#177)

Rodríguez, Victor M. (describing the "Racialization" of the Porto Ricans in the U.S.), 111, 112, 137; (Bib. #178-#180)

Rosario, Carmelo Natal (autor of: *Exodo Puertorriqueño: (Las Emigraciones Al Caribe Y Hawaii: 1900-1915)*), (published in San Juan, Puerto Rico: 1983), 131-132

Rosario-Rivera, Raquel (see her Archival Research in Puerto Rico and the identification of over 285 Porto Rican Immigrant's names in Hawaii in the early 1900s), 27-28, 37-38, 40, 45, 71, 74, 99, 226, 245; (Bib. #181)

Ruiz, Vicki L. ("*Nuestra América*: Latino History as United States History" article), (2006), 53; (Bib. #182)

_____. ("Why Latino History Matters to U.S. History" article), (2009), 53; (Bib. #183)

Russell Sage Foundation in 1913 and Porto Ricans, 119-120; (Bib. #184)

Sacramento, CA area newspapers and Porto Ricans (1884-1899), 25-26, 59-60, 82; (Bib. #185-#187)

-(The City of), 25, 80, 83, 94, 97, 129, 150 (Exhibit 6), 202-203, 235; (Bib. #8, #185-#187)

San Ciriaco Hurricane in Porto Rico and its devastating agricultural and economic effects on Porto Rico (on August 8, 1899, and thereafter), 9-12, 25-27, 34, 37, 39, 52, 115 139 (Footnote 8), 206, 207, 211, 215, 223, 239; (Bib. #187) (Bib. #34, p. 5, 48, 463)

San Diego (the City) and San Diego County:

-(1868-1915), (*Index to Obituaries and Death Notices in the San Diego Union (1868-1915) and the San Diego Herald (1851-1860)*), 83, 84; (Bib. #193, #197)

Directory of San Diego City and County for 1893-1894, 83, 201, 226, 236; (Bib. #194)

San Diego City and County Directory: 1895, 83; (Bib. #195) (B.L.A. Munroe cited as a Salesman)

-(Puerto Rican Population in 1900, 1910, 1920, and 2000), 169 (Table 1), 170, 226

-(*1906 San Diego City and County Directory*), 83; (see also: Bib. #29)

-*San Diego County California Census Index 1900*, (Evelyn Jean White, Editor), 84, 226, 236; (Bib. #135; #391)

-SD County (Puerto Rican Population & Community in 2010), 5; (cf.: Bib. #359; #381)

-County (Puerto Rican Population in 1900, 1910, 1920, and 2000), 169 (Table 1), 170

-SD County, (*The Great* Register *of San Diego County for 1894, and of 1866-1898)*, 83-84, 201, 227, 236; (Bib. #28; #196)

San Diego Genealogical Society (*Index to Obituaries and Death Notices in San Diego Union (1868-1915)*) [Database] (2013), 5, 83-84; (Bib. #29, #193-194, #197)

San Francisco Area newspaper articles, (cf.: 88-91); (Bib. #198-#231, #233-#245, #326-#352)

-Area newspapers (*e.g.*, Redwood City, CA) (1951-1978); (Bib. #161 - #163, #358)

-Area newspapers (*San Mateo, CA*) and Marine Cty., (1859, 1910, 1976); (Bib. #243-#244)

San Francisco, CA (Porto Ricans and pre-1906, as well as post 1906, San Francisco Earthquake), 117-120; (cf.: Bib #34, p. 90, 93-94, 100, 102-105, 109-110, 114, 124, 129, 141, 229, 240, 244, 452, 456)

-(the 1910 Federal Census population figures for Porto Ricans), 77, 121-123

-(Puerto Rican population in 1900, 1910, 1920, in 2000), 169 (Table 1), 170

San Francisco Census Enumeration Districts in 1910 and Porto Ricans, 125-126, 220; (Bib. #121, #123, # 230) [According to an Internet article authored by the U.S. Federal Census, in 1910 "the Census Bureau began to delineate Eds (enumeration districts) to follow the boundaries of legally or administratively defined entities such as villages, cities, wards, and minor civil divisions (MCDS)," (from: a personal e-mail received by this author from the Serra Research Center, San Diego, CA Library System, June 21, 2010)]. (sources: *IPUMS USA (Minnesota Population Center (MPC))*, "1910 Census: Instructions to Enumerators"; Dept. of Commerce and Labor, Bureau of the Census, *Thirteenth Census of the United States 1910: Population by Counties and Minor Civil Divisions 1910, 1900, 1890,*" (1912); (pages 2-12, 4, 35, 40)) [These two sources are not cited in the 1st Edition of this Book]

-S.F. Census Dist. #32, pages: 96-97, 99, 104-106, 110, 126

-S.F. Census Dist. #33, pages: 96-97, 103, 104, 106-107, 110

-S.F. Census Dist. #37, page: 100

-S.F. Census Dist. #39, pages: 96, 97

-S.F. Census Dist. #41, pages: 96, 97, 99-100, 110, 104-105, 110, 126

-S.F. Census Dist. #44, page 103

-S.F. Census Dist. #45, pages: 95-97, 99-100, 104-106, 110, 125-126

San Francisco City Directory (1852, Sept.), 80; (Bib. #232)

San Francisco County and the 1910 Federal Census, 121-123

San Francisco Earthquake (of 1906), 4, 31-32, 64, 97, 115, 117-120; (Bib. #91, #184, #209, #228, #230)

-(of 1906) (and Porto Rican Relief), 119-120; (Bib. #184, #230)

-San Francisco Earthquake Relief Corporation (1906) (and Puerto Ricans), 119-120

San Francisco Municipal Reports For the Year 1872-73, Ending June 30th, 1873 (Board of Supervisors, 1873), 80, 81, 201, 228; (Bib. #20)

San Francisco Relief Survey publication (relating to Porto Ricans and the 1906 San Francisco Earthquake), 120; (Bib. #184)

San Jose, CA (The City of), 29, 39, 91, 94, 96, 107, 147

Sanabria, Carlos ("Labor Migration from Puerto Rico 1900-1930 and the origins of the Puerto Rican Community in New York City") (Master's Thesis, Hunter College, N.Y.), 15; (Bib. #188)

Sánchez Korrol, Virginia, 21, 52-53, 69, 87, 130; (Bib. #189-#192)

Schmitt, Robert, *Historical Statistics of Hawaii.* (1977), 8, 69, 109, 204; (Bib. #246, #247)

Schnack, George F. ("*Subjective Factors in the Migration of Spanish from Hawaii To California*"), (Master's Thesis), (Leland Stanford Junior University; today it is: Stanford Univ.), 46; (Bib. #248)

Schomburg, Arthur A. (Arturo A. Schomburg and the "citizenship question"), 135; (Bib. #249, #360)

Seabury, Joseph B. (*The World and Its People – Porto Rico: The Land of the Rich Port*), (1908), 10; (Bib. #250)

Senior, Clarence, 17, 44, 61, 63-65, 121, 134-135, 139; (Bib. #268-271)

Silver, Patricia, 5, 54, 175 (Bib. #55); (Bib. #272)

Silvestrini-Pacheco, *et. al.*, ("Sources For The Study of Puerto Rican History: A Challenge to the Historian's Imagination"), 53; (Bib #273)

Smith, Claude A. ("Further Remarks on the Mode of Infection in Uncinariasis"), (1905); (Bib. #353)

Social Clubs and Organizations (Porto Rican) (in California) and in Hawaii, 32-33, 126-129, 140 (Footnote #12), 188-189, 204-205; (Bib. #40 - #41, #90, pp. 176, 183-186)

-and Organizations (Porto Rican) (in Hawaii), 32, 33

Social Definitions (of the concepts of "Race", and of "Ethnicity", have historically changed over time from 1898-1994, according to Sociologist Clara E. Rodríguez), 137 (Footnote 5); (Bib. #175)

Spain, 2, 6, 18, 40, 43, 46-47, 53, 61, 81, 83, 84, 104, 133, 135, 138, 146 (Ex. 5), 147, 195, 196, 197, 210, 219, 222, 224, 228, 239; (Bib. #231, #375; see: #34, p. 44, 47-48, 80, 102, 129, 328, 371-372)

Spaniards (from Spain) laborer's immigration to Hawaii, 18, 57; (Bib. #34, p. 1-2, 9, 14, 16, 17, 18, 21, 22, 42, 129, 210-211, 219, 331, 449; Bib. #105; #248; #295,; #297, pp. 7, 18, 19, 64, 80ff.; #407)

Spanish (from Spain) Diaspora in the United States (1848-1948), 18, 46, 196, 224; (Bib. #307; #248)

Spanish-American War (1898) and Porto Rico (sometimes referred to as the: Spanish-Cuban-American War), 11, 12-13, (cf.: 133 (Footnote #1)); (Bib. #362)

Stanford University, 167 (Exhibit 21), 168; (Bib. #248); *California State Board of Health Weekly Bulletin* (Jan. 32, 1925, Vol. III, No. 51, this is an extract of an address delivered at Stanford University Medical School, Jan. 23, 1925)

State Census Records (1992) (by Ann S. Lainhart, Genealogical Publishing Co.), 80; (Bib. #95)

Stead, Alfred ("The Labor Question in Hawaii: An Object Lesson To American Statesmen"), (1902); (Bib. #354, #405)

Strikes (a strike at the Pioneer Mill [Plantation] in Lahaina, Hawaii, on April 4, 1900, and at the Olowala Plantation near Lahaina, and on other plantations), 21, 22, 24, 25, 36; (cf.: (Bib. #104))

-(Porto Ricans and other Ethnic Groups used as "Strike Breakers" in Hawaii), 22, 25, 36; (cf.: #104) (cf.: *Bulletin of the U.S. Department of Labor –No. 46, May 1903, p. 709)* (Wash., D.C.: GPO)

Summary of one of the major research goals of this book, 129-130, 229

-of Puerto Rican Migration from (Hawaii to San Francisco, California: 1901-1925), 85-86

Surplus labor in Porto Rico (as a factor in emigration), 2, 15, 17, 26, 35-36; (Bib. #34, p. 255)

Tate, William (born in Puerto Rico, a wood chopper by occupation, and was living in CA, and he was cited in the 1870 Federal Census), 82

Teaching U.S. Puerto Rican History (by Virginia Sánchez Korrol, 1999), 53; (Bib. #191)

Teresa Whalen, Carmen, ("Colonialism, Citizenship, and the Making of the Puerto Rican Diaspora: An Introduction"), 21, 57, 59, 68, 69, 77, 140 (Footnote 11), 145, 229; (Bib. #274)

The 1852 State of California Census, 7, 15, 79-80, 82, 146, 150, 162 (Exhibit 18), 236; (Bib. #8)

The 1900–1910 time periods in California and selected population figures, 68-69

The Organic Act of 1900 (which established the labor contract system; thus, Japanese laborers felt free to make demands for higher wages, reduced hours, in Hawaii), 21-22; (see: Bib. #30)

Thurston, Lorrin A. (ex-Judge and ex-Attorney General of the Hawaiian Islands), 112-113

Treaty of Guadalupe Hidalgo (1848) (Simon M. Mezes and Mexican Land Grants in California in the 1850s San Francisco Bay Area, along with its related Legal Court issues), 81; (cf.: The National Archives, National Archives and Records Service. General Services Administration, (1978), "Private Land-Grant Case Files in the Circuit Court of the Northern District of California 1852-1910", (Roll 28, Cases: …*Mezes v. Greer*….) (Microfilm Publication T12207) (pp. 004, 005, 0561-0563, 0582-0584, 0587) (this is about the "Pulgas Rancho" 1850s court case) (I purchased this Microfilm from the Archives for about $135.00) (I purchased this "primary source" in 2016; this is a digitized copy of this 1850s court case)

Treaty of Paris (Dec. 10, 1898) (which **ceded** Porto Rico to the United States), 25, 133, 135, 220; (Bib. #34, p. 47-47)

21st Century [Twenty-First Century] Research Technology, Tools and Advances, 18-19

Uncinaria Americana (Porto Ricans in California and in Porto Rico) (a devastating disease afflicting Porto Rican plantation laborers) (aka: ***Uncinariasis***) (aka: hookworm disease), 115, 116; (Bib. #61, [continued: *Uncinaria Americana*] #62, #63, #316, #321, #353)

U.S. Commonwealth on July 25, 1952 (Puerto Rico) (or *Estado Libre Asociado*, in Spanish), 12; (Bib. #54)

U.S. Constitution (the 14th Amendment) (and its effects on both Puerto Rico and Puerto Ricans), 15-16, 31, 57, 87, 137 (Footnote 5); (Bib. #16, #122), (cf.: pages 11-12, the U.S. Supreme Court "paradoxically defined the Island as 'foreign to the United States in a domestic sense', neither a state of the American Union nor an independent country…."), (cf.: Bib.#224)

    -the U.S. Supreme Court, and the U.S. Congress (their effects on Porto Rico and Porto Ricans), 11-12, 12-13, 15-16, 21, 51, 57, 135 (Footnote 3), 137 (Footnote 5); (Bib. #16, #42, #43, #122, #200, #211, #227, #329, #361)

United States (Puerto Rican population in 1900, 1910, 1920, in 2000), 169 (Table 1), 170, (see also: 144 (Exhibit 4))

U.S. Supreme Court Justice (Supreme Court Justice Sonia Sotomayor, of Puerto Rican heritage, raised in the Bronx, New York, i.e., the "South Bronx" area), 51

Vázquez Calzada, José L., 12, 34-35, 72; (Bib. #308-#312) (note: also cited as, José L. Vázquez)

Vega, Bernardo, 16, 75; (Bib. #306)

Wages and the standard of living (in Porto Rico), 9-11, 25, 35, 118, 213, 224; (Bib. # 25, pp. 757, 764-765, 776ff.; #186; #302, page 11,"Wages and Standard of Living" in Porto Rico. This document summarizes wages as follows: "Wages in Porto Rico are very low" (cited: 1906) (see: 24)

    -in Hawaii (Porto Rican Celestino Garcia being disenchanted with his wages), 40, 41

    -(low) (in Hawaii), 9, 22, 40, 46, 118, 210, 233; (cf.: Bib. #254, pp. 64, 69, #295, "Wages: average, occupations, average hours of labor, and nationality of employees in each industry", pp. 513, 514, 592-662; #392) (cf.: pp. 24, 35, 39, 44, 113 in this 2016 Edition book)

Waialula Sugar Mill Plantation (O'ahu, Hawaii), 35

Wailuku Plantation (in Hawaii); (Bib. #34, p. 133)

Wealth and "Per Capita Wealth" (in Porto Rico - 1909) (and/or "lack thereof"), 47; (Bib. #304, pp. 13-14, Chart titled, "Per capita wealth of principal countries compared with Porto Rico". Among the 14 countries cited, Great Britain was first with $1,442.00. Porto Rico was last at only $182.00, with the United States at fourth at $1,123.00, "Labor Conditions in Porto Rico")

Where did all these California Puerto Ricans come from?, 64-65

White versus non-White Immigrants, and plantation laborers, to CA and to Hawaii in relation to Porto Ricans/Puerto Ricans and its subsequent historical effects, 23, 36, 53; (Bib. #173)

White versus non-White Labor (relating to immigrant labor), 23, 36

Women in Hawaii (on December 23, 1900, the first arrivals of Porto Ricans in Hawaii), 8

    -(Porto Rican women in California), 9, 13, 49-50, 64, 85, 89, 101-102, 119; (Bib. #209, #219, #236), (cf.: Bib. #337, #332)

-(Porto Rican women in Hawaii), 8, 23, 27, 29, 40, 48-50, 64, 85, 230; (Bib. # 141, #337) (cf.: p.113)

-(Porto Rican women while living in Porto Rico, and in Hawaii), 8, 10, 27, 31, 35, 39, 68, 212; (Bib. #129; cf.: #227)

-(possibly the first Porto Rican Postmaster in Porto Rico; she worked in this position in Adjuntas, Porto Rico), 31

-(two-thirds of women were unemployed in Porto Rico in 1899, out of 183,635 of the total unemployed population), 10, 35, 68

World War I (and Porto Rican Veterans of), 29, 30, 32, cf.: 148 (Exhibit 5b), 234; (Bib. #34, p. 233)

Zealandia (the *SS Zealandia*) (a ship which transported the Porto Rican immigrant laborers to Hawaii in March 1901), 28, 231, 232; (Bib. #204; see: Bib. #34, p. 90, 113, 118, 122, 124, 128, 164)

Selected Names of Porto Rican Immigrants and their Children in CA, and in Hawaii

Note: In addition to the "Selected Names" which are listed below, pages 60 and 95-110, of **this** book, I have numerous *other* names in several different types of "Lists" which provide the names of **other** Porto Rican Immigrants, (cf.: p. 154, Exhibit 10; p. 155 Exhibit 11) [**Note:** the number following the name(s), is the page number within **this** book]:

Abril, Mariano ("a prominent Porto Rican" and the editor and proprietor of *La Democrata* newspaper in [Caguas] Porto Rico, 41; (see: Bib. #34, p. 124, 160); **NOTE:** Mr. Abril was **not** an Immigrant himself);

- Acevedo, Francisco, 40;
- Agostini, Julio, 40;
- Aguilar, Nicolas, 29;
- Alas, Providencia, 40;
- Andujas, Pedro, 28;
- Aponte, Mario, 127;
- Arbelo, Ramon (stayed in California on Dec. 14, 1900; "can read and write Spanish", and placed with the "kind fathers of Santa Clara College"), 89;
- Avilés, Emilio (was "a member of the first contract labor expedition" scheduled for Hawaii in Dec. 1900, however, he stayed in San Francisco, CA instead, and was from Arecibo, P.R.), 32;
- **"Baby Silva"** (this is how the 1910 Census identified this baby (2/12 months old); her mother was born in Porto Rico, and they immigrated in 1904, and they lived in California in 1910), 107;
- Bargas [?], Q., 29 (spelled in the original) [probably: Vargas];
- Beauchamps, Dolores (passenger on the ship, the *Zealandia*, on her way to Hawaii in March 1901, while marrying Francisco Beauchamps on this ship on her way to Hawaii), 28; (see: Bib.#34, p. 122);

- Beauchamps, Francisco (passenger on the ship, the *Zealandia*, on his way to Hawaii in March 1901, while marrying Dolores Beauchamps [no record of her maiden name cited in the newspapers reviewed by this author] on the ship), 28; (see: Bib. #34, p. 122);

- Beltran, Frederick, 28;

- Berríos, Enrique, 127;

- Berríos, Evaristo, 127;

- Berríos, Juan, 127;

- Blair, Clara (born in Porto Rico and she immigrated to the U.S. in 1850; the *1900 U.S. Federal Census* (for California) cited her), 80, 83, 144 (Table 4, "Notes");

- Bonilla, Manuel, 127;

- Burtardes, Clalio (aka: Olalio Curtardio), 123;

- Caedeno, F. (aka: Nancisco Santiago), 29;

- Caedeno, M. (Bib. #34, p. 154), 29;

- Camacho, Lorenzo, 29;

- Cancio Martínez, Juan, 29;

- Caravallo Vegas, Nicolas, 29-30;

- Cencel, Candido, 29;

- Cartes, M., 29;

- Cruz, Domingo, 32;

- Cruz, Vicente, 28;

- Cuotodis, Valentine (Porto Rican's name cited in the book *San Francisco Deaths 1865-1905: Abstracts from Surviving Civil Records. Vol. I. Surnames Starting with A-D* (published: 2010), 97; (Bib. #357)

- Dufish, Edward (born in P.R. and immigrated to the U.S. in 1852; his name appeared in the *1910 U.S. Federal Census* (for California)), 80, 81, 219, 235;

- Emilio, Don, 32;

- Espiel, Ysidro (stayed in California on Dec. 14, 1900; "can read and write Spanish"), 89;

- Feliciano, Dionisia, 29;

- Feliciano, (Rev.) Juan C. (Juanito), 29;

- Feliciano, Salomon, 29;

- Fino, Pedro, 29;

- Fraticelli, Carlos (Porto Rican poet in Hawaii), 29-30; (see: Carr 1989: Bib. #34, pp. 258,

- [continued] 291, 319; #356) [*Note*: Dr. Carr "…conducted several 'personal interviews'… with Charles Fraticelli"….];

- Garcia, Celestino (the first Porto Rican who earned enough money to leave Hawaii and returned to San Francisco, CA, in Nov. 1901, after being disenchanted with wages on the plantation in Hawaii), 40-41, 230;

- Garcia, Paula, 32;

- Guzman, Manuel, 29;

- Irizarry, Mercedes, 127;

- Jesus, J. (aka: Baldo Velsope), 29;

- Jimenez, Lorenzo, 28;

- Jose Torres, Maria, 28;

- López, Josie ("parents came in the first Hawaiian migration and resettled in San Francisco just before the 1906 earthquake"), 32;

- Lucena, Lorenzo, 29;

- Lugo, Juan (he had come on the 1900 migration from Yauco, Porto Rico. He was one of the Protestant Ministers), 29, 32;

- Lugo, Panchito, 29;

- Lugo, Ramón, 127;

- Madura, F.J., 28;

- Maldonado, Margaret (in 1927 she was teaching at Honomu, in Hawaii, and she had a long career as a school teacher in Hawaii), 29;

- Maltines, Johann, 29;

- Martínez, Marcelino, 127;

- Medina, Jorge, 127;

- Mendez, Ramon, 29;

- Mezes, Dr. Sidney E. (cited as: Sydney E. Mezes in a book which he was a part of), 147, 148;

- Milán, Dr. [Don?] Ramón, 127;

- Mitta, Ramon, 29;

- Montes, Julio (the Hawaiian Puerto Rican immigrant who wrote a letter in 1901 in Hawaii), 73;

- Montijo, Hermophenes, 29;

- Morales, Catana [Cataña?], 32;

- Morales, Jose (stayed in San Francisco, CA on Dec. 14, 1900, and was interviewed by the *San Francisco Chronicle* on Dec. 15, 1900), 67, 87, 91;

- Morales, Rafael, 32;

- Muniz, Ana, 28;

- Orsatelli, Judith, 32;

- Olivieri, Milliano S., 29;

- Olivieri Sanchez, Manuel, 29, 30, 31, 214 (and the Territorial Supreme Court of Hawaii and the struggle to functionally and practicably acquire U.S. Citizenship rights);

- Orsatelli, Judith, 32;

- Ortiz, Hilda (she was at the Ookala School in 1924-25, and she had a long career as a school teacher in Hawaii), 29;

- Ortiz, Panchito, 29;

- Pagan, Jesse, (was born in Hawaii in 1924. Was president of PRUMA in the Bay Area thirteen times), 32, 33;

- Pagan, (Rev.) Jose , 29;

- Pagan, Maria, 28;

- Patinao, Ramon, 28;

- Perez, Juan (stayed in California on Dec. 14, 1900, however, "he later joined his parents in Maui, Hawaii" thereafter), 28, 88, 93, 94; (Bib. #34, p. 104, 453)

- Perez Troche, Domingo, 31;

- Perry, Mingo (he was born: Domingo Perez), 31, 33;

- Quinones, Emergirdo, 29;

- Quinones, (Rev.) Ramon, 29;

- Ramos Borrero, Juana, 31;

- Ricardo Centerio, Jose, 29;

- Rivera, Eusebio, 127;

- Rodriguex (*sic.*), Ezequial, (name written in the original), 28 [probably: Rodriguez family name];

- Rodríguez, José (Porto Rican World War I Veteran), 32;

- Rodríguez, Olagario [or Eulagario Rodríguez] (he was interviewed by newspaper reporter, in Dec. 1900, by Mr. Livernash), 93;

- Rodríguez, Ramon, 127; (cf.: 100)

- Rodriguez de Olivera, Julia, 32;
- Rosa, John F., 29;
- Ruiz, M. (aka: Martin Cortes), 29;
- Salsules, Francisco C., 29;
- Sanchez, P. (aka: Eselle Rivera), 29;
- Sanchis (*sic.*, in original), Manual O., 29 [probably: Sanchez family name];
- Santiago, Alfred "Freddy", 29;
- Santiago, Carlos (Bib. #34, p. 194), 29;
- Santiago, Julio, 33;
- Santiago, Luis, 127;
- Santiago, Ramon (stayed in California, near Napa, on Dec. 14, 1900; "he wrote a letter to his father in Porto Rico"), 90, 93;
- Santiago, Santos, 127;
- Tomás Rodriguez, Jose (WW I Veteran), 32;
- Torres, Asiscio, 127;
- Torres, Eusebio, 37;
- Trochez, [Andalecio] (also: Troche), 30;
- Velazquez, C., 29;
- Velez, Miguel, 29.

List (persons born in Puerto Rico, who *also lived in California* from 1850-1900):

- Benzon, Charles F. (He was listed in the *1900 U.S. Federal Census*, and he lived in San Francisco, CA. He was 19 years of age, Race: Black), 83, 154 (Exhibit 10, a copy of a *1900 U.S. Fed. Census* page), 83, 144 (Exhibit 4), 219;

- Blair, Clara (the *1900 U.S. Federal Census* listed her as having been born in "Porte Rico" [*sic*] Porto Rico and she immigrated to the U.S. in 1850, and she lived in "Sacramento City, Sacramento, CA", in 1900), 80, 83, 144, 219, 232, 235;

- Camacho, Ben (He was listed in the *1900 U.S. Federal Census*, and his family lived in "Soquel Township, Santa Cruz, CA". He was 24 years of age; R: White), 83, 144, 154 (Exhibit 10), 219;

- Dufish, Edward (the *1910 U.S. Federal Census* listed him as being "black", and that he was born in Puerto Rico, and immigrated to the U.S. in 1852. He was a barber, and lived in Los Angeles, CA, in 1910, and his occupation was a Barber), 80, 81, 219, 232;

- Hernandez, Rafael (He lived in San Francisco, CA according to the *1880 U.S. Federal Census*, and was born in Puerto Rico Island". His occupation was listed as being a: "Cigar

[Hernandez, Rafael continued] Maker"), 83, 209, 219, 235-236, (cf.: p. 14);

- Mezes, Simon M. (aka: S.M. Mazie; S.N. Mazie; Simon Montserrate Mezes, S.M. Meces), 1, 4. 6, (he was born "about 1828" in Porto Rico. In 1852 he resided in San Francisco; he was a Banker in Porto Rico), 79-84, 143 (*1870 U.S. Federal Census*), 146 (Photo of Mr. Mezes), 147-151 (Ex. 5b – Ex. 7), 162, 245; (Bib. #96, #119 (Vol. III, p. 382-383), #118, #162, #163, #185, #358, #375, #398, #400, #403, #404, #419-#422), 195-198, 208, 213, 219, 220, 229, 241, 242, 375. Importantly, Mr. Mezes' name(s) appears in the 1860, 1870, and 1880 *U.S. Federal Census*, as well as being listed in the *1852 State of California Census*; Note: The 2nd Edition portion of the book shows that S.M. Mezes was born in 1823, (cf.: pp. 196ff);

- Munroe, Alphonso B. L. A. (listed as having a: "Nativity as Porto Rico"; lived in both Los Angeles and in San Diego, and was cited in the *1900 U.S. Federal Census* (for California)), 83-84, 144, Exhibit 4), 154 (Exhibit 10), 208, 219, 226, 236; (Bib. #28, p. 81; #135, #388, #391, cf.: pp. 84, 226), (Note: This is the Census' spelling of his name, aka: Monroe, B.L. Alphonso). The *Directory of San Diego City and County* for the following years __all__ had his name spelled as: B .L.A. **Munroe**, 1897; 1899-1900; 1901; 1905; 1906; 1907; 1908; and 1909; he was not listed in the *1910 City Directory* for San Diego. The 1*906 City Directory* listed Mr. Munroe as: Blanfort L A Munroe. Mrs. M O Munroe (i.e., Mr. Munroe's mother) was *only* listed in the *1906 City Directory*. Finally, Mr. Munroe's newspaper "Death" notice in the *San Diego Union* (April 25, 1910), cited Mr. Munroe as being "…a native of Martinique Island"), **_contrary_** to all the aforementioned documents (see: Bib. #391, the *San Diego County California Census Index: 1900,* in this Book; cf.: pp. 84, 226; Bib. #135).

Further, the *Great Registers, 1866-1898* record also shows that Mr. B L A Munroe in 1888 lived in Los Angeles, and that his voting No. was 7450, his occupation was listed as being a Teacher, and that he was naturalized "by naturalization of Father" (no date was listed), and that his country of nativity was **Porto Rico**, and was 37 years of age on the "Date of Registration" on 9/11/1888. He resided on Hayes Street; (see: Bib. #28, p. 28); Note: "2016" Update-- Blanford L. A. Munroe (aka: B LA Munroe) is listed in the 1892 publication titled, "California, Voter Registers, 1866-1898", contrary to what I wrote in the 1st Edition, (p. 83);

- Munroe, M O (she is Mr. Alphonso B. L. A. Munroe's mother) (both names appeared in the *1900 U.S.* Federal *Census* (for California)), 83-84, 144, 154 (Exhibit 10), 219, 236; (cf.: Bib. #28, #29). (Note: This is the Census' spelling of her name) (Note: aka: Monroe, M O);

- Portorico, Mcenty [the Census spelling of this name!], (He lived in San Francisco, CA and was cited in the *1900 U.S. Federal Census*) 83, 144 (Exhibit 4), 154 (Exhibit 10), 219, 236;

- Rodigez, Charles (the Census spelling of his name in the 1900 Federal Census). In 1900 he lived in San Francisco, CA and he was 57 years of age, Race: White,), 83, 144, 154, 219;

- Spence, R V (she was listed in the *1852 State of California Census*, and it listed her as being born in Porto Rico "about 1847", and she resided in San Francisco, CA). (Note: this is how the *1852 State of California Census* cited her name), 80, 219;

- Tate, William (the *1870 U.S. Federal Census* listed Mr. Tate as being born in Puerto Rico; his occupation as being that of a Wood Chopper; lived in San Rafael, Marin, CA), 82, 219, 229;

- Vanryn, John M. (also cited as: John M. Van Ryn) (he was listed in the *1860 U.S. Federal* Census, and that he was born in Puerto Rico; the *1860 U.S. Federal Census* listed him as being a "Professor of Languages" in Los Angeles, CA), 81, 141 (Exhibit 1), 142 (Exhibit 2), pp. 219, 236.

List (Names of the "at least" 64 Immigrants that Stayed in California on December 14, 1900), (*Note: the following names below are written as they appeared in the newspapers in Dec. 1900. The children's names of these Immigrants were not mentioned by their respective first names; their respective **ages**, where known, are in parenthesis*) (see: pages 88-91, 87-92, in this Book):

1) Agosto, Jose, 91;

2) Arbelo, Ramon (22), 89;

3) Barreto, Carlos (16), 89;

4) Billafana, Carmelia, 89;

5) Colon, Joaquin (14), 88;

6) Cruz, Victorian, 90;

7) De Soto, Aurelio (34), (see: Bib. #34, p. 452);

8) Espiel, Ysidro (26), 89;

9) Figueroa, Maria, 89;

10) Figueroa, Mateo, 89;

11) Flores, Juan (15), 89;

12) Gimenez, Petronila, 88;

13) Gimenez, Serafin (4 ½ year old boy), 88;

14) 14-21) Guadaloupe, Senora, along with: "they will remain with their '**Seven** Little tots'" (all unnamed) (this is how the newspaper identified them, although one of these seven was identified as being twelve-day-old "Miguela baby"), 88;

22) Guez, Fabian, 89;

23) Heresadia, Juan, 90;

24) Hernandes, Mateo, 91;

25) Ignosund Berreto, Blanco, 91;

26) Heredia, Ignosunty, 89;

27) Lopez, Eusabia, 90;

28) Martin, Mrs. Ramon (the wife of Ramon; newspaper did not provide her first name), 90; (Ramon and Mrs. Martin had **two** children, one 3 *days old;* thus they are **#29** and **#30** among the "list" of the "at least" 64 immigrants that stayed in CA in Dec. 1900);

31) Mr. Ramon Martin (husband of Mrs. Ramon Martin), 90;

32) Marzan, Lola Dolores (16), 88;

33) Marzan, Emelio, 88;

34) Medina, Juan, 91;

35) Miguela, Senora [Señora?], 88, 102;

36) Miranda, Felix, 89;

37) Morales, Jose (18), 67, 87, 91;

38) Morales, Salvador, 89;

39) Nunez, Francisco, 91;

40) Ortiz, Ramon, 90;

41) Ortiz, Mrs. Ramon, 90 (had a **baby**; newspaper did not identify the baby's first name);

42) Pacheco, Nicomedes (23), 89;

43) Panilla, Santiago (14), 88 [Note: the author determined that Santiago Panilla/Parnilla/Padilla is most likely the same person]. (Dr. Norma Carr wrote that Santiago Padilla was age 12 to 14 years old), [the "family name" could possibly be: Padilla];

44) Perez, Juan (12), 28, 88, 93, 94; (see: Bib. #34, p. 104, 453);

45) Puty, Claudino (19), 88;

46) Reyes, Eduardo, 90;

47) Ribera, Gregoria, 91, 238;

48) Rodriguez, James, 91;

49) Rodriguez, Jose, 31, 32 (*possibly* in the 1st Expedition in 1900 to Hawaii; WWI Veteran);

50) Sanchez, Vicente, 89;

51) Santiago, Louis, 91;

52) Santiago, Mrs. Louis (the newspaper did not provide her first name), 91;

53) Santiago, Ramon, 90, 93;

54-59) Soto, Sisto, 90 (plus **5** children of Mr. & Mrs. Soto), 94;

60) Soto (Mrs. Soto) (the newspaper did not identify her first name), 90, 94;

61) Torres, Francisco, 89;

62) Trinoe, Francisco, 91;

63) Valentin, Manuel, 89;

64) Volentico, Eugenia, 91.

Oct. 2016: "New" Reference *Citations [mostly]* not *cited in the 2013 Bibliography, nor in the "Bibliography Addendum" Section (pages 191-194) of this Book*   10/28/16

Note: the Bibliographic number of #368 follows Bibliographic number #367 which is the last cited Bibliographic source number in the 1st Edition of this printed book in March 2013 (see: page 194 in this 1st Edition, as well as page 194 in this 2nd Edition of this Book, as well).

368) *Annual Report of* the Governor *of Porto Rico for the Fiscal Year ending June 30, 1907. (1907).*

369) *Annual Reports of* the *War Department for the Fiscal Year Ended June 30, 1900.* (1902), Part 13. Report of the Military Governor of Porto Rico on Civil Affairs, (see: section: "Hurricane Relief", on the deadly and economically devastating hurricane in Porto Rico on Aug. 8, 1899, p. 210ff.).

370) *Annual Reports, War Department,* (1918), *Report of the Governor of Porto Rico to the Secretary of War 1918.* ("Rejection of Citizenship" and the World War I selection draft), (pages 569-570), (Vol. III, Appendix VIII) (In Three Volumes).

371) *Bulletin of the Bureau of Labor.* (1911), "Fourth Report of the Commissioner of Labor on Hawaii", see: pages 673ff) (May 1911), (No. 94).

372) *California State Board of Health Weekly Bulletin.* (1925). "Migration and the Spread of Disease", (January 31, 1925, Vol. III, No. 51, page 1).

373) Cifre De Loubriel, Estela, (1962). *Catálogo De Extranjeros Residentes En Puerto Rico En El Siglo XIX.* (Ediciones De La Universidad De Puerto Rico) (Rio Piedras, [Puerto Rico]).

374) _____, (1964). *La Inmigración A Puerto Rico Durante Siglo XIX.* (Instituto De Cultura Puertorriqueña: San Juan De Puerto Rico). (see: pages LXXVI, LXXX (this Table on this page shows that a total of 7 Foreign Immigrants arrived from *Luisiana* (the spanish spelling) "a Puerto Rico En Siglo XIX" (the early 19th Century)), LXXXI, LXXXIII). (*note*: she was a researcher and autor and was also a "*Doctora en Filosofía de la Universidad de Madrid; Catedrática Asociade e Investigadora del Departamento de Historia de la Universidad de Puerto Rico*).

375) Fredricks, Darold, (2008). "Simon Mezes – shrewd attorney". *San Mateo Daily Journal* (Printed from The Daily Journal) (November 10, 2008), (accessed: 1/19/2011 on-line). Mr. Darold Fredricks [incorrectly] wrote: "…Simon M. Mezes [was] originally from the Basque area of Spain, Mezes came to California in 1850 from Puerto Rico…."

376) *Gaceta de Puerto Rico*, (1897). *Gaceta de Puerto Rico. Periodico Oficial Del Gobierno.* (Año 1897, Número 1, Image 1, page 1. Under the Table/Chart titled "Junta de Obras del Puerto de la Ciudad de Ponce" lists the ship called the **_Arkadia_**. (see: Chronicling America – Library of Congress; http://chroniclingamerica.loc.gov/lccn/2013201074/1897-01-01/ed-1/s...). (accessed on: 4/10/2016). (Image provided by University of Puerto Rico, Rio Piedras Campus, Library).

377) *Harper's Weekly.* (1905), "We should do Something for Porto Rico at Once", (September 30, 1905, Vol. XLIX, New York City). This article references Mr. Santiago Iglesias, Mr. Samuel Gompers, the American Federation of Labor, as well as Porto Rican laborers as an "army of idle workmen", and that "…600 Porto-Ricans [in the original] died monthly from starvation [in Porto Rico]".

378) Hasemeir, Wayne, Geraldine D. Moser, and Colleen Norby, (1999). *History of the San Francisco Bay Region by Bailey Millard. INDEX OF VOLUMES ONE, TWO AND THREE In Two Parts. PART 1 – INDEX of the Biographies, PART 2 – Every Name Index of all Volumes.*

Genealogical Society of Stanislaus County, Inc., Modesto, California.

379) Hernández de Noboa, Milagros and Carmen Judith Nine Curt. (1988). "Puerto Rico Discovers Its Hawaiian Colony". *OAH Newsletter: Organization of American Historians*. Vol. 16, No. 1 (February 1988, pp. 6, 18). "… by 1900 labor recruitment facilities had been opened in San Juan, Ponce and Aguadilla.… Frequently it was those who had been dwelling in the Puerto Rican mountains who responded most enthusiastically to [the recruiter's] appeals. They came in their thousands from Adjuntas, Yauco, Ponce and Lares to the port at Guánica and elsewhere…with the first boat load sailing on November 22, 1900…only 56 reached Hawaii.… The emigrants sailed from Puerto Rico to New Orleans [then to]…the Hawaiian sugar fields. The San Francisco newspapers of the day turned out to be a prime [*primary*] source for accounts of the Puerto Ricans' saga."

380) History Task Force. (1982), "La Colonia Puertorriqueña en California", reprinted from the: *La Correspondencia* (Puerto Rico), (3 de Noviembre de 1923), (cited in: *Sources for the Study of Puerto Rican Migration – 1879-1930*. Centro de Estudios Puertorriqueños).

381) Instituto de Edtadísticas, (2013). *Puerto Rican Diaspora Atlas: 2010*. (Estado Libre Asociado de Puerto Rico, October 2, 2013, San Juan, Puerto Rico) (Idania R. Rodriguez Ayuso, MS, *et. al.*), (https://www.estadisticas.gobierno.pr).

382) *Journal of Heredity, The*. (1919), "Race Mixture in Hawaii" (2nd Series), (February 1919, Vol. 10 (issue 2), pp. 90-95). Porto Ricans in Hawaii are identified.

383) *Journal of the Executive Council of Porto Rico*. Volume I. (1901), Executive and Legislative Sessions, June 28, 1900 to January 31, 1901. Meeting of the Executive Council Held on June 28, 1900. (This publication identifies the "number of inhabitants" breakdown for each of seven Districts, i.e., the "territorial districts" in Porto Rico, including the identification of the various "municipal districts", and population, in Porto Rico).

384) King, W.W. (1901), "PORTO RICO: Inspection of immigrants at Ponce during the week ended December 22, 1900", (January 18, 1901), *Public Health Reports (1896-1970)*, (Vol. 16, No. 3, p. 128). (Published: Association of Schools of Public Health). ("On December 26 (1901) the Steamship ***Arkadia*** left this port [Ponce] with 380 immigrants for Hawaii, via New Orleans. One vessel was inspected and passed.… There is no change in sanitary conditions.") (signed by: The Surgeon-General, U.S. Marine-Hospital Services).

385) *La Correspondencia* (Puerto Rico newspaper), "La Colonia Portorriqueña de California cuenta con dos grandes sociedades que trabajan por el mejoramiento de nuestros compatriotas residentes allí". (1925), (12 de Octubre de 1925), cited in: Bib. #90, pp. 183-186) (from: *Sources for the Study of Puerto Rican Migration – 1879-1930)*.

386) Loveman, Mara, (2007). "The U.S. Census and the Contested Rules of Racial Classification in Early Twentieth-Century Puerto Rico", (*Caribbean Studies*, Vol. 35, No. 2, July-December 2007: 13ff.).

387) Loveman, Mara and Jeronimo Muñiz, (2007). "How Puerto Rico became White: Boundary Dynamics and Intercensus Racial Reclassification." *American Sociological Review* (72(6): 915-39).

388) Munroe, B.L.A. (aka: B.L.A. Monroe). (1895), In the Superior Court of the County of San Diego, State of California. Case Number C8728. (signed by Mr. Munroe on: 6/1/1895, as one of the "Defendants"). (**Note:** There are two other Superior Court Cases filed in San Diego County; **Note:** The first page of this July 1, 1895 court filing had his name as being spelled Monroe, and then it was later changed to Munroe in this aforementioned cited legal document).

389) *New York Times, The.* (1901), "Sufferings of Porto Ricans. 387 Islanders, Going to Hawaii, Arrive at New Orleans Weak, Sick and Starving". (January 3, 1901: 2). (re: the *Arkadia*).

390) _____. (1910), "Steamer Missing with 41 Aboard: All Hope Abandoned for Porto Rican Liner ***Arkadia*** by All but the Captain's Wife." (December 10, 1910). (emphasis added).

391) North San Diego County Genealogical Society and Carlsbad City Library, (1981). *San Diego County Census Index: 1900*. (Evelyn Jean White, Editor; Genealogy Reference Section Area) (see: Ref Family Research 312White). The name of B.L.A. Monroe (as opposed to his "correct" surname of Munroe, appears on page 84). She correctly pointed out that: "There will be discrepancies in the index due to difficulty in deciphering the names for various reasons. Accuracy is limited by the difficulty in reading some of the handwriting of the census takers, and by the census takers' phonetic (and sometimes creative) spelling…." (Chula Vista Historical Society, Chula Vista, CA) (Bib. #135).

392) *Nurses' Associated Alumnae of the United States* (Eight Annual Convention of the *Nurses…*), George Washington University, Wash., D.C., May 4 and 5, 1905, "Minutes of the Proceedings", pp. 756-763, "Developments in Visiting Nursing", by Miss Lucy Fisher, Visiting Nurse, United Charities, San Francisco. ("…Miss Kane's energy has been used in the care of the Porto Ricans. A large colony of these people was imported from Porto Rico by the sugar planters of the Hawaiian Islands. The contract to pay the Porto Ricans a fair amount of wages for their labor was never kept, so with the hope of bettering themselves they keep coming from Hawaii to our city [i.e., San Francisco]…. Dr. Herbert Gunn says this extremely important work for San Francisco of eradicating this disease uncinariasis…could not be accomplished if it were not for Miss Kane's strong influence over the Porto Ricans. The other nationalities in this Telegraph Hill district are the Spanish-speaking people…and the Porto Ricans").

393) O'Brien, Matt. (2010). "1910 census provides a snapshot of olden-day East Bay". *Contra Costa Times (ContraCostaTimes.com)*, 03/15/2010 (accessed: 5/19/10).

394) Poblete, Joanna. (2014), *Islanders in the Empire: Filipino and Puerto Rican Laborers in Hawai'i*, (University of Illinois Press: Urbana, Chicago, and Springfield) (cf.: Chapter 1. "Letters Home: The Failure of Puerto Rican Recruitment", pages 25-46; Chapter 3. "Indefinite Dependence: U.S. Control over Puerto Rican Labor Complaints", pp. 75-94; Chapter 6. "Limited Leadership: Roles of Puerto Rican Labor Agents in the Plantation Community", pp. 139-161. *Note:* Puerto Rican migration from Hawaii to California appears on page 92.).

395) Pui Lai, Kum. (1936), "Fifty Aged Puerto Ricans", Andrew W. Lind *Social Process in Hawaii*. (May 1936, Volume II, Honolulu, Hawaii, U.S.A.; pages 25-27). "Ever since the arrival of the main group of immigrants in 1901 [to Hawaii]…. In this preliminary study the writer will deal only with the **aged** in the Social Service Bureau."

396) Rasmussen, Louis J. (1965), *San Francisco Ship Passenger Lists*, (Volume I). (Baltimore, Maryland: Deford & Company) ("…the names of passengers arriving by vessels in the Port of San Francisco during the period of 1850 to 1875") (S.F. Historic & Genealogy Bulletin).

397) *Report of the President of the Board of Health of the Territory of Hawaii for the Eighteen Months Ending December 31, 1902*, (1903), "Report of the Inmates of Oahu Insane Asylum…."

398) *Reports of Cases Adjuged in the Supreme Court of Porto Rico"*. (1904), Antonio F. Castro, Secretary and Reporter. Volume 7. May 14 to December 24, 1904. San Juan, Porto Rico. Bureau of Supplies, Printing and Transportation. [*Note*: **Simon M. Mezes'** father, [Juan] Simón Mezes, is cited in a Court case involving the father buying land in Puerto Rico in 1834, see: page 33]. (Cited in: *Schulze & Co., In Liquidation, v. Estate of Castro*. Appeal from District Court of Mayagüez. No. 81. – Decided May 1904. "Action to Recover Possession", pp. 27-37) (accessed on October 29, 2014,

from: Google Books)]. (Emphasis added)

399) Ribes Tovar, Frederico. (1970), *Enciclopedia Puertorriqueña Illustrada, Tomo II. The Puerto Rican Heritage Encyclopedia. Volume II.* (San Juan, P.R., pp. 20, 249, 259, 301).

400) Rivera Maldonado, Tony (APG). (2013), **Preliminary Research Results into The Birth Place of Simon Mezes of Belmont, California**, (de Ribera Researchers: P.O. Box 13042, Las Cruces, New Mexico 88013-3042; Research Project No. 13-016). (Member: (APG) Association of Professional Genealogists) (Specializing in the Genealogy of Puerto Rico, and Genealogical Investigations). (September 16, 2013) (**Revised**: September 25, 2015). (Sociedad Puertorriqueña de Genealogia).

401) Sáenz and Karen Manges Douglas, (2015). "A Call for the Racialization of Immigration Studies: On the Transition of Ethnic Immigrants to Racialized Immigrants". *Sociology of Race and Ethnicity* (Vol. 1(1): 166-180. "What is clear, however, is that over time, the color line between nonwhites---Asians, blacks, and Mexicans---and whites became more important than the division between old and new European immigrants", (p. 168).

402) *San Francisco Chronicle. (*1900), "No Restrictions for Porto Rican Laborers: The Immigration Bureau Decides that they are Citizens and therefore have a Right to Land". (December 1, 1900: 1, Vol. LXXII).

403) San Mateo County Museum, (undated). Hand-written notes, and typed-written notes, (author unknown), Topic: S.M. Mezes [aka: Simon M. Mezes] and Sidney Edward Mezes (his son) with a brief "history" covering S.M. Mezes, as well as on Sidney E. Mezes. Covered under Sidney's name are sub-topics such as: Ancestry, Parentage; Education and Schools; Religious Turmoil; and Mr. Mezes' Death (S.M. Mezes). (San Mateo County Museum, 2200 Broadway, Redwood City, CA 94063) (Received by this author on: 4/30/2015). (SMCHA [San Mateo County Historical Association] 74-155.3).

404) *Stanford Historical Society Newsletter*. (1983). (see: section relating to Simon M. Mezes, a "Spanish-Puerto Rican attorney", pages 2, 3), (Spring 1983, Volume 7, No. 3) (by Dorothy Regnery).

405) Stead, Alfred. (1902), "The Labor Issue in the Islands: Alfred Stead's Exhaustive Article as it appears in the Current Collier's Weekly. A Careful Review of an Economic Problem which presents many phases of special interest to Statesmen in Washington". *Pacific Commercial Advertiser* (Dec. 11, 1902: 1-4). (His racial-oriented statement: "…Attempts to introduce Porto Rican laborers are now being made… *Negroes* have been tried, but have caused endless trouble…It has never been found feasible to induce large bodies of *white* immigrants to come, though the authorities tried hard to induce *white* immigration." (emphasis added)

406) *Sugar in Hawaii: A Guide to Historical Sources* (Compiled and Annotated by Susan M. Campbell), (1986). (Edited by Linda K. Menton) (The Hawaiian Historical Society, Honolulu). "Selected Chapters"/Sections: Indexes (Archives of Hawaii. Immigration Records Card Index; Archives of Hawaii. Subject Index Card File; Bibliographies; Selected Articles in Periodicals; Newspaper Indexes; Selected Articles in Newspapers; Government Publications; Annual Reports; Business Records; Oral History, p. 68-69; Maps and Blueprints; Directory of Libraries and other Research Institutions.

407) *The American Sugar Industry and Beet Sugar Gazette*, (1909). "Hawaiian Sugar Chat", (August 1909, Vol. XI, No. 8: 348). It stated, in short: "Several Portuguese and Porto Rican [as well as Spaniards] families, which had become discouraged with conditions in California, will also be brought back to Hawaii by the Territorial Board of Immigration." (accessed via: *Google*)

408) *The Associated Charities of San Francisco: Annual Reports 1904-1910.* (undated). The Porto Ricans are cited in four (4) pages within these *Annual Reports.* (Blair-Murdock Co: S.F.).

409) The Editors of *TIME-LIFE Books*, (1970). *1900-1910. This Fabulous Century.* (Vol. I), 1970 – Reprinted. (*Time-Life Books*, New York). Has Tables on: Population (for the U.S. [as well as for each of the 45 States, and for the then **Territory of Hawaii**], Immigration [from Europe and from Asia], Labor, Transportation, Business, Communication, Government for 1900, and for 1960. *Note:* "In 1900…the average American worker earned **22 cents an hour**…fewer than 150 miles of paved highway existed in the whole United States," (page 6). (emphasis added)

410) *The Louisiana Planter Sugar Manufacturer: A Weekly Newspaper devoted to the Sugar, Rice and Other Agricultural Industries in Louisiana*, (1903). "Porto Rico", (June 6, 1903, New Orleans) (Vol. XXX, No. 23: 367). It stated, in relevant part: "The Federation of Labor has complained to Governor Hunt that quite as bad a state of affairs exists on several Puerto Rican sugar plantations as is alleged exists in Hawaii. The Porto Ricans in Hawaii frequently write to Porto Rico a tale of woe but this comes closer home and will doubtless have immediate attention…. Porto Ricans are so prone to complain that the foregoing rather startling statements are to be taken with at least a grain of salt until they are shown to be true." (accessed via: *Google*)

411) *The Washington Post.* (1905), "Porto Ricans and Filipinos", (July 30, 1905: 2), Fourth Part: pages 1-12. "…Porto Rico became a Territory of the United States on July 25, 1901 but not subject to the United States Constitution. By a decision of the United States Supreme Court, rendered December 2, 1901, which sustained the right of Congress to impose customs duties on Porto Rican products imported into the United States and a separate tariff for Porto Rico, the natives and citizens of Porto Rico are not citizens of The United States…."

412) *Third Report of the Board of Immigration* to *the Governor of the Territory of Hawaii.* (1911), "European Immigration".

413) Tovar, Frederico Ribes, (1970). *Enciclopedia Puertorriqueña Ilustrada Tomo II*/The Puerto Rican Heritage Encyclopedia Volume II. (Plus Ultra Educational Publishers, Inc.: San Juan, P.R.).

He stated: "it is only since 1908, when they began to keep the pertinent statistics, that official data on Puerto Rican migration to the continental United States have been available", (p. 20).

414) U.S. Bureau of the Census, (1932). *Fifteenth Census of the United States: 1930. Outlying Territories and Possessions. Number and Distribution of Inhabitants.* Washington: G.P.O.

415) U.S. Bureau of the Census, (1933). *Fifteenth Census of the United States: 1930 Population Volume II. General Report Statistics by Subjects. Washington: GPO.*

416) Vélez, William. (2014), "California and Hawaii's First Puerto Ricans, 1850-1925: The 1st and 2nd Generation Immigrants/Migrants", (*CENTRO Journal*, Center for Puerto Rican Studies), "**Book Review**", (Spring 2014, Volume XXVI, No. I: 196-198).

ORAL HISTORY INTERVIEWS (for future research by Researchers and Scholars)

417) **Center for Oral History**, (1977-05), "Puerto Ricans" (APPENDIX, Vol. II), Social Science Research Institute, University of Hawaii, Manoa. Publisher: Honolulu (accessed online, in 2016). The Puerto Ricans interviewed were Trinidad Marcella (housewife, age 65), and Alfred (Alfredo) F. Santiago (retired foreman, Waialua Sugar Company, age 68) [**ORAL HISTORY INTERVIEW**, Tape No. 1-58-1-76, pp. 115ff]. While both were born in Hawaii, both of their parents had emigrated

from Porto Rico (Puerto Rico) in the first decade of 1900. Mr. Santiago "was Puerto Rican-Portuguese, and was born in Honolulu on May 12, 1908. His father came with his four brothers from Puerto Rico and married a Portuguese women from the Big Island," since his first wife had died. He began working for the Waialua Sugar Company in 1923 working as a mule driver, locomotor brakeman, and foreman, from which he retired after 50 years from it in 1973. Mr. Santiago did not know what year his father arrived in Hawaii from Puerto Rico. His mother was born in Pauuilo, Hawaii. (emphasis added)

Ms. "Tana" Rios was interviewed on March 30, 1984, and she indicated that while she was born in Kohala, Hawaii on May 2, 1914, her parents came from Puerto Rico to Hawaii in 1901 [see: Tape No. 11-50-1-84; page 729ff.]. "As an infant, 'Tana' was taken by her grandmother to live in Maui's Green Camp...."

Mary Rios' ORAL HISTORY INTERVIEW on March 28, 1984 [Tape No. 11-47-1-84 and 11-48-1-84] indicated that Mary (Salcedo) Rios was born on January 13, 1909 at Paauhau, Hawaii, the Big Island, and that her parents came to Hawaii in ca. 1901 [circa?] from Puerto Rico, (see: pp. 797ff.). She was a "homemaker and a former fertilizer factory worker. She was 75 at the time of this interview." Both of "her parents lived in Paauhau's Puerto Rican Camp and labored in the sugarcane fields...."

418) **Norma Carr's** 1989 Dissertation and her "Oral Interviews" which she conducted, and referenced in her Dissertation (contact: the University of Hawaii for possible acquisition of these copies) (names of interviewees which she recorded or transcribed) (Bib. #34, *page 216*):

Luis Cruz (held on 1/21/1978; on tape, 80 minutes);
Daniel Feliciano (held on 9/30/1978; 38 pages);
Manuel Guzman (held on 4/25 and on 8/12/1976; on tape; English parts transcribed, 37 pages);
Marcelina Salcedo (held on 8/11/1976; on tape, 50 minutes);

Page 258 in Dr. Carr's 1989 Dissertation:

Daniel Feliciano (held on 9/30/1978; unpublished manuscript, consisting of 38 pages);
Charles Fraticelli (held on 1/27/1978; unpublished manuscript, 65 pages);
Daniel Maldonado (held on 11/11/1976; unpublished manuscript, 65 pages);
Julio Milan ("Notes on conversations in the 1980s");
Alfred Santiago (1976; Manuscript, Waialua Oral History Proj., Univ. of Hawaii; Ethnic Studies);
Solomon Vegas (held on 2/20/1978; unpublished manuscript, 53 pages);

Page 291 in Dr. Carr's 1989 Dissertation:

Joseph Ayala (held on 6/29/1978; unpublished manuscript, 67 pages);
Antone Carvalho (held on 3/17/1978; unpublished manuscript, 86 pages)
Monserrate Feliciano (held on 12/21/1977; Tape, 50 minutes);
Charles Fraticelli (held on 1/27/1977; unpublished manuscript, 65 pages);
Daniel Maldonado (held on 11/11/1976; unpublished manuscript, 65 pages);
Adolph Samuels (held on 2/3/1978; unpublished manuscript, 60 pages);

Page 319 of Dr. Carr's 1989 Dissertation:

Joseph Ayala (held on 6/29/1978; unpublished manuscript, 67pages);
Joseph Bulgos (held on 6/1/1978; unpublished manuscript, 36pages;
Charles Fraticelli (held on 6/27/1977; unpublished manuscript, 65 pages);
Manuel Guzman (held on 4/26 and 8/12/1976; Tape and a unpublished manuscript, 65 pages);
Daniel Maldonado (held on 11/11/1976; unpublished manuscript, 65 pages);
Raymond Pagan (held on 8/5/1978; unpublished manuscript, 53 pages);
Adolph Samuels (held on 2/3/1978; unpublished manuscript, 60 pages)
Queenie Samuels (Notes; United Puerto Rican Association of Hawaii. Minutes of the Officer's Meetings and the General Membership Meetings of the PR Civic Association: 1940-1960).

Special Genealogical Primary Sources Relating to S.M. Mezes' Birthplace in Puerto Rico

419) Source: *Bautismos Book – 1818 (1818-1825, B)*. "Libro 11B De Bautismo De La Catedral De Nuestra Señora De La Candelaria De Mayagüez. (1818-1825)". (folio 213) (por Dennis De Jesús Rodríguez, Investigador Histórico, Mayagüez, Puerto Rico, Año 2005). (Coleccion Documental Y Archivo Demografico, Emilio C. Garces Vazquez). (LB 11B, F213, - 1.jpg) (305K).

Obtained this document in the December 16, 2013 *Report* (revised: September 25, 2015) from Genealogist, Tony Rivera Maldonado (APG) (see: Bib. #400, above). This document is a copy of a transcription of the **original** Church Baptismal Book record which listed S.M. Mezes' having been baptized in Mayagüez, Puerto Rico on January 31, 1824, while listing his parents as: Juan Simón Meces and Maria del Carmen Moreno; this is transcribed by: Dennis de Jesús Rodríguez.

NOTE: Puerto Rican Genealogist, Orlando Bodon-Echevarria (The Hispanic Genealogical Society of New York (HGSNY) Member / Principle Administrative Assistant at the Brooklyn Public Library, New York City) sent me an e-mail on Oct. 26, 2015, wherein he provided me digitized pages from the aforementioned *Baptismal Book – 1818 (1818-1825, B)* wherein S.M. Mezes' father, D. [Don] Juan Simon Meces, is cited in one of the paragraphs, and stated: "…*Yo el infrascrito Cura Rector de ella bauticé solamnemente y puse óleo y crisma a Simón que nació… hijo…de Don Juan Simón Meces y Doña María del Carmen Moreno de esta feligreses….*" (p. 213); cf.: Rosario-Rivera, 1995.

420) Source: *Bautismos Book – (1825-1830)*. "Libro 15 De Bautismos De La Catedral De N. S. De La Candelaria De Mayagüez . (1825-1830)". Nov. 10 de 1825, por Dennis De Jesús Rodríguez, Investigador Histórico. Mayagüez, Puerto Rico, Año 2005. Coleccion Documental y Archivo Demografico) (Transcribed by Dennis De Jesús Rodríguez), (see: Bib. #400, p.23).

421) Cipriani, Count Leonetto. (1962), *California and Overland Diaries of Count Leonetto Cipriani From 1853 Through 1871…* (Translated and edited by Ernest Falbo, The Champoeg Press: MCMLXII [1962?]). A contemporary of S.M. Mezes, and who made a reference to S.M. Mezes [incorrectly cited by Count Leonetto Cipriani in his book as "Megas", (see: pages 65, 70 (footnote 12))]. (Note: "In Cipriani's handwriting 'g' and 'z' look alike, cause [causes] confusion….", (p. 70)).

422) Source: *Libro 6 De Matrimonios De La Catedral De Nuestra Señora De La Candelaria De Mayagüez, Mayagüez, Puerto Rico (1820-1833)* (LM6, F49, 20 May 1822). This book is a copy of a transcription of the **original** Church Matrimonial Book record which listed S.M. Mezes' parents having been married in Mayagüez, Puerto Rico on May 29, 1822, (Bib.#400, p. 19), (see: Bib. #400, pp. 20-22).

423) Bancroft Library, University of California, Berkeley. Collection Number: *BANC MSS C-B 833*. Folder 18. (Antonio María Osio Papers). "Contrata, Nov. 14, 1850. Agreement with S. Sterrett and S.M. Mezes re Santa Clara Mission Orchard."

Exhibit 22

Weekly Alta California, Number 52, 29 December 1849 — Page 3 Advertisements Column 2
[ADVERTISEMENT]

Halleck, Peachy & Billings, Attorneys and Solicitors, San Francisco. Office, the room at present occupied by Peachy & Billings, on the north side of Sacramento street, between Kearny and Dupont sts. Mr. Billings Commissioner for New York, Massachusetts, and Connecticut. H. WAGER HALLECK, ARCH'D CARY PEACHY, FREDERICK BILLINGS. January 1, 1850.   9-24

King, Bowie, Bell & Judah, Attorneys and Counselors at Law. Moffatt's Buildings, corner Clay and Dupont streets, San Francisco. T. BUTLER KING, CHAS. P. JUDAH, H. RAY BOWIE, EDWIN BELL.   9-2

Robinson, Arnold & Sewell,

Shipping and Commission Merchants, foot of Pine street, San Francisco, Upper California.   1tc

Z. H. ROBINSON,   A. ARNOLD,   W. D. SEWALL, JR.

Henrichson, Reincke & Co.,

General Merchants, San Francisco, corner of Sacramento and Kearny streets.

O. F. CIPRIANI,   H. REINCKE,
H. W. HINRICHSEN,   [1tc]   S. M. MEZES.

WATER-PROOF BOOTS.—The subscriber, in acknowledging his obligations to the citizens of San Francisco, Sacramento city and the people of California generally, for their continued patronage, would again call their attention to his greatly increased stock of Water-proof Boots, of his own manufacture, made of the best selected grain leather, cowhide, kip and calf skin, and by superior workmen. Having

Exhibit 23

U.S. Department of Homeland Security
U.S. Citizenship and Immigration Services
Genealogy Program Mailstop 2206
Washington, D.C. 20529-2206

 **U.S. Citizenship and Immigration Services**

August 29, 2016

Case Number: GEN-10127880

Daniel M. Lopez
518 Hotz Street
Spring Valley, CA 91977

Dear Daniel Lopez:

Your index search request was received in this office on December 10, 2015, regarding Simon Monserrate Mezes born December 25, 1823 in Puerto Rico. We completed a thorough search for records based on the information you provided. Unfortunately we found no matching index reference. Our search included all variations of the subject's name with the same results.

As noted on our website (www.uscis.gov/genealogy) under About Index Search Requests, while USCIS indices do contain entries for some individuals born earlier than 1850 the majority of the entries refer to individuals born since *ca.* 1875. Furthermore, as explained on our website, our index searches and records generally cover immigrants who arrived after 1892 and/or naturalized after September 27, 1906.

Naturalization activity prior to September 27, 1906, was under the exclusive jurisdiction of the courts. Naturalization records may be found in Federal, State, or local court records. Practice and procedure varied greatly over time and geographical location, and as a result the best information on how to find pre-1906 naturalization records is usually available from local sources. For more information on State and local courts, contact the State or county historical or genealogical society in the location where you believe the immigrant naturalized. For Federal court records, contact the National Archives or see their webpage at http://www.archives.gov/genealogy/naturalization/. We do apologize that we could not be of further assistance to you.

If you should have any additional questions about your request from USCIS, please direct your inquiries to this office at the above address or send them to Genealogy.USCIS@dhs.gov. Always note your case identification number on the correspondence.

Sincerely,

Lynda K. Spencer
Chief, Genealogy Section

Exhibit 24

CERTIFICADO DE PARTIDA DE BAUTISMO

Yo, el infrascrito, Sacerdote de esta parroquia de la Sta. Iglesia Catedral de Mayagüez
I, the undersigned, Priest of this Parish of the Holy Cathedral of Mayagüez

NUESTRA SEÑORA DE LA CANDELARIA
OUR LADY OF CANDLEMAS

CERTIFICO que en el Libro **11B** del Registro de Bautismos, folio **213** número marginal **no consta** se halla la siguiente partida:

En el día **31** de **enero** del año **1824**, yo, el Rvdo. **Manuel G. Casuela** bauticé a **Simón** que nació en **no consta** el día **25** del **pasado** del año **no consta**, hijo **o** de don **Juan Simón Meces** natural de **no consta**, vecino de **Mayagüez** y de doña **Mª del Carmen Moreno** natural de **no consta**, vecina de **Mayagüez**

Padrinos:
- D. Feliz García
- Da. Mª Moncerate Suarez

De que doy fe **Manuel G. Casuela**

Para que conste, firmo y sello en Mayagüez, Puerto Rico, el día **14** del mes de **abril** del año **2015**

P. Rawlins Mazueta Mevin
Párroco - Coadjutor

MP 9324

PRIMERA COMUNION — First Holy Communion
Fecha: ___ Iglesia: ___ Lugar: ___

CONFIRMACION — Confirmation
Fecha: ___ Iglesia: ___ Lugar: ___

☐ **MATRIMONIO** — Marriage
Con: ___ Fecha: ___ Iglesia: ___ Lugar: ___

☐ Con: ___ Fecha: ___ Iglesia: ___ Lugar: ___

☐ Diaconado — Iglesia: ___ Lugar: ___ Fecha: ___

☐ Ordenación Sacerdotal — Orden: ___ Lugar: ___ Fecha: ___

☐ Profesión Religiosa — Orden: ___ Lugar: ___

Certifica

Doy fe

NOTA: *No tiene notas al margen.*

Sello Parroquial — Parroquia La Candelaria, Mayagüez, P.R.

Exhibit 25

Certificado de Matrimonio

Santa Iglesia Catedral
Nuestra Señora de la Candelaria
Mayagüez, Puerto Rico

Certifico que: D. Juan Simón de Meses Edad: no consta
I certify that: age

Hijo de: D. Simón   y D. Maria Pillate
son of   and

y Da. Mª del Carmen Moreno   Edad: no consta
and   age

Hija de: D. José   y Da. Manuela Ramos
daughter of   and

CONTRAJERON MATRIMONIO
Were united in Marriage

El día 29 de mayo de 1822
on the   day of   the year

Por el Rvdo. Manuel G. Casuela
by the Rev.

Testigos: D. Antonio Frasinet
Witnesses

y D. Manuel Vidó
and

Según consta en el Libro de Matrimonios de esta Iglesia:
as appears in the Marriage Register of this Church:

Libro: 6   Folio: 49   Núm. no consta
Book   Page   No.

Doy fe hoy, el día: 14 de abril de 2015
Dated on the   day of   the year

Sello Parroquial   Rvdo. P. Paulino Yazuelas Merino
                      Rev.

MP 9325

Exhibit 26

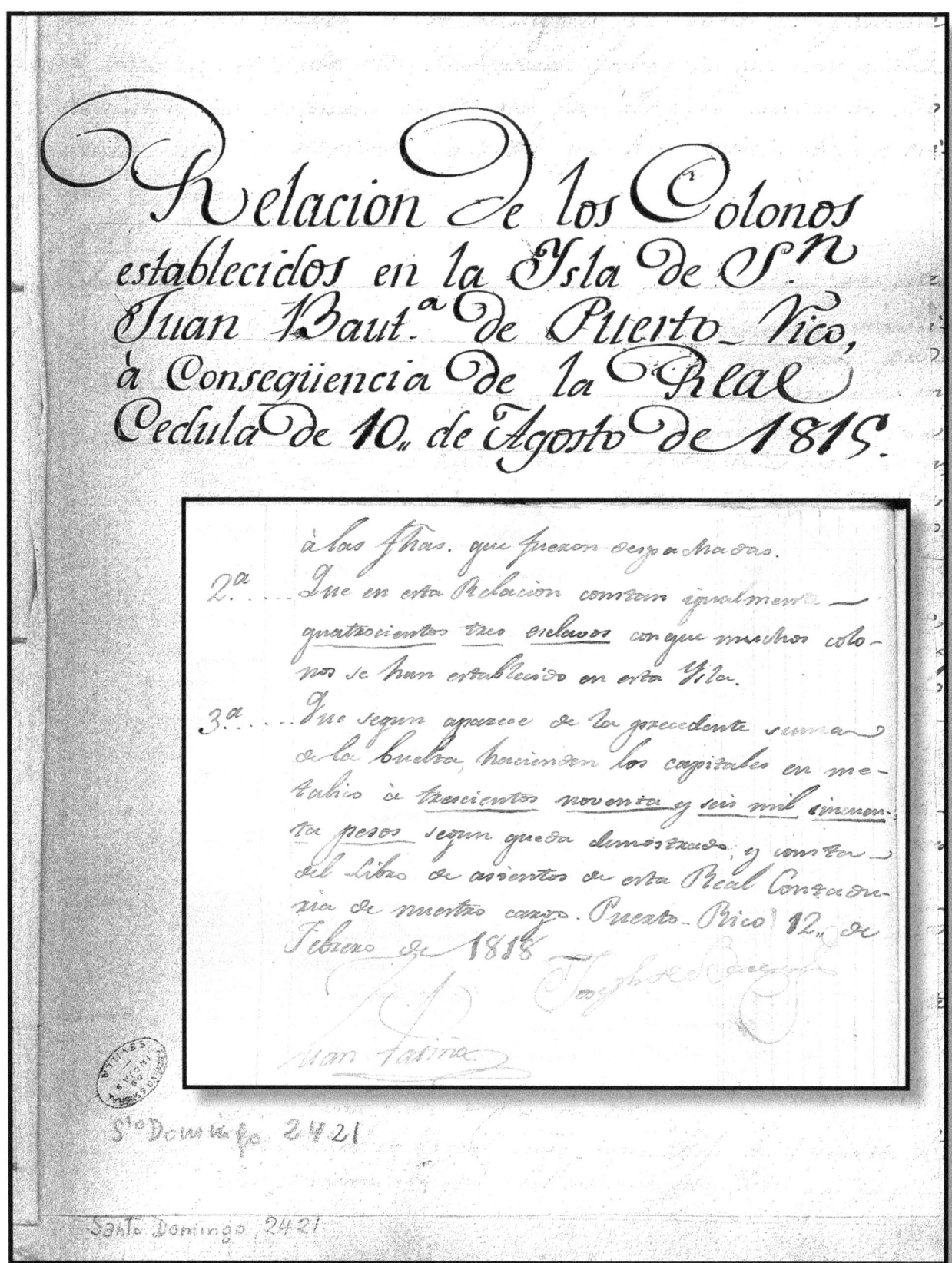

Relacion de los Colonos establecidos en la Isla de Sn Juan Bautª de Puerto Rico, á Consegüencia de la Real Cedula de 10 de Agosto de 1815.

Exhibit 27

LIBRARY OF CONGRESS

Head, U.S. Monographs Section
U.S./ANGLO DIVISION

September 15, 2014

Mr. Daniel M. Lopez
518 Hotz Street
Spring Valley, CA 91977

Dear Mr. Lopez:

On behalf of the Library of Congress, we want to thank you and acknowledge the generous donation of your publication, ***California and Hawaii's first Puerto Ricans, 1850-1925: the 1st and 2nd generation immigrants/migrants.*** We are happy to inform you that the publication was selected for addition to the Library's General Collections, and was assigned Library of Congress control number: **2014432068.**

Once again, thank you for your interest in enriching the collections of the Library, and your most kind donation.

Sincerely yours,

Bridgetta C. Jenkins
Head, U.S. Monographs Section

Enclosure: Printout of record

101 INDEPENDENCE AVENUE, S.E. WASHINGTON, DC 20540-4274
202-707-6352 (Voice) 202-252-2725 (Fax) bjen@loc.gov (E-mail)

Exhibit 28

WIDENER LIBRARY
of the Harvard College Library

January 12, 2015

Mr. Daniel López
518 Hotz Street
Spring Valley, CA 91977

Dear Mr. López,

On behalf of the Harvard University Library, I would like to take this opportunity to thank you for your generous donation of *California and Hawaii's first Puerto Ricans, 1850-1925*. We are delighted to add this volume to our collection.

Best wishes,

David Leyenson
Assistant Librarian for Western Europe
Widener Library Collection Development
Harvard University
Cambridge, MA 02138

COLLECTION
DEVELOPMENT

HARVARD UNIVERSITY
CAMBRIDGE
MASSACHUSETTS
02138
USA

T 617.495.2425
F 617.496.8704

Exhibit 29

UNIVERSIDAD DE PUERTO RICO
Recinto de Río Piedras
Sistema de Bibliotecas
PO Box 23302
San Juan, Puerto Rico 00931-3302

October 23, 2014

Mr. Daniel M. López
518 Hotz St.
Spring Valley, CA 91977

Dear Mr. López:

We are pleased to have received two copies of the *"California and Hawaii"s First Puerto Ricans, 1850-1925: The 1st and 2nd Generation Immigrants/Migrants"*.

Thank you for your kind donation and your interest in the enrichment of our collection, Library System, University of Puerto Rico.

Cordially,

Jorge I. Ortiz Malavé, MLS
Head, Acquisitions Section

Patrono con Igualdad de Oportunidad en el Empleo M/M/V/I

ESTADO LIBRE ASOCIADO DE PUERTO RICO
INSTITUTO DE CULTURA PUERTORRIQUEÑA
BIBLIOTECA NACIONAL DE PUERTO RICO

PO BOX 9024184
SAN JUAN DE PUERTO RICO 00902-4184

November 6, 2014

Mr. Daniel López
518 Hotz Street,
Spring Valley, CA 91977

Dear Mr. Daniel López,

Thank you for the donation of your book titled: California and Hawaii's First Puerto Ricans, 1850-1925.

The book is already catalogued and processed in our Library system locally. This book is a very important contribution to the study of genealogy of Puerto Ricans especially for people that come to our Library to research their family and ancestors.

I am including the electronic address of the Sociedad Puertorriqueña de Genealogía, webmaster@genealogiapr.com so you can also contact them.

With regards to the donation, I have to consult on this matter. I will let you know.

Also, I have included the brochures of the library and a brochure of the Eugenio María de Hostos Room.

Sincerely,

Madeline Saavedra Marvez
Librarian I

Visite el portal cultural de Puerto Rico en:
www.icp.gobierno.pr

Centro
Center for Puerto Rican Studies

Understanding, Preserving and Sharing the Puerto Rican Experience in the United States

HUNTER COLLEGE   **CUNY**

December 3, 2014

Mr. Daniel M. Lopez
518 Hotz Street
Spring Valley, CA 91977-5710

Dear Mr. Lopez,

On behalf of the Centro Library and Archives, I would like to thank you for your generous donation(3 copies) of your book:

California and Hawaii's first Puerto Ricans, 1850-1925: The 1st and 2nd generation immigrants/migrants
[National City, CA : D. M. López], 2013, c2012.
194 p. : ill. ; 28 cm.
Call #: E184 P85 L67 2013

The book is a valuable addition to our collection, and is an excellent resource for students and researchers conducting studies in the area of the early migration history of Puerto Ricans to California and Hawaii.

Again, thank you again for your gracious donation and your continued support

¡Muchisimas Gracias!

My Best Regards,

[signature]

Félix A. Rivera
Reference and Film Librarian
Centro Library and Archives
Hunter College
Silberman School of Social Work
2180 Third Avenue @ 119 Street
New York, NY 10035

Centro de Estudios Puertorriqueños · Hunter College, CUNY · 695 Park Avenue, Room E1429 · New York, NY 10065 (212) 772-5688 · Fax (212) 650-3673
Centro Library & Archives · Hunter College, CUNY · Silberman Building · 2180 Third Avenue at 119th St., Room 121 · New York, NY 10035 (212) 396-7874 · Fax (212) 396-7707

centropr.hunter.cuny.edu

Exhibit 32

The New York Public Library

Daniel M. Lopez

*My colleagues and I gratefully
acknowledge your generous gift of*

**2 copies of "California and Hawaii's First Puerto Rican's, 1850-1925
The 1st and 2nd Generation Immigrants/Migrants"**

*Please accept our thanks for your help in
developing the Library's resources.*

**Denise Hibay
Susan and Douglas Dillon Head of Collection Development**

July 21, 2015

In accordance with Federal income tax law we inform you that no goods or services were provided in return for your charitable contribution to the Library.

Materials given to the Library are subject to the Library's "Policy on Gift Materials", which can be found at www.nypl.org. The Library reserves the right to use or dispose of unsolicited materials in any manner it deems appropriate.

www.ingramcontent.com/pod-product-compliance
Lightning Source LLC
Chambersburg PA
CBHW080334170426
43194CB00014B/2558